THE LIFE OF A LONG-DISTANCE WRITER

THE LIFE OF A LONG-DISTANCE WRITER
THE BIOGRAPHY OF
ALAN SiLLiTOE

Richard Bradford

Peter Owen
London and Chester Springs

PETER OWEN PUBLISHERS
73 Kenway Road, London SW5 0RE

Peter Owen books are distributed in the USA by
Dufour Editions Inc., Chester Springs, PA 19425-0007

First published in Great Britain 2008
© Richard Bradford 2008

ISBN 978-0-7206-1317-9

A catalogue record for this book is available from the British Library.

Printed and bound in Slovenia by
DZS-Grafik

For Amy Burns

CONTENTS

List of Illustrations	8
Acknowledgements and Preface	9
Introduction	11
Part I Family	15
Part II A Man Abroad	63
Part III The Road to Success	121
Part IV The Unsettled Radical	183
Part V Judaism and Israel	231
Part VI Old Haunts	299
Bibliography	379
Index	381

ILLUSTRATIONS BETWEEN PAGES 208 AND 209

Portrait of Alan Sillitoe in 1968 wearing his signature collarless cotton shirt
Sillitoe and his sister Peggy
Sillitoe, aged seven or eight, with comments by his sister Peggy
Sillitoe's parents, 1950
Grandad Burton
Grandmother, Mary Ann Tokins, 1889
Sillitoe in uniform, 1947, with a wireless operator's badge
Sillitoe in the Butterworth radio hut, Malaya, 1947
Sillitoe, Malaya, September 1947
Postcard from Sillitoe to his father from Majorca, 1953
Ruth Fainlight and Sillitoe, Majorca, 1954
Ruth Fainlight and Sillitoe with an unknown companion, Majorca, 1954
Sillitoe, Hertfordshire, 1959
Sillitoe, Harry Saltzman and Ruth Fainlight on the set of *Saturday Night and Sunday Morning*, 1960
Brian Sillitoe, Norman Rossington, Albert Finney and Michael Sillitoe on the set of *Saturday Night and Sunday Morning*, 1960
Norman Rossington, Sillitoe's mother and Shirley Ann Field on the set of *Saturday Night and Sunday Morning*, 1960
The 1960 Pan paperback edition of *Saturday Night and Sunday Morning*
Sillitoe, Ruth Fainlight and David Sillitoe, Tangier, 1962
Sillitoe and Karel Reisz, London, 1963
Sillitoe at Lake Baikal, Siberia, 1963
Postcard to Brian Sillitoe from Moscow, 1963
George Andjaparidze, Sillitoe's companion on the road in the Soviet Union, June 1967
Outside the Moscow Writers' Club, 1967
Sillitoe at Wittersham, Kent, in the early 1970s, with David, Sue and a neighbour's daughter
Sillitoe with producer Graham Benson at Ollerton Colliery, Nottinghamshire, 1976, the set for the BBC television adaptation of the short story 'Pit Strike'
Yehuda Amichai, Ruth Fainlight and Sillitoe, Israel, 1977
With Kingsley Amis at the Imperial War Museum, London, 1987
A pause during a return visit to the Malayan jungle in 1988, where Sillitoe would prepare notes for *Lost Loves*
Sillitoe with Bernard 'Bunny' Sindall in France, October 1990
Portrait of Sillitoe by David Sillitoe, 2000
Publicity card for a BBC 2 television series *My Generation*, broadcast in 2000, featuring various cultural figures who helped shape post-war Britain
Sillitoe in his London study with a bust by Bernard 'Bunny' Sindall

ACKNOWLEDGEMENTS
AND PREFACE

Thanks are due primarily to Alan Sillitoe for authorizing me to write this biography and for providing me with such generous amounts of time and assistance. Ruth Fainlight too has been hospitable, helpful and indulgent.

Dr Amy Burns is deserving of special gratitude. From the early stages of the project when she assisted with the practicalities of research, involving trips to interviews and archives and the sourcing of material, to its near completion at which she has provided advice and support, her help has been invaluable.

Alan Sillitoe's own *Life Without Armour* and *Raw Material* deal selectively with aspects of his life up to the end of the 1950s. I sometimes cite passages from these, but the substance of my account comes from interviews, many with Alan Sillitoe himself, correspondence and unpublished documents, some in library archives, some privately held.

The following have been patient and helpful interviewees: Tamara Dragadze, Dannie Abse, Jeffrey Simmons, Jeanetta Sindall, Helder Macedo, Suzette Macedo, Margaret Drabble, Patricia Parkin, Ronald Schlachter, Betsy Blair, Doreen Haslem (née Greatorex), Hilary Bussey, Lucia Graves, Brian Sillitoe, Michael Sillitoe, David Sillitoe, Susan Sillitoe, Ruth Fainlight, Joanna Marston.

Roy Davids helpfully collated and forwarded much of the voluminous correspondence between Alan and his brother Brian, and Michael Sillitoe has provided me with valuable passages of his childhood diary and some of his later correspondence with his brother Alan. Professor H.M. Daleski has shown great generosity in his assistance with the research for the book, particularly in his provision of Alan's letters to him, reflecting their close friendship of more than thirty years. Hilary Bussey and Ronald Schlachter have entrusted me with originals and copies of their correspondence with Alan Sillitoe, and Joanna Marston generously collated and forwarded some copies of correspondence between Alan Sillitoe and her late grandmother Rosica Colin, his first agent.

The Lilly Library, University of Indiana, is home to an illuminating and vast archive of notebooks, typescripts, manuscripts and correspondence to and from Alan Sillitoe, covering the period between the late 1950s and the mid-1990s. I am immensely indebted to it both for allowing me access to all this material and for copying pieces for my private scrutiny. The Emory University Library has been equally helpful in offering me access to correspondence between Ted Hughes and Alan Sillitoe, and between Hughes and Ruth Fainlight.

Alan Sillitoe himself has provided me with documents and manuscripts – particularly correspondence between himself and H.M. Daleski and his brother Brian – that have been of immense value in the preparation of this book, and he has endured, selflessly, several hours of relentless interviewing.

The University of Ulster's generous provision of a permanent Research Professorship has allowed me the time to complete this biography. Professor John Gillespie, Head of the School of Languages and Literature, Professor Robert Welch, Dean of the Faculty of Arts, Professor Bernie Hannigan, Pro-Vice Chancellor, Research, and Professor Richard Barnett, Vice Chancellor of the University of Ulster, deserve special thanks for agreeing to my contract. Professor Pól O Dochartaigh has been of great assistance regarding travel for research. Rosemary Savage, also of the University of Ulster, has helped greatly, and I am indebted to James Ryan, an excellent editor.

If the source for a quotation is not cited it has been taken verbatim from recorded interviews conducted between February 2006 and November 2007 with individuals acknowledged in the list above. In citations following quotations from correspondence the following initials are used:

AS	Alan Sillitoe
BS	Brian Sillitoe
MS	Michael Sillitoe
TH	Ted Hughes
CH	Carol Hughes
RF	Ruth Fainlight
BD	H.M. 'Bill' Daleski

It has been agreed by all parties concerned that certain individuals be referred to only by pseudonyms – notably 'Sally', 'Janet' and 'Pauline'.

INTRODUCTION

We are in Alan Sillitoe's study, in the flat in Notting Hill where he and his wife, the writer Ruth Fainlight, have lived since 1971. He has just agreed, tentatively, to take me on as his biographer and I am wondering where to begin. So I switch on the tape machine and ask him: 'Tell me about your day.'

'I'm a lazy, slow-moving morning sort of bloke. I get up by alarm clock at a quarter to eight, drink a glass of (what's called pure but isn't) orange juice, then do ten or so minutes of jumps and press-ups, etc. – a comical sight for any looker-on, though I lock myself away for them – listening to the news in the meantime. After that, still in my dressing gown, it's breakfast, for which I always have an appetite, either "continental" or English cooked. If I'm in the country the *Guardian* is on the doorstep, but in London I have to go out for it, though not before (at both places) a shower and hair (what there is of it) wash. After going through the paper (to see if it's my birthday, or whether I died the day before), by which time it's getting on for ten, I go into my "study" (when did I ever study?) and light the blissful first pipe of tobacco. Not to do so before ten is my way of cutting down, but I don't feel like it till then anyway.

'So in my study I look at the table and spend half an hour picking up paper-clips and razor blades and pencils and putting them in a small glass tray. I empty the ashtray and set it in its place, put one book on top of another, make the pile of unanswered letters more shipshape, fill my fountain pen and do all sorts of little clearances till there's plenty of space around my elbows and for the pile of paper on which I am to write.

'During decades of knowing Robert Graves I noticed, on staying overnight at the house in Deyá, how in a similar way, before starting work in the morning, everything had to be neatly in place on his desk. Could this habit have grown from his experience as Orderly Officer in the Army? Equally, could mine have come about organizing the logbooks, pencils, etc., as a radio operator at my desk?

'As if I've already done a day's work, I begin to think about coffee. So the day begins, at the end of which something has been achieved, however much or little, because by then it's most likely eleven o'clock at night.'

Sillitoe loves maps, and his study offers an atlas of his life and temperament. In the middle of his desk – 'Actually,' he corrects me, 'it's an old dining table' – is a seventies vintage electronic typewriter. He once dallied, for a day, with a word processor. 'It [the typewriter] has an eraser,' he explains, meaning that he regards on-the-spot corrections as something of an indulgence. His first drafts are in longhand – ink, not ballpoint – and then he goes to the typewriter to do at least two, perhaps three, new versions of the original.

Next to the machine are loose papers, anchored to the desktop by a horseshoe fashioned by his maternal grandfather Burton, a Nottingham farrier, to fit the misshapen hoof of a lame horse. Burton, sixty years dead, is an enigma and has been Alan's spectral companion since his childhood, appearing regularly in his writing. To the side is a communications receiver that he uses to tune into all manner of coded communications, some of which, one assumes, should have been better protected. (For example, his short story collection *Alligator Playground* took its title from the call sign used in the first Gulf War to warn RAF pilots of imminent hostile encounters.) Alongside the receiver is his Morse key, retained from his own time in the RAF, and employed by him, addictively, particularly late at night. 'Sometimes it's a form of therapy. If I can't write I tap out a few words in Morse, not knowing where they'll go or if anyone will pick them up. Perhaps God, the gods, or whoever, will reply with a poem or a splendid opening sentence of a novel.'

Facing him across the desk are bookshelves floor to ceiling and window to doorway serviced by a librarian's ladder. Along with the books are his RAF cap badge and a bottle of rare Russian vodka, 'Putinka, 50% by volume'. 'I enjoy a few shots with supper. Wine leaves me with a hangover next morning, but vodka sharpens the senses and doesn't.' It is his favourite drink, a taste he acquired in the 1960s on several visits to the Soviet Union, journeys which, as we will see, were exploratory and transformative. Most writers begin with a political allegiance that through maturity, fame or bloody-mindedness mutates into something else. Sillitoe saw, asked questions and made up his own mind.

On the most accessible shelf a twenty-two-volume encyclopaedia betokens his verdict. It is a vast compendium of everything one might wish to know of the doctrine, the history, the culture, even the sheer refusal to conform, that makes up what it is to be Jewish. 'It is wonderful,' says Sillitoe. 'If I look up something, or just open a volume at random, I'm usually sidetracked on to another subject before I can get to what I really want to find out.' Next to the encyclopaedia is a small library of books about Nottingham and Nottinghamshire. Silllitoe relishes travelling and while his anchorage has since the late 1950s been London he has always felt at home in the East Midlands, never losing any opportunity to drive there and see his family.

This year he will be eighty, but there is something about him that recalls the magnetic, slightly alarming qualities of his literary creations. We have been talking of East Midlands regiments in which our respective relatives served in both world wars and he is searching the drawers for a file on the

Sherwood Rangers Yeomanry. 'Oh!' he observes, turns to me and in his hand is a Second World War vintage Luger, confiscated, apparently by one of his reckless cousins, from a Wehrmacht officer. 'Does it still work?' I enquire, shifting uneasily in my chair. He glances at it. 'Well, if ever there's another census or if Blair [this was pre-Brown] sends around one of his apparatchiks to measure us up for ID cards . . . it would be interesting to find out, wouldn't it?' Yes indeed.

In appearance he seems little changed from the figure who came from nowhere to prominence in 1958: slim, alert and still wearing the same black leather waistcoat that has featured continually in photographs over the last five decades. So much for the man, at least for now. But what of the writer?

There are states of mind which by their nature abjure an alternate condition, let alone a means of improvement. In private we tend to encounter them as depression or what used to be called melancholia, and like everything else known or surmised they will be found in literature. Writers such as Dostoevsky are routinely invoked as witnesses to their potency. But no writer in English has handled them with such pitiless transparency as Sillitoe. Yet he never leaves the reader feeling that despair is the only option. He is not an evangelist, he has no religion, no political formula for bettering himself or his readers, but somehow the energy of his writing can make the worst seem bearable, sometimes perversely enjoyable. He is a writer who obstinately resists classification. When evaluating the quality of his work one searches – inevitably and often despite oneself – for points of comparison and contrast, and the familiar circuitry of assessment always breaks down. His characters, his narrative trajectories, sometimes his syntax, appear ungovernable, obtusely indifferent to our standard expectations. Not since Blake has a writer in English so deserved the accolade of idiosyncratic self-reliance, and while Blake built a parallel universe of ideas as a haven from the world he loathed, Sillitoe, courageously or stubbornly, refuses even to replace the systems he despises with alternatives of his own devising.

Arthur Seaton of *Saturday Night and Sunday Morning* is an energized, unfocused individual whose existence is embedded in a single mantra – 'Don't let the bastards grind you down.' Too frequently, and too easily, the grinders-down are seen as those above Seaton, not just the people who own the factory in which he works but also those who have, by birthright or enterprise, avoided having to spend their lives there too. In truth, however, Seaton's spectrum of intractability and self-determination cannot be reduced to such petty designations as class. The very notion of being beholden to someone else – which involves the possibility of being told, even asked, to be or do something in particular – stirs within Arthur a rage that is apolitical and indomitable. The novel has been subjected to numerous exegeses as a mid-twentieth-century pioneer of a new wave of 'working-class' fiction, but its analysts blind themselves to the irony of their undertaking: Arthur Seaton would have loathed them. He distrusted systems of any kind, and if condescending intellectuals had wandered into his world and offered him political enlightenment they would have received as much of his bile as those who had shackled him day by day to his lathe.

It is for this reason that a life of Alan Sillitoe is such an enthralling prospect. Certainly a knowledge of what went on outside and beyond the books won't alter the significance of the words on the page, but because his writing is so closely interwoven with his temperament we are offered a rare opportunity. We will be able to witness an artist at work, and more significantly observe something rare indeed: a decent, generous and modest man producing outstanding literature.

Many have known him longer than I, and better than I can claim to do, but during the period I have worked on this book he has offered me an uncommon, yet for him characteristic, abundance of friendship and honesty.

PART I
FAMILY

ONE

Alan Sillitoe was born on 4 March 1928 in Nottingham, the son of Christopher Archibald Sillitoe and his wife Sabina (née Burton). The Sillitoes already had one child, Peggy Eileen, aged two, and would after Alan have two more sons, Brian and Michael, and another daughter, Pearl.

The family's council house was little more than ten years old, a comfortable red-brick semi-detached of the kind that was becoming available for the first time to the urban working classes as a relief from the cramped indignities of back-to-backs and tenements. Sillitoe's memories of this rare instance of good fortune are brief and largely vicarious. He associated the building with one incident when, aged about nine months, he was stricken with a horrible croup-like condition and had to be hurried to a nearby doctor through a snowstorm, wrapped in a blanket held under the coat of his mother's sister Edith. His mother was herself too weakened by some unrecalled illness to venture out, and neither woman felt it necessary thereafter to explain the absence of his father, an indication of much that would follow. Sillitoe senior drifted from one unskilled labouring job to the next and after a long period of unemployment was obliged to vacate the council house, his rent arrears having become too vast even for the relatively tolerant local authority.

For most of the next decade – at least until the outbreak of war presented Christopher Sillitoe with unavoidably regular employment – the family moved, with all of their possessions stacked into a handcart, between the kind of dwellings which Dickens had improved upon and would have tested the credulity of Orwell's readers. Frequently all six of them would occupy the same room with as many as four similar-sized families in equally cramped quarters in the same building, sharing a single hall and landing and an unsanitary outside lavatory that might be emptied once a week. Among this ghastly mosaic of enforced transience Sillitoe can fasten upon few enduring memories. The only non-utilitarian objects to accompany them were two pictures of fishing boats, wedding presents from his mother's brother. Despite being regularly pawned they seemed to signify at least a degree of continuity. Eventually they would be sold. He recalls also a boy only slightly younger than himself who would spend most of his time on the landing and stairs where he defecated relentlessly and with no apparent heed to the effects upon others in the house who, according to Sillitoe, concurred in the hope that he might one day 'shit himself to death'. He was about seven years old and in every other respect entirely normal. In the same building an unemployed man would spend all day at the window staring blankly and unnervingly at passing girls who worked at the nearby Players factory. Eventually they began to mock him but he uttered not a word in response and his expression never altered.

So frequent were their moves from one abhorrent dwelling to the next that Sillitoe has no reliable recollection of their addresses; most were so dire that the 'mangonels of slum clearance rumbled not far behind' their usually hasty departure. Alfreton Road, to the east of the city, was a thoroughfare regularly crossed, one house was flooded most winters by the nearby River Leen, and Albion Yard, which no longer exists, was a playground of sorts. He remembers the names of two other infants, Billy French and Amy Tyre, with whom he and his sister would spend time in the Yard. He did not see either of them again, but their names resonate because at least when the four of them could meet at the public water taps Sillitoe and Peggy would not have to endure the presence of their father.

Sillitoe writes of his father in *Life Without Armour* and *Raw Material* with a mixture of caution, fascination and disbelief. He attacked Sabina regularly, remaining indifferent to the physical injuries suffered by her and the emotional effects upon their children; punching her in the face and kicking other parts of her body when prone was his routine. Christopher Sillitoe's bouts of rage had no obvious cause, at least not for those who endured them. Sabina, in the manner of most working-class wives of the time, never provoked him and – heroically, pitiably – made herself the target of her husband's blows whenever she feared he might vent his unfocused anger on the children. Sometimes she failed, and Sillitoe will always associate their cramped quarters with a particular plea desperately uttered by his mother: 'No, no not on his head!' 'From the beginning', Sillitoe reflects, 'my emotions were divided between hatred for my father and pity for my mother'. The latter brought with it the emotional routines of sadness, loss and regret, but one has the impression that his loathing for his father carries a far more taxing retinue of questions. He was someone who 'seemed to have the mind of a ten-year-old in the body of a brute', and Sillitoe 'experienced twinges of despair at my mother having met him and given me birth' (*Life Without Armour*, pp. 3–4). Yet 'To forgive the deed is the first step towards illumination' (*Raw Material*, p. 159).

In order even to initiate some notion of forgiveness Sillitoe later looked into his father's own experiences before his marriage and found himself puzzled by the apparent incongruity between the savage presence of his own recollections and the Sillitoe family background. His paternal great-grandparents were John Sillitoe, a tinplate worker from Wolverhampton, and Mary Jane Hillary, daughter of Henry Blackwell, a Nottingham hosiery warehouseman. Family legend presented them as exemplars of robust working-class self-sufficiency, and their son Frederick, Sillitoe's grand-father, became a successful businessman and retailer, buying hosiery at stock prices, employing a small workforce and selling the finished goods through his shop in Trafalgar Street, Nottingham. Frederick and Ada Alice had eight children, six boys and two girls, of whom Christopher was the youngest, and it is here that the story of the Sillitoes begins to resemble an opaque piece of fiction, where threads of narrative either extinguish themselves completely or take on a fragmentary enigmatic character. Sillitoe knew only two of his uncles properly, Edgar and Frederick, and met just one of the other seven, Bert, the second eldest, when he, Bert, was in his eighties and Christopher was dead.

Uncle Frederick, through connections with his father's firm, became a lace designer and eventually came to regard himself more as an artist than a craftsman. Finding small satisfaction with the provincial tastes of Nottingham he moved to London and, shortly before the outbreak of the First World War, travelled through Germany where he uncovered a satisfy-ing alliance between appreciation of imaginative design and the pragmatics of commerce. During the war he convincingly affirmed that his religious convictions – assiduously absorbed from the strict Christadelphian sect to which his wife belonged – discharged him from engaging in any form of violence. He was accepted as a conscientious objector. From 1916 to 1918 he worked as a farm labourer in Lincolnshire and spent the rest of his life making just enough money from what he perceived bitterly as the 'trade' of hosiery design while aspiring to his true vocation as a painter.

Uncle Edgar served in the First World War and survived the conflict as a prisoner of war. He too had benefited from his father's business, and before the war trained successfully as an upholsterer. However, for Eddie, like many of his contemporaries, the conflict had an enduring and largely unrecog-nized effect. He would sit for hours, brooding and staring into space, and when asked what troubled him claimed not to know. He married during the early 1920s but his wife left him within a few months, insisting that his state of mind, which he was unwilling or unable to discuss, made her own life unbearable. For the remainder of his existence Eddie worked only when he had to, usually to fund his addiction to alcohol. He had no permanent home, sometimes sleeping in charity shelters, now and again in derelict buildings, and occasionally sharing cramped quarters with his brother Christopher's family. He became known as Eddie the Tramp and would eventually become the model and inspiration for Sillitoe's compelling short story 'Uncle Ernest'.

What fascinated, indeed confounded, Sillitoe was how some logical connection might be found between his father's ghastly presence and his origins. It was never explained to him, for example, why Christopher was totally illiterate. Sillitoe, first out of fear and then pity, never put the question to his father, and his mother, apparently, had never been inclined to ask him. Bert, Eddie and Frederick were reasonably well educated and indeed Frederick was responsible for offering Sillitoe, then aged twenty-one, advice on the best authors to sate his growing appetite for serious literature. How could it be, wondered Sillitoe, that a man who could recommend to him the likes of Chekhov and Dostoevsky had come from the same background and environment as his own paternal 'brute' who was never able to read or write a word? All that could be established from his brothers – and with some reluctance – was that Christopher had as an infant suffered from rickets, a disease that was generally a consequence of malnutrition, ill-treatment and neglect, states that would not normally be found within families of the lower-middle, mercantile classes. A 'fable', as Sillitoe puts it, that he dragged out of his uncles had it that Christopher had been, as the youngest child, placed in a high chair at his pre-infant stage and made to spend most of his early years there. As a consequence he became, aged about nine or ten, effectively a cripple and obliged to 'learn' to walk with the assistance of irons on his legs. At the age of thirteen, and now walking with sticks, he was allowed to attend school, his first proper excursion into the outside world which lasted barely two months. Thereafter he was treated much like a slave, being allocated those jobs in his father's shop – principally moving machinery, rolls of cloth and furniture – that required no more than physical effort and robotic alertness. This would, thought Sillitoe, account for the immense muscularity and strength in his arms and shoulders, a physical attribute inconsistent with his otherwise feckless manner and causing his son to recall how in their crowded room he often felt 'something like . . . a courtier in the cage of an orang-utan' (*Life Without Armour*, p. 3). Bizarrely, when Frederick senior died in 1921 Christopher was chosen by the other brothers to take over the business. The rationale for the decision is lost among the swirling myths that make up Sillitoe's knowledge of his family history. Frederick had his artistic ambitions, and apart from Eddie the rest had moved out of the area, so perhaps Christopher was placed in charge partly because no one else wanted the job and partly as a result of a collective feeling of guilt about the injustices visited upon him as an infant. In any event this period of authority and independence – the only one of his otherwise desperate life – was brief. Within months Eddie had persuaded him that he, being sufficiently trained and more experienced in the trade, would be better able to keep the business afloat. In truth he hoped that running the firm would relieve him of the responsibilities of proper employment while funding his alcoholism. Catastrophe was guaranteed, and the company closed in little more than a year.

As Sillitoe enquired more deeply into the details of his father's past – a quest which began in his teens and intensified when he came to write his memoirs – so the feared uncommunicative presence of his childhood gradually mutated into something more enigmatic and pitiable. He was not, concluded Sillitoe, mentally subnormal or unbalanced. He spoke rarely but because that 'minor civilized grace of curiosity' had been damaged beyond repair in his childhood he had come to regard language as a disposable convenience. His maxim was ' "See all, hear all, say nowt" – with no compensation of self-expression' (*Raw Material*, p. 93). His utterances were reflexive, brutalized extensions of instinct and frustration, but Sillitoe believes that had the intelligence he had been born with survived the neglect and ill-treatment of his formative years he would have turned into an adult even worse than the one he became; the residue of inarticulate kindness and generosity at least 'served to torment him after he had bullied someone unjustly' (*Raw Material*, p. 94). There is little doubt that Christopher's parents created a world unto themselves so suffocating and unnerving as to provoke in their children a need to escape at the earliest opportunity. Rarely did Frederick or Eddie speak of their childhood, as if some things were better left unsaid. Christopher himself became the unwitting prisoner of these memories, one of which involved his mother waking one morning with her eye having rotated backwards into her head. She did not visit a doctor and was found dead a few months later at the foot of the staircase. Her death certificate recorded that she was riddled with cancer but the bruises she had acquired caused most to believe that Frederick senior had modified a long-established custom of their marriage. He had relieved her suffering by kicking her down the stairs. Sillitoe dragged this story from Eddie, Frederick and the few remaining friends and relatives who knew his paternal grandparents. Christopher had never referred to it at all. It seemed as though he was observing some punitive vow of silence, unable to free himself from the enclosed memory of this horror story even by speaking of it.

Sabina was one of eight children from the marriage of Ernest Burton and Mary-Ann Tokins. Ernest came from several generations of Nottinghamshire country stock and Mary-Ann's grandparents had emigrated to Huntingdonshire from Co. Mayo during the Great Hunger of the 1840s. Sillitoe always refers to Ernest as Burton, as though a Christian name or the familiar Granddad would be inadequate for so imperious a figure. He was born on 1 May 1866, had little formal education, and from his early years was trained by his father as a blacksmith. He made a living from the agricultural infrastructure that remained through his life largely undisturbed by the burgeoning industrial centres of Nottingham and Derby and as an individual he could have stepped out of a novel co-written by Hardy and Lawrence.

He was made up of contradictions and incongruities and he fascinated Sillitoe as someone who bore an oblique resemblance to his father but was in almost every respect an improvement on him. While work, for Christopher, was an obligation undertaken, when unavoidable, with glum indifference, Burton seemed to embody a turbulent link between the steel of his trade and the creatures he shod. In his later years he worked in local coal mines as a farrier, shoeing pit ponies and the horses that still laboured underground, and by the time Sillitoe, then aged about ten, got to know him he was semi-retired in his sixties and living in a cottage near the village of Radford Woodhouse on the estate of Lord Middleton. Though this was only a mile or so from the Nottingham conurbation through which the Sillitoes conducted their dispiriting odysseys, the Burtons offered Sillitoe the rough magic of another world.

The story of Burton's wooing of Mary-Ann, preserved for Sillitoe by his maternal aunts and uncles, would not seem out of place in *Far from the Madding Crowd*. Mary-Ann had been put into service aged thirteen and within four years was working as cleaner and barmaid at the White Hart in the village of Lenton. Burton, tall, self-consciously lean and muscular with glistening thick fair hair and brown eyes, eclipsed the other men in the bar by his presence. He asked Mary-Ann for another beer to put out the 'spark in his throat from a day's smithing' and told her he loved her. She thought at first he was drunk or mocking her, but the cool steadiness of his manner suggested neither; unnervingly he repeated his declaration day after day and within a week proposed marriage. Eventually she responded by pushing a florin over the counter and asking him to buy her a pair of black gloves from a shop in Nottingham for which she'd been saving for months. Would he, she wondered, put aside his strident masculinity and go shopping for women's gloves? He downed his pint and returned two hours later with the gloves, elegantly wrapped, plus the florin. The next day he again asked her to marry him and she said that she would. Had Burton turned out simply to be an exciting alternative to the feckless brute at home then his effect upon Sillitoe would have been predictable; he would merely have had cause to reflect upon the injustices of fate and genetics. But Sillitoe found that there were as many parallels between Burton and his father as differences. He could indeed be far more savage and pitiless than his son-in-law, and this for the young Sillitoe turned him into a figure of compulsive fascination, perhaps the most influential presence of his early life.

Like Christopher Sillitoe, he was illiterate, but he never treated this as a disadvantage. He worked with his hands. If he wanted to communicate something he spoke forcefully, and he had a command of language which paid no heed to the ascendancy of the written text.

To gain such a thing [literacy] he would not be prepared to pay the price of giving up a certain central feeling of quality and aloneness. To recover from pneumonia after refusing an inoculation that promised to save you from what was said to be certain death might feel like victory indeed. And to live one's life without being able to read or write in a world that shouted how damned you were for not having those gifts must have given one an untouchable sensation of great value. [*Raw Material*, p. 26]

Sillitoe sensed that Burton's obdurate indifference to literature was an index to some imperious rebellious aspect of him that in truth he admired. Among Burton's generation illiteracy was not uncommon, but Sillitoe sensed that in his case literacy was not something he had been denied, rather he had abjured it. Being able to read and write, aside from its practical benefits, sets one inexorably on the first rung of the ladder of cultural improvement. Once you move beyond the basics there is no going back and, more significantly, your past is something you can only perceive as inferior. Reading more, writing more, increasing your capacity to do both and proving an ability to appreciate such undertakings by others is for the working classes a rejection of what they once were in exchange for a system designed and maintained by the elite. Sillitoe did not idolize Burton's heedless attitude towards culture. He recognized that as a model of behaviour it was contradictory and self-destructive – he was himself from the same stock as Burton and had become his antithesis, a professional writer. Yet at the same time he admired in him a refusal to associate with anything resembling a collective condition or state of mind. Burton never joined a society or a union, and he viewed the Army as an abomination

and thought that anyone who joined or allowed himself to be ensnared into it was even lower than a dog. He did not feel threatened by foreign power or alien system, and he would not have protected any government which felt itself in danger or which told him that he was in danger. He owned no property and lived by his labour and skill, so saw little connection between the government and the people. When his eldest son Oliver enlisted during the Great War he only forgave him because he was killed, for even Burton was not so hard of soul that he could hate the dead. [*Raw Material*, p. 11]

As for God, from his youth Burton, when asked, maintained that beyond mortal existence there was nothing; no afterlife, significance or ultimate meaning. You were born and eventually you died, and that was it. It was remarkable that an uneducated man, who had no time even for folk philosophy, had insulated himself completely from any kind of belief, all the more so in an area where some sort of affiliation – to Anglicanism or more likely to the vast number of Nonconformist alternatives that thrived there – was a routine feature of working-class life. None the less he made sure that his children all attended Sunday school, and his reasons for doing so became part of the legend. A few hours on Sunday afternoon in the empty cottage, after dinner and beer, could be spent with his Mary-Ann. Though it was perhaps not planned as such, the knowledge that their parents were engaged in rampant sexuality while they had to endure a dreary afternoon of spiritual enlightenment was a far more effective means than a course on Mill, Huxley, Darwin and Nietzsche to instil in most of the Burton family a general disillusionment with organized religion.

Politics and politicians he treated with easy contempt. Unlike God, they existed, but he was convinced that every one of them had a negligible effect on his life. He shoed horses and he shaped iron, and rather than look beyond that to his position in an undoubtedly oppressive economic system he preferred to ignore what went on beyond the world he knew. If the Union Jack were flown at a local festival he cursed it, and if his children brought home from school their own miniaturized version of the national flag he told them to 'hurl the bloody thing away'. 'As a man you had your work and your family – though you may well like one and not the other. But the country you lived in, in the form of its government, was always threatening both with destruction, so he did not see how anyone could be wet-eyed about it' (*Raw Material*, p. 36).

One should not, however, assume that Sillitoe's fascination with Burton took the form of cultish idolatry. The man excited him, certainly, but along with this came distaste. One of Burton's part-time jobs involved the ringing of bulls and pigs. Those few with the strength and courage to subdue such animals usually undertook this task reluctantly: even the largest bull would scream at the pain inflicted. But Burton loved the job. He would spend all day ringing animals for farmers at Wollaton Park, and to all who witnessed the spectacle his delight was evident. The dogs he kept at home were treated similarly. If they fell asleep in front of the fire Burton's boot would soon have them yelping and running for the door, and he would reduce his children to screams, tears and pleas for mercy on the animal's behalf when he performed his favourite trick of placing his fist around the largest dog's snout until the beast writhed and convulsed.

For his family he was a benevolent dictator, given to occasional moments of violence and unpossessed of anything resembling a set of beliefs. The three daughters were bullied, but his verbal assaults were rarely accompanied by more than a slap. As they reached their teens he showed general disapproval for the young men whom they had, allegedly, courted or on some occasions brought home. Morality played no part in this; Burton simply found it difficult to envisage a man good enough for his girls. Most of them were, in his view, weak or 'soft as shit'. Of an evening the cottage turned into a comedy of double bluffs as one of the sisters would, with the assistance of bedclothes, descend from a bedroom window for a few hours out with her boyfriend, fully aware that Burton, in bed, knew what they were up to. As long as they were not caught, however, his authority remained unchallenged.

Oliver, his eldest son, was from childhood treated warily, as a potential threat to Burton's supremacy. At the slightest prompting he would receive a closed fist or a kick, ostensibly to prepare him for the generally unforgiving nature of life. He too, with Burton's grudging approval, trained as a blacksmith and soon after taking a job at a sawmill near Wollaton left home without leaving an address. Through friends in the area, Mary-Ann learned that he was sleeping in the loft of the mill and began sending his sisters to him first with food and then with messages that were he to return he would be welcomed by all, including his father. For a year Burton restrained himself, treating his eldest almost as an equal, until Oliver brought home his first girlfriend. Burton, aged forty-seven, still possessed the build, raw charm and sexuality of a man twenty years younger and within a week he had seduced his son's girl. The year was 1914. Whether the girl felt anything much for Oliver is uncertain – no one surviving in the family can recall even her name – but he had tasted that mixture of independence and romantic *naïveté* that comes with a first relationship and then watched his father snatch it away. Knowing how much Burton loathed politics, nationalism and the military, he found the perfect opportunity to revenge himself and enlisted with the Army as a blacksmith. Three months after joining up he was dead. Burton was in his stable, shoeing a horse and surrounded by two or three other men, probably the animal's owners, when his youngest daughter, aged twelve, arrived. Before she spoke a sense of anticipation and dread seemed to animate the place. The horse became agitated and the girl had to shout repeatedly to be heard: 'Oliver's dead, our dad.' 'I bloody well knew it!' he replied. So unnerving was his tone that all present felt unable even to speculate on whether he was disclosing a premonition or cursing fate.

The news had first been received by Mary-Ann, unofficially, via neighbours whose son had jointed the same regiment. The telegram arrived two days later as the entire family had just sat down for a subdued, mournful Sunday dinner. Later that week came the body, to lie coffined and uniformed in the living room, and Burton forbade public displays of grief. 'There'll be no bleddy blawting in this family,' he decreed, and for anyone who weakened: 'I'll kick 'em from arsehole to breakfast time.'

Oliver had not fallen in combat. He was stationed barely two counties away in Berkshire. Someone had fed whisky to one of the horses which then ran wild around the stable yard. Oliver tried to calm it and was killed by a single blow to the head from one of its iron-clad hooves. Burton knew then, but would only speak of it decades later, that there was an ominous quality in the parallels between the events surrounding Oliver's death and the trade to which he owed his existence. It was almost as though the horses he had so long subdued and controlled had in a single stroke revenged themselves.

Out of a mixture of fear and duty, the family restrained themselves until the day of the funeral. Florrie Voce, a neighbour, pushed through to the still open coffin, looked into the face of the 22-year-old and screamed her distress. The children began weeping, Mary-Ann sobbed to herself quietly in a corner, and for the first and only time in his life Burton cried.

He often treated Mary-Ann badly but she was the only human being to whom he conceded respect. On one occasion she heard that he had been visiting a pub near Wollaton for more than drink; that a woman had met him there several times. Mary-Ann went after him, ordered the woman to leave and told him that if he did not follow her back he need not return at all. To impress others in the bar he promised to come home and cause her to regret what she'd said. When he caught up with his wife by the lane near their cottage he was seen by one of his children to raise his hand, but Mary-Ann did not flinch and spoke directly to his face. His arm dropped and they returned together in silence. No other living creature had ever successfully resisted him.

By the time Sillitoe got to know Burton his children were adults, Sillitoe's maternal aunts and uncles, all of whom contributed to a fabric of tales whose principal subject would entertain his grandson with his own version of events. Burton's family did not censor their accounts of his treatment of them and of the temperament which seemed to possess him, and these stories would have been particularly fascinating for Sillitoe because the seventy-year-old he encountered appeared so unusual. Certainly the powerful presence, usually seated in the oak chair in front of the fire, corresponded to the figure in the family's tales and Sillitoe had no particular reason to doubt their truth, but a question would have nagged at him even though he was too immature to address it. Why was it that Burton seemed to have taken such a liking to him? Burton, rarely given to humour or geniality, had never conferred a nickname on any of his children, but Sillitoe received one. When staying at the Burtons' he would spend much of his time roaming through the scrubland, wild orchards and thick copses that surrounded the cottage, and though he never returned with prey Burton renamed him Nimrod.

Even today Sillitoe recalls that there was something about Burton's linguistic mannerisms that set him apart from everyone else he knew. With the exception of one or two of his teachers his world was made up of people for whom the Nottinghamshire dialect was a routine feature of existence, but Burton, without changing its vocabulary or pronunciation, seemed to command it in a way that others rarely achieved. He didn't introduce Sillitoe to such terms as 'clambed' (hungry), 'mardy' (a tendency to whine without cause), 'windy' (cowardly) or 'snatched' (perished with cold), but when he used them their routine familiarity seemed to acquire a graphic quality.

Sillitoe would recall that Burton didn't so much speak as inhabit his particular brand of English. He and his grandson appear to have developed a channel of communication which, if not quite exclusive, was noticeably different from conventions that obtained in Burton's exchanges with practically everyone else. Sillitoe later remarked that Burton 'took to me because I ran errands, cleaned his Saturday night dress boots, and sometimes amused him by reading from the newspaper' (*Life Without Armour*, p. 21). The flat transparency of this statement indicates that there was far more to it than that. What Sillitoe does not say, but is evident by implication and stark omission, is that the laconic hostility that accompanied Burton's daily interchanges with the rest of the human race – his closest family included – had been substituted for something else with Sillitoe. He did not become the old man's confessor – not exactly – and he was shrewd enough to know that the fearsome, sometimes vile presence who inhabited versions of Burton's past and was lodged in the memories of his long-suffering family was authentic, even though it differed from the more genial figure who seemed to have been waiting decades to disclose itself to him. And here we locate the key to why Burton so beguiled Sillitoe during his childhood and endured as a formative influence beyond that. He was an embodiment of the essential dynamic of storytelling; unnervingly believable yet at the same time a figure who existed beyond the confines of the routine, the familiar and the predictable.

Sillitoe recalls that in the Burtons' parlour a glass-fronted case was filled with novels – mostly popular and historical fiction of late Victorian/Edwardian vintage with titles such as *The Lamplighter* and *John Halifax, Gentleman*. He was fascinated, mainly because there were no books whatsoever at home, wherever that happened to be at the time, and it was in the same parlour that he began reading his first ever novel, 'a boy's yarn about smugglers called *Dawn Raiders*'. He has no recollection of the name of the author, but what he does remember is that this first encounter soon became a preoccupation.

In 1938 the BBC dramatized *The Cloister and the Hearth* by Charles Reade and Dumas' *The Count of Monte Cristo* and the entire Sillitoe family would listen to the weekly half-hour episodes each tailored to achieve a greater degree of narrative tension – and the family's suspension of disbelief was intensified by a growing fear that they might not find out what happened at the end of these stories; reality seemed about to intervene. Christopher had purchased the wireless on the never-never and as the final episode neared so anxiety regarding his repayments intensified. As if chasing fiction to its source, Sillitoe and his siblings did their best to obtain weekly copies of the *Radio Times*. They read it not just to check the schedules; advertisements for unobtainable foods – Horlicks, Golden Shred or preparations completely unknown and exotic – became supplements to the fantastic adaptations. In the *Radio Times* Sillitoe also learned of the source of *The Count of Monte Cristo*, that before he heard it dramatized it had begun life as a book by a Frenchman called Alexandre Dumas. He became obsessed with the original and obtained from his primary school teacher, Mr Salt, the first book he ever owned, *History Day by Day*. From this he familiarized himself with the history behind Dumas' story, without paying too much attention to the distinction between literature and life. He was nine years old, and by the age of ten he had managed to save enough pennies to buy a copy of the novel from the basement of Frank Wore's second-hand bookshop in central Nottingham. Manically he went through Dumas' original, testing it against his memory of the BBC version and his own nascent impressions of nineteenth-century France. Next came Hugo's *Les Misérables*, Rider Haggard's *Beatrice*, *She*, *King Solomon's Mines*, etc., and soon after that he discovered the local public library, there to borrow and rapidly devour everything else available by Dumas, Hugo, Haggard, plus the lighter menu of Crompton's 'William' stories, G.A. Henry, Herbert Strang, Jules Verne and Conan Doyle.

Sillitoe's father became unnerved by his new interest, sometimes threatening to throw the book into the fire and more routinely knocking it off the table and across the floor. The easy explanation, which Sillitoe acknowledges, is that he saw his son's precocious absorption as a reminder and reproach to his illiteracy. What is striking, however, and Sillitoe never mentions this, is the contrast between the house in which his interest in stories and reading was sparked and the one where it matured. Burton, also an illiterate, was happy to share his home with so many books all of which provided entertainment for his wife and children; he seemed indeed to regard them with comfortable indifference, as if he already knew enough tales of his own.

TWO

Sillitoe has since his childhood maintained an extraordinary fascination with maps. It is intriguing that he first became aware of them during 1937–8, the period when his parents' marriage reached its nadir. His father seemed in a permanent state of depression and resentment, a condition from which he sought relief by violently assaulting his wife, every day. It seems both horrific and inconceivable that a nine-year-old might, having pondered the sheer futility of his existence, consider suicide as a legitimate option, but Sillitoe did so, finding refuge only in the bitter hypothesis 'that my parents might go out one day and fall under a bus', or more practically with his now regular excursions to Burton's cottage. There, looking through the books that his aunts and uncles had won as Sunday school prizes, he became less concerned with their stories and subjects than with their ability to shift the mind if not the body to somewhere else. He began to scribble on the inside covers and flyleaves and create his own maps of the places that the book had enabled him imaginatively to visit. He gave shapes and names to locations such as Greenland, Dreamland, France and Wonderland, and this sense of the map as a channel between the known and the fantastic was maintained when he consulted the atlas for authoritative surveys of America, China and the Pacific: the security of what he found on the page licensed inventions in his mind.

Burton, amused by his grandson's obsession, promised him something special and dug out from an old sideboard two Ordnance Survey maps of the immediate location and area surrounding the cottage. These, he explained, had been acquired some decades earlier when there seemed a remote possibility of Burton purchasing the house from the estate of Lord Middleton, but monies were insufficient and the opportunity was withdrawn. Suddenly, Sillitoe found himself with a guide to what had previously been improvised excursions. Ever since he first visited the cottage he had amused himself by finding new routes through the surrounding undergrowth and crossings of the feeder brooks for the nearby River Leen. Now he took command of the territory. He became a self-taught map-reader, charting his position among the actual gradients and landmarks against their miniaturized versions. He wrote, almost six decades later, that 'It is difficult to know at such times [during early childhood] how our birthplace fits into the scheme of the world map. Until we have put down surveys with the purpose of identifying our location there seems so much uncertainty in our lives.' He goes on to explain that his own early family life was fragmented, unfocused, with no foundation in religion or any other kind of belief which might address his questions, the only reliable aspect being the monotony of violence, suffering and despair. 'Such a loss, if that's what it was, meant that I wanted even more than most to belong on the map, though only under my own idiosyncratic terms' ('Maps in a Writer's Life', unpublished lecture given to the Ratti Institute, Como, October 2005, p. 6). The psychological and imaginative promptings of maps, their ability to balance the logic and specificity of knowing against a sense of release as the eye and then the mind seek escape and adventure provided Sillitoe with a form of deliverance from the enclosed world he was obliged to share with his father and mother.

One day he found Peggy, his elder sister, kneeling before the bed praying, a sign of utter desperation given that neither of them had been instructed even in the existence of God. '. . . she turned to me half ashamed and said: "It's the only thing to do, our Alan. You should do it, as well, then perhaps *he* won't hit her any more.' His reflections on the incident are revealing, particularly in the way he focuses upon the nature of location and place. 'Supposing God to exist somewhere – a titanic misty figure at the edges, remote and pitiless, but no less God for that – it was nevertheless hard to believe that such prayers could be in any way answerable.' He felt for his sister, loved and pitied her, but his mind worked differently; if God was impossible to find, how could he exist? All that could be relied upon were the pragmatics of particular routes and methods of escape. 'So I ran from her, screwing back my tears at knowing she didn't even have the Burtons' cottage for a refuge' (*Life Without Armour*, p. 32). He acknowledges that the cottage and its environs provided only temporary compensation for the ongoing horrors of home, but what is also apparent is that it had a special significance, as the place in which he first discovered, through maps, that the mind, the imagination, can provide at least a form of escape from what at first seems unendurable.

The worst episode of all came in 1938. Christopher had for several months been working as a labourer for the Furse Electrical Company who paid him approximately ten shillings a week more than he had previously received on the dole. He made himself voluntarily redundant and as a consequence was disqualified from any form of government relief. The family was reduced to living on parish hand-outs, had just enough food and coal to keep them alive and, occasionally, a few second-hand clothes. Sabina, out of anger or defiance, probably both, went to a pub in the middle of town with her elder sister Edith, and came back with enough money to supplement their meagre resources. Sillitoe never quite had the inclination to ask her if this was prompted by desperation – there were no other obvious sources for money – or was a means of revenging herself against Christopher; probably, he thought, something of each.

Once Christopher became aware of her activities there was, predictably, a noisy and violent exchange witnessed by the children. Sabina emptied her handbag of the money she had obtained over the previous few weeks, threw it in his face and left. Christopher sat for days staring into the fire, not speaking a word and moving only to visit the lavatory or go to bed. Peggy ran the household on money sent from her absent mother's takings until after little more than a week Sabina was brought back by the man – an otherwise unobjectionable figure – with whom she had been living. The family was restored to the already dreadful condition that had obtained for as long as any of the children could remember: attrition replaced crisis.

Peggy, Sillitoe and Pearl (aged respectively twelve, ten and eight) had been introduced to the most pitiless face of adulthood before reaching adolescence; for Brian, only six, the incomprehension of infancy offered some protection, and it is significant that his only clear recollection from the period is of his brother Alan. 'It was terrible, and even the things I can't remember directly I found out later from the others. For all of us, though, Alan was like a proper dad. We'd all get into his bed and he'd tell us stories. They seemed to go on for ever. One man, called Handley, was always there, he was an adventurer but he survived. Alan named one of his characters in his novels after him. Listening to Alan meant that we didn't have to think about everything else. He was a good storyteller even then, and we felt safe listening to him. He took us under his wing, just by telling stories.'

For all the children the effects of their parents' altercations, alongside a state of relentless deprivation, were ghastly, but for Sillitoe these incidents had a special significance as yet another dimension of what seemed like an unfolding of two stories, each involving similar circumstances and characters while following separate trajectories, their only dependable constant being their single witness, Alan Sillitoe. For most ten-year-olds a catalogue of violence, poverty and likely marital break-up would have registered as both horrific and unsurpassable; they would have had little opportunity to measure this against anything else. For Sillitoe, however, the events of 1937–8 seemed tailored to invite comparisons with another story. There appeared to be striking similarities between recent events at home and the crises and transitions that had beset the Burton family, notably Burton's making off with his son's girlfriend which prompted Oliver to enlist and led ultimately to his death, and Mary-Ann's confident intervention in her husband's further attempts at infidelity. Differences in detail were overridden by a shared notion of a struggle for power and ascendancy, and what was blindingly evident was that the Sillitoe household involved a resigned acceptance of humiliation, despair, lassitude and pain which seemed rooted in Christopher and had an immobilizing, denigrating effect on everyone else. The Burton house was by no means an idyll – even as a child Sillitoe did not blind himself to the fact that its head was possessed of a special brand of self-absorbed cruelty – but as he compared the actions and reactions that made up its history with their counterparts at home he found in the former a dynamic, albeit frequently harsh and savage, that was preferable by far to the biddable hopelessness which seemed to inform his immediate experience. Later this same sense of anarchic energy, unfocused but betokening a refusal to submit or conform, would become the quintessential feature of the character and the book that launched Sillitoe's career as a writer, Arthur Seaton in *Saturday Night and Sunday Morning*. Before that this unique sense of there being no alternative to what most children would accept, if not name, as fate had a crucial influence upon the formation of his own character. Much later he prefaced his first piece of self-evident autobiographical writing, *Raw Material*, with a quotation from Rabbi Akiba ben Joseph: 'All the future is foretold, but freedom of choice is given to everyone.' Succinctly put, this is the conundrum that has taxed theologians and everyone else since the Book of Genesis. Why care about our actions and their effects if everything is predetermined? For Sillitoe, ben Joseph unwraps the paradox by stating that each of us has a duty, a part to play in the formation of that which is foretold. The only reason that our destiny is unknown to us is that we have yet to make the decisions that will determine its foretelling. Sillitoe had some knowledge of the Old Testament, which seemed oddly familiar in the sense that its stories and parables appeared to correspond with many of his own experiences.

Late 1938 vouchsafed the Sillitoes a degree of stability in the option to rent a terraced house which at least allowed for some privacy. It had three bedrooms – one for the parents and one for each pair of sisters and brothers – and an outside lavatory to be used exclusively by its tenants. It was adjacent to the Raleigh bicycle factory, which would, for periods ranging from six weeks to four years, eventually employ each member of the family. Living space and income were again strained with the arrival of their third boy, Michael, in 1939, but Christopher was undeterred in his apparently quixotic attitude to long-term employment. He lasted a week with the British Sugar Corporation and after two and a half months as a labourer with Thomas Bow and Co., Builders, winter arrived. He found that mixing concrete and shifting bricks and hard core in inclement weather was unendurable, and left. Sillitoe returned again and again to his decaying editions of *Les Misérables* and *The Count of Monte Cristo*, principally to remind himself of how social injustice antedated the 1930s and affected places other than the East Midlands and to take some vicarious pleasure from a story driven by the desire for vengeance.

It was assumed, at least by most of Sillitoe's family, that school was simply an obligation offering some preparation for whatever type of manual work, most ambitiously an apprenticeship, would be available for a fourteen-year-old. Mary-Ann Burton, however, suggested that Sillitoe should sit for the local authority Free Scholarship examination. His parents did not object since they had no real idea of what this involved. If they had they would probably have shown less indulgence since a successful candidate could stay at school until the age of seventeen or eighteen, and if their initial promise was maintained they could take the appropriate entrance examinations for higher education. Mary-Ann had for some time noticed that Sillitoe was unlike virtually all of the children she knew, her own included. She had never urged the latter to remain at school for longer than they had to and though she and Burton himself were strangers to the demands and advantages of a formal education both recognized that Sillitoe combined an uncommon desire for knowledge with a natural instinctive intelligence. The examination was the equivalent of the eleven-plus, demanding a higher than average intellectual capability along with a basic grounding in the disciplines that would be studied more intensively thereafter, in all probability at Nottingham High School, effectively the local grammar. A small feeder class was set up in Sillitoe's primary school for those thought competent enough to try for the examination, and everyone in it, apart from him, came from the ambitious respectable branch of the local working class. 'We,' as his brother Michael would later reflect, 'were in a class of our own. It was impossible to fall any lower.' For various reasons – educated and doting relatives, Sunday school, the extracurricular assistance of charitable societies and the Workers' Educational Association – Sillitoe's fellow examinees were far more prepared than he for the sections on mathematics, grammar and modern languages. With pennies donated by Burton and Mary-Ann, Sillitoe had visited Wore's bookshop and purchased a *Pitman's Guide to French Grammar*. He already had a French–English dictionary and now he attempted to teach himself the mechanics and conventions of how languages work, heroically tackling the complexities of French syntax without any prior instruction in the abstract structures of English. He was fascinated by the experience of attempting to exist in another linguistic landscape, because he now had a primitive knowledge of foreign words and their operations to add to his imagined conspectus of lands and experiences elsewhere. Despite or probably because of his idiosyncratic efforts he failed the exam, but his marks were close enough to the border for him to be encouraged to sit again in the winter term of 1939. Once more, however, his energetic single-minded attempts at autodidacticism proved incompatible with formal expectations and he prepared himself for Radford Boulevard Senior Boys' School, the pre-war equivalent of a secondary modern, from which everyone departed without qualifications aged fourteen.

Much has been written about the nature and effects of class mobility, and Richard Hoggart's classic *The Uses of Literacy* reflects, circa 1957, the general consensus on what the consequences could be for someone who took the escalator from the proletariat to its preferred alternative. 'In part they have a sense of loss ... they are emotionally uprooted from their class, often under the stimulus of a stronger critical intelligence or imagination, qualities which can lead to an unusual self-consciousness before their own situation' (Hoggart, p. 292). In Hoggart's findings – and indeed his experience – upward mobility from the bottom end of working-class existence could often cause unease and a sense of identity crisis and even lead to psychological breakdown. The phrase which irritates – because it amounts to an insult – is that which describes the upwardly mobile class-jumper as eventually having to cope with a 'stronger critical intelligence or imagination'; in short, in order to become more cultured and intelligent one must suppress innate inhibiting features of your humble background. It would be too easy to perceive this as a token of bourgeois conservatism, but it functions just as effectively, with added hypocrisy, as the means by which the enlightened, cultured leftist intelligentsia retains its own brand of clubbishness, ensuring that only the right sort of intellectual aspirant can gain membership.

The classic example, from the beginning of this century, is D.H. Lawrence, a writer whose background and location often prompt misguided comparisons with Sillitoe. Lawrence, aged twelve, won the same scholarship which forty years later Sillitoe failed to secure and went on to attend the same school, Nottingham High, for which the latter had ambitions. Lack of money forced Lawrence to leave aged fifteen but after working as a clerk and pupil teacher – the latter post secured by his mother, herself an ex-schoolteacher – he eventually took up a scholarship at Nottingham University College. Lawrence's introduction to middle-class culture did not on the face of things cause him to exchange his origins for literary ventriloquism but in truth he became the kind of radical who was exciting enough to appeal to the fashionable iconoclasts within the literary establishment without being too garish or uncouth to cause them embarrassment. The fact that he could write, from experience, of a world that those who came to idolize him – particularly the members of the so-called Bloomsbury group – knew only by vicarious observation added greatly to his appeal, yet it was his ability to combine a penchant for raw, mystically emboldened sexuality with the kind of humourless prophecy pioneered by George Eliot that secured his place as a favourite among the conceited radicals of 1920s British intelligentsia. Lawrence is a writer who has divided critics since his death, mainly because he wasted much of his undoubted literary talent as a polemicist for a grotesque irredentist philosophy of being. His status as almost a significant writer was secured by his division of allegiance to what he had been and what he found himself becoming. His past provided him with a store of original narratives and perspectives while his initiation into the world of Huxley, Morrell, Murry, Mansfield, Russell et al. offered him an audience whose culture he pretended to renounce but, in truth, to whose music he danced.

Hypothesis can lead to mischievous dissembling, but one must none the less wonder what would have happened to Sillitoe had he won the scholarship to Nottingham High School, received proper, formal instruction in the languages and sciences and gone on to university. He might have become a linguist or an engineer, but let us assume that his nascent literary interests developed alongside his passage through the education system. It is possible that works bearing some resemblance to *Saturday Night and Sunday Morning* and the short stories of *The Loneliness of the Long Distance Runner* volume – drawn as they are from his personal memories – would have gone into print but they would not have been as striking, as bitterly original as the pieces that we have. The quintessence of Sillitoe's early work is its magnificent lack of allegiance. It is focused upon working-class life but it refuses to recognize a culture that might exist beyond it and avoids forlorn signals to victimhood or anxious definitions of itself in relation to some repressive correlate. Sillitoe was the first ever to create a portrait of working-class existence which eschewed any responsibility to define itself, and this was due in part to his taking the route that he did at that first important crossroads in his life in the summer and autumn of 1939. He did not choose to fail the examinations – he was inevitably disappointed – but as a consequence he took a first step towards the uncompromising individuality that is the imprint of his writing.

Sillitoe: 'At the time I felt I had let myself down, but even if I'd passed, the kudos would soon have been replaced by rebelliousness. I wanted the satisfaction of being able to get to grammar school but once there I wouldn't have been able to put up with the regimentation and conformity. I'd have loved to prove I was capable of getting in but I'd have hated being there and I'd have got out.'

For Sillitoe the outbreak of war seemed a continuation, with some variants and even improvements, of the world as he knew it. Its first year involved little more than military attrition and public speculation and provided an abundance of material for his interest in maps, landscapes and their geopolitical correlates. BBC reports on the state of the British Expeditionary Force and its French counterpart, while for obvious reasons incomplete, became the inspiration for exercises in map reading and annotation. Most adults had some memory of the previous conflict which had ended barely two decades earlier and greeted this one with weary resignation; it was out of their hands, conscription had yet to be announced and with the widely publicized developments in mechanized warfare it was unlikely to last long. None the less, anxiety soon displaced insouciance as the Germans overran the Netherlands and Belgium with unprecedented speed and efficiency. Within months the battered remnants of the Expeditionary Force had been evacuated from Dunkirk, France had fallen and only twenty-two miles of sea separated Britain from the combined forces of the Axis powers who now controlled most of central and western Europe.

Within a year unemployment was virtually abolished, and though prosperity was out of the question the basic wage for the ordinary working man did not fall any lower than its already dismal 1938–9 level. Christopher was sent straight from the Labour Exchange to work as a labourer building air-raid shelters, having already as he put it 'swung the lead' to avoid military service; he had in fact convinced the recruitment board that he was forty, four years beyond his actual age.

THREE

Sillitoe's recollection of his parents' discussion on whether or not to evacuate four of their five children – Michael, aged six months, was not in these circumstances classified as a child – is, he admits, clouded by subsequent exchanges with his sisters on what exactly was said, but it might have been written by Samuel Beckett, with some small assistance from Kafka. Sabina and Christopher, for once agreed on a matter of mutual concern, were distraught at the prospect of themselves being killed – everyone by then assumed that Nottingham would be a prime Luftwaffe target – and thus never able to see their children again. Sillitoe and Peggy were only later able to reflect upon the darkly comic logic that underpinned this peculiar prognosis; perhaps their parents had some intuition of a happy state as yet unenvisaged by theologians or philosophers, inverse bereavement. Troubled, they considered the pragmatic benefits of allowing them to go; they would through a government-sanctioned initiative still have a family but be excused the time, money and effort that normally went into looking after it. Christopher brought the exchange to a close by declaring that they would let them go '. . . and see what happens'. Sabina agreed, providing a glint of rational tenderness with her comment that this would at least prevent the Germans killing all of them.

Along with twenty or so others from the locality Sillitoe, Peggy, Pearl and six-year-old Brian were put on a bus which took them through Sherwood Forest to the small mining town of Worksop. Every other child had with them the recommended provision of at least one spare set of clothes and underwear, pyjamas and enough food and drink to cover them for unforeseen overnight delays. The Sillitoes left with the clothes they stood up in, plus a pasty to share between them, a few sweets and government-issued gas masks. In Worksop Church Hall names were called and siblings separated apparently at random, some staying in units of two or three and others being taken away on their own. Without explanation or the opportunity to say a proper goodbye Sillitoe was driven by car to a terrace that resembled the one he had left that morning. This one, he was told as they arrived, was called Sandhill Street. Mr and Mrs Cutts were only a few years older than his parents and once again he found himself in what seemed like a living hypothesis – superficially a version of his home life but with key aspects shrewdly modified. The Cuttses' house was of the same period and design as his though a little more spacious, and it was furnished and decorated in a manner that reflected routines of quiet affection and permanence. Cutts was self-employed, selling fruit and vegetables from his handcart in the town, and his wife made use of this produce in a daily menu of basic nutritious meals. Sillitoe's abiding first memory of the house's interior was the appearance and smell of a stewpot on the kitchen hob. Aside from another evacuee who stayed only for two weeks Sillitoe seemed, without trying too hard, to belong in the household. Breakfast, the same hour every day, would be porridge and toast, the main meal a hot dinner at midday, a sandwich and perhaps some tinned fruit for tea and then supper between seven and eight.

Within a few weeks he had become Mr Cutts's occasional assistant, helping him wheel the cart through the narrow cobbled streets of Worksop. Other days he would be free to roam the surrounding countryside; no maps this time but a feeling of adventure and independence greater than that he had enjoyed around Burton's cottage. Now, aged barely twelve, he was beyond anyone's control. The Cuttses showed sufficient concern to make him agree to return for meals at the appointed times, but whatever else he did was up to him. He began drawing his own maps, tracing the mosaic of hedges, roads, streams, pitheads and church spires that made up the landscape, but his cartographer's instincts were overtaken by a more powerful attraction. No one knew who he was and everything he encountered seemed the more fascinating for that. At the end of Sandhill Street was some open ground in which he found three caravans, oval framed, brightly decorated and drawn by horses. The people accepted his visits without much comment and did not object to his becoming friendly with Laura, who seemed to be around his age. It was, he thinks, his first infatuation. They were too young to form a close friendship, let alone an adolescent relationship, but he knew even now that they recognized similarities in each other. For Laura, separateness, a life lived outside the settled community to which her family sold crockery, was the given, all she had known. Sillitoe sensed that her world echoed his burgeoning instinct, something that as yet he was not able to properly rationalize let alone articulate. Laura's family – he was never told nor did he ask her surname – were by heritage and choice itinerants yet they seemed to belong in the landscape in a way that reminded him of Burton; they didn't own it, nor were they beholden to it. What excited him most was their lack of allegiance to anywhere in particular; whenever they wanted to, Laura informed him, they could just go.

The Cuttses offered yet another variation upon his home life and his experience of the Burtons. Mr Cutts was the breadwinner but he seemed to share the governance of the household with his wife, which in any event constituted only the two of them – their only son was in the Army. Neither had received much of a formal education but each had what would later impress Sillitoe as a rare combination of innate wisdom and generosity. While Mrs Cutts prepared their tea he began offering her tentative reports on his excursions and the people he had met, Laura in particular. She showed genuine interest and reprimanded him only once, for using the single term he knew from home to describe his new friends. 'Gypsy', she explained, was insulting. Sillitoe was reminded of this when the word 'travellers' began to enter the currency of political correctness more than thirty years later, and he remains awed by Mrs Cutts's apparently personal coining. Cutts himself appeared something of an enigma. In some respects he reminded Sillitoe of Burton, a well-built, confident man with a voice powerful enough to raise his customers from their beds. He enjoyed a full plate of food and consumed impressive amounts of beer at the table and in the local pubs. Yet he never gave orders, made threats or, beyond an easy conviviality, appeared drunk. When the time came for Sillitoe to enrol at the local secondary school Cutts went with him and introduced him to his class teacher. On the way home he told him that the two of them, though not friends, had known each other for more than twenty years. He, as sergeant major, had served with the teacher, then a captain, in the South Nottinghamshire Hussars in the Salonica campaign of the Great War. They had been spared the mind-numbing horrors of the Western Front but Cutts harboured no illusions about what now faced Britain. This, he confided to Sillitoe, would be a different kind of war because the enemy was not just another country. It was much worse than that.

His parents, through naïveté or incautious optimism, took a different view and only three months after his arrival the Cuttses received a letter from Sabina, their first and only one, informing them that she would be coming to Worksop in a few days with a view to taking Sillitoe home. Over tea she made it clear that everyone she knew in Nottingham were now of the opinion that the war had reached a stalemate and the cities were safe. Cutts disagreed and offered a prescient account of Germany's potential and objectives. Undeterred, Sabina insisted that all of her children should return. Sillitoe still remains puzzled by the whole episode with regard to both his parents' motives and his own feelings. Sabina's and Christopher's decision seemed unselfish – indeed the return of four children would ensure that they remained at their usual point, just above the poverty line. Perhaps the gesture reflected, at last, something akin to love and commitment, though if it did it seemed a characteristically English kind of disclosure in that nothing was actually said. Aside from the curious nature of his parents' act Sillitoe came to regard his time with the Cuttses as yet another insight, uncommonly vivid for someone his age, into the mischievous nature of fate.

Once they were all at home he began to exchange stories with his sisters. They, apparently, had been sent out to a farmer near Worksop, been obliged to share a room – in effect a converted sty – with about four others and used virtually as servants. Gradually, he came upon similar stories from children who had returned to Nottingham later in the war. Each dire anecdote prompted a comparison with a collateral act of generosity from the Cuttses. She, for example, had provided him with a new pair of trousers and shoes within a week of his arrival, and was tactful enough to avoid any comment on the fact that the ones that made up his entire wardrobe were beyond repair. Tales from friends of their being obliged to dig allotments and clean scullery floors chased into sharper focus his memory of how one day Cutts had taken him to see his teacher, 'the Captain', after school and both had suggested that he have one more go at the scholarship exam. He had mentioned his previous attempts in response to the Cuttses' enquiries into his interests. The more he heard of what others had been through the more it seemed to him that his months with the Cutts had been sanctioned by an omnipotent farceur. He had been shown a glimpse of another life, led by working-class people who transcended the patronizing folklore of socialism, and he had then watched the shutter close.

Barely into his teens, Sillitoe had neither the resources nor the inclination to reflect on what his time with the Cuttses meant but the episode matured with him and contributed to his unorthodox, bifurcated perception of class and identity. He grew to loathe those who sustained position and power by exploitation but reserved an equal contempt for others who perceived and portrayed the exploited as incapable of shaping their own lives.

Back at home the world he had known a few months earlier was seemingly unchanged yet touched by a hint of the bizarre. Christopher as usual was incapable of sustaining long-term employment except that now he was never unemployed, driven from one job to another by the wartime labour shortage. For a fortnight or so either side of Sillitoe's return he was doing basic menial labour at the local sugar-beet processing factory, satisfied in being able to bring home several bags of sugar from his shift, a valuable supplement as rationing became more severe.

Arthur Shelton was Sillitoe's age and had been his closest friend outside the family since before evacuation. Arthur's father was a self-employed joiner and though they lived barely a street away from the Sillitoes the Sheltons always had enough money to feed and properly clothe their children. They had, moreover, not for one second procrastinated on whether to send Arthur out of Nottingham: their family would stay together come what may, and Mr Shelton made use of his experience as a builder to construct a formidably strong Anderson shelter. Sillitoe and Arthur did not keep their respective home lives secret, but each, by tacit agreement, never commented on what they knew. They were equable companions and soon after Sillitoe's return they spent a good deal of time cycling around the countryside, fascinated by the feckless state of emergency that had informed provincial

England. The landscape they knew so well now had unobtrusive sandbagged trenches placed at what appeared to be key strategic points – notably cross-roads, bridges and railway junctions – and manned by soldiers who didn't seem to know exactly what they were waiting for beyond the regular arrival of a lorry bringing bread, butter and tea. The fact that all this was observed at close quarters by two twelve-year-olds, keen to see what sort of weapons the soldiers had and whether they thought an invasion was imminent, made everything seem faintly absurd, almost quaint.

Almost; but the Sillitoe family seemed to act as a magnet for the aberrant or inopportune. Sillitoe came home one day from school to find that the already crowded household had now acquired an official lodger. Sillitoe never learned his name but after a week of him sleeping on the sofa his mother explained that she had gone out for bread and found him standing nervously in a shop doorway, having made a rather forlorn attempt to hide his uniform under an overcoat. He had asked her if she knew where he might get a cup of tea and she, without hesitation, had told him that 'yes, me duck' she did; across the road at her house, where he would also be safe from the prying eyes of those in the locality who might deal with him less sympa-thetically. He had, he explained, been attached to an anti-aircraft artillery unit and gone absent without leave. Sabina did not press him on his reasons for doing so but she asked Sillitoe for his ID card. Children were rarely required to show theirs and dealt with indulgently when they lost them. She rubbed out Sillitoe's name and date of birth and got a typist at the Raleigh factory to replace them with false ones. With proof of his civilian status the soldier attended the local labour exchange and Sabina advised him that if he found work he could then get lodgings in the area and spend the rest of the war in relative anonymity. Christopher was of course aware of what was going on, or at least most of it, but he allowed his wife to take charge. When the soldier was arrested he claimed to have stolen the ID card before meet-ing Sabina and stated that neither she nor any of the family knew that he was on the run. He was sent to prison and had he not protected them Sabina, Christopher or both would have faced a custodial sentence. They knew the identity of the neighbour who had informed on the soldier, a man who continued to greet them with the same disingenuous good humour before and after the soldier's arrest.

Sillitoe would come to reflect on this incident as evidence of something in his family – genetic or inculcated, he was not sure – that involved an unpremeditated sympathy with anyone who seemed the victim of authority. Perhaps when Sabina saw the soldier he reminded her of her brother-in-law Eddie who had deserted, hid in the countryside near Burton-on-Trent, been arrested and sent back to the Western Front. He survived but never recovered. It was not that the Sillitoes were pacifists or appeasers; insofar as they knew much at all about politics they were aware that defeat by Nazism was a horrific prospect. Yet at the same time they felt able to reconcile this with an equally powerful empathy with a desperate lad, barely out of his teens. For the first time Sillitoe began to feel for his parents something close to respect, and he would recall all of this when planning the early drafts of *Saturday Night and Sunday Morning*. The episode is not recreated verbatim but intriguing traces of it can be found in several passages; principally in Chapter 7 where the young man breaks the undertaker's window and is subsequently detained by a group of people, most enthusiastically women, whose desire to have justice done is bogus and who revel in the opportunity simply to punish, irrespective of the nature of the crime.

Sillitoe's brief collusion in sheltering the hapless deserter was followed by an altogether more morally ambiguous coda, the arrival of his two cousins. Burton's grandsons, both just old enough to have been called up, had deserted before completing basic training. They had burned their uniforms, Army pay books and ID cards at their mother's house and for most of 1940–41 ventured out only at night. They would sleep during the day in the houses of relatives, calling in on the Sillitoes about once a fortnight for some food, a wash and the use of empty beds. For a few hours between his return from school and their departure they would entertain Sillitoe with stories of their nocturnal activities. Mainly they broke into shops and warehouses or anywhere they suspected that rare and rationed goods were stored. Such organized crime as existed in Nottingham was now focused upon the black market, and Sillitoe's cousins contributed energetically to this concealed economy, sometimes rewarding the Sillitoes with leftovers from the night's thefts and sales. It was all as exciting as anything by Haggard, Doyle or Dumas, and Sillitoe, as yet having had no opportunity to reflect on the unrealness of fiction, felt inspired. He purchased from Wore's a *Pitman's* guide to shorthand. Shorthand proved too complicated to master single-handedly but he remained clear in his objective and took out a book on how to become a writer from the public library at the top of the street. He would assemble material from their tales and from his first-hand knowledge of them – mannerisms, accent, age, hair colour, height, etc. – and try to make a story from it. This was his first attempt at fiction and despite his adolescent uncertainties it was prescient. He assumed, while never having discussed 'the novel' with anyone, that the author should be an unobtrusive choreographer, should enable the words on the page to resemble as closely as possible things and events witnessed. Grand gestures and the invocation of moral absolutes did not seem necessary. The reader should be offered the equivalent of what he, Sillitoe, listened to and observed; judgement was their business. Fifteen years later this same programme would underpin the drafts of his early ground-breaking fiction, but at the time his mother was more concerned with the consequences for all of them if these luridly accurate accounts were scrutinized by a particular type of reader, a policeman, and, following her nephews' example with their uniforms and documents, she burned the lot.

Sillitoe's remaining two years before leaving school constituted a patchwork of the routine, the quixotic and the faintly bizarre. The most concentrated air raid on Nottingham occurred in May 1941, causing more than two hundred fatalities. By then the family had become used to sirens announcing night-time visits from the Luftwaffe, and even if their targets eventually turned out to be Coventry or Birmingham the Sillitoes would spend eight-hour periods crowded into their backyard Anderson shelter, damp, freezing cold and lit only by a flickering, smelly oil lamp. The very name of these improvised dugouts became a joke because in truth they would have provided no 'shelter' whatsoever from bombs falling in the vicinity. Sillitoe's clearest memory of the May air raid is of his father standing on a wall and silhouetted against the glow of fires barely a quarter of a mile away. He was, for once, enjoying himself, noting that many of the successfully bombed targets were factories which over the past two decades had either employed him or refused him work.

In late 1941 the cousins – still today referred to as 'Aunt Edith's boys' to spare potential embarrassment to living relatives – were caught by the police, served a year for theft and went on to do time in a military prison for desertion. After being returned to their units they went AWOL once more and resumed their criminal careers until caught once again. They ended the war on the front line, serving in an armoured division on the North German plain, and they were, according to Sillitoe, not greatly different from most other young men of the area; true, they had at first elected not to fight, but so did conscientious objectors, and they had only stolen goods from businesses and never done physical harm to other people. They were not moral exemplars but Sillitoe still detects something much worse in the man who took malicious satisfaction in handing over the other deserter.

FOUR

The war in Europe began to offer Sillitoe a peculiar blend of wish fulfilment and self-instruction. Previously his interest in maps would be confounded by a lack of any other frame of reference. From the dated *Baedekers* and *Guides Bleus* from Wore's bookshop he could work out the political and topographical contours of places such as France and Germany but his sense of what actually went on there was hazy and tenuous. Now however he had a story, supplied variously by newspapers, by wireless and the Pathé newsreels which accompanied his occasional visits to the cinema. The event which enthralled him most was the German invasion of the Soviet Union in June 1941. The unpronounceable names of regions and towns suddenly came to life in reports of the German advance, and Sillitoe knew that, despite the fact that the Soviet armies were retreating constantly until the winter of 1941, this would be the turning point of the war in Europe. His teacher, Percy Rowe, lent him a copy of G.D.H. Cole's *Post-War Europe* and while much of it remained beyond his grasp he became aware of how vast were the natural and industrial resources of the Soviet Union and more significantly that its winter had the capacity to defeat the best-equipped and most determined military forces – the legend of Napoleon's retreat was a mainstay even of primary-school treatments of history.

In the library he found a book of Russian folk tales, and the one he recalls most vividly had the Devil, disguised, offering the inhabitants of a steppes village all the land that they could walk round during a single hot August day. Each was beset by various levels of greedy ambition and died in the attempt to overreach the limits of human endurance; all but one. A Jew walked for a few hundred yards, rested, set out to his right and repeated the exercise twice more as everyone else disappeared into the far distance to collapse from thirst and exhaustion. Sillitoe was fascinated for two reasons. The story fed his growing fascination for a group of people about whom he had no clear understanding. He had marvelled at stories from the Old Testament read aloud by teachers in primary school and had a vague sense of the Jews as a tribe which pre-dated the Christian era. Did they still exist? He had heard of a reasonably well-off Jewish family in Nottingham for whom Arthur Shelton's mother had done cleaning work, but quite how these figures related to the almost fantastical race of the Old Testament was a mystery. Later he began to suspect that the Russian folk tale was tinged with anti-Semitism, in that it implied that only Jews would be possessed of sufficient levels of cunning and earnest calculation to temper the emotions which claimed the other villagers' lives. But when he first encountered it as an innocent reader who had yet to learn of the Holocaust his response was empathy and admiration. This man had after all outwitted the Devil and was guilty of nothing more than an abundance of common sense.

There was something else too that caused the image of the walking Jew to fix itself in his imagination. He was not yet old enough to contemplate what travelling and the implied notion of freeing oneself from a rooted existence involved, but he knew it attracted him. The map would be his index to elsewhere and for the first time he had come upon a figure – real or symbolic, he was not sure – who corresponded with this as yet unfocused ideal of travel as a form of controlled destiny.

Sillitoe completed his formal education for good in March 1942, only just fourteen. He had shown himself to be one of the best in the class and in the previous year received praise for an essay on how the Russians might reverse the German advance – plagiarized, he admits, from the wireless – and the day he left school the headmaster presented him with a black leather-bound copy of the King James Bible in recognition of his 'achievements'. Before the age of ten he had formed a primitive sense of there being nothing of any significance beyond the tactile world, that death was the end of everything, but the Bible he was given on his last day at school remains with him today. He is still uncertain of how someone whose lack of faith remains resolute has since the day he received the book treasured it as a source of inspiration – hardly a week has gone by over the past sixty-five years without his reading it. He always goes to the Old Testament and invariably feels strengthened by the experience. Before Christ there was doctrine and belief but both were matched by examples of self-abnegating decency and strength; the choice to be and do what you judged best and the courage to endure the worst were as important as overarching rules.

The Raleigh factory had been a charmless constant in the Sillitoe family's peripatetic existence for as long as Sillitoe could remember. Now it produced armaments along with bicycles and a week after he had walked through the school gates it gave Sillitoe his first full-time job. First he was told to chamfer – that is, file away the rough edges – brass shell cases and within a month he was upgraded to machinist. Parts for artillery pieces were sent to his bench, already marked for drilling, and it was his job to secure these in a vice, follow the instructions to insert the designated size of bit and bring down the massive drill. The perforated plates and hubs would then be transported off and bolted together in another part of the factory.

It was not the worst kind of repetitive factory work – it demanded some skill – but the job was none the less a classic instance of the supposedly dehumanizing effects of the production line. Sillitoe, however, enjoyed himself. It was not that he felt fulfilled – though he took some satisfaction from the knowledge that each piece he helped produce would in all likelihood kill Germans; his pleasure was more perverse, a mixture of self-absorption and masochism.

Many of his more experienced workmates complained that the factory's system of piecework – payment by the number of items produced rather than by the hour – was just another scheme dreamed up by the bosses to dupe the more gullible workers; they knew how much it was physically possible to produce and they set their piecework rates at just enough to tempt the money-grabbers into working themselves into a state of exhaustion. Sillitoe agreed, to an extent, but saw piecework as a personal challenge and set about attempting to produce more and better pieces than anyone else. He wanted the money, certainly, but he got almost as much pleasure from taking the factory on at their own game.

Soon he earned himself a modest reputation for levels of endurance and efficiency that belied his appearance; he was a pale, skinny teenager who could easily have been mistaken for an eleven-year-old. Word even reached his father, who at the time had work in a different part of the factory, and Christopher would occasionally visit his son and nod with grudging approval at what he had himself produced and the speed at which his son turned out shell cases and other parts.

Sillitoe had a rough idea of what the political divide between left and right involved – though for the war years party politics at government level had effectively been suspended – and he was fully aware that for people of his class and locality politics was one-dimensional, Labour and the trade unions. The same instinct that prompted his attitude to piecework resurfaced when soon after starting work he was approached by the shop steward and informed that his threepence-per-week membership fees for the union would be deducted automatically from his pay. 'What if I don't want to join?' asked Sillitoe, and the shop steward, recovering his composure – no one asked him questions like that – informed the disrespectful youth that he did not have a choice. It was, he said, 'the law'. At the time the only Marx Sillitoe had heard of was Groucho but he remembers vividly the feeling of bitterness that following being told he had to be part of an organization that seemed just as faceless and dictatorial as the factory itself. He returned to his bench after urging the union official to 'fuck off and get dive-bombed'.

His first wage packet came to one pound twelve shillings, which he handed unopened to his mother who provided him with half a crown pocket money. As the months went by and his weekly income gradually increased, so did his percentage, and he was by the end of 1942 taking girls out to the pictures and still managing to save ten-shilling notes which he stored in his King James Bible, Old Testament only. His first girlfriend worked at a factory producing uniforms, but their families had known each other for decades.

Her name, then, was Doreen Greatorex. Doreen: 'There was Alan and me and his friend, Arthur Shelton, and Dorothy. Arthur would marry Dorothy. We made up a foursome quite often.' What did you do? I ask. 'We didn't have enough money to do much at all. Sometimes we might have enough for the pictures. Mainly we just larked about. We might take bikes out at weekends, sometimes go rowing.' It sounds all very innocent, I observe. 'It certainly *was*,' Doreen states, before laughing. There is a coincidence, more than a coincidence, that compels a question. Arthur and Doreen? Doreen Greatorex and the delightful Doreen Greatton of *Saturday Night and Sunday Morning*? 'Yes,' Doreen concedes, 'Alan's family, particularly his sister Peggy, have told me many a time that she was based on me.' We will hear more from Doreen – the real one – later, but there was a reason why Sillitoe chose her as the model for the woman to be played with such captivating allure by Shirley Ann Field. The Doreen of the novel is Arthur's refuge from a rampaging sexuality that is fed as much by bitterness as desire. This is how he remembered Doreen Greatorex. After they drifted apart his relationships became anything but virtuous.

He bought more maps and pre-war out-of-print guidebooks to virtually every part of Europe, and on one occasion was just in time to pick up for free a city-centre travel agent's entire stock of brochures for the fashionable parts of the Continent. Alluring photographs and accounts of the Côte d'Azur, the Alps, the spa towns of southern Germany, Paris, Biarritz and even Berlin seemed like a faintly macabre joke given that these destinations had been visited by, among others, British tourists, barely three years earlier; many of the brochures were dated 1938. Sillitoe's lathe-bound fantasies were made predominantly of a curious mosaic of images, some drawn from pictures and descriptions of a continent unaware or wilfully ignorant of its imminent dreadful fate and others, via the BBC and Pathé, often featuring the same location in the grip of a nightmare.

Sillitoe knew that the only way he could change his life was by first joining up and when the war ended setting out on his own. By now the USA was involved and even the most pessimistic within his own community were beginning to acknowledge that however long it took the overwhelming combination of the Soviet Union and America would bring about the defeat of Germany. He was too young for active service and even if he contrived to alter the dates on his ID forms his build and appearance, barely five feet six and cheekily amiable, would undo any heroic attempt at deception. To add to his frustration he found himself transferred to the part of the Raleigh plant that still assembled bikes. These were for military use but they wouldn't actually kill anyone.

To move to another factory meant a Ministry of Labour form in which the applicant had to offer a convincing case for the transfer. Sillitoe stated that he was a better worker than most and needed to be doing more for the war effort. The form was dispatched to the silent hinterland of bureaucracy and would probably have remained there had not Sillitoe organized an unofficial sit-down protest. His co-agitators wanted to move mainly because they had heard of less taxing or better-paid jobs elsewhere, but Sillitoe's primary motivation was an evolving addiction to contrariness. His desire to participate in the production of real armaments was genuine enough but it was accompanied by a dissentient characteristic in his personality that would attend virtually all of his opinions and beliefs in adult life. He would in due course commit himself wholeheartedly to a number of fundamental causes, but in each case commitment would be qualified by perversity. It seemed as though any pure belief brought with it a threat to individuality, and this same temperamental characteristic would become a feature of his writing, often causing umbrage in critics who expected capriciousness to be more predictable.

His next job was with A.B. Toone and Company where plywood and timber were cut, planed and nailed and bolted together as basic units for invasion barges and Mosquito fighter bombers. Union membership was again compulsory and piecework was replaced by an hourly rate. Sillitoe was slightly worse off but took some satisfaction from the knowledge that the things he was helping to make were designed exclusively for assault rather than defence, that the war was now being taken to Germany. Mainly he worked as a labourer shifting six-foot-by-three, half-inch-thick boards from one bench to another and obliged to work as fast as the man on each either finished their job or shouted for another board to start the next. It brought to mind the family story of how his father had been forced to spend days shifting rolls of cloth and furniture and hence developed a wrestler's upper body strength. Despite the slightly dispiriting parallel Sillitoe relished the opportunity to build muscle on his skinny frame.

Everyone in the family, apart from Brian and Michael who were too young, was now in some sort of employment. Sabina finally had the opportunity and indeed the money to run the house in an orderly manner, and food, though very basic, was never in short supply. Sillitoe grew stronger and spent many of his tea breaks and dinner hours in the company of a boy he had last known at primary school. Bill Towle had acquired the physique of a Rugby League player, solid, stocky and fast, and set about teaching Sillitoe the rudiments of self-defence: boxing, knife fighting and the less disciplined skills of doing as much damage to someone else as possible.

It was not that Sillitoe felt particularly insecure about his relative slightness. He had never been fearful of anything much, his instinctive reaction to the inevitable presence of bullies and their like being indifference. But adulthood would be far more dangerous and brutal than anything he might have faced at school, and with a provocative personality like his, physical conflict seemed inevitable.

He enjoyed his knockabouts with Towle. There was something about violence that seemed to guarantee release. 'You were on your own, your fate was in your own hands and even if you stood no chance of defeating your opponent, just doing them some harm would bring satisfaction.' And yet again one senses in Sillitoe's first addictive experience of brutality, albeit without rancour, the kernel of the peculiar passage in *Saturday Night and Sunday Morning* when Arthur is ambushed by the two off-duty soldiers and beaten up. It involves an account of physical conflict of a kind unprecedented in literature and for that matter unrecorded anywhere else. Arthur knows he is outnumbered, he does not particularly enjoy being beaten up or inflicting retributive pain on his aggressors. But he never gives in and as a token of his utter obduracy he even refrains from telling the reader what he feels or thinks.

Sillitoe's relationship with militarism has always been paradoxical. To an extent the armed services characterized a good deal of what from adolescence onwards he treated with anger and contempt. They were the agencies of the ruling élite, guaranteed to reinforce the class system of society and deny the ordinary soldier any sense of individualism; Sillitoe knew from his family and neighbours of what had occurred only two decades before, and the regular visits by the pitiable, ghostly figure of his uncle, Eddie the Tramp, bore immediate testimony to the horrific effects of mass conflict even upon the physically unharmed. As a teenager, however, he was able to set all this aside. Not until the newspaper reports of 1945 disclosed what had happened in the camps liberated by the British and US forces – the full extent of the Holocaust would not become apparent until even later – did he and everyone else come to recognize the true evil of the regime against which they had battled as much with grim resignation as moral zeal. So in 1943–4 Sillitoe's fevered determination to get involved was, though creditable, possessed by something of the elemental and primitive.

Bill Towle, precociously strong and agile, had enrolled with the local Home Guard and Sillitoe tried to join the same platoon. He knew that the threat of invasion had largely passed and that such units were now little more than morale-boosting clubs for those too old for proper service, but they had also been issued with proper weapons, Lee-Enfield rifles and Thomson sub-machine guns, and Sillitoe was itching to get his hands on one. Unfortunately and despite being toughened up by work at Toone and Co. he still looked fourteen. The captain advised him to come back in two years.

What followed could be described as Sillitoe's characteristically perverse initiation into adulthood. Aside from individuals with priestly ambitions the mid to late teens involve a spiral of competing, raging instincts in which sex usually predominates. For Sillitoe this explosive mixture was supplemented by two equally compulsive imperatives: he wanted to travel and he wanted to fight.

FIVE

On 1 October 1942 Sillitoe and Arthur Shelton enrolled with the local wing of the Air Training Corps. The adjutant, Flying Officer Pink, offered them a rough account of the roles which they, as potential recruits, might fill, if found sufficiently competent, from ground staff through the air crew functions of navigator, wireless operator, gunner, bomb-aimer and even pilot. Flying Officer Pink then asked whether or not they cleaned their teeth on a daily basis. Sillitoe confessed to an irresponsible lack of dental hygiene and was advised by Pink that if he were to go further in the service something would have to be done about this. He promised that he would do his best.

They were told that if they got through the four-week probation they would be issued with uniforms and cadet cap badges and admitted to the training course for a Proficiency Certificate Part 1, involving basic weapons training, elementary navigation skills, map reading and the formalities of square bashing. Sillitoe invested in a new toothbrush and though the absurdity did not properly register at the time he subsequently became intrigued by how his seniors had focused upon the state of his teeth as the key determinant of his probation. He got through and, teeth glistening, became qualified to fly in combat aircraft and fire a rifle.

He recalls the former vividly. In February 1943 he and about ten other recruits were sent to RAF Newton, eight miles east of Nottingham, and introduced to the disheartening spectacle of a De Havilland Dominie, a plywood, twin-engine biplane of pre-war vintage. The youngsters had been instructed on how to use their parachutes, and each took their place on a bench within what was technically the fuselage but reminded Sillitoe of a large garden shed. The pilot was a Pole who set about his task with unaffected disinterest, wandering over to the plane while still in avid conversation with his friends and taxiing for take-off like a man with other things on his mind. Once airborne he offered a display of what an experienced pilot might do with a plane. Sillitoe loved it. The Trent, the urban landscapes that cut into the greensward of the East Midlands countryside, church towers and steeples – all of these he had known, through his interest in maps and his bicycle rides through the locality. Now points of recognition were tinged with the sublime. Within a second he would glimpse a particular village and its spire and a moment later the broader span of the whole eastern region of England, from Nottingham to the North Sea, would fill an enlarged canvas. It was the most exciting moment of his life so far. Everything and elsewhere appeared almost immediately available, and the episode was further enriched by its personnel. The pilot took the youths back to the canteen to join his comrades for a meal, stewed meat of unspecified origin cooked in hot peppers and served with the strangest dumplings any of them had come across. Newton was staffed entirely by expatriate Polish pilots, most of whom had fought heroically, recklessly, in the Battle of Britain two years earlier and were now awaiting their next major assignment involving, they were convinced, the liberation of their native land. This whiff of untrammelled non-Englishness – the Poles, all officers, were carelessly informal and familiar and so unlike their English counterparts – combined with the opportunities for raw freedom further convinced Sillitoe that he would and could shake himself free of the region in which he was born.

For the next two years Sillitoe's world involved precipitate moments of excitement set against a backdrop of unrealized ambition and the predominance of the mundane. Advanced ATC training involved target practice with 303 Lee-Enfields and, most thrillingly, 'hedge-hopping' flights in twin-engined Oxford trainers. Sillitoe would sit behind the pilot, confounded, exhilarated and petrified in equal measure as the plane seemed capable of avoiding hillsides treetops and electric pylons as a matter of routine. He took his new girlfriend, Sally, to the pictures, politely introduced himself to her parents – her father was a miner and her mother worked short shifts at a local factory – and she in turn introduced him enthusiastically to sex. She was more than a year older and didn't bother even to acknowledge what some would call morality. Her parents, non-churchgoers, felt much the same, and the only propriety observed was that she and Sillitoe would make use of the front room sofa when the former were out at the pub and be decently dressed when they returned. She was attractive, uninhibited and good company, but inevitably, Sillitoe being a fifteen-year-old male, this was not enough. He had started to go to dances and was well resourced by savings stashed in his Old Testament. Now he had experienced sex the predatory instinct seemed as exciting as the act, and soon he fixed upon Sally's antithesis. Janet didn't work in a factory, her manner was aloof and slightly precious and she treated Sillitoe as an indulgence to be tolerated until something better came along. What he first took for shyness turned out to be a guard against the banalities of everyday exchange; she was articulate and opinionated. He was besotted, and even more so when it became evident that she would resist his attempts to have sex with her. He took her for bicycle rides, to dinner, romantically, in a village pub, wrote her letters assuring her of his commitment and telephoned the office where she worked to declare his undying love. All he wanted, of course, was sex, its prospect being the more fanatically desired as its likelihood faded. But he had as a consequence become dismissible, and he was discharged via her sister who informed him that it was her sibling's wish never to see him again, let alone inform him of this in person. His 'self-esteem' was, as he put it, 'damaged beyond repair' for approximately two days; 'and then I returned to a girl who enjoyed fucking with a steadiness of purpose that fully satisfied me until after I joined the Air Force two years later'. In the ATC thrills, non-sexual but equally compulsive, abounded. For two days he did intensive training at Syerston and a Canadian warrant officer, called Rome, allowed him to take control of a Douglas Dakota, one of the planes that were being used in rehearsals for D-Day less than a year hence. He and other young recruits were used as guinea-pig crews for the new Hamilcar gliders that would eventually land airborne troops inland from the Normandy beaches. Dakotas released them at eight hundred feet and the glider pilot would deposit a score or so of quivering and expendable teenagers on to rough fields, sometimes through hedges and on one occasion a greenhouse. The fear, the machinery, the danger were all very real but it was not quite active service.

The Normandy landings took place barely three months after Sillitoe's sixteenth birthday. The advance through Western Europe would, it seemed, be slow and costly, and later that summer he witnessed a train drawn up in Nottingham, its coaches filled with severely injured British and US troops back from northern France. One question gnawed at his impulsive temperament during this period: would the war last long enough for him to take part in it? He feels guilty about this still, knowing that in order for hostilities to have endured until his eighteenth birthday many more lives would have been lost. At the time, however, self-reproach was sidelined by exhilaration.

In early 1944 he had obtained his 'release' from Toone's plywood mill and started at Bert Firman's engineering works, picking up where he had left off at the Raleigh factory. This time, however, he had more autonomy, specifically his own lathe at which he was responsible for producing parts, from design, for the Rolls-Royce Merlin engines that powered Spitfire fighters and, in units of four, carried Lancaster bombers over Germany. The Raleigh factory had provided the kernel for what would eventually become Arthur Seaton's daily routine, but Sillitoe's two years at Firman's offered the model for Arthur's unconstrained hubristic state. It was at Firman's that Sillitoe first experienced what in *Saturday Night and Sunday Morning* would be described as the 'favourable rhythms' of factory work (p. 37). Arthur certainly did not derive any standard form of pleasure or sense of achievement from his job, but he did not feel like an automaton either. His work required skill and concentration but at the same time he felt a bitter satisfaction in being able to master and transcend the challenge and to create a mental space that was his alone.

Turn to chamfer, then to drill, then blade chamfer. Done. Take out and fix in a new piece, checking now and again for size because I'd hate to do a

THE LIFE OF A LONG-DISTANCE WRITER

thousand and get them slung back at me by the viewers. Forty five bob don't grow on trees. Turn to chamfer and drill, then blade chamfer, swing the turret until my arms are heavy and dead. Quick as lightning . . . [p. 36]

Arthur copes with the boredom of production-line work by detaching himself from the present and making use of the 'raw material' of his other life outside the factory: 'a compatible world of pictures that passed through your mind . . . often in vivid and glorious loonycolour, a world where memory and imagination ran free and did acrobatic tricks with your past and with what might be your future' (p. 38). Such as: 'Brenda, I can't wait to get at her. It serves you right duck for being so lush and loving. And now this chamfer blade wants sharpening, so I'll give it to Jack this afternoon . . . Brenda and me'll play merry hell in all the beds and nooks we can find. Bloomers flying, and legs waving in Strelley Woods, no matter how cold it gets' (p. 37).

One of the striking and unprecedented features of the novel was that having set himself against the demands of his job Arthur refuses to function as a stereotypical working-class figure. For him the ability to cut himself off does not prompt thoughts about the grim injustices of his background and condition, imagined projections of what he might one day become professionally or intellectually; and he certainly has no time for thoughts about the benefits of socialism. He thinks about sex, about drink, about fist-fights, and a whole regiment of individuals cross the screen of his delighted inner consciousness, from his cuckolded – by him – colleague, to his fat, malicious neighbour. And all that Arthur does is watch. Certainly he registers elemental feelings – principally desire and contempt, less frequently pity – but he never bothers to confer anything resembling significance upon this private retinue of images. Sillitoe recalls his time at Firman's in a phrase that could have been uttered by Arthur: 'I cared for no man, and cared not whether he cared not for me as I stood before the lathe with sleeves rolled up and, a thousand times a day – though the magic of turning out each separate object never left me – released the bar an inch toward the middle, spun back the turret, pushed the chamfer tool . . .' (Life Without Armour, p. 75). Even the movement of the syntax seems to incorporate an interplay between the 'favourable rhythm' of the task and an obdurate sense of nonconformity.

Saturday Night and Sunday Morning is set in the late 1950s, and part of its success comes from Arthur's and the narrator's indifference to circumstances that appeared to reduce everyone else to a state of dull ennui or powerless resignation. Sillitoe achieved this effect through an act of imaginative time travel. As a sixteen-year-old, at Firman's, he was a nucleus of raging instincts, demands and desires. He had enough money to drink, go to dances, behave as irresponsibly as he wished, and sex was ever-present. At weekends he risked his life and derived excitement from the ever more

54

demanding operations with the ATC, and all the time he was counting off
the months towards his eighteenth birthday and trying to work out if the
war would end first. Detach the main figure at the centre of this from its
most powerful motivating force – the war and the sense of excitement and
fear that it seemed capable of injecting into all other aspects of life – and take
him to a point approximately thirteen years later, when the thrill and immediacy of conflict had been replaced by drab predictability, and you have the
vividly anomalous presence of Arthur Seaton.

Sex and death have always enjoyed a magnetic companionship in literature, albeit to the relish of some and the equal displeasure of others. What
Sillitoe did with Arthur was to preserve the dynamic of this relationship yet
disguise its provenance.

> While standing at the lathe my mind was lively with fantasies recreating
> flights made under blue sky and above cumulus cloud-fields, and then
> being told on the radio telephone, after the pilot had mysteriously lost
> consciousness, to bring the kite in on my own. Or I would stow away in a
> Lancaster and, a gunner being wounded, take over his station and shoot
> down a German night-fighter. More often there was a lascivious reappraisal
> of sexual encounters from the recent past, and revelling in others yet to
> come. [*Life Without Armour*, p. 78]

The very real recollections of this passage could easily be transposed with
those of Arthur except that Lancaster bombers and the thrill of being close
to death in airborne combat didn't feature in his workplace imaginings and
visualizations.

Sillitoe's mental landscape was not made up entirely of chimera and
fantasy. In April 1945 he heard of the Fleet Air Arm 'Y Scheme' (he still has
no idea what the letter stood for) in which seventeen-year-olds could, if found
sufficiently mature and competent, be drafted into a fast-track air crew training programme and be flying within a year. He had been seventeen for
approximately a month. Entrants might even, if good enough and irrespective of their educational background, become pilot officers. Sillitoe
applied immediately, passed the medical examination and was informed that
he would be required to attend for the entrance exam at 13–15 Nantwich
Road, Crewe, on 2 May. As the train carried him through Stoke and the
Potteries, he was tormented by memories of the high school scholarship
examinations. The questions were just as taxing but the manner in which
they were asked suited him better. He was required to face a three-man board
of officers for the best part of forty minutes and respond to a crescendo of
questions on issues as diverse as geometry, basic navigation, Morse code, his
sporting preferences and knowledge of British history. The randomness was

deliberate, designed to test a candidate's ability to maintain focus while facing a bewildering, illogical sequence of tasks, a fundamental requirement for air crew. This was followed by a more familiar written examination, essentially an IQ test that would pick out weaknesses not evident in the oral exchange. During lunch in the mess he remained pessimistic about his prospects, expecting that yet again his almost complete lack of formal education had let him down. Later that afternoon he was summoned into an office where a junior officer, maintaining a cold impersonal manner, issued him with a naval identity card and informed him that he would be called up for flying training at HMS *Daedalus*, Lee-on-Solent, at an unspecified later date.

He was elated, but within four days of his interview the war in Europe was over. VE Day, 8 May, was celebrated in Radford much as it was everywhere else in Britain. Church bells, previously muffled, rang for the first time in six years, makeshift bunting indicated at last a licence for abandon, bands of various sorts played while everyone ate and drank as much as was available. Sillitoe remembers good weather, outdoor tables and virtual strangers kissing. Even his father seemed affected by a spirit of release and geniality, maintaining an uncommon degree of good humour well into the night. He lost his false teeth on the way home and Sillitoe, impressed by his performance through the day, gave him enough from his Old Testament stash of notes to purchase replacements.

Ostensibly the defeat of Germany didn't mean that his future with the Fleet Air Arm would be affected; at least he received no formal notification that his call-up to HMS *Daedalus* would be postponed. But he had enough common sense to know that priority would now be given to the redeployment of resources and skilled servicemen from Europe to the Pacific. So despite the promise of a hitherto only imagined ambition – becoming a pilot – he began to reorient himself to the guilty, even macabre process of clockwatching, estimating the likelihood of a Japanese surrender occurring before the powers that be turned their attention to pilot trainees for Pacific-destined aircraft carriers.

Again he became driven, unfocused. His actions were in no sense malicious or irresponsible – he caused no one harm – but at the same time he seemed capable of immunizing himself from the routine and the conventional. One day he found himself at Mrs Cutts's front door, having cycled the twenty miles to Worksop and given her no notice of his visit. She first seemed a little puzzled but greeted him kindly, gave him tea and told him of how her own son, though still in the Army, looked likely to survive. Mr Cutts was upstairs taking a late afternoon nap – yes, he still worked from the cart – and Sillitoe asked her not to disturb him. Recollection, indeed intuitive affection, soon caused her to suspect the real reason for his visit. Laura, she informed him without prompting, had moved on with her family a year ago.

She did not know where, but she could see from the expression on his face that he too would soon be off.

An abundance of lust – customary for most male teenagers – played some part in all this, but at the same time something else was involved. He was happy with Sally. Both earned enough to support a lively social life attending dances, nights out in the pub and the cinema at least three times a week, and they had sex at any time and anywhere that was possible without causing offence or arrest. But listen to Arthur Seaton, or at least apprehend his reflections recorded by Sillitoe.

As soon as you were born you were captured by fresh air that you screamed against the minute you came out. Then you were roped in by a factory, had a machine slung around your neck, and then you were hooked up by the arse with a wife. Mostly you were like a fish: you swam about with freedom, thinking how good it was to be left alone, doing anything you wanted to do and caring about no one, when suddenly: SPLUTCH! – the big hook clapped itself into your mouth and you were caught. Without knowing what you were doing you had chewed off more than you could bite and had to stick with the same piece of bait for the rest of your life. [*Saturday Night and Sunday Morning*, p. 219]

And so it was for Sillitoe. Anything even mildly predictable, albeit otherwise illicit, had to be undermined. It didn't matter that his attempted seductions of other girls were unscrupulous, let alone pitiably unsuccessful. He was their architect; he ran his own life.

For a few months he trod a fine line between self-absorption and directionless anarchy. He did overtime at the factory, equalled his father's wage of £6 per week. It was not that he needed the extra money but excess had become part of his mindset, and the work represented a challenge; he would stay at it longer than anyone else and his product would always be faultless. Politics was talked about on the shop floor and a poster of the local Labour candidate was taped to the wall above the boss's desk, as much to annoy Bert Firman as a serious reflection of ideological commitment by his employees. The *Herald*, the *Mirror* and the *News Chronicle* all contributed to an atmosphere of cosy radicalism, and Sillitoe's workmates took to using words such as 'nationalization' and 'the Welfare State' as if they were discussing the weather. The Labour triumph of 1945 involved a very English brand of radicalism – considerate, weary and circumspect – but none the less Sillitoe found himself becoming infuriated by the promises of the new age. He conceded that in basic terms of health and income the people he lived among would be more secure under the new Labour government, yet being told what sort of social group you belonged to, how you'd been exploited, and of the collective benefits to come he took as a threat to his by now vehement sense of individuality. He didn't need to be advised that he belonged to something in order to be rescued from it: 'on reading of an egalitarian society coming about I did not quite understand what was meant, having never felt anything except equal, at least. To be told that I was equal was as impertinent as being informed that I was not' (*Life Without Armour*, p. 86).

He found himself one afternoon in the rear turret of a Lancaster bomber, now shifted from its combat role to transport. The four massive Browning machine guns were still in place and he squeezed the triggers, half hoping that someone had neglected to empty the magazines. Never previously interested in sport, he applied himself to weekly inter-flight football matches, compensating for his relative lack of skill with ferocious, almost maniacal energy. On hearing from the touchline an officer advising him to 'Chase the ball, Sillitoe. Don't hang about,' he came close to asking him 'what the fuck he thought he'd been doing this last hour or so' and following up his verbal assault with a fist. His mood, indeed his general state, was explosive, and arriving at weekend camp in July 1945 at Syerston he passed out and remained semi-conscious for the best part of a week. At the time no one offered him an explanation for what had occurred – it was far more serious than a faint – and, relying as much on common sense as retrospective advice, he assumes that his body simply rebelled against the unremitting torture to which he had subjected it. Some weeks after being released from the sick bay he was on an advanced Navigation course in RAF Halton, Buckinghmashire. While there he became mildly besotted with the station warrant officer's daughter and, he thought, she with him. He saw her regularly at weekends, was on one occasion invited to take tea with the family, and retains a vivid memory of her: slim figure, angular pale features and red hair; but not her name. No one had heard the wireless that day, and a recruit he had known at school cycled from the nearby village waving a newspaper. A bomb of gigantic, previously unenvisaged destructive power had obliterated the Japanese city of Hiroshima. Two days later Nagasaki was also wiped from the map, and Japan surrendered.

He visited London, for the first time, with fellow cadets to take part in VJ Day, the official celebration of the end of the Second World War. Train and bus fares were waived for anyone in uniform, and he recalls being among the crowd around the Queen Victoria Memorial as the royal family appeared on the balcony of Buckingham Palace. In *Life Without Armour* he comments enigmatically on how, above all else, he was fascinated by the Underground, 'at how only a second or so seemed to pass between one station and the next, making it difficult to know whether the time was short because there was nothing in my mind, or whether it was due to the density of my reflections' (p. 87). The image is eloquent and ungovernable. He is, self-consciously, present at a moment of epic historical significance yet he is preoccupied by something which seems a perverse imitation of his own hidden contemplations. He now knew that his dream of glory was gone, but it was a thought that he felt obliged to chase away and the Tube seemed an appropriate emblem for what was happening in his head. Everyone's emotions that day would have been tinged with something partial and unique – loss, regret, relief and so forth – but few if any would have admitted to disappointment, and as the train sped him beneath the capital he felt a compensating sense of anonymity, like a politely silent spectre at the feast.

He spent the next few months in a state of resignation and reflection. Superficially he lived and behaved much as he had for the previous two years, applying himself to his job at Firman's – albeit less manically – taking time off for further ATC training and enjoying nights out plus energetic sex with Sally. Inwardly, however, he was taking stock. His life so far had been made up of events and experiences that were unexceptional for children from poverty-stricken families. He had coped as best he could but like others in similar circumstances he was powerless to alter the state he was in or even envisage such an alteration. The war introduced him, cruelly certainly, to the potency of independence, but now he was returned to what seemed at worst atrophy and at best a predictable form of betterment. His eighteenth birthday was a month away when he wrote to the Fleet Air Arm requesting information on the present status of those who had been selected for air crew training before the cessation of hostilities. The reply confirmed what he had suspected. There was no longer an urgent requirement for air crew and the forces were investing in specialist training only for those who would commit themselves to a service career. He would be required to sign up for seven years minimum, with a further five for reserve service. The war had been over for barely six months but what had previously seemed like a thrilling compulsion with expectations of self-sufficiency and independence now resembled factory work in a uniform.

Firman, his boss, wanted to keep him on, tempting him with the prospect of being on reserved occupation – that is, doing work vital to the national interest. He chose to sever his connection with the Fleet Air Arm and re-muster into the RAF. Then he left the factory and for eight months worked at Langar aerodrome as an air traffic control assistant – happy to do anything connected with aviation, even though his temporary civil servant salary was only half of what he had earned in the factory.

The break-up with Sally seems to this day to him something that was inevitable, though he remains resolutely undecided on whether it was willed or destined. At the time he had evolved a mindset – which might without too much pomposity be termed an existential manifesto – in which fate and choice were indistinguishable. 'I shied off thought, instinct telling me that it could too easily lapse into worry, which could give way to uncertainty, and even degenerate into fear. And I wasn't having any of *that*. Such feelings were either a compound of self-indulgence and wisdom, or a shameful supineness in someone who by now ought to have known better, though I would not have cared to have anyone tell me which it was, wanting only the maximum amount of freedom within which Fate could have free play.'

He remembers attending her sister's wedding and at the reception in the local Methodist church hall feeling disturbed that they too were a couple, officially recognized as such, and on the conveyor belt to a ceremony like the one just witnessed. She seemed pleased by the prospect, or was he imagining this? She had not actually suggested anything. Was his own contempt for convention causing him to turn her into a feared agent of conformity?

After eight weeks of basic RAF training – which he strolled through, having learned all of it and more with the ATC – he returned to Nottingham in July 1946 for two weeks' leave, now a full-time serviceman.

The image he recalls most vividly from the period between the end of the war and his departure overseas comes from his visit to the cinema with his cousin Jack. Jack, Burton's grandson, was two years older and had served with the infantry in Germany and Italy. Now demobbed, he wanted to see what had become the most talked-about performance of Shakespeare in living memory, in which Olivier as Henry V, particularly with the famous battle speech, seemed capable of projecting unremembered history into the present; everyone said that Olivier's Henry reminded them of Churchill, despite the physical differences. Sillitoe recalls that Shakespeare's language seemed at once magnetic and impenetrable. The fact that he only half understood it did not concern him, but what stayed in his mind was a visual effect, the flights of arrows disappearing into the sky and, somewhere else, annihilating apparently superior French forces.

For all their many and manifest differences as writers it is intriguing that Larkin and Sillitoe should have taken from the film something that Shakespeare had not envisaged in its performance; the same image provoked in both (Larkin in 'The Whitsun Weddings') a comparable notion of fate as a combination of act and accident, impulse and uncertainty.

Sillitoe already had a basic familiarity with radios and Morse code, and this became his specialism. His time in the RAF as a radio operator satisfied and tested the same part of his temperament that had attracted him to maps. Morse fascinated him because of its oddness, and its poetic rhythms. It enabled people maybe hundreds of miles apart to communicate in a manner that preserved the particulars of the message but which stripped it of anything resembling ostentation; it was a paradox, language which allowed unlimited communicative transparency with a guarantee of anonymity. His attraction to Morse would eventually influence his manner as a writer. The wireless itself provoked a hitherto unacknowledged compulsion to listen in. This propensity was not voyeuristic; instead he began to feel that his role as silent witness to all manner of things made his purpose as a human being a little more unvexed and fathomable. Even before leaving for his posting abroad he developed an ability to intuit and fix upon signals in the same way that a hunter reads the landscape or a fisherman the stream. His tastes became egalitarian: weather forecasts, messages between aircraft pilots and sea-goers, encoded military orders, staccato, repetitive signals that seemed to mean nothing at all but which obsessed him all the more with their persistence and hint that for some purpose, somewhere one human being might well have been attempting to contact another. Sillitoe has remained an avid listener. The personal radio set he carried with him through Europe during his 1950s odysseys enabled him to witness history being made, particularly in Suez and the Middle East, in a way denied to everyone else not directly involved in the unfolding narrative. Today in his study in north-west London he will take a break from work, make some tea and tune in. The Russians still have radio officers in their larger aircraft, and his records of what went on between the USA and supposedly official forces in both Gulf Wars would make the standard investigative journalist drool. His desire to bear witness to the fabric of global exchange was fed by the same characteristic that, as a writer, would make him so difficult to classify – an attendance to detail but with a collateral respect for its independence. He will describe but rarely turn the description into a conceit or inform it with laboured significance. 'There are few writers', commented the *Literary Review* on his career following the publication of *Life Without Armour*, 'who can rival Sillitoe when it comes to the business of [simply] noticing things.'

In early summer 1947, after almost a year as an enlisted RAF serviceman, Sillitoe and other signals staff were taken by lorry from their transit camp in Burtonwood, Lancashire, and put on a train that took them south. Even after arriving in Southampton and being issued with full kit and rifles they did not know for certain what their destination would be, though the inclusion of khaki shorts indicated that it would not be Continental Europe.

PART II
A MAN ABROAD

SIX

Even after boarding the *Ranchi*, a 1920s merchantman refitted as a troop ship, all they knew was that they were going to South East Asia. The Indian sub-continent was moving rancorously towards independence but there was much of the region that, if not still a full remnant of the now rather thread-bare Empire, involved a post-war British military presence. A few of his comrades, unnerved by the lack of information, speculated among themselves and worried over what they would say in letters home: 'Dear Mother, I'm on a ship . . .'? Sillitoe, however, found that the experience offered an unprecedented form of contentment. There was a routine: vacate hammock at about 6.30 a.m., shower, dress, prepare kit for inspection, fold away hammock. Next would come a basic but very enjoyable breakfast of bread, marmalade, eggs and sausage, and after that the officers found that they rapidly ran out of ideas to occupy the time of the NCOs and servicemen for the rest of the day. Occasionally they might be told to perform basic tasks normally undertaken by the ship's crew – hosing down and cleaning decks, for example – but this soon took on the absurdity of such shore-based exercises as painting stacks of coal to match the colour of the rest of the barracks, and in any event the seamen began to resent these repeated intrusions upon their regime. For much of the time the troops were left to themselves. They played games, from cards to a cramped, improvised version of football, or exchanged stories about their pasts. Some, very few, read books, and Sillitoe remembers one man who seemed preoccupied exclusively with his notebook. It might have been a diary or something more ambitious but it was certainly an obsession, the man's pencil seeming to virtually keep time with the movement of the ship. Whether he was recording events or inventing them Sillitoe never discovered. At the time he did not really care.

He was discovering another permutation upon his fixations with the lathe and the wireless. Both – the former through obligation, the latter choice – had provisioned him with a private landscape from which he could observe and reflect. In the Bay of Biscay he watched Spanish fishing boats exchange signals with the *Ranchi*, official ones to confirm their position in relation to the larger vessel and informal waves from crewmen. Then came similar trawlers with Portuguese flags, and after that Gibraltar, gateway to the Mediterranean, hot and uncharacteristically stormy. His most enduring memory of Suez was the sight of a man dressed in traditional Arab robes riding a camel. He looked like something from his childhood picture books made consummately real. Not once did he acknowledge the presence of the

12,000-ton vessel barely two hundred yards away from him, and to Sillitoe the question of whether this act of indifference was deliberate or involuntary was of no consequence. He was more engrossed with what seemed a respectful moment of empathy, shared and unacknowledged.

In Malaya Sillitoe used the forces library regularly, without troubling himself whether or not the books available corresponded to any orthodox classifications of significance. He found Wodehouse funny and, as one might expect, H.G. Wells appealed to his growing appetite for the fantastic. Warwick Deeping and P.C. Wren allowed him to pass the time when not engaged in duties that demanded his attention, and *The Diary of a Nobody* seemed as amusing as Wodehouse, though for different reasons.

Fascinatingly it was during this period that he first encountered Robert Tressell's *The Ragged Trousered Philanthropists*. A corporal, also a wireless operator, from Liverpool whose name Sillitoe no longer recalls offered it to him. Appropriately, the copy with dog-eared, loose pages belonged to no one in the unit. They had simply passed it around and the corporal told him that he ought to read it because 'it's the book that won the '45 election for Labour' (*Mountains and Caverns*, p. 145). In 1965, having made his name as one of the new wave of 'working-class' novelists, Sillitoe was asked by Panther to write the introduction to the first paperback edition of Tressell's novel. It is a masterpiece of well-meant disingenuousness, in that he commends the book as the first unreserved presentation of capitalism and the class system as abominations while remaining cautiously ambivalent on its value as literature.

When he first read the novel in Malaya he was impressed by Tressell's ability to provide key roles for figures who in everything else he had read either existed on the periphery or more often seemed not to exist at all. Tressell's painters and decorators are presented as individuals with particular inclinations, idiosyncrasies and life histories. Sillitoe appreciated that for the first time he was encountering in a book the kind of people who had so far made up virtually all of his experience – outside books – but he also noticed the contrast between the central character, Owen, and everyone else in the novel. Owen appropriates sometimes entire chapters in his attempts to persuade his fellow workers that the only solution to their apparently hopeless state is their collective recognition and support for a new political and economic system. Critics, usually the Marxist kind, have toiled for decades over what precisely Tressell was attempting to achieve and how his work corresponds with various formulae evolved by Marx, Engels and subsequent theorists. None of them has dared to recognize that Owen is, deliberately or not, an unsettlingly patronizing presence. He does not so much talk with his fellow workers as preach at them, assuming the kind of moral authority and intellectual superiority we usually associate with the priesthood.

In his 1965 piece Sillitoe obfuscates, politely, on the role and effect of Owen. 'A tragedy cannot be written about creatures of the jungle, only about those who try to get out of it – or those who succumb to it not knowing that it is possible to transform it. Therefore Owen is the most tragic figure in the book' (*Mountains and Caverns*, p. 150). 'Just tragic, or slightly infuriating?' I asked Sillitoe. He smiled and nodded. Was he, when first coming upon Owen in Malaya, I went on, reminded of how he himself had reacted when anyone had attempted to convince him that a set of ideas, socialist or otherwise, could solve anything? There was, for example, his encounter with the union official at Raleigh. He acknowledged that he was, but at the time he had treated this with relative indifference, having no clearly formed ideas nor 'caring less' about what literature was supposed to be or do.

Within a year of reading *The Ragged Trousered Philanthropists* Sillitoe had decided to ignore the trades and careers that seemed obligatory for men of his background and become a writer. But he had certainly not become a convert to Tressell's missionary zeal. To treat the working class as a group characterized by the various shared consequences of victimhood was, in his view, akin to racism. Even those who pitied the proletariat saw it as made up of types rather than individuals, a condescending element of socialism's middle-class heritage that Sillitoe has always loathed. He was certain that it was not Tressell who set him on the road to his new vocation, but something in Malaya did contribute to the transition, and in a number of his novels he ponders the question of what this was.

Sillitoe's main duties involved monitoring and shepherding local RAF exercises or longer flights to or from Australia, and soon this role was extended to include the civil airliners of BOAC, KLM and Qantas on recently opened routes between Europe and the Pacific. As always he drew a certain amount of taciturn satisfaction from his role as listener and anonymous correspondent, and he thinks that perhaps there was some 'small connection' between this familiar task and its new context that 'made me want to do something unusual'. He began to sense that the slightly perverse pleasure he derived from reaching into a kind of oblivion, via Morse, might now find a more substantial, genuinely exciting counterpart.

Sillitoe's friends and colleagues in Malaya – particularly Peter Spruce, Bill Brown, Ron Gladstone and Ronald Schlachter – found him straightforward and unexceptional with no pretensions to be or do anything particularly different from the rest of them, but when each revisits the period there does appear to be something about him, hardly notable then, that hints at nonconformity. Ronald Schlachter recalls: 'One time he [Sillitoe] was seconded to the direction-finding unit – air traffic control in modern parlance – of the adjacent civil air base. I don't know how he managed it but he always reported for duty in his civvies, his whites, because when it was time for his tea break he would wander into the passenger lounge, read the paper and help himself to refreshments. He would be sitting around with colonial civil servants and their wives and nobody knew who he was. Well, they thought he was a passenger, but when they boarded the plane he slipped out and prepared it for take-off. Typical Alan. The thing was, he didn't talk about it – I only found out when I asked him why he wasn't wearing his uniform – he just did it because he wanted to.'

The Education Corps ran language classes in Malaysian and Sillitoe was among the tiny minority who showed any interest. His comrades were satisfied, even impressed, by his explanation that some fluency in the local language would give him a distinct advantage with the Eurasian taxi-dancing girls at the City Lights club in Penang, the magnet for virtually all servicemen on leave in the region. Having never been taught English grammar he did not have a point of comparison for its demanding South East Asian counterpart. He attempted instead to memorize statements verbatim, pick up clues to understanding through repetition, and he hoped to be able to recognize enough key signals in replies to keep an exchange going. The taxi-dancing girls were more amused than impressed. But was flirtation, possibly seduction, his only motive? 'No, it wasn't,' he replied. 'I wanted to know more about where we were, and their language provided an obvious insight. But I was as fascinated by the landscape as the culture, which is why I set out with Bill Brown and, later, on the Kedah Peak expedition.'

Bill Brown was another wireless operator and while they were still at the flying boat base of Seletar on Singapore Island he and Sillitoe began to spend their spare time building a raft, mainly from the pieces of plywood and aluminium left over from decommissioned Mosquito fighter-bombers based there during the war. Two long-range drop tanks, plus some boards, became a dangerously unstable catamaran. They abjured a sail, preferring home-made paddles, and within an hour after setting off into the estuary of an adjoining river they were sinking. Without even announcing his presence a Malaysian fisherman drew his sampan alongside, rowed them to a swamp-less piece of shoreline and, withdrawing again to his own world, returned their clumsy gestures of thanks with a brief 'sketch of laughter'. Bill had been a willing participant in the escapade but it was not he who had come up with the idea.

It was Sillitoe too who suggested the ascent of Kedah Peak. This was a single 4,000-foot mountain rising out of the jungle twenty-seven miles north of Butterworth. Few if any of his comrades bothered even to acknowledge it, but for Sillitoe it began to exercise a special degree of fascination and compulsion. He was not then disposed to ruminate upon let alone articulate this sensation, and for this reason the Kedah Peak expedition is a pivotal moment in his discovery of writing as a vocation. The episode is used in precise detail in Sillitoe's third novel, *Key to the Door* (1961). He returns faithfully to the planning for the trip, the amount of kit carried by those involved and the story of how six adventurous, misguided men pit themselves against an unwelcoming landscape and come close to death in the process. The most intriguing passage is Brian's – that is, Sillitoe's – exchange with fellow radio operator Knotman, who was older than the rest and had done time in Africa. In the novel Knotman becomes the predominant figure, sometimes the provocateur, with Brian as the unsettled questioner.

Brian asks, 'I give in. What does Gunong Barat [Kedah Peak] mean?' and Knotman tells him that he, Brian, wants to climb mountains because he has no clear ambition to do anything else, 'but [you] think you might as well get something out of life'. He adds that Brian is 'just an idealist, meaning you give in to worldly values without dirtying your hands on them' (p. 273). Knotman is a sophist without pretensions capable of drawing from his friend anomalies and paradoxes that would otherwise stay hidden. Sillitoe dismantled his private inclinations and susceptibilities, remembered from Malaya, and reassembled them as the dialogue between Brian and Knotman.

Wordsworth in the ode 'Intimations of Immortality' set the precedent for alluding to an experience that is all the more profound because it antedates one's ability to properly articulate it. The paradox, as he implied and demonstrated, lies in the fact that in order to allude to it one is obliged to write about it. In *Key to the Door* Sillitoe puts a new twist upon this because what might normally be seen as a handicap becomes for him an opportunity. The mythology of untainted epiphanous moments has taxed writers for the simple reason that for most of them the innocence that supposedly precedes formal education never existed. As a consequence in their attempts to re-create this myth they are obliged either to lament its absence, hypothesize patronizingly about how others – usually the gloriously uneducated peasant or working classes – might enjoy it or, like Joyce, invent new ways of writing in attempts to capture raw transparency. Sillitoe, however, had an advantage over his generally middle-class counterparts. Aged twenty he was an intelligent, unorthodox individual. He was aware that somehow he was going to escape the predictable routines that seemed to have swallowed the lives of everyone he knew. He would not simply rely on material ambition, better himself and climb a few rungs up the social ladder. He would eventually become a writer, but, almost uniquely, he had at his disposal sharply defined recollections of adult experience that occurred when his knowledge of literature was random and unfocused and any notion of practising this curious vocation was non-existent. So for him the perplexity that follows writers into their attempts to stand outside literature, to create a state of mind that they had never in all honesty experienced, became a resource. There were two Alan Sillitoes, one who during the 1950s and after applied himself to literary production, and the other the aggressive, unfocused figure who both antedates and accompanies Sillitoe the writer. Sillitoe had occasionally sent out anonymous improvised statements via Morse to no one in particular and wondered what would be made of them – the equivalent of a context-less overheard remark from an invisible speaker. In the novel Brian does this with passages from Coleridge and Wordsworth; on night-time guard duty in the jungle with Knotman, when both are attempting to smother their fear of hostile presences, Brian recites to himself passages from Dante's *Inferno* (pp. 337–8); when on a beach with his Malayan lover Mimi, a taxi-dancer, she draws Chinese lettering in the sand and introduces him to haiku poetry (p. 275). Sillitoe in Malaya had become familiar with a random selection of fiction writing but his knowledge of verse was scant and tenuous; his fascination with the nature and mechanics of poetry along with a self-willed tour of the canon would occur after his medical discharge in 1949. Why then did he elect to blend an otherwise faithful facsimile of himself circa 1948 with the later erudite version?

Brian's literariness is undemonstrative; he neither makes it conspicuous to his comrades nor takes much care to hide it; and Sillitoe is conducting an experiment with materials to which his background offered him unique access: transpose his present-day, late 1950s, early 1960s presence – a man who has read, thought about and written a good deal – with the same figure of barely a decade earlier, shrived of this cultural baggage, and see what happens. He was in effect making use of the novel to address a question that has taxed writers and teachers for centuries: does literature make us better or even different people? Commendably he does not settle upon an easy conclusion, yet a hint of scepticism is evident throughout.

SEVEN

During the period that Sillitoe and his comrades explored the jungle and eventually attempted to climb Kedah Peak, attacks on British units by nationalist, mostly Communist, insurgents increased, and after their return all bases, Butterworth included, were obliged to regard security as involving more than the perfunctory routines of guard duty. When manning his radio at night Sillitoe would drape a network of tin cans on wires through the bushes and trees surrounding his hut. On one occasion he saw someone or something moving through the undergrowth. It must, he thought, be human. What else would be sufficiently cognizant of his clumsy warning system to avoid setting if off? He fired a shot and the noise alerted a unit of the Malay regiment brought into Butterworth as official defence during what had become a state of emergency. Sillitoe denied having fired his weapon and to this day remains unsure whether his bullet made contact or even if anyone was there at all.

His only other involvement with the insurrection occurred later in 1948 when from June to August the RAF began to carpet-bomb parts of the jungle suspected to contain guerrilla encampments – a half-hearted precursor to what would happen two decades later in Vietnam. The RAF used Lincolns, enlarged versions of wartime Lancasters, and Sillitoe was one of the ground contacts whom they called upon as a static answer point to check their position as they roamed the jungle in the hope of depositing bomb loads at positions identified by Army intelligence. On one occasion he and a direction finder operator in Singapore were ordered to take cross-bearings on what were believed to be transmissions from a guerrilla broadcasting station; the Lincolns were directed to the point where their two bearings crossed. His description in his 1972 essay 'National Service' of what happened is beautifully coy and evocative: 'somehow my hand couldn't quite find the middle ground for a satisfactory QTE . . . in spite of my inner thoughts I had done my best' (*Mountains and Caverns*, p. 57). Done his best to do what? His duty as a radio operator? Or to ensure that 'another load of bombs [were] wasted on empty forest'? I ask him now. 'Maybe both,' he answers. 'The bearings were as exact as could be made – professional pride and good training wouldn't allow any other.'

In *Key to the Door* both incidents resurface, first of all in a passage where Brian is almost killed by a guerrilla wielding a kris, a crude scimitar-like blade generally used for clearing undergrowth. Brian disarms him, has the opportunity to shoot him but instead tells him to run away. Later he and several of his unit are involved in a small-arms exchange with a guerrilla column.

He fires into the trees or the ground, anywhere but towards the likely location of his combatants. After releasing the kris-wielding guerrilla Brian tries to make sense of what he has done, searching without success through his personal experience for a precedent that in some way explains his apparently spontaneous act. "'What did you do in the war, dad?' 'I caught a communist and let him go.' 'What did you do that for then?' 'Because he was a man.'" (p. 418). During his final meeting with Mimi he confesses to her that 'I couldn't kill him. And later in the ambush I didn't aim for anything. I fired where nothing could be hurt. It took some doing, but I held back. I did it' (p. 436). He is begging her to respond, to provide him with something that resembles a rationale, a motive, even one that he might reject. Instead she simply listens and returns the question to him. '"Why?" she said at the end of it. "Why?"' (p. 436).

Mimi, a prostitute, is an unillusioned pragmatist for whom Brian's attempt to turn his experience into a grand existential gesture is incomprehensible and faintly ridiculous. Like Knotman she embodies the cynical aspect of Sillitoe's temperament. Altering the coordinates for RAF Lincoln bombers was much easier than sparing the life of someone, yards away, who was quite capable of killing you. Sillitoe's personal experience had taught him that idealism was cheaply purchased, and in the novel it is by Brian pretentiously mismanaged, a not entirely accurate account of events but without doubt an honest one.

In *Life Without Armour* he describes a morning in Penang when the dawn sunlight seems capable of transforming not just the colours but the very nature of the landscape. Prompted by nothing he could properly recognize he wrote about fifteen lines of what from his retrospective knowledge of verse he assumes it must have been a poem, of sorts – why else would he shape his impressions into lines instead of sentences? The lines are now lost but they were, arguably, a rare sighting of that literary holy grail, the creative act untainted by the mannerisms of high culture. Sillitoe does not lament their loss – he is pragmatic enough to recognize that unalloyed impressionism generally results in formless nonsense – but what he does retain from Malaya is the conviction that there were aspects of him that would be for ever incongruous. In particular he has come to regard his profession as a writer as comprised of magnetic and incompatible pairings: artistic vocation and job, impersonality and temperament, candour and misrepresentation. The polarities are numerous, kindred, and buried in virtually all of his work. At one point in *Life Without Armour* he shifts from the predominant mood of impartial disclosure and offers a paragraph on Malaya that is a fascinating reflection on something it never mentions.

> Some kind of change in my life must have been taking place within the agreeable trance of duty done and leisure enjoyed, a spirit clandestinely

deciding what my fundamental obtuseness would not be able to deny when the moment of reality came. There was no intimation that such was on its way, because a vague day-to-dayness was the whole of my existence, and I belonged to where I was to the extent that such feelings as weighed on me from time to time did not allow me to see the future, or imagine anything that I could not bear to contemplate. [p. 122]

It is as though he is here attempting something similar to his experiment with chronicling in the novel, in this case recovering the complex fabric of emotions that would soon enlist him as a writer, but preserving their original, dynamic lack of focus.

Orders came through in 1948 that Sillitoe and those posted to Malaya at the same time would be returned to the UK in July and shortly afterwards demobilized, irrespective of whether this fell short of their designated two years' service. Flight-Lieutenant Power, in charge of Signals, summoned him to his office and asked if he would be willing to stay on for another three to four years. The enquiry was made without even the implication that either Sillitoe or the service might benefit from his continued presence. Sillitoe, in retrospect, is slightly bemused by how he chose his reply. He was, having no great ambition to be anything else, happy in Malaya doing a job he found 'compatible' with his temperament; a return to what he had left in Nottingham involved the prospect of rejoining the routines he had witnessed as a child and teenager. Did the flight-lieutenant's attitude, I asked Sillitoe, play even the slightest part in his decision to leave the RAF, touching in him that anarchic, bitter instinct to react against anything sanctioned by authority? 'Yes,' he answered, 'I think it did. It's a long time ago but there was something about him . . . Well, whatever it was, it made you want to go against it.'

Soon afterwards, when he had time to reflect on what he had done, he started to cast around for alternatives. He could, he had heard, take further exams and become a wireless operator in the merchant navy, and word had it that the Royal Canadian Air Force would pay at least twice as much as the RAF for trained signals men. In truth, however, his speculations were partly a means of compensating for a potentially rash gesture and a way of passing the time until the likely became the inevitable, when he boarded the troopship home. This he did on 23 July at the Empire Dock, Singapore. His experiences on the troopship *Dunera* were a replay of those on the *Ranchi*, superficially at least. This time there was no sense of curiosity and anticipation, but nor did Sillitoe feel that what was about to happen next would be predictable or dreary. He recalls, crossing the Bay of Biscay, gazing out towards the landmass of southern England that was still invisible and days away. 'I felt at the summit of my power (and indeed happiness) as if I had already lived for ever and saw a kind of future that only those who live from day to day can envisage – empty but without end . . . The beautiful morning had ended, but with everything coming my way' (*Life Without Armour*, p. 137).

EIGHT

What had come his way showed up about three weeks later on an X-ray taken at RAF Warton, Lancashire. Tuberculosis is one of those conditions with a history and aura that often occlude their clinical actuality. In the 1940s it was still regarded as both hereditary and infectious, a twentieth-century equivalent of leprosy whose sufferers were isolated from the rest of the community in sanatoria. It was seen as a disease of the neglected and the weak, something that fate or natural justice visited upon those who for some reason had it coming to them. Sillitoe is honest about how the stigma of the condition was almost as distressing as what it might do to him. 'It seemed almost inconceivable that someone like me should be tainted with the disgusting disease of consumption'. In truth anyone could acquire TB. It is an infection caught, like influenza, from someone else, a carrier. For many it lies dormant, and is eventually eradicated by the body's natural defence mechanisms. For others, however, it can infect and destroy cells in key parts of the body, most frequently the lungs, and if untreated will result in death. The acquisition of the disease and its subsequent progress are purely matters of chance. Sillitoe learned more about it later in his life but at the time it seemed an unendurable injustice, and a shameful one at that. He remembers crossing Manchester in uniform – looking as smart and as confident as all the other servicemen on leave or in transit – and feeling like a fraud, as though he were carrying a guilty secret. He began to fixate upon the possibility that his X-ray plates had been mixed up with another man's, as much a means of assuaging his damaged 'pride' as sidelining a fear of death. When he returned to Nottingham for two weeks he lied to his parents and siblings, telling them a vague story about how he would need to 'convalesce' in a service hospital following his time in Malaya, hinting vaguely at malaria or battle fatigue, and he did not even try to contact his old girlfriends.

He was almost relieved to be able to return to Warton and face his dilemma head on. He read a few books – principally Priestley and Wells – randomly shifting through them without giving much attention even to their potential as entertainment, and finally turned to his King James Bible. The likelihood of death had not caused him to revise his commitment to atheism but the Old Testament bore witness to the sometimes elemental courage of others faced with similarly dire prospects, God or no God.

Further, more intensive X-rays showed that he was 'TB positive', his left lung was on the point of collapse and his right showed signs of infection. It was, he recalls, like enduring a rambling, digressive death sentence; the decision was predetermined and irrevocable but would, it seemed, be delayed.

Penicillin, the world's first antibiotic, had proved to be an effective cure for acute bacterial infections such as pneumonia and septicaemia, but against TB it was powerless. Not until 1952 with streptomycin did the medical profession have any means of controlling let alone curing the condition. In 1948 the only known 'treatment' was bed rest, confinement to a sanatorium with other sufferers. If your body was disposed to combat the infection then it would be assisted in its struggle by having no other commitments. If it was not, you died.

Sillitoe was sent to RAF Wroughton in Wiltshire, an airbase with a hospital unit set aside exclusively for servicemen with TB. His most vivid memory of the journey is of leaving the train at Swindon. The station seemed deserted except for one other person waiting to board the same train, having come from the hospital to which he, Sillitoe, was destined. This man was in a coffin.

It was during the few days between his return to Warton and departure for Wroughton that Sillitoe found his vocation. He became a writer. He had begun an account of the ascent of Kedah Peak and he would return to it over the next six months, mostly when propped up in bed. The original typescript (typed by Flight-Lieutenant Hales, commander of his ATC squadron in Nottingham, Sillitoe having composed it in longhand) is a fascinating document, by degrees gnomic and revealing. He would eventually send it to *Geographical* magazine and to the more popular *Wide World*, neither of them literary journals in the strictest sense, topography and travel being their remit. Both turned it down, without explanation, but one suspects that they were unsettled by the unevenness of mood. For the most part Sillitoe provides a scrupulously impartial account of the expedition, almost as though he was writing a report for his superior officer. At the same time, however, there is something about the manner in which detail, narrative and reflection are choreographed that shows an impulse – unwitting, subdued, who knows? – to inform the report with a momentum of its own. There is a passage, one could call it the thematic apogee of the story, in which Corporal Ron Coleman volunteers to cross a ledge of a rock face that will allow them to bypass a three-hundred-foot gorge. It is not until we get to this point that we realize how vital, indeed heroic, the moment has become. They are running out of food and water, and if Coleman can get through a stream will be only hours away. The passage is striking because it comes upon you so unexpectedly. The narrator, Sillitoe himself, has until that point maintained a studiedly unruffled tone, but as soon as we encounter the tense moment of Coleman's crossing – he falls and almost kills himself – a charge ignites all that we have previously read. It is a precociously effective reversal of mood and perspective; suddenly it seems as though the narrator's sober constancy is a mask for subdued panic.

A passage from the essay, barely a page and a half long, was eventually published in *Scribe*, the journal of the Nottingham Writers' Club, in April 1951, and in 1957 Sillitoe himself adapted and read part of it for a special programme on the BBC Home Service (10 April 1957). Versions of it have reappeared, usually disguised, in several of his novels, and if proof were needed of its totemic significance for its author then sufficient will be found in *The Open Door* (1989), the sequel to his autobiographical *Key to the Door*. Here it is reprinted in its entirety, an almost verbatim copy of the original typescript, the only major changes being the alteration of the names (pp. 64–73). The document was important to him because it was his first serious attempt to write anything and it was prompted by his being informed that he might quite soon be dead.

Sillitoe would spend almost ten months, between October 1948 and July 1949, in the Wroughton sanatorium waiting for something to happen. His 'treatment' involved bed rest and a solid diet of meat, vegetables and beer. Bottles of stout were issued shortly after breakfast and made available throughout the day, as were, amazingly, all types of smoking material – cigarettes, cigars, pipe tobacco. As long as they were careful to avoid setting fire to their sheets and blankets the men could smoke in bed. Even before a connection between smoking and respiratory damage, cancer in particular, had been scientifically proved, common sense indicated that the bombardment of often threadbare lungs with regular doses of tobacco fumes might not have been entirely beneficial. Sillitoe surmises with hindsight that the rationale, of sorts, was that TB would in any event have the final say and victims might at least be allowed some contentment while awaiting its decision. Sillitoe enjoyed a regular supply of Malayan cheroot cigars and, more captivatingly, the attention of a ward orderly.

She was – is – a confident, tall woman around a year older than he and from a different social background, educated lower middle class. Hilary Bussey retains a vivid recollection of when she first saw Sillitoe. 'Most of the patients were thin – service, rationing and TB combined saw to that – but Alan looked particularly gaunt and though he was not withdrawn – he got on well with everyone, staff and patients included – he seemed oddly separate. Perhaps a little lonely, but no more than that. Someone who was resigned to living in a world of their own.' The most enduring memory of their brief relationship was that for each of them their differences, while apparent, were of no significance at all. Hilary recalls: 'My stepfather was a professional classical musician. We weren't rich but we lived comfortably and the house was well stocked with books. In fact I used to bring back copies of all sorts of volumes – philosophy, literature, history, art history – for Alan after I'd been on leave. I wanted to study art and become a painter after I'd left nursing, but it wasn't to be. Anyway, Alan and I talked of our respective ambitions. He said he wanted to write, he was certain of that even though as he admitted he had no clear idea of what this meant, let alone how he would earn a living. We talked about our childhoods and backgrounds but neither of us had any time for class or status. We didn't deliberately sideline our differences, we just didn't pay them any attention.' They enjoyed each other's company, he escaping via a ward window to meet her at a spot – on the Downs or in a village pub – arranged during their apparently chaste exchanges in the ward. These assignations, he comments, 'probably did more for me than anything prescribed by the medics'.

Sillitoe came closest to death when X-rays disclosed that his more infected lung had worsened considerably, had developed extensive lesions, and he was informed that surgery was the only possible means of arresting an otherwise terminal decline. The technique involved cutting away the worst affected parts, deflating the lung and thereafter injecting air to flatten it and maintain its redundant state. Previous experience had shown that lungs relieved of their usual function and workload would sometimes heal themselves. After being wheeled back from theatre and returned to his bed Sillitoe 'celebrated' with a bottle of stout and a cigar.

Even if he survived, his prospects seemed limited and dispiriting in that he was told that the things he'd enjoyed as a boy and in the forces – climbing, walking, cycling, swimming, indeed anything that combined exertion with discovery – would for the foreseeable future be impossible. The sense of elation and optimism that had accompanied him through the Bay of Biscay was unfocused but it was driven by his conviction that he could combine the necessity of making a living with enjoying himself. Now, it seemed, only the dullest supine kind of job would be possible. Making a world from language would at least be some compensation for losing control of the real thing. Was there, I ask him, some connection between him facing this cul-de-sac and his sudden commitment to writing?

'Yes, yes . . . I think there was. In fact there must have been. I went into the sanatorium with some vague notion of sending a report of Kedah Peak to a geographical journal, or in truth probably doing it as a way to pass the time. When I left the idea of being a writer meant something much more. So I'd agree, it was transformative.'

So much so that he set about becoming a literary autodidact. On the library cart he found an apparently unused copy of Bertrand Russell's *History of Western Philosophy* and from this he manically attempted to absorb all major ideas from Socrates to Nietzsche. What, he wondered, did such abstractions have to do with telling stories? Starting as close to the beginning as he could he ordered works by Xenophon, Tacitus, Sophocles, Virgil and Homer – in translation inevitably – all the time finding parallels between them and the stories he already knew well from the Old Testament of his ever-present King James Bible. Soon the laborious chronological approach seemed counterproductive – he was becoming more intrigued by enduring patterns, archetypes that writers of all periods found taxing and compelling. Kant's *Critique of Pure Reason* – lent by Hilary – had much in common, so he thought, with Wilde's *De Profundis* and Fitzgerald's *Omar Khayyam*. Next he hurried, transfixed, between passages from Shakespeare and Wordsworth's *Collected Poems* and compared both with Voltaire's *Candide* and de Maupassant's *Bel Ami*. Then he went to Tolstoy, Turgenev and Dostoevsky, and found further clues indicating a sense of community among writers, shared preoccupations; not something that he felt as yet able to define or articulate but detectable none the less. He moved closer to home, that is Britain and the present day, first with Thackeray, then Dickens, Maugham, Shaw, Wells and Huxley, an eclectic mix certainly but all the more exciting for that; he was searching for something, and his fascination increased with its elusiveness. It was, he recalls, a massive reckless undertaking pursued without guidance or prior knowledge of genre, period or the canon. Instead he charted his own path through this unknown fascinating landscape of texts. Introductions to collections offered him a rough guide to such notions as Romanticism or the Renaissance which he found by degrees informative and distracting, preferring to make up his own mind about the value and significance of a writer's work. He ordered a copy of Egerton Smith's *The Principles of English Metre* from Sisson and Parker's bookshop in Nottingham. He realized that poetry, or at least most of it, involved arbitrary rules and conventions of its own and since his commitment to his new vocation was all-inclusive he set about teaching himself the basics of scansion, prosody and sound pattern. His twenty-first birthday present from an ATC friend, John Moutt, again at his prompting, was Auden's *Tennyson Selection*, so with Smith as his guide he began looking for stress patterns, testing his abstract knowledge of that bulwark of English poetry, the iamb, against its use by a versifier who combined, infuriatingly, conservatism and eccentricity.

He purchased a reconditioned Remington portable typewriter for £26 – a fortune in those days; four times as much would have bought him a decent car – and began to write poems. First he attempted to play by the rules, shaping whatever he had to say according to his recently acquired lexicon of poetic theory and practice. He could have dealt with the inhibiting pressures of convention had his urge to express himself clashed with them, but that was the problem: he did not really know what he wanted to say. His memories were comprised mainly of facts the like of which had, as far as he knew, been treated as unsuitable for poetry, and the rest was hypothesis and unrealized ambition. There was of course Hilary, so he began to write poems about and sometimes to her, terrible unwitting versions of how Edward Lear might have sounded had he suffered a bout of solemnity or enchantment. Free verse he had heard of – he cannot remember how or whose work he had read – and with the energy and reckless exuberance of the born explorer he began to see if the poem could build a structure of its own without the assistance of abstract regulations. He destroyed the original poems not long after composing them – like most good writers he was able even at this early stage to evaluate his own work with merciless impartiality – but there is an unapologetic memorial to them in *The Open Door* (p. 128):

> I don't know where I'm going
> I only know where I am,
> But Fate will get me, like a fox
> That knows how to open a hedgehog
> Like a child its toy-box.

The recreation of one's aspirations, forty years hence, as a heroic failure to control the medium must be commended. Brian is too self-absorbed to assess dispassionately the quality of his work. All he can do is think, and write, about his own fate and his dependent relationship with his current girlfriend.

NINE

The pneumothorax operation seemed after only a few weeks to have improved Sillitoe's condition and by spring 1949 'bed rest' had been altered from regular confinement to his being able to wander around the sanatorium much as he wished, at least during the day. After his release in July his remaining time as a serviceman was largely a formality; six weeks of the two months up to his official demobilization were spent on leave in Nottingham.

His armed services disability pension began at £3 11s a week; he moved back into the family home and paid his mother £1 a week for food. Sabina and Christopher seemed on unaccountably good terms, most of the time, and during the day both went to work, as did Pearl, Peggy and Brian, all at the nearby Raleigh plant. Michael, aged ten, was the only one still at school. He still has his diary, with notes, from the summer of 1949 when his brother came home, and Alan features in almost every other entry. 'August 16. I went with my brother Alan to Newstead Abbey and we saw the abbey house, where Lord Byron lived who was a poet too.' I asked Michael if the 'too' refers to Alan. 'Oh yes. He used to write a lot of poems. But what I remember most is Alan as a storyteller. As you'll see he would take me out ["Mon Aug 10. Downtown with brother Alan"; "Fri 29 July. Clifton with brother Alan"; "Tues 23 Aug. Boating with brother Alan at Highfields Lakes, Beeston"]. It was odd because it didn't feel as though I was with an adult. It was better than school. Alan was a mine of information – the history of the area, the names of places and their associations and so on – but he would also keep a tale going for the duration of the trip. He would improvise, tell one part of a story – they were fantastic but believable, involving animals and humans – then pause for half an hour and I'd be wondering what would happen next. We had a great time.'

With the rest of the family at work Sillitoe had the house to himself for most of the week and he worked for the best part of three months on what would be his first publication. He sent 'No Shot in the Dark' to the *Nottinghamshire Weekly Guardian* at the end of December 1949 and had to wait almost seven months for a reply. It was published on 26 August 1950 and it reappeared eleven years later in Chapter 21 of *Key to the Door* (pp. 309–11). Sillitoe's habit, becoming almost a ritual, of revisiting his earliest work and reinscribing it in his later autobiographical fiction was fed by many impulses. Predominantly, as a mature experienced writer he relished the prospect of seeing if he could make sense of the makeshift figure of decades before.

In 'No Shot in the Dark' he tells of how he, as Brian, shoots a pi-dog which had been scavenging near their wireless hut in Malaya. Ninety per cent of the story is pure documentary realism unfurnished with emotion, reflection or rhetoric and this is counterpointed against the few moments when the shooter's feelings – compulsive, confused, guilty – are allowed to intrude. The effect upon the reader is magnetic. As the unostentatious prose catalogues the rifle being loaded, the first shot missing the dog and the dog being pursued into the jungle we find ourselves bitterly impatient for some trace of what is going on in Brian's mind. In our own we gather an abundance of emotionally charged questions. We want to ask him why he is doing this, what he feels, and Sillitoe brilliantly hinders our enquiries until the end. Remarkably the piece, largely unaltered, fits seamlessly into the texture of *Key to the Door*, which goes some way to explain why Sillitoe had used it in what was his fifth major publication. It reinforced his belief that the nature of what you write is a reflection of your disposition and temperament, irrespective of the attainment of formal skills. He had written it in 1950 at a time when he cared little about reproducing the mannerisms of fashionable or classic fiction – these would inform and inhibit much of his writing during the early fifties – and instead allowed the subject of the story to determine its pace and temper. Sillitoe never really understood his own actions, even with the benefit of hindsight, and therefore felt that to clad them with a superstructure of motive and emotion was dishonest. This was an approach that he had not encountered in his eclectic wanderings through literary culture and for that reason he stifled it. Why not then remind himself that the unorthodox method that brought him acclaim antedated *Saturday Night and Sunday Morning* by at least a decade? Unobtrusive craftsmanship was the real Alan Sillitoe.

In autumn 1949 he contacted his old friend Hales and they talked of his plans for the future. Sillitoe stated, bluntly, that he wanted to make a living as a writer and Hales invited him home to meet his wife Madge whose collections of poems had just, in early 1950, gone into print with the Fortune Press, quite possibly the most bizarre publishing outfit of the twentieth century. Its owner (and also its editorial director, sole copy-editor and sales manager) was L.S. Caton, a man who when not publishing was involved in tax fraud and semi-legal property speculation. The 'literary' output of the Fortune Press provided a respectable counterbalance to its money-making part, pornography. None the less its authors during the late 1940s and early 1950s included Philip Larkin, Kingsley Amis, Alun Lewis, Julian Symons, Dylan Thomas, Roy Fuller and C. Day Lewis. Caton could spot talent. Madge Hales's collection *Pine Silence* was part of this new wave, characteristically abrupt, transparent and unaffected. Sillitoe was impressed, and at the Haleses' prompting he joined the Nottingham Writers' Club. There, however, he encountered a rigorously maintained commitment to experiment. Modernism in 1950 was still very much the vogue with aspirational writers, particularly in the provinces; it was a touchstone for endeavour, its impenetrability guaranteed it immunity from the ordinary reading public and secured its status as an exclusive art form. Sillitoe dutifully introduced himself to Joyce and Woolf. He had, thanks to Hilary, come upon the latter's *A Room of One's Own* when confined to the sanatorium and he was intrigued to notice the difference between the robust accessible manner of this early feminist polemic, of which he greatly approved, and her fiction which he found both ponderous and unapproachable. The early Joyce he enjoyed, particularly the short stories, but as the ascent towards more intimidating peaks of obsessive complexity grew steeper the less he wanted to tag along. This at any rate was his instinct, but understandably, given his background, an equally powerful impression stayed with him that in order to properly appreciate and therefore practise literary art he must in some way reinvent himself.

He recalls that his first impulse when starting D.H. Lawrence's *The Rainbow*, with its description of Ilkeston church tower as the mute focus for the life histories of the surrounding countryside, was shock and recognition. He had been there and seen it and for the first time he felt a solid connection between a work acclaimed as literature and the world he knew (*Mountains and Caverns*, p. 134). The sensation was short-lived in that Sillitoe began to suspect, first with *The Rainbow* and more so with his later fiction, that Lawrence was not so much writing about Nottinghamshire and its people as using both as conceits, points of departure, for an intellectual landscape which belonged to the literary aristocracy.

His impression that most art was practised from beyond the horizons of his own very ordinary existence was bolstered by his encounters with Uncle Frederick, his father's brother, of whom he had been told much as a child but never met. In 1936 Frederick had left his wife, children and career as an embroiderer in London and returned to Nottingham. When Sillitoe got to know him in 1950 he had installed himself in a two-room studio in the middle of the city, changed his name to Silliter and was making a living as a painter, specializing in landscapes of Constable-style Englishness with a slightly decadent Impressionistic touch. Frederick provided his nephew with a potted history of Western art, allowing him access to his considerable library of illustrated guides to all major artists from the Renaissance to the present day. He also added a commentary, implying that creativity involved an almost obligatory commitment to unusual behaviour, frequently involving sex. Gaudier Brzeska, George Sand, Eleonora Duse, Gabriele d'Annunzio, Verlaine, Baudelaire were all cited as exemplars of the commendably aberrant. Frederick himself seemed a living anomaly. His original persona had been that of reliable family man, a solid Christadelphian whose beliefs excused him, as a conscientious objector, from active service in the First World War. Now he wore a skull cap and perused the Old Testament, more as a fabric of exotic narratives than a touchstone to faith. Sybil Cotton was almost half Frederick's age, he being sixty-five, and was often present, casually dressed, during Sillitoe's visits. 'My model,' said Frederick when he introduced them, raising his eyebrow – a superfluous gesture given that he did not do portraits.

Frederick beguiled his nephew. There weren't many bohemians in Nottingham in 1950; the affected radicalism of the Writers' Group members was a hedge against the dullness of their otherwise ordinary lives in banks and offices, and Frederick seemed to Sillitoe to have come from another world. When he offered Sillitoe advice on his ambition to be a writer his words seemed gnomic and sagacious in almost equal measure. The only 'indication of success', he proclaimed, is 'money'; what editors want in a story is a 'slice of life'. Sillitoe was at the time too awestruck to admit to puzzlement but on reflection he concedes that he had difficulty in reconciling his uncle's performance as a throwback to *fin de siècle* Paris with his commercialist dogma. He approved, in general, of the idea that literature should be something that people wanted to read and buy, but what kind of 'life' was it supposed to draw upon to secure popular appeal? His programme of self-education suggested that honest representations of ordinary life in painting, literature or any other media were rare. It seemed that even if populism, sales, were indicators of success then it was evident that most people did not want to read accounts of themselves. It was only later in sanguine maturity that Sillitoe would reflect upon Frederick as a suspect, perhaps dissimulating, figure rather than someone who at the time seemed to offer release from the monochrome world of 1950. Maybe it was pure coincidence that his commitment to Christadelphian pacifism had come so close to the outbreak of war, but if mendacity had been involved he had, apparently, lied magnificently, at least until he felt it opportune to find another role more suited to his inclinations. Though Frederick can be excused of anything resembling malicious intent his influence upon Sillitoe at the time was not beneficial, provoking him as he did to search for inspiration in narratives and states of mind that were remote, dissociated and alien. Sillitoe would, eventually, respond by allowing echoes of Uncle Frederick to animate one of his most peculiar creations, Michael Cullen of *A Start in Life* (1970) and *Life Goes On* (1985). Cullen's life is the picaresque made modern. He is aware of such abstractions as morality and probity in the same way that he apprehends light and darkness; conscious of them, certainly, but not particularly concerned.

Sillitoe's first attempt at fiction would be called 'By What Road?' and it reflects the crippling diversity of influences that at the time were beginning to displace anything remotely connected with the real Alan Sillitoe. He concedes a circumstantial resemblance between the central character, John Landor, and himself but this was an unavoidable expediency. He wanted a reliable narrative backbone and unless he resorted to plagiarism all he had was his own. Landor has just returned from three years of military service abroad and is desperately attempting to make sense of the events that have taken place in his absence. His mother died shortly before his return and has intimated in her last letter to him that Ralph, his father, is harbouring some distasteful secret; and the novel's collocation of sub-plots is anchored to Landor's search for the truth about his family history. Landor's old girlfriend, Helen, is a woman who shares his interest in literature and the arts, while Ada, his more recent loved one, works in the local factory and treats his aspirations as a passing affectation. Helen is, he admits, based predominantly upon Sybil, Uncle Frederick's 'model', with a trace of Hilary, his girlfriend from the sanatorium, and Ada is a confection of every other woman in the locality whom he had pursued, successfully or otherwise. His problem was that he could not quite work out how to reconcile his raw material, based mainly on real people and events, with a perception of literary writing drawn from a dizzying mosaic of exalted authors. Hence we come upon such unwittingly comic mismatches and graftings as the love-triangle of Helen/Sybil, Tom Ransom (bitter, unpredictable artist)/Uncle Frederick and John Landor/Sillitoe. Each attempts to outdo the other with utterances that parade every high-cultural reference point and existential crisis from Homer to Camus. Landor comes across as a humourless version of Evelyn Waugh's Ambrose Silk and Tom and Helen are a stricken double act lifted from Huxley's *Point Counterpoint*. The conclusion is, to put it mildly, bizarre. The suspicion that John's father might in some way have been responsible for his mother's death is mooted but hastily bypassed in pursuit of a much more macabre denouement. Irrespective of whether he sent her to the cemetery, his true compulsion involves revisiting her tomb and making up for whatever their sex life lacked pre-mortem. Being an unfastidious sort Ralph has also acquired a living girlfriend, Moira, who on discovering his nocturnal habit is suitably horrified, implores him to cease, even attempts to seek a 'cure' and is murdered for her troubles. Ralph, more from fear of what will happen when apprehended than guilt, pre-empts the authorities and hangs himself.

Sillitoe had some acquaintance with the works of Poe but he cannot to this day explain why he and the novel had fixed upon such an unprecedentedly morbid scenario, necrophilia particularly. Given even cursory access to Sillitoe's background and family history psychoanalysts would of course have a field day. I will not labour the point with comparably predictable speculation, except to say that somewhere in all of this he was without doubt getting his own back. The novel was not entirely unrealistic in that its reckless disdain for credibility was fed by Sillitoe's having witnessed, being part of, a family that seemed to belong in a particularly grotesque brand of fiction. The more experience he gained of human beings in their scattered chiaroscuros of types and potentialities the more Christopher seemed an anomaly without explanation, and now that he had got to know his father's brother it became even more difficult to believe that the two of them had come from the same planet let alone the same gene pool. Hence turning Christopher into a grave-robbing necromancer seemed to add only a slight twist of the Gothic to an already unfathomable spectacle.

Once again a measured recollection of the time surfaces in his later fiction, specifically *The Open Door* (1989). When planning the novel Sillitoe set himself a particular task. The years between his being diagnosed with TB in 1949 and his departure for Europe in 1952 were without doubt transitional. What fascinated him forty years later was how he elected to take particular routes, make specific choices, from the maze of possibilities which faced him. Calculation, chance, fate? How had an irreverent autodidact barely out of his teens with a single story in the local newspaper become, circa 1990, one of the most formidable and respected presences in the literary establishment? It could, he concedes, quite easily have gone wrong, the landscape of literary aspiration being one where the bodies of the desperately ambitious far outnumber the even moderately successful survivors.

One thing is clear. If the Brian who sets off for France at the end of *The Open Door* does not reconsider the kind of writer he thinks he can become he will not succeed.

In the novel Sillitoe executes a superb exchange between an almost omniscient narrator, himself with benefit of hindsight, and the character who will in due course invent this figure. There is a wry passage in which Brian, using the sanatorium as a refuge from the distractions of vulgar existence, tries to immerse himself in two millennia of high culture, with occasional breaks for passionate, exalted sex with Rachel the ward orderly, based on Hilary. Then one day in walks a visitor from his Nottingham life, his cousin Bert. '"Hey up, then yo'!" he called, in the Radford accent Brian had hoped never to hear again. Yet at Bert's appearance he came back to life. The hemlock store of his childhood with its adventurous suffering still lodged in him, and his hand went out for the shake . . .' (p. 103). There follows an exquisite sequence in which Bert treats Brian to a cascade of remarks about the qualities of the nursing staff who in his opinion are 'longing for a bit of the mutton dagger'. Brian is by degrees embarrassed, unsettled and ashamed of himself for feeling that a man who is part of his life ought not to belong there. Later he reflects:

It was almost as though he had dreamed Bert's visit, not good these days at remembering recent events. They hid. Or he hid them, if they had too much significance. In Nottingham Bert had been put away, goodbye for ever. Brian didn't know why, had done it without thought, yet however final the parting, it hadn't been final enough, because when Bert clowned up the ward it was as if the decision to get him out of his life had been no more than a fantasy, and he was glad. [p. 107]

We are offered glimpses into Brian's troubled state of mind – particularly the dilemma of how to reconcile the person he is, one who in truth has much in common with Bert, with the person he aims to be – while at the same time we are left with the tantalizing question of whether Brian's perception of this is as clear as ours. Sillitoe, when he was a version of Brian, perceived Bert and his world as alien to his ambitions as an artist, but Sillitoe, post *Saturday Night and Sunday Morning*, knew otherwise.

The episode which is easily the most intriguing in the book is near the end where Brian is about to board the train which will take him south to the ferry for France. He has with him a few changes of clothes, his typewriter and a letter from a publisher tactfully turning down his manuscript as 'not suitable' for their list. Seeing him off is his youngest brother Arthur, still at school but looking forward to entering the real world with a factory job and his own money. This is a brief snapshot of the young Arthur Seaton who will resurface with bitter potency eight years after his elder brother's departure for the Continent. Their parting exchange offers a far more poignant insight into this period of Sillitoe's life than anything in his memoirs.

Arthur looked at him. 'Are you going away with a woman?'
'What makes you think that?'
'I would be – if I was yo!'
'Well I'm not. I'm going by myself.'
'You'll be lonely, wain't yer?'
'I expect so.'
'You'll soon have a woman, I bet.' He hauled the case into the compartment and found his brother a seat.
'Write me a letter, our Brian.'
'I will. Don't get into too many fights. And don't get any women pregnant.'
'Don't worry about that. I'm not daft.'
'If you do I'll be back to sort you out.'
Arthur bit his lip, showing anguish.
'Got your platform ticket?'
He nodded.
Brian pulled the window down to answer his farewell. [p. 353]

One senses that Brian's fatherly advice is not meant to be taken seriously by either of them, more wry prediction than admonishment. 'Write me a letter, our Brian,' asks Arthur, and he will, just as he'll 'be back to sort you out', both being coded references to the document written in Europe that will eventually bring Brian/Sillitoe back to England, *Saturday Night and Sunday Morning*.

TEN

In *The Open Door* Brian has a number of affairs, some corresponding closely with Sillitoe's – particularly his relationship at the sanatorium – others inventions. Paul Henderson, who owned a small bookshop in central Nottingham, befriended Sillitoe, a regular customer, and introduced him to his Saturday night open house session where anyone of his acquaintance interested in the arts would call in, talk and have a drink. In the novel Paul becomes Tom Boak and in Chapter 22 he and Brian are alone in the shop talking of Turgenev, Forster and Lawrence.

> Brian's back was to the door, and he heard the bell go. 'My God, another customer,' Tom said. 'My heart can't stand two in one day. It must be the rain.'
> A heap of books slid on to the lino as he stood up to greet a tall abstracted woman holding an empty shopping basket and an umbrella. 'Can I pay for these?'
> Tom took them from her. 'Everybody seems mad on Lawrence today.' Brian noted the heavy lids to her eyes. Lizard eyes, he said to himself, though they weren't so obvious when a smile put life into her face and showed the bow-like shape of her lips. She opened her New Look coat in the dense air, a brown frock buttoned down the middle and fastened by a belt. Her hair was held back by a ribbon, showing a large amount of pale forehead – as he had observed on seeing her in the foyer of the Continental Cinema. Her remark that she loved Lawrence's works suggested that he'd have to read them, even if only to find out something about her. [p. 247]

They are introduced. Her name is Anne Jones, but the figure in Sillitoe's mind as his wrote the passage was Ruth Fainlight, the woman he would marry. They met in exactly the same circumstances in Paul Henderson's shop and were introduced by the proprietor. No other woman in the book is described with quite so much absorbed attention to detail as Anne Jones, and this is not a submission to nostalgia, simply an accurate record of fact. Sillitoe had found many women immediately attractive but none had combined this with the elusive fascination generated by Ruth at their first meeting.

Ruth Fainlight was twenty when she met Sillitoe, and had been married – recklessly and disastrously, as she now observes – for little more than two years. She was not officially separated from her husband but the fact that they sometimes lived in the same property was an unavoidable contingency. She was born in New York City, in the Bronx, in May 1931 to what she describes as an 'aspiring lower-middle-class Jewish family'. Her mother had been born in what is now Ukraine – then part of the Austro-Hungarian Empire – and had come with her family to the USA as a small child. Her father was born in London. He had gone to America (South America first, then north to the USA) as a young man, where he met his wife. Her recollections of those early New York years are fragmentary, given that her mother and father moved to England when she was five, but she vividly remembers her mother's sister Ann with whom she spent much time in her infancy and during those later periods in the USA as her 'anchor' in the country of her birth. Sillitoe's choice of a forename for Ms Jones thus requires no comment. From 1936 the Fainlights lived in North West London; 'less exciting and cosmopolitan than the Bronx, no doubt, but at the time I was too young to notice the difference'. In 1941, however, she, her mother and younger brother Harry returned to the USA as 'British refugees' – her father served in the British Army during the war. After their mother's injury in a road accident she and Harry went to live with Aunt Ann who now had a spacious house just outside Washington, DC – her husband worked for the Office of Strategic Services (the forerunner of the CIA). 'I attended art classes for schoolchildren every Saturday morning at the Corcoran Gallery of Art in Washington, and I'd listen with Aunt Ann to the opera matinée broadcasts from the Metropolitan Opera House in New York. She loved opera and her shelves bulged with books. I read everything I could, and writing, painting and drawing seemed simply things that you did. One of mine, a poem, was read on a New York children's radio programme. I was eleven.'

When her father was demobilized in 1946 the family returned to England to find a place they hardly recognized. 'There was a sense of relief, atrophy and resignation. That was understandable, given what the country had been through, but what I noticed most of all was how one-dimensional England was, compared with the US. My mother's family had emigrated to the States from a city that had previously been in Poland, Roumania and the Ukraine depending upon the period. And the people we knew in the States all seemed to have come from different backgrounds; we knew Greeks, Italians, Poles, and Jews of every hue.'

Opposites attract, as the well-worn cliché has it, but with Sillitoe and Ruth it would be more accurate to say that they recognized in each other a dissatisfaction with the regimented, the predictable and the humdrum. She found in him something that seemed resolutely unorthodox, and completely different from everything else she had encountered since her return from the USA. He had never met anyone like her, a woman at once rootless, unaffiliated and magnetically unpredictable.

In the novel Anne is without doubt different from all of the other women whom Brian leaves behind. During his moments with Pauline, Rachel, Nora and Lillian we can discern a mixture of lust, love, guilt and hesitancy, all accompanied by a subtle countercurrent of control; as individuals they are predictable and transparent enough for him to take command of his feelings, sincere as these might be. Anne, however, is by degrees captivating and threatening; as it becomes ever more apparent to Brian that her feelings for him are potent and unguarded so we discern on his part a burgeoning sense of unease. He is attracted to her physically, fascinated by her as an individual but unsettled by the enigmatic aspect of her that despite his intellectual assurance remains beyond his comprehension. The disclosure that she also wishes to become a writer is dropped into the narrative in a cursory manner with little attendant comment, but thereafter we notice a gradual heightening in Brian's self-protective instincts.

Never before had Sillitoe met a woman who so closely resembled himself. Certainly he shared a good deal of temperamental, social and sexual affinities with his previous lovers, but the part of himself that was always indisputably his, that he kept from them and indeed everyone else, he suddenly found mirrored in Ruth. By excluding her avatar, Anne, from his journey to Europe Sillitoe is not so much rewriting the past as discriminating between the world that he had chosen to share with those disposed to read his book and the one he shared with Ruth. She too was evolving a literary presence, and four decades later the idea that he might attempt to annex her artistic evolution to his own was unconscionable. 'She seemed to be two people who, if they got to know each other, might become a single person. He didn't want to see her again' (pp. 333–4). Anne leaves the novel, but with Ruth he began his first and last long-term relationship.

They spent as much time in each other's company as possible. Her marriage was little more than a formality, but she still shared a house with her husband in Nottingham and so, when not obliged to make use of traditional 'courting' locations such as pubs, cafés and the cinema, she and Sillitoe gratefully accepted the Hendersons' invitation to treat their house as their own. Paul Henderson and Ruth began to read 'By What Road?' which Sillitoe had completed in January 1951. Their approach was lateral, exchanging chapters of the 100,000-word, 400-page longhand draft, opinions on what sort of direction it seemed to be taking and a growing sense of unease about the most tactful way they could break it to Sillitoe that this was a ludicrous blend of pretentiousness and grotesquery. He took it well, fully aware that in embarking on his new vocation he had become like the proverbial bull in a china shop.

He was, he now admits, recklessly prolific. He tried everything, involving himself in apparently inexhaustible permutations of manner, theme and subject matter. Between 1950 and 1952 he wrote approximately forty short stories and at least as many poems, and adapted some of the more plausible elements of 'By What Road?' to another novel, 'The Deserters'. His problem, essentially, was that he remained oblivious to a paradox that informed his project. He was convinced that the best, most significant literature was animated by its author's presence and state of mind, but virtually everything he had read seemed to have been shaped by a background and outlook that bore no resemblance to his own and was populated by people, narrators particularly, whose intellectual *hauteur* and manner seemed entirely alien from the world he knew.

His options were being systematically foreclosed and inhibited by a tradition that offered no precedent for the kind of work that he so desperately wanted to produce. Indeed, having talked with Ruth about lack of focus they decided in November 1951 to take a bus trip to Eastwood, known by everyone in the locality as Lawrence's original home and the subject of much of his fiction but not yet turned into a shrine by academics and devotees of literary celebrity. They had read the biographies and had found from local sources that Willie Hopkin, once a friend of Lawrence, was now an alderman of the borough and still living a few streets from where he and Lawrence had grown up. They had written to him and he agreed to meet them. He invited them into the sitting room for tea and talked of the young man who had 'disappeared' from Eastwood, gone on to become famous and indeed infamous, *Lady Chatterley* still at the time being banned. Willie Hopkin was more than twenty years older than Lawrence, a scion of the nineteenth-century community of miners whose lives were indescribably grim and usually short. Sillitoe recalls that he had little to say of Lawrence that was not already in the public realm, that he showed no great affection for him, nor for that matter any antipathy. What endures in his recollection of the visit is a sense of discordancy. He had always felt, from his first encounter with Lawrence's fiction, a degree of empathy; the places, the landscapes were tantalizingly familiar. Yet he was also slightly puzzled by the characters who often came across as marionettes, trained to work according to Lawrence's thematic plan rather than faithful reconstructions of the folk that Willie, and Sillitoe, had grown up with. Meeting Willie Hopkin gave concrete proof to his suspicions. It was not that Willie bore a grudge against his old friend or resented his success, just that he reminded Sillitoe of how different the real people of the area were from their Lawrentian counterparts.

The Eastwood episode raised further questions for him about Lawrence but did little to resolve his own dilemma. Instinct told him that he would write in a way that was different from the authors whose works had over the past three years left him awestruck and ambitious, but how? Even the one book which seemed exclusively addressed to and about ordinary people, Tressell's *The Ragged Trousered Philanthropists*, was, he began to realize, commendably fraudulent. Tressell meant well, but that was his problem because beneath the patina of literature was a sermon on the exploited; it was fiction but fiction made use of to raise the consciousness of its readers, and there was a whiff of condescension about that.

As Sillitoe sat in the bedroom of his parents' house, the rest of the family at work or school, he tried constantly to find connections between the life to which he as an individual bore witness – this he knew would provide the substance for his work – and the worlds created by past and contemporary practitioners of the craft to which he aspired. He became by degrees infuriated and dispirited. He had read Dickens, Bennett and some Gaskell. Ordinary people, those at the bottom of the social scale, all featured, but it seemed to him as if they had been allowed into these books as visitors, their status and rank made vividly apparent by the contrast between the way they lived and spoke and the more sophisticated fabric of the novel where they seemed to exist uncomfortably, precariously, despite the indulgences of their authors.

He began to look around for stories, vignettes, images; something that was durable, and which did not carry the sub-generic stamp of the characteristically 'working-class' experience, with all its predictable entailments. One day, on his way to Wore's bookshop he saw a man he recognized leaving a lodging house that, from the outside, looked barely habitable. It was Uncle Eddie, whom he had last known during his early teens. Sillitoe could not be certain, but his uncle seemed to be wearing the same greasy cap and ragged trench coat that he remembered from more than ten years before. They talked for a while, Sillitoe tactfully enquiring if he needed any money. Eddie, unoffended, said thank you, but no; he was earning enough to keep himself. He pointed to his bag of upholsterer's tools. He was in fact on his way to a job just across town.

A few days later Sillitoe, alone again at home, began to write a story.

A middle aged man wearing a dirty raincoat, who badly needed a shave and looked as though he hadn't washed for a month, came out of a public lavatory with a cloth bag of tools folded beneath his arm. Standing for a moment on the edge of the pavement to adjust his cap – the cleanest thing about him – he looked casually to left and right, and when the flow of traffic had eased off, crossed the road. His name and trade were always spoken in one breath, even when the nature of his trade was not in question. Ernest Brown the upholsterer. ['Uncle Ernest', in *The Loneliness of the Long Distance Runner*, p. 55]

Without disclosing his special interest he mentioned to his parents that he had bumped into Eddie and enquired casually as to whether they had heard much of him during his, Sillitoe's, time away. They had not seen him lately but they exchanged glances and said that they had heard, without saying from whom, that a while ago there had been 'some bother' involving a couple of girls. 'What sort of bother?' asked Sillitoe, feigning *naïveté*. 'You know what sort,' his father replied. Somebody had alerted the coppers. They'd watched and warned him and that was it. Sillitoe did indeed know 'what sort' of bother had been visited upon Eddie, or he at least surmised that he did. A mixture of sadness and anger accompanied his recollection of Eddie's terrible life, of how he had enlisted in 1914, deserted twice, and on the second occasion set himself up in a tent in Robin's Wood. Sillitoe's father, then fourteen, would cycle out to him with hot puddings, meat and cans of tea prepared by their mother. Both times the police had found him, probably at the prompting of informers 'doing their duty', and after his second capture prosecution by military court had been waived, given that his regiment, the Sherwood Foresters, was in urgent need of as many men as possible. He arrived in France just in time to take part of the memorable assault on the German trenches on the first day of the Battle of the Somme.

Despite being uncooperative and gnomic on most matters of family history Christopher did seem willing to open up to him on Eddie's personal experiences. Of all his brothers he probably felt closest to Eddie, sensing perhaps that fate seemed to have singled out both of them for rough treatment. Eddie had given him a detailed account of what had happened that day. As they stood in the trench waiting for the order to advance he in particular seemed burdened with something heavier than the seventy pounds of equipment that each soldier carried. Two nights earlier he had been summoned by his commanding officer and informed that he was a marked man, he had a record as a deserter, and if there was the slightest evidence of slacking he would be tried and shot. To reinforce the message the officer had recited the names of men who had over the past two years been summarily executed for dereliction of duty.

He had no clear recollection of what happened as he and the rest of his battalion tried to cross the quarter-mile between the two sets of trenches. 'About from the White Horse to the Boulevard pub. We might as well have been trying to get to the moon,' he told Christopher. But he knew that when he regained consciousness, in a foxhole several hours later, he was gripped by a special kind of fear. He had lost his rifle and was certain that what the German gunners had failed to achieve his seniors would make up for if he returned unarmed and relatively unscathed. He could not remember how and when the Germans captured him but he felt that, comparatively speaking, they treated him with kindness.

In the story Eddie's history is distilled into passage of tragic, poignant brevity.

> Ernest remembered little of his past, and life moved under him so that he hardly noticed its progress. There was no strong memory to entice him to what had gone by, except that of dead and dying men straggling barbed-wire between the trenches in the first world war. Two sentences had dominated his lips during the years that followed: 'I should not be here in England. I should be dead with the rest of them in France.' Time bereft him of these sentences, till only a dull wordless image remained. ['Uncle Ernest', p. 57]

No particular motive is disclosed or implied when Ernest befriends two schoolgirls in his local café, but we, as readers, have already been granted a private knowledge of his past and his state of mind. The two girls must seem to offer him fleeting glimpses of an undamaged life. He wants nothing from them, except perhaps the acknowledgement that he too exists and shares, or rather might have shared, the world they take for granted. Others, it seems, perceive the exchanges as anything but innocent, the police arrive, give him a brutal warning, and he leaves the café in search of drink 'that would take him into the one and only best kind of oblivion'.

The story is one of the finest in the language, combining understatement with crisp evocation as magically as anything in Joyce's *Dubliners*. Over two weeks in early 1951 in the back bedroom of a terraced house in Radford Sillitoe wove together different filaments of actual experience – particularly Eddie's history and the inclination among some to spy and inform for no better reason than pure malice – into a brief, thirteen-page piece where so many elemental registers coexist: hopelessness, hope, victimhood, persecution, and most of all the horrible spectacle of a man who seems to have spent his entire life, despite himself, as the prey, the hunted. Astonishingly he was not aware of what he had achieved. During this period he sent vast numbers of stories and poems to virtually every publishing outlet he could find, many addresses supplied by Paul Henderson. 'I tried my luck with a total of eighty items up to February 1951, after which I stopped taking note' (*Life Without Armour*, p. 157). Astonishingly 'Uncle Ernest' was not among the drafts that he sent. Why? I asked him. 'Probably because it seemed too rooted in the world I knew to be a worthwhile offering.'

There can be few, if any, cases of innate genius hindered by the burdensome presence of convention that compare with Sillitoe's during these years. He was inordinately preoccupied with a story called 'The General's Dilemma' which in July 1950 won him first prize in the Nottingham Writers' Club short-story competition. At just over 2,500 words it was the nucleus for what would eventually become his second full-length novel, *The General* (1960). The eponymous officer has taken command of a train containing an orchestra sent to play for enemy troops. His orders, which he keeps secret from his captives, state that he must execute all prisoners, military or otherwise, yet he prevaricates and tells them to play for him. Following their performance he is further troubled by the order, and his delay in carrying it out leads to him too becoming the victim of his own totalitarian regime. The piece resonates with echoes of Dostoevsky, whose fiction Sillitoe regarded at the time as far superior to virtually anything produced in English. Dostoevsky's figures embodied a civilization, a collective state of mind, on the cusp of apocalyptic change, and Sillitoe acknowledges that 'The General's Dilemma' took its cue from *The Brothers Karamazov*. Instead of the novice monk, the atheist intellectual and the dissolute soldier, each of whom embodied nineteenth-century Russian trajectories of collapse and turmoil, we encounter the General, torn between his allegiance to his profession, the ideology of his state and the almost mystical power of art to open deeper channels of compassion and empathy. In the story the protagonists are unambiguously the democratic West and the Soviet Union and, given that at the time Europe and the USA were still too transfixed by the last war to be fully, neurotically conscious of the potentialities of its Cold successor, it was immensely prescient. It was not, however, the type of thing that a population, still rationed and stumbling through the aftermath of 1945, wanted to read, at least in the view of the five publishers to whom he sent it as a work in progress for something more substantial. Even the magazines to which he offered it as a short story in its own right sent it back.

Sillitoe treated his writing as a vocation, but this carried none of the self-consciousness or bohemianism that we customarily associate with the novice artist. He dressed as he always had, associated with the same type of people in pubs and clubs, and when he attended the WEA, the Hendersons' soirées or meetings of the Nottingham Writers' Club he felt no unease whatsoever regarding the fact that virtually everyone else, though local, was self-evidently middle class. 'I virtually lost the rough edges of my Nottingham accent when I became an air traffic control assistant at seventeen. There had to be no ambiguity as to what you said to incoming aircraft about to land.' Stubbornly, precociously, he refused to acknowledge that class and upbringing were of any significance compared with guts and innate capability, and here he faced a dilemma, albeit one that he could only properly discern and acknowledge about a decade later. Dostoevsky and others he admired dealt with the absolutes of existence – and this Sillitoe believed was the essential duty of the writer – but he was not as yet capable of taking a leap from the techniques and exemplars of the enormous number of books in which he had immersed himself to the coarse material that he, personally, knew more intimately than any other writer past or present.

In 1949 his cousins, Jack and Ernie Adkin, took him to a Notts County game, the only football match he would ever attend. What stuck in his mind from the event was less the activity on the pitch, which in any case was largely obscured by fog, than the presence of a man next to them in the terrace whose loud bitterness at County's performance (they lost 2–1 to Bristol City) seemed to Sillitoe to be a pressure valve for something far more malignant and unfocused. Within a fortnight this figure became Lennox in a short story provisionally entitled 'Cock-eye' and which would eventually be published, with few changes, as 'The Match' in *The Loneliness of the Long Distance Runner*. (A French translation was published in *Carrefour* early in 1954.) In this the narrator follows Lennox home from the match where eventually and in front of his children his blend of rage and resentment is visited upon his wife, whom he beats to the floor. She leaves, with the children, and no explanation and certainly no justification are offered for the sort of individual that he has become. The genesis of the story is an example of naturalism at its best. Lennox after the match is not based upon a particular person but Sillitoe knows and knew of plenty who had simply gone bad, his father included. It is not as impressive a piece as 'Uncle Ernest' but it came together by the same means.

Sillitoe was a watcher, but he was not by temperament an analyst. He observed the people he knew and encountered without feeling that what he saw – variously puzzling, complex, tragic, immutable – could be fully explained. Certainly he was aware that poverty, social injustice if you wish, forced people to do things they might in other circumstances not have done, but it was surely not as simple as that. If the repulsive Lennox could be reduced to explanation, his foul behaviour made to accord with some socio-political formula of victimhood, then by implication everything else about the 'working classes' could similarly be hollowed out as a function of some-one else's perspective, and the latter, however benign or sympathetic it might claim to be, would assume command of its subject and as a consequence deny it any real claim upon independence, even significance. This is why Sillitoe refuses to offer the reader any clue to the psychological make-up of Lennox. He certainly does not want us to sympathize with him, but by conceding that he is a function of his dire, pitiful circumstances he would have connived at the worst kind of class consciousness – that generated by the concerned intellectual who none the less deals with the poor in the way that anthropologists treat apes: they might be like us, to an extent, but they aren't really in control of their actions.

People do not live in classes and masses, nations or groups. They are all of them individuals. When I see a long stretch of sand along a sea shore or river bank I know that not one grain is the same as any other, even though there are more than anybody can count. [*Mountains and Caverns*, p. 159]

This was written twenty-five years after he drafted 'The Match'. In the years between 1949 and 1952 he would have come up with the same observations, but at the time he felt rudderless. His instincts and his commitment to the dignity of the individual were as secure and powerful as they would be in 1975 and are today. Yet to channel these into his writing then, indeed to make good literature from the lives of those outside the cultural mainstream without distorting or patronizing them, was something that had never before been attempted, let alone achieved in English writing. It was for this reason that during this three-year period Sillitoe assembled a file of drafts based almost exclusively on the world around him which he kept to himself. While he was bombarding publishers and journals with pieces like 'The General's Dilemma', all wearing various badges of high cultural rank and affiliation, he was also turning out early drafts of some of the pieces which at the end of the 1950s would launch his literary career.

'The Fishing Boat Picture', another minor classic in *The Loneliness of the Long Distance Runner*, was also conceived in those years. Casually he asked his mother about the two pictures of boats that she and Christopher had been given as a wedding present and which during the 1930s had to be pawned on an almost fortnightly basis to buy food. They had, apparently, sold them when he was abroad, for a decent sum. He felt no great emotional attachment to them but at the same time they acquired inspirational magnetism and he began to build a story around them. He imparted some factual details – the picture of the story is also routinely pawned – yet he also allows this object to move as a mute, deadened witness between the tragic individuals in whose care it is placed. It is brilliant work, but like 'Uncle Ernest' and 'The Match' he kept it to himself, as indeed he did the original draft for 'Mimic', which would not be published until 1973.

In spring 1950 he spent two weeks with his Aunt Amy in Kent. Her husband Richard Richardson, a coal miner, had been killed in a motorcycle accident two years earlier. Four of her eight children were still at home and Amy ran the household from their wages. It seemed as though the arrangement in Nottingham had been moved south, with Sillitoe given one of the bedrooms to use as a study while his cousins were at work, but Sillitoe detected a slight but tangible difference. No one objected to having him as a guest, and his cousins, two of them close to his age, treated him as family, yet he could not help but sense an air of puzzlement on their part about why this young man who came from the same stock as themselves should spend all of his time crouched over a table writing and reading. It was not that he was studying for examinations or had a particular objective, at least not one that they were familiar with. He had told them he had decided to become a writer and they were decent enough to abstain from questions about what he was writing and how exactly he expected to make a living from this. At home his parents tolerated his eccentricities and his brothers and sisters had known him long enough and were sufficiently concerned with getting on with their own lives to bother themselves too much with what Sillitoe did with his. In Kent, however, it was as though a politely surreal hypothesis was being enacted. The easy-going, unpretentious relative appeared to be at home with the family, yet in one respect seemed to belong somewhere else.

Two of his cousins were helping to repair some woodwork in the village church and it was here that Sillitoe met the vicar, though he no longer recalls the clergyman's name. Their conversation on this day and on several occasions afterwards bypassed any customary enquiries as to their respective backgrounds – these differed conspicuously – their state of health or the weather. Instead the vicar, scholarly in appearance and bespectacled, began an account of his recent undertaking, the life story of his dog, now dead, in verse. Sillitoe, unfazed by this apparent visitor from the late eighteenth century, enquired with genuine interest as to the nature of the verse form. 'One long and two shorts per foot,' answered the cleric. 'Indeed,' mused Sillitoe, wondering if the man's faith in the ability of English to reproduce classical quantitative measures equalled his belief in an almighty presence. He was aware also that the question had something of the alleged freemason's handshake about it. Would he, it implied, know the name of this measure and announce himself as part of the club of recondite prosodists? 'Oh yes,' he went on, 'the dactylic hexameter. Used so well by Homer, wasn't it?' He later suspected that one of his cousins had, innocently enough, indicated to the vicar that they might have a common interest, which prompted him to wonder if, for others at least, he seemed to be playing different roles simultaneously. Certainly the working-class autodidact, familiar with Homeric metre and committed to the vocation of writing, was not without precedent but generally they appeared in books written by people from the same social set as the vicar.

Matters which might have left others indifferent fascinated Sillitoe and fed his voracious appetite for new material. He began to make notes and recalled that his uncle Richard's nickname had been 'Mimic'. He wasn't, Aunt Amy explained, particularly good at imitations but he was harmlessly addicted to them. Suddenly these two peculiar narrative trajectories became for Sillitoe components of an immensely unsettling story. Its subject's ability to imitate others is by degrees affable exhibitionism and a means of protecting himself from his own elemental state of mind, and as the latter gradually engulfs the former we follow him towards a tragic, nihilistic end point where no trace remains of his original identity. The 1950 draft underwent numerous revisions over the subsequent two decades but its essential features endure. At this stage, however, 'Mimic' would follow other impressive material – including such nuggets as the drunken staircase episode destined eventually for *Saturday Night and Sunday Morning* – into drawers and files rather than envelopes for publishers. Again one suspects that his reluctance to try to publish the piece was fed by an anxiety that it was of indeterminate status, literally without precedent. One could, if forced, find correspondences with Kafka, but this would oblige one to distort the essential character of each man's work. Sillitoe's story is just as frightening, but it does something that Kafka never attempted or achieved. Sillitoe creates a split-screen effect in that we at once feel trapped along with the mimic inside his head yet are also aware of the world outside him where the mundane particulars of life – working-class life – attain a desperate importance.

ELEVEN

Even as an unpublished apprentice Sillitoe had begun to resent Lawrence. He did not begrudge him his decision to leave, to experience the world beyond Nottinghamshire, but he suspected that he had been motivated by a kind of inverse snobbishness. He needed the transparency, rawness, even the occasional brutality of his origins for his writing, but he had no desire to maintain personal contact with them. Hence a helping of guilt accompanied Sillitoe's growing intuition that in order to regenerate his regime of prodigious unsuccess he too needed a new environment. He was not certain how exactly this would assist him but his relationship with Ruth influenced both of them in what happened next.

At the beginning of 1951 Ruth had gone to Brighton to stay with her family, not exactly the final break-up of her marriage but at least a relief from having to endure a sham. They exchanged letters almost daily and met when they could, spending a week together in a boarding house in Folkestone at Whitsun. One day they walked to Dover and on the beach Ruth read Matthew Arnold's indecisive meditation on that same surrounding mass of shingle. Arnold's manner and execution awed each of them but they exchanged his lament on the ebbing of faith for something more pragmatic. The day was clear and discernible in the distance was what amounted to another world. They talked of what each would like to see – Paris, the Louvre, the Côte d'Azur, Italy – and speculated on how going abroad would free them from attendance to respectability and subterfuge; England at the beginning of the 1950s provided few comfortable opportunities for cohabitation, especially when one of the partners was still married to someone else.

After Folkestone they continued to exchange thoughts on the benefits of elsewhere, but gradually practicality began to overrule hope. Where would they live; what would they live on? Sillitoe's disability pension was guaranteed until 1953 at least but he had no idea of how he might draw this when travelling through Continental Europe. As a compromise he spent three weeks in October 1951 hitchhiking around Cornwall in the hope that some cottage rented to holidaymakers during the summer might be available for next to nothing for the forthcoming winter. That autumn was inhospitably bleak, which did little to endear the windswept, treeless landscape to him, and owners of properties were either uncontactable or unaccommodating: what on earth, they seemed to wonder, did this person want with self-contained quarters in the rural South West during the winter?

A week or so after his return to Nottingham Ruth wrote to him; she had found in *The Lady* an advertisement for an unfurnished house in south-east France. The rent, £48 per year, would swallow up approximately a quarter of Sillitoe's pension, and the first three months would need to be paid in advance. The owner summoned the potential tenants for interview at her Kensington residence. Mrs Corbetta was English but had married an Italian during the war and they now spent their time between London and the grand villa for which the property to rent was effectively the housekeeper's quarters. Treating with patrician insouciance Sillitoe and Ruth's claim to be a respectable married couple, Mrs Corbetta assured them that a few pieces of basic furniture, a bed included, could be found for them from the main house, gave them the address, just outside Menton in the Alpes Maritimes, and stated that she and her husband would meet them there on 14 January 1952.

Did they have an idea of what Menton and environs would be like? I asked Sillitoe. 'I looked it up in my *Blue Guide to France*. The description was brief and evocative of the usual images of the French Riviera . . . palm-lined gardens, grape vines, lemon trees and so on. But you never know a place until you see it.' Indeed, and even the most indulgent travel guide could hardly do justice to this place. Equidistant between the Italian border and Monaco, the town enjoys the enviable reputation of being the warmest and sunniest in France. Even in the nineteenth century when the fishing village expanded to become a winter retreat for wealthy families from northern Europe it maintained, compared with Nice and its neighbour Monte Carlo, a reticent modesty; Queen Victoria visited on several occasions.

They boarded the Newhaven ferry on 10 January, a rough crossing causing him to deposit his three-course celebratory meal of farewell in the English Channel. Two days earlier he had said goodbye to his family, who by now had come to treat his idiosyncratic behaviour as routine; that's Alan for you. The Dieppe train took them to Paris, and after a bus trip across the city they set off from the Gare d'Austerlitz for the south. They travelled third class but their discomforts gradually faded as the landscape became more exotic. In a day Burgundy and the Rhône Valley were exchanged for Provence, and winter seemed to have been left behind. It was not sunbathing weather but the clouds dispersed and a refreshment of colours, from the luminous pink of the mountains to the enduring blossom of lemon and orange trees, elbowed aside memories of the grey north. In his 1977 notebook he recorded:

This morning it is 25 years since Ruth and I set off for the South of France – leaving Hastings for Newhaven on a wet and windy morning to get free of her husband and many other things. It was a real see-saw into the unknown – certainly a see-saw of a ship that took us over the water into Mimosa-land. [Private notebook, 10 January 1977]

Their house, Le Nid, was a four-room cottage with an external staircase linking the ground floor to the two upstairs bedrooms. On an average day, after Sillitoe had spent a few hours gathering logs for the main fireplace and thus securing them against the bitter January weather, he and Ruth would go through the ritual of cladding themselves in at least two more layers of clothing in order to get to bed. The Ministry of Pensions accepted Sillitoe's claim that he had moved to the Riviera on the advice of specialists – the climate and altitude would assist with his breathing – and arranged for his pension to be sent to France, which meant that they had an income of sorts. None the less they soon found themselves dealing with unfamiliar problems. Sillitoe's life so far had by any estimation been rough but the basics of existence – food, drink and shelter – had always been provided by others; often he paid, but his family or the RAF did the rest. Suddenly he was on his own, except of course for Ruth who also faced a fresh set of obligations. She too wanted to write, and she had abandoned her marriage and her conventional lifestyle for an uncertain future. Now they had to set about looking after themselves in a region where they knew no one.

On one occasion they walked across the border into Italy, approximately eight miles, following the advice of the Corbettas' concierge that in Ventimiglia touts would exchange francs for lire, bypassing currency and exchange controls. They would, he promised, earn enough to buy around twice the amount of food, clothes and wine that their francs would have got them back across the border. Within two weeks of their first cross-border excursion – from which they returned with prodigious amounts of ham, pasta, cheese and wine – the Italian authorities clamped down, and the touts stayed at home. On their last trip a shifty character, whom they had seen before doing business at Ventimiglia railway station, drifted towards them from an alleyway and suggested a different sort of transaction. He had 'goods', he said, mainly jewellery and wristwatches, and showed them his prize item, a lady's watch, Swiss made, which he would sell them for, well, virtually nothing in francs and which, over the border, they would be able to exchange for at least six, seven times as much. Ruth would wear it for the next four years. It was not that she liked it much, but what else could they do with an item that every French jeweller or second-hand shop they visited recognized as of suspect provenance? For food they would go down into Menton's old town. Everything was fresh, stallholders having no refrigerators for storage, and they choreographed their visits carefully, picking up reduced-price fruit and vegetables as the market closed down at midday and returning later to take their pick from the unsold stock at the *boulangerie*. If they were lucky they would also meet returning inshore boatmen prepared to part with some mackerel or sea bass for a few centimes. Meat as a rule was beyond their budget and even when desperate for a stew Sillitoe drew the line at the cheapest, as an image of Burton flicked into his mind. Shoeing horses, even in his idiosyncratic manner, seemed more respectful than eating them.

Their situation seemed by turns idyllic and inauthentic. The mythology of the writer-as-bohemian-and-traveller was well known to each: Byron, Hemingway, Joyce and of course Lawrence all appeared obsessed with the prospect of somewhere else, even if their work was informed by what they had left behind. Neither was particularly impressed – there seemed too much performance and affectation – but now they found themselves in almost identical circumstances. They worked hard and quite successfully on their French and most of the locals they met – barkeepers, bakers, stallholders, fishermen – respected their efforts and treated them companionably, one café owner at the village of St Agnes never charging them for a glass of his locally produced table wine. Yet, without asking, they also drew the interest of the expatriate community which while not outnumbering the locals seemed more confidently conspicuous and behaved as if the refinement that had drawn them to this inspiring region put them a notch above those who had merely been born there. In spring a German painter called Gowa – who introduced himself without then, or ever, offering his first name – moved into one of the towers of the main villa, as was his annual habit. Robert Culff, an Englishman, arrived shortly afterwards to take up residence for the summer in one of the rustic chalets on another part of the estate. He too was a painter, who also wrote fiction and verse and was, fortunately, buttressed by a private income. Stan Noyes, a young American, lived in nearby Nice and came over to give a reading of his work-in-progress at Menton Library, attended exclusively by expats; Noyes's only significant publication would be a novel based on his experiences of rodeo in the States. At one reading was Nick Nicholas, a Russian of minor aristocratic stock who as a teenager had fled the Soviet Union and ended up in London to become a naturalized Englishman. Sillitoe never learned his original name but his adopted one was, as he informed everyone, a respectful tribute to the murdered Tsar. He was writing his memoirs, and his English wife Muriel was toiling away on a novel based on her pre-Oxford, Bloomsburyesque experiences in the 1920s which struck Sillitoe as a cross between Waugh and Woolf, with murmurs of restrained very English lesbianism. It was never published.

Everyone, Sillitoe thought, was playing roles, an impression confirmed when he received a note from a Mr Boak, then staying at the Royal Westminster Hotel in Menton. Boak had been told of Sillitoe and Ruth by Hales of the Nottingham Writers' Club; Boak owned a tyre factory in the city, and in the Menton community of artists seemed something like a patron or philanthropist, albeit of the otiose sort. Would they, he asked in his note, care to join him and his wife Dolly for dinner at the Royal Westminster?

Sillitoe went alone, for the food, and found that the Boaks were in fact affable and transparent. Sillitoe was glad to accept Boak's gift of a £5 note and a Havana cigar as they said goodbye. It should be noted that in *The Open Door* aspects of Henderson and Hales are merged in a character called Boak: learned, witty and condescending.

What kind of writer, Sillitoe asked himself, was he becoming? Before leaving Nottingham he had burnt the vast majority of his more ambitious attempts at the novel-of-ideas, saving only 'The General's Dilemma' and 'The Deserters'. The latter would in due course be dismantled and rewritten as *Key to the Door*, and he continued to work on it in France. He also tried something new. 'Man Without a Home' is a novella, or to be more accurate a fictional vacuum into which are drawn chunks of his experience since crossing the Channel. The main character is an embarrassingly pretentious English painter, involving fragments of Culff and Gowa but showing traces of Sillitoe behind the masks.

One person who remained unaffected by the self-absorbed ambitions of the expatriate artists was a friend of Gowa, Ilse Steinhoff, a literary agent down from Paris. She too was fascinated by accounts of this new version of Lawrence, visited him and was shown the draft of 'Man Without a Home'. She mistook it for satire and was cautiously impressed. On being asked what else he had done Sillitoe went to a stock of stories and fragments kept from the Nottingham bonfire whose common feature was that he had previously never shown them to anyone, let alone forwarded them for publication. 'Uncle Ernest' and 'The Fishing Boat Picture' fascinated her. This, she suspected, was the true voice of the farceur of 'Man Without a Home' and she took copies of all, the latter mostly at Sillitoe's prompting, to Paris. She wasn't aware of what it was about 'Uncle Ernest' that compelled her attention. A hint of Camus? Sartre? Perhaps, but it was something that she had never before encountered in English. Whatever its nature and provenance, Sillitoe remained largely blind to it. During his period in France he never once returned to the material which he had salvaged from Nottingham, material which would in due course provide him with the kernel for his almost overnight success.

A typescript which no longer survives, 'No Peace among the Olives', was co-written by Sillitoe and Ruth and was their version of a private living parody. While cooking, cleaning the house and gathering firewood they would amuse each other with caricatures of two other famous refugees from England. Sillitoe played 'Bert' and Ruth 'Frieda'. She did a fair Germanic accent and he dressed solemn pretentious statements in Nottinghamshire colloquialisms. Only later did he recognize the similarities between 'Man Without a Home' and 'No Peace among the Olives', the latter resembling a ruthless caricature of the former's veneration of art's tragic obligations.

Ruth wrote poems and worked on draft material for *A Forecast, a Fable*, a small book eventually published in 1958. She began to evolve an idiom that can best be described as mid-Atlantic in tone and internationalist in breadth and perspective. Her background sometimes prompts comparisons with Plath, but in fact there are few parallels between her work and that of her near contemporary and eventual friend. Sillitoe also worked on his poetry but this was even more affected by erudition than his fiction. He prided himself on having mastered the peculiarities of English metre but by temperament he was drawn to creating patterns shaped more by instinct than abstract regulation.

Ruth's aunt in America sent them food parcels and Sillitoe's mother and his sisters Peggy and Pearl scraped together enough for packages of tea and other such items unavailable in France.

Their only reliable, constant companion was Nell, who can claim to be one of the most travelled and best-connected cats in literary history. She would accompany Sillitoe to Majorca and Spain, there eventually to reside as permanent guest of a farmer, and she would be commemorated, and transgendered, in Sillitoe's later tales for children concerning the adventures of Marmalade Jim.

After ten months, in October 1952, Ruth left. If they had any future, and she thought they did, she needed a divorce – something that, certainly in the 1950s, required the close attendance of solicitors and the presence of interested parties; it could not be conducted from the security of the Mediterranean.

Sillitoe had never lived on his own before and he became mildly obsessive regarding cleanliness and order. The routines of family existence, school, work, military service, even attendance upon that new thing, a partner, had suddenly been exchanged for solitude, and he compensated. On visiting the town he wore a tie, visited the local barber to keep his hair as militarily short as possible and patrolled the interior and grounds of Le Nid as though he were fearful of imminent inspection – cleaning, tidying, even painting. He went for walks, enjoyed the landscape, and sometimes, unavoidably, met other expatriates. He was not unhappy, far from dissatisfied, but at the same time his life seemed askew. He missed Ruth yet felt a guilty satisfaction at being entirely without links to anyone and anybody. He wrote to her, almost daily, and sprinted down the rough, walled stairway that linked the cottage to the road to collect her replies. He hoped that what they could eventually become would be permanent; but where? How would they keep themselves?

Sillitoe met the Tarrs, John and Dorothy, who would in due course inspire a number of his more dubious, eccentric characters. John Tarr, aged about sixty, had recently retired from an executive position in the Monotype Corporation. Print, typography, the physical characteristics of visible language obsessed him and he treated Sillitoe to a detailed account of his long-term project, a multi-volume study to be entitled *The History of Printed Letters*. He had already published a trade textbook called *Printing Today*, along with several manuals of instruction for those wishing to master Chancery script. He had a substantial pension, plus income from property in Kensington, and he conceded that the book, for all its scholarly significance, might have to be published privately. Dorothy, like almost everyone else in the locality, had written a novel.

Sillitoe took to John Tarr, initially because there was something about him which mirrored his own preoccupation with mildly eccentric topics: Morse code, maps and typography all seemed to stand at a quirky angle to the routines of communication. The better he got to know him, however, this echo of a character from an Ealing comedy, played no doubt by Alec Guinness, began to fade into something more obtuse. John's enthusiasm for print was matched by his affection for Stalinism. Orwell, in his view, was guilty of treachery. Avowing sympathy with the working classes yet betraying them by advocating half-hearted socialism was, he proclaimed, a characteristically bourgeois act of hypocrisy. Pre Hungary 1956 it was almost de rigueur for those with any claims upon a liberal humanist outlook – which among the educated British included virtually everyone apart from self-confessed Conservatives or resolute devotees of apathy – to regard the Soviet Union as at its worst a wounded behemoth with good intentions. John Tarr, affable and engaging as he was, was Sillitoe's first proper encounter with a phenomenon that would in due course infuriate him as an individual and influence him as a writer: the presumptuous, condescending assumption by middle-class intellectuals that they could rescue the 'working classes' from their dreadful plight. Sillitoe, mischievously, played games with Tarr's menu of stereotypes. Tarr's apparent respect for his intelligence was, he suspected, bolstered by his friend's image of him as a worthy curiosity, a heroic but entirely predictable example of working-class ambition. During their lengthy conversations on the state of Britain Sillitoe would follow John along familiar routes involving complaints about the state of the Labour Party, now in opposition, and the trade unions, emasculated and ineffectual as they evidently were, and then offer his own opinions. These included the suggestion that striking pickets should be shot and police given the power to summarily detain those suspected of harbouring Communist sympathizers. He was not entirely antagonistic to John's left-wing affiliations but he drew satisfaction from unsettling his standard model of the proletarian outlook. Later, much of his most successful fiction would be driven by this same urge to disrupt complacent perceptions of class and behaviour.

Alone in Menton he began to experience for the first time the compulsive draw of writing as a substitute for everything else. He maintained attendance upon the necessary routines of existence – he cleaned, shopped, cooked, fed Nell and so on, kept in touch with people that he and Ruth had got to know, the Tarrs in particular, and wrote her letters – yet he slipped gradually from the world he inhabited to the ones he invented.

He pressed on with 'Man Without a Home' and 'The Deserters', both destined to fail because of their divided allegiances. Threads of autobiography and rough naturalism contrasted uncomfortably with aspirations to a novel of ideas; Lawrence, Hemingway and Huxley are ill-suited companions. Ilse Steinhoff had become his unofficial agent and he bombarded her Paris address with everything he could lay his hands on. She indulged his enthusiasm for the novels – going through the motions of trying to interest publishers and failing, predictably. What interested her most was something in Sillitoe's fragments and short stories that she had never encountered before: hope-less, sometimes sordid pictures of ordinary life shot through with an electrifying defiance. These were not hymns to moral outrage at the state of the dispossessed – he knew even at this stage that writing about things would not improve them – but in his hands characters seemed to enjoy a bitter independence. Ilse was friendly with several people on the editorial board of *Carrefour*, arguably France's leading literary magazine of the time, and they too soon became fascinated by the short pieces. This was 1952, Amis, Wain and Larkin would not introduce themselves to the reading public for a year or more and their curious combination of anti-establishment mischief and conservative technique had yet to stir the surface of British literary culture. But here the *Carrefour* editors found something most unusual, a version of Camus who had turned an unapologetic spotlight on to territories that the curators of Britishness normally kept under wraps. 'Uncle Ernest' stunned them, but it would have to be translated into French. They exchanged other fragments, one describing drunkenness and nausea and another an attempt to bring about an abortion with a hot bath and a bottle of gin, both vividly realized and neither carrying an inkling of expla-nation or comment. A third offered a vignette – for them astonishing – of how ordinary people in a provincial working-class city dealt with a black soldier – tolerance was not even an issue; they just didn't care that much about what he looked like. Were these, they asked Ilse, the parts from which something bigger – a novel? – would be assembled? She didn't know, nor at the time did Sillitoe. Eventually they would resurface as key episodes in *Saturday Night and Sunday Morning*. How perverse and intriguing it is that the French intuited immediately the power of a text that had yet to find coherent shape, one moreover that publishers in Sillitoe's home country would treat as unacceptable – it would in due course be rejected by eight London publishers.

Carrefour asked Ilse if her unusual English friend had written anything that might form a bridge between the English and French urban working classes – football, for instance? She wrote to him and he remembered that one of the pieces that he had saved from the fire in Nottingham was 'The Match', dug it out from the chest of papers that he thought would never again see light, let alone a typesetter, and forwarded it. With a characteristically Gallic pairing of exuberance and insouciance *Carrefour* announced that they would publish 'Uncle Ernest' in 1953 and promptly lost it. Luckily Sillitoe had kept a carbon. 'The Match' would appear on 15 September 1954; Sillitoe's first published piece of fiction was in French translation, though the illustration offered what *Carrefour* thought was an authentic representation of a provincial English football ground in all its dreary greyness.

TWELVE

He still has no clear recollection of what prompted him to set off for Spain. The notion of the literary expatriate, the bohemian exile constantly eschewing the familiar in pursuit of enlightenment, was as he now knew largely an indulgence of the comfortably-off dilettante. He did not expect that what awaited him five hundred miles down the Mediterranean coast would – aside from language, architecture, a cheaper cost of living and an impoverished, ineffectual brand of fascism – be much different from what he had known in Menton.

It could have been the Tarrs, who had taken a lease on a villa in Majorca – warmer in winter and much cheaper than France, they advised – or perhaps it was a less accountable feeling, irresponsible dislocation. For the time being he had no allegiances to anywhere in particular, so why not go somewhere else? Letters from Ruth contributed to this; the divorce was in progress but proving tortuous and time-consuming and she didn't know when she would rejoin him.

He arrived in Palma, Majorca, on 30 January 1953 and took the train to join the Tarrs at their spacious Villa Catalina in Soller. His largest piece of luggage was a wooden chest which he had made himself just before leaving Menton. This along with his Remington typewriter, two battered leather suitcases and Nell's box – she had come too – joined him on the pavement outside Soller station where he sat waiting for a tram to the Tarrs' house. Unprompted, a woman from the adjacent butcher's shop had brought him a chair from their kitchen.

Sillitoe insisted on contributing to the Tarrs' food bills and other expenses and John provided him with a well-appointed room in which he could write; it contained the extensive library which John had recently paid to have shipped from their Kensington house. Sillitoe's weight had fallen to 130 pounds and his cough seemed to be worsening – the latter was not helped by a particularly cold and damp Mediterranean winter, not to mention Sillitoe's now almost continuous attachment to his pipe, with occasional breaks for a cigar. Taking a pragmatic view of things, he registered with a doctor in Palma recommended by the British consulate, and asked for refills of medicine for a pneumothorax in the hope that they might kick-start his sluggish right lung. No immediate improvement was evident, but after the treatment his doctor advised him nonchalantly that the better weather of spring would turn things around.

No correspondence survives from this period, except a black-and-white postcard of Soller which Sillitoe sent to his father. Christopher had not become literate, not quite, but Sillitoe wrote clearly on the card, in prominent capitals, three sentences that he thought Christopher might decode from his primitive familiarity with signs and labels. One cannot help but be moved.

March 24th

DEAR DAD
HOW ARE YOU?
ALL RIGHT, I HOPE.
I THINK OF YOU
A LOT, SO BE
HAPPY.
    YOUR LOVING
      SON,
        ALAN

A few weeks after Ruth had left Menton Sillitoe decided to spend an afternoon on the beach and soon found himself chatting to a young fair-haired Englishwoman who introduced herself as Brenda Mullan. She worked for the Foreign Office, was holidaying with a French family and was suitably impressed when Sillitoe told her he had left England to become a writer and had produced two novels and several short stories, none as yet in print. They spent the afternoon walking and Sillitoe took her to see the house where Katherine Mansfield had stayed. Later she returned with him to Le Nid for tea and a glass of wine. Nothing happened, he insists, but inevitably when a man and woman in their twenties spend a day together a degree of flirtation attends their exchanges on background, tastes, prospects and their agreeable surroundings. His harmless day out with Brenda involved, involuntarily or not, a testing of the water; nothing specific or reckless but without doubt the exploration of a hypothesis on what he might be inclined to do now that Ruth was away.

After a month or so in Majorca his private sense of fecklessness began to find a welcoming milieu. He had read a fair amount on Spain, particularly the Civil War and the Franco dictatorship – he found Orwell's *Homage to Catalonia* gripping and tragic – but his preconceptions soon started to disintegrate. Certainly there was abundant evidence of militarism, but it seemed a hapless parody of its Italian and German antecedents. Uniformed soldiers could be found everywhere in Barcelona – from which he disembarked for Palma – but it was difficult to tell if they were on duty or on leave. Apart from the fact that they were uniformed and armed their manner

indicated young men beset by aimlessness. Majorca had felt the reverbera-
tions and effects of the Civil War but as the island outpost of a still backward
economy it maintained a strong allegiance to pre-twentieth-century Spain:
politics was less important than looking after its own insulated fabric of fishing, farming and wine making. Sillitoe and the Tarrs would, at the weekend,
go into Soller to eat at cafés – a meal and several bottles of wine costing
roughly the same as a pot of tea in central London – and sample the nightlife.
The latter involved the kind of folk music and swirling-skirts dancing that
would within a couple of decades become a staple of the tourist industry;
then, it was undiluted and magnetic.

Sillitoe and John Tarr now spent more time together than they had in
Menton. They often stayed on in the bar in Soller, Dorothy being unable to
match their capacity for talk and drink, and John would, with Sillitoe's growing appreciation, move to the piano and perform everything from English
music hall to high opera. One night they postponed John's musical enter-
tainments to introduce themselves to a person who, the bar owner informed
them, was also a literary man. He was Oxford educated, in his fifties, but
had exiled himself from mainstream academia – his links with which were,
they suspected, tenuous – and now intended to complete a ground-breaking
book on Nietzsche. John Tarr was hypnotized and embittered by this
prospect. Nietzsche, he argued, had made fascism intellectually respectable
and, even worse, had detached philosophy from any sense of responsibility
to the ordinary man, unlike Marx of course. Sillitoe was fascinated, though
certainly not by the vigour and complexity of their exchanges. How, he
thought, can two apparently sane, intelligent individuals become locked
into this spiral of self-indulgence and still take themselves seriously? He felt
as though he had become a spectator upon a world which defied rational
comprehension. The locals – or at least most of them – seemed to go about
their business with an insouciant calm, unconcerned with such issues as the
meaning of life, yet the region appeared to encourage in visitors an addiction to literary ambition, intellectual veracity and collateral misbehaviour.
Such moments of detachment were rare given that Sillitoe had himself joined
this dance of high-minded debauchery.

One cannot help but notice the parallels between Sillitoe and Tarr and
the friendship formed three decades later between the anti-hero Cullen
and the egregariously bad Claude Moggerhanger in A Start in Life and Life
Goes On. These novels are, appropriately enough, modern-day versions
of the Spanish picaresque and Sillitoe admits today that when he wrote
them memories of his year of hedonism in Majorca played some part. 'Yes.
I carried something forward into those novels. John Tarr was my foil, just
as Moggerhanger is for Cullen. I was for a while determined to cause
havoc.'

He was drinking in a hotel in Soller, it was early March 1953 and the spring climate had, as his doctor predicted, improved his health. He fixed upon a woman, dark haired, slim, attractive and roughly his age, who was speaking English. He walked over and introduced himself. By then he had come to realize that there was something about him – by no means the usual repertoire of the charmer – that aroused in women if not immediate attraction then at least curiosity. He cannot, as usual, remember her name, but what stays with him is a vivid mutual recognition of unrestraint. She was either a trainee nurse or a medical student. This information lodged temporarily; his interest was elsewhere, and he certainly recalls her rather solemn pronouncement that she was bisexual. His reply that, so what, he too enjoyed sleeping with women, appeared to decide things, at least for the brief duration of her stay, and off they went for a couple of days in Ibiza.

And then there was Pauline. (This is not her actual name, but private records and first-hand accounts testify to her existence.) She was ten years older than Sillitoe, American and married with one seven-year-old daughter. He describes her as 'handsome and beautiful as a Russian princess' and from the moment they met one lunchtime at a café on the plaza he was besotted. Her husband was, it hardly needs be said, producing the Great American Novel, an undertaking which preoccupied him fully. This pleased Sillitoe since it effectively blinded him to the real interests of their new family friend – also it seemed an apprentice novelist – who would entertain their daughter with readings from his work in progress for children, *Big John and the Stars*.

Pauline was flattered and fascinated by Sillitoe's attentions, and their occasional assignations soon became a serious affair. They would meet at various times of the day. He recalls, 'I no longer lived at the Tarrs' place, but had taken a room in the town of Soller, and we went there.' Sometimes he would dine with the family at their house and he recalls with barely disguised relish the exchanges between secret lovers, cuckold and dangerously inquisitive seven-year-old. Did he not feel some guilt, or at least unease? 'Some, and less than I should have done. But that year I seemed immune from standard responses to anything.'

During his time in Spain Sillitoe kept a diary, albeit at irregular intervals and certainly not in any predictable format; sometimes there would be two-line aphorisms on the state of mankind and on other occasions meticulous accounts of the garden, the weather and what he would have for dinner. The entries do not even comprise a separate document, being scattered among plans and manuscripts that reflect his myriad literary endeavours of the 1950s.

One of the earliest entries is undated but is in the same folder as the original manuscripts of *Big John and the Stars*, which places it during the period when he began his affair with Pauline. He begins:

I always write up my diary in the morning, usually around nine o'clock. This is because I like to give things a chance to simmer down before writing about them. I suppose this is cheating, that one is obliged by the duty of keeping a diary to write things down while they are still hot. [Private diary, undated]

One suspects that his attention is here straying from the diary itself to literature in general and in particular the incessant concern of all writers – how to close the gap between the world and the word. Then he slips back to the implied question of why he feels duty bound to his diary given it is not intended for public disclosure. 'It is a duty you owe to any bloody snoopers who will eventually read it.' He is referring of course to me, dear reader, and you, and he adds, 'It is a duty you owe to yourself.' Further down the page it becomes clear why he has prefaced the entry with a brief disquisition on truth, representation and ethics. He is out with Pauline:

Yesterday, then, we watched the Corpus Christi procession. I was feeling tired what with the work I had done. But I felt I had to see the procession. We stood by the road edge among the other watchers with [Pauline's daughter] on my shoulder. Seven years of age but not too heavy.

The little boys came first with drums and bugles, all dressed in white, followed by four maidens bearing an image of Christ. Then youths with candles, and men with candles and a band with the priest swinging his censer; and as everybody went down on their knees I did so too. Out of courtesy. And as well as looking at what was passing I saw the looks on the women's faces; ecstasy. My heart went cold to see them. I could have wept at the same time. How do they do it? I remembered an expression on [Pauline's] face, but did not look at her.

It is imperfect, improvised, but a kernel of genius is evident. His capricious attraction to an alien culture and belief system interweaves with personal registers – the parallel between him supporting the daughter of his married mistress on his shoulders and the maidens carrying shoulder high the image of the Crucifixion requires no comment. He ties these strands together gradually at first but the thread begins to tighten as the image of the women's faces, engorged with the pleasure of spirituality, reminds him of something recently experienced by the woman next to him.

In early summer he gave up the room in town and moved in with Jim Donovan at a large bourgeois house called Casa Jolana. Jim was an Englishman only just nineteen and set upon a career as an artist. The house was massive, four spacious ground-floor rooms and six bedrooms, but the woman who had offered it to him, Jup Van Dreil, had done so on the understanding that they would live and work in the servants' quarters in the attic. She herself occupied the better, cooler part of the house, having arranged to look after it for its wealthy Dutch owner until he decided to move south. It was rent free so Sillitoe and Jim agreed to live in the hot roof, each of their rooms offering a small window with an enticing view of the sea. In August Donovan returned to London and Sillitoe and Pauline would treat the attic as their own, at least during the day. Jup Van Dreil noticed but feigned indifference.

Sillitoe's unfettered lifestyle was reflected in the motley nature of his literary output. He produced poems fitfully and distractedly, went back again to 'The Deserters', now four hundred pages long and rejected with cursory comments by Macmillan and Gollancz. He finished *Big John and the Stars*, sent it to the BBC – potentially as a series for children – and to Heinemann; it came back by return of post. The *Nottingham Weekly Guardian* said they would like a couple of pieces – travel guide style – on Majorca, which they published and the BBC wrote asking if he would come to London to read, on air, a condensed version of his article on the ascent of Kedah Peak. He wanted to do so but the prospect of travelling across Europe by train for thirty-six hours and at a cost that would only be half covered by the minuscule fee caused him to turn them down. The producer, part-time, who had written to him was called John Wain. Within a few months he would recruit other unpublished figures to his Third Programme readings and launch their careers: Kingsley Amis, Philip Larkin and Donald Davie included.

Surprised and inspired by the enthusiasm of the French, Sillitoe at last started to think seriously about what he called his 'Nottingham Fiction'. He began and in a week completed 'Mr Raynor the School-Teacher', based, he claims, on recollections of a real figure who presided over a class of recalcitrant thirteen- and fourteen-year-olds. Raynor divides his time between retributive tasks for his pupils and staring at an abundantly stimulating retinue of shop girls who appear in the windows of Harrison's Drapery across the road, an image adapted from his memory of a less scholarly figure from his early childhood, mute, possibly disturbed, who spent his days watching girls who passed his doorstep on their way to the Raleigh factory. It is in its own right a superb short story, a crisply executed vignette of desuetude, lust and bitterness, and while Raynor might in part have grown out of Sillitoe's hypotheses on what had created the choleric manner of one of his teachers one senses that the story also collects something of its dynamic from contemporaneous events. Raynor's detestation of his charges is caused, it seems, by his perception of their aggressive philistinism, but Sillitoe choreographs the story so we begin to suspect that something deeper and unstated is at work. Raynor's knowledge of uninhibited sexuality is largely hypothetical; he watches with the full knowledge that he will never be part of it. Simultaneously he has to deal with a collection of boys on the cusp of manhood. We are never told but we feel that his loathing for his class boils with envy: they in a few months will leave, forget his tiny fiefdom and join the world of the girls across the road. Consider the passage in which he takes against the misbehaving Bullivant:

> 'Y'aren't gooin' ter 'it me wi' that,' Bullivant said again, a gleam just showing from his blue half-closed eyes.
>
> Robust. An eye for an eye. The body of the girl, the bottom line of the sweater spreading over her hips, was destroyed in silence. His urge for revenge was checked, but was followed by a rage that nevertheless bit hard and forced him to action. In the passing of a bus he stepped to Bullivant's side and struck him several times across the shoulders with the stick, crashing each blow down with all his force. 'Take that,' he cried out, 'you stupid defiant oaf.' [pp. 75–6]

When he wrote the story Sillitoe was behaving like an unruly embodiment of its parts. He had carried into it the subversive energy of Bullivant and his peers, but now he could both match Raynor intellectually and take satisfaction that the latter's ineffectual hypothesis, sex, was now his, Sillitoe's energetic routine.

In early summer Tarr asked Sillitoe if he had any opinions on Robert Graves, who lived, so Tarr informed him, barely ten kilometres away near Deya. His acquaintance with Graves's work was, he admitted, fragmentary but he certainly knew of *Goodbye to All That* (1929), a radically honest account of public-school cruelty, marital breakdown and, significantly for Sillitoe, the horror of First World War trench warfare. He knew some of Graves's poetry – by degrees unpretentious, tough and eloquent – and read the Claudius novels for the first time in Malaya, lent to him by Schlachter. All and more were available in John Tarr's library. Then he wrote to him, asking if they might meet, and enclosed some samples of his own verse. Why didn't you send him some fiction as well, I ask? 'I didn't want to bother him with too many words.' Graves replied, and the letter survives:

> Dear Mr Sillitoe,
>
> I should have written before but have been plagued with work, primarily an 1100pp book on Greek myths . . . thank you for showing me those poems. There is something unusual, and good, about them . . . I live here [at his country house] during the school terms . . . This is in case you feel like calling. [Indiana Archive]

He did, they agreed a date, and Sillitoe busied himself reading *The White Goddess* (1948) which argued that the female muse is the vital counterpoint to maleness and that literature had been coarsened by her displacement. Sillitoe was not sure that he agreed with Graves's thesis but he admired his disrespect for orthodoxy.

Sillitoe rode the whole distance to the Graves's remote farmhouse on a bike he had hired for a few pesetas. Graves was hospitable – they went rapidly from lemonade to Spanish brandy – informal and willing to discuss Sillitoe's writing and plans. Nothing Graves said – he averred that the poems might benefit from being honed to a 'point of simplicity', a tactful, honest suggestion, but Sillitoe did not really know what he was getting at – made any difference to his self-reliant programme of work. This and successive meetings were of no practical benefit to Sillitoe but he and Graves became friends and Sillitoe and Ruth have stayed in close contact with the Graves family since then. If Sillitoe gained anything from their first encounters it was a feeling of confidence. He had met people with literary ambitions in Nottingham and around the Mediterranean, yet apart from informal encounters with agents and letters of rejection from mainstream publishers he often wondered if he was destined to remain on the margins of the literary commonwealth; at least until he met Robert Graves. Graves never paraded his eminence, considerable as it was, and as their friendship developed Sillitoe began to feel not simply that significant writers were ordinary and approachable but that the mythology of art as the special gift of the elect was flawed. Graves was self-evidently good at what he did but as a man he was no different from anyone else that Sillitoe had befriended in the past. True, the badges of class showed through in their respective accents and manner, but neither had cause to notice.

A small bridge had been crossed. The fact that Sillitoe felt not even the slightest inclination to remodel himself as a version of Graves or anyone else of his class and generation reinforced his certainty that he, Alan Sillitoe, could write in a way that suited him best, untrammelled by precedent, fashion or convention, and that one day if what he produced was any good someone would appreciate it.

Meanwhile his personal life began to resemble a tale written by someone with a taste for the baroque. He continued a regular correspondence with Ruth and as his affair with Pauline intensified so did his pleas to his partner in London that they should resume life together as soon as possible. It was and still is Sillitoe's habit to compose personal letters – notably those to friends, family members and fellow writers – in longhand, keeping his typewriter for newspaper editors, publishers and correspondents with whom he has had no previous contact. Bizarrely – or appetizingly, if one can abide psychoanalysis – his most desperate statements of intent to Ruth were typed.

In early September 1953 he asked Pauline to leave her husband, and with their daughter come to live with him. He was not sure where – they would probably remain in Majorca, he thought – nor how exactly his RAF pension could sustain them, but they would manage somehow. He was certain that success, and money, as a writer would come eventually. Pauline too treated their relationship as much more than an exciting brush with infidelity. She felt something for Sillitoe that was lacking in her marriage, yet she was also a pragmatist. Any risks that she took would also change the lives of others, and while her husband could probably survive she did not intend to involve their daughter in an act of such recklessness. She turned him down but they did not break up. Sillitoe recorded in his diary: 'Do I love her? [Pauline] I do not, but nor do I wish to end this. I feel we are circling each other, magnetised and cautious. It is like a bullfight with [Pauline's husband] as the only, blind, spectator.' At the beginning of October Pauline and her family left Majorca for Malaga and two weeks later Sillitoe followed them. With Mike Edmonds he shared a flat, again to be used for afternoon liaisons with Pauline, sometimes followed only hours later by Sillitoe's arrival at her house for dinner as the avuncular friend of the family. It soon became evident to Sillitoe that Pauline's husband knew or at least suspected that something was going on, though he apparently never mentioned this to his wife and certainly not to Sillitoe. While nothing was said at these assemblies much was implied, glances exchanged, unvoiced suspicions lodged. Sillitoe remembers the period vividly, but much as an actor might be reminded of his most outrageous performance; he relished it, lived it, but it was not really him.

He recalls also that he felt his private world had become informed by a provocative illogic, as though the balance between compulsion and responsibility either disappeared completely or had become farcically distended. Shortly after he and the Tarrs had moved into Villa Catalina, for example, John answered the door to find there a priest, in full regalia, and attended by two altar boys, who then entered unbidden and proceeded to sanctify each room, reciting Latin formulae and swinging a crucible of rancid-smelling incense. He appeared to be purging the place of evil spirits – a not uncommon local custom when residences changed hands, apparently. John, devotee of Stalin and committed atheist, appeared immobilized; it was as though his mid-twentieth-century ultra-rationalist sensibility had despite itself been silenced by a visit from the Middle Ages. For Sillitoe it all seemed darkly appropriate; this had after all been the house in which his relationship with Pauline had begun. Later during their affair his abiding memory of the room in which they would meet was of a crucifix. A sculpture of Christ on the cross was set in an aperture in the wall just above the bed. Recessed, it could not be removed, and it seemed designed to remind occupants of the room that though they had closed the door against the world something else stood in mute witness to their presence.

Sillitoe had never had much time for abstract morality but his ongoing regime seemed to involve more than instinct. Something else appeared to be at work and it occurred to him that the fact that he was behaving in such a way in the most repressively Christian country in Europe was if not accidental then a reason for self-scrutiny. As a consequence he turned to his Bible and concentrated deliberately on the Old Testament.

He would select passages at random 'much like my mother's old system . . . when she closed her eyes and, holding a pin, pricked the page of a racing paper to choose a horse on which to place sixpence or a shilling at the local bookies' (*Life Without Armour*, p. 193). He favoured the Old Testament because in his view it was less peremptory than the New. It allowed for occurrences and individual actions that could never easily be explained even by the prophets, and his adoption of his mother's betting system provided another level of security against having to take instruction. Who knew what would turn up and how it might affect his present state of mind? Indeed his anarchic though not irreverent engagement with scripture became the compass for his behaviour and it is intriguing that during the hours before he asked Pauline to leave her husband he stumbled upon the verse from the Book of Samuel that would later provide the title for his memoirs: 'And they cut off his head, and stripped off his armour, and sent it into the land of the Philistines round about, to publish it in the house of their idols, and among the people.' Irrespective of its original significance Sillitoe traced through the sentence a deeply personal thread of irony. He was living as if the moderating organs of circumspection and rationality had indeed been removed and he had already decided to exist without the layers of protection – physical, emotional and psychological – that most of us take for granted. There are in his notebook passages which record his private reflections on justice, morality and God.

> Do I believe in God? Yes, unconditionally. God is my driving force, my inexhaustible machinery, my fear and passion, the sane and insane phrases drumming in my brain. God is my right to love two women, live as I wish, and choose my own words . . . He makes me happy to be alive and to be melancholic; fills me with too much love and too much hate . . . I am my own God . . . God is all that I am or ever can be. Sometimes I fight with him, curse him . . . but in the end he wins, and always will win, because God is on my side, and I am God and we are one, together and the same. My brain is God, and my pen is his priest. [Private notebook, undated, circa winter 1953]

This is incendiary stuff, even by the standards of Nietzsche or Sartre, and certainly not the kind of thing with which the so-called 'Fifties generation' of British writers are customarily associated. Also, one senses a presence here which is less a reflection than a projection of Sillitoe, someone who bears a close resemblance to the figure who would make his author famous but was as yet as much an impulse as an idea.

PART III
THE ROAD TO SUCCESS

THIRTEEN

It is impossible to say when exactly the collection of fragments and vignettes based partly on observed experience began to mutate into *Saturday Night and Sunday Morning*. The earliest complete draft is dated as 1956 but this involved a rewriting and extension of existing material and it is evident that as a character capable of taking control of his story Arthur Seaton was born two years earlier during Sillitoe's season of unrestraint. Pauline and her family left Spain for good in mid-December and little more than a month later Sillitoe began a story provisionally entitled 'Once in a Weekend'. At the time it seemed destined for his growing collection of Nottingham-based short stories, but with a few alterations it would eventually become the opening chapter of his first published novel. It sets the tone perfectly for what will follow.

The narrator betrays little of how the events register for their begetter Arthur Seaton, but he does not have to. Arthur has a presence that we usually only encounter outside fiction in real people, the kind that incites a spectrum of feelings from disgust through fear to a begrudging sense of awe. Sensation sidelines any requirement to know them personally. While there is no clear sense of purpose or premeditation behind the narrative – it is as though we too are in the bar, witnessing events with no suspicion they might be choreographed by a single agency – Arthur's personality imparts to it a barbarous logic. His behaviour in the pub combines belligerence and hedonism with a hint of the self-destructive, and one is impressed by how Sillitoe carries Arthur's magnetic singularity into the second part of the chapter. After leaving the pub he visits his mistress Brenda, and next morning he treats her son Jacky as though he were his own. He refers to Jacky's real father, Jack, as 'that bastard' for no other reason than he is guaranteed regular sex from Brenda and such homely delights as the bacon and egg breakfast that Arthur hurriedly enjoys before departing through the front door as Jack enters via the scullery – a droll exercise in status reversal. In all other respects Jack is the epitome of decency, and, sadly for him, guileless predictability; hence Arthur's dangerous allure for Brenda as her lover and, more innocently, for Jacky as his mysterious uncle.

Inevitably the parallels between the chapter and the twelve months of Sillitoe's life that had preceded its composition prompt the question. 'More than a coincidence?' I ask him. 'Yes, the scenario is borrowed, if not quite the personnel.' What does he mean? 'That relationship – involving myself, Pauline and — [he will not name Pauline's daughter] – has something of

Arthur and Brenda and Jacky about it, though Brenda as a character draws as much on memories of women I'd known in Nottingham.'

When he wrote the piece as a short story Sillitoe had no plans to enlarge it, but within six months he was thinking about Arthur's friendship with Jack. For most of the book they remain on convivial terms, working in the same factory and exchanging banter, with Arthur sometimes trying to provoke Jack by setting his own irresponsible, licentious habits against the latter's regime of steady resignation. And all the time the jibes trail a bitter subtext: not only is my bad lifestyle more enjoyable than your routine of domestication and overtime, I'm also screwing your wife. One cannot help but note the similarities between Arthur and his cuckolded workmate Jack and two other men who shared a trade – writing – and indeed a woman. Did Sillitoe taunt Pauline's husband? 'No. I was more concerned with ensuring that he had no suspicions about Pauline and me.'

This exercise in dissimulation was for Sillitoe emotionally taxing in that his exchanges with his male host were affable and transparent – each had a genuine interest in the other's work and its progress – while also calculated to protect him from suspicions. Sillitoe today recalls such events without pride, as an unfortunate imperative. 'Unless or until Pauline left him, we had to lie. That was it.' But there is sufficient evidence in *Saturday Night and Sunday Morning* that necessity brought with it a residue of guilt and dejection. Arthur bears no malice towards Jack. Indeed he almost admires his strength of purpose and rectitude. But despite himself he can't leave Brenda alone, nor can he offset his determination – perhaps subliminal – to provoke the cuckold's anger and take the deserved consequences. It is almost as though in the novel he takes pleasure, contrite pleasure, in being beaten up by off-duty soldiers acting on behalf of Jack and the husband of another of Arthur's conquests. Nothing like this happened in Spain, of course, but the sense of guilt which informs the Nottingham fiction originated there.

In the novel Arthur is promiscuous but, having no steady girlfriend of his own, not strictly speaking inconstant, which causes one to wonder why he carries into his various quests and misdemeanours such an undertone of self-loathing. He pities Jack, but not that much. It is as though he is paying his penitential dues to some other unspecified presence.

In late January 1954, three months after Pauline had left the area, Sillitoe received a letter from Ruth stating that now her marital and financial matters had been settled she would in about a fortnight take the train through France to Barcelona. She had never visited Spain before and she thought the city, just across the Pyrenees, seemed a good place for him to meet her. It was barely half a day's journey from his current address in Malaga.

Sillitoe arrived on 17 February, the day before Ruth's train was due. He would find a hotel for them before meeting her at the station, and he admits that he has no proper explanation for what happened next. As he booked a room at the reception desk of a cheap hotel in the Old Town two men, dressed film noir style in dark raincoats and trilbies, moved into position on either side of him, obviously intent on blocking any hurried departure. Without stating who he was or on whose authority he acted, one of them showed him an official-looking identity card, and also revealed a holstered sidearm. Sillitoe was addressed by name, informed that he was under arrest and marched about a kilometre to what he later learned was the central police station. As he approached its steel-framed door and barred windows, however, it seemed to him more like a prison. For the subsequent twelve hours he was subjected to a persistent interrogation which resembled Kafka's *The Trial*, in equal measures pointless and sinister. The opening questions regarding his full name, date of birth, profession and reason for being in Spain – he was, as he stated truthfully, a writer surviving on an RAF pension – were run through in a perfunctory manner; it was as though they already knew the answers. These were then rehearsed with supplementary enquiries on his location at particular times, exact residential addresses over the previous year and so on.

For about half an hour one of the questioners meticulously examined Sillitoe's typewriter as if suspect persons were known to conceal vital material beneath the keys and within the mechanisms of these instruments. At no point did any of them indicate the reason for his detention or what information they hoped to obtain, and after several hours Sillitoe decided that the appropriate response was to play the role of the half-witted Englishman abroad: candid, artless and perplexed. He is not certain if this sapped his interrogators' energy, but as darkness fell – the 'interview room' had an intimidatingly small window – there were a number of notable silences and absences. Were they, he wondered, waiting for confirmation by phone or telegraph of something from somewhere? At about 10 p.m. his luggage and papers were returned to him and he was told that he was free to go. Again no explanation was proffered either for his being detained in the first place or for his release. He recalls that when he asked for his French *carte de séjour* – which more than eight hours before had been carefully scrutinized on the table before his eyes – the officials stated that no such document had been found on his person or retained by them. An appropriate coda, he thought, to a mildly surreal experience.

Fifteen years later when Sillitoe decided to turn his hand to the contemporary picaresque, memories of his time on the loose in Spain vied for contention with literary antecedents from the same country. At the end of *A Start in Life* Cullen is sent to jail, framed by his one-time mentor Moggerhanger but accepting his fate as simply that, an event to be endured; he had enjoyed many others. There are, self-evidently, parallels between the incident in Barcelona and the conclusion of *A Start in Life*, but a less obvious and more intriguing echo occurs in a piece he wrote less than a year later and which would eventually appear in *Saturday Night and Sunday Morning*.

Chapter 9 constitutes one of those moments in a novel that could be the result of either recklessness or measured genius. A decision is too close to call because in either event the text as a whole is enriched by the contrast between what we expect to happen and what does. The chapter is brief and it takes Arthur outside his usual environment to a barracks where he is being put through basic training for National Service. The really puzzling passage follows his return to his billet from the local pub. A raging thunderstorm seems to bother him slightly, and before he can reach his bunk he collapses on the barrack-room floor. Next morning he awakes, strapped to his bunk with webbing. On being asked why he has been tied up, his comrade, Moore, states that he is not and then, having conceded that he is indeed detained, tells him a slightly fantastic story of how during the night and in a semi-conscious state Arthur had lashed out at the CO – 'kicked him right in the nuts' – and that the latter had ordered him to be immobilized. Arthur does not believe him and insists that since he is now demonstrably harmless he should be released. Moore refuses and leaves him alone. His next visitor is the orderly officer, who appears to have no knowledge of the night's events. 'What are you doing still in bed?' he asks Arthur, who answers, 'I'm badly. I don't feel well. I got pains in my head and stomach and I feel as though I'm tied to my bed' (p. 144). The OO believes him and leaves, grumbling that he will have the sergeant move him to sick quarters. As these competing accounts of whether he is truly detained and what might have led him to this condition circulate around him, Arthur settles into a state of complacent indifference.

The passage seems on first impression to be a brief excursion from the novel's predominant mood of rough naturalism to a combination of Gothic and farce, but though the tenor changes we find that we have in fact been shown a little more of the real Arthur Seaton. He neither asks for explanations for life nor offers excuses for his part in it. And he does not complain:

> The door slammed and the billet was silent. The OO forgot to send the sergeant, and Arthur stayed in bed till tea-time, obliviously sleeping, forgetting that he was tied up, the hours passing with such pleasant speed that he remarked to Ambergate later that they should leave him be, that he could think of no better way to spend his fifteen days, provided they gave him a drink of tea and a fag now and again. [p. 144]

The piece preserves all of the unnerving resonances of Sillitoe's detention in the Barcelona police station. For Arthur and Sillitoe logical expectations of what happens next are disrupted by an occurrence apparently choreographed by figures committed to the unforeseeable and inexplicable.

I ask Sillitoe: 'Did the incident in Barcelona inspire the curious passage in Chapter 9?' 'Yes,' he answers. Case closed. The next question is more complex. Does he feel that what happened in Barcelona was a fitting conclusion to a brief period of excess? 'No. It was just a coincidence. A few bumbling caricatures of the Gestapo had nothing better to do than harass Britons who had been resident for more than a fortnight. Gibraltar probably had something to do with it.' I believe him of course but, as Arthur would testify, truth can be unreliable.

The next day he met Ruth at Barcelona railway station. She had stayed in Paris en route and met Ilse Steinhoff, who gave her £12. This was Sillitoe's payment from *Carrefour* for 'The Match' which would appear in French in a few weeks. For a writer without any public recognition it was a generous fee and it enabled them to spend an unhurried three days together at the hotel where he had been arrested. They had not seen each other for almost a year and a half.

Ilse Steinhoff had tried to interest Continental publishers in his work, but she had few contacts outside Paris. In 1954 he had met the English novelist Charles Chapman-Mortimer in Malaga. Unlike most of the aspiring writers of the region Chapman-Mortimer already had a decent reputation – his novel *Father Goose* had won the James Tait Black Memorial Prize in 1951 – and he advised Sillitoe that to stand a reasonable chance of getting into print he must persuade an established London agent that his work was worth promoting. Generously he agreed to read some of it and then, perhaps, act as an intermediary. He did not see any of the Nottingham fiction but he was impressed by 'The General's Dilemma'. It was, he thought, ambitious in that it did not toe the line of any recognizable British fashion or antecedent, and he wrote to his own agent in London, Rosica Colin, introducing and recommending Sillitoe to her. She too saw 'The General's Dilemma' but was more interested in the short stories he also forwarded, some of which would appear in *The Loneliness of the Long Distance Runner* and others that would be refashioned as parts of *Saturday Night and Sunday Morning*. Like Ilse Steinhoff she was bewitched and bemused. The quality of the writing was self-evident, but selling to publishers work that belonged within no recognizable tradition was all but impossible. It was not until the emergence of figures such as John Braine that Rosica would find a benchmark for promoting Sillitoe; he had pre-empted Braine and in other respects surpassed him.

For various reasons, Sillitoe had never felt particularly at ease on the Spanish mainland. His first night in Malaga, sharing a flat with Mike

Edmonds, was memorable in that while they were out for a drink their two-room basement apartment was burgled. The thief had not broken in but instead used either a fishing rod or something resembling it to pull jackets, trousers, underwear and a wallet containing £3 – all Sillitoe's – through a broken pane in the window. Sillitoe knew he would never see his goods again, and the manner in which the police treated their report – contemptuous indifference – left him with the impression that the town had something intrinsically nasty about it. Poor people seemed to prey upon each other – their flat was in the roughest, cheapest area and clearly the burglar was waiting for new residents – and no one else cared. The Barcelona incident, though tinged with the absurd, left a stain on his memory of the city, and Alicante, where he was also to stay for several weeks at the beginning of 1958, seemed like Malaga to have an insidious stench of inhospitality about it. He grew to feel that the Franco regime had since the Civil War become something of a languorous curiosity – why else would so many aspiring and allegedly enlightened expatriate writers be drawn to the place? But scrape the surface and an unbroken seam of cruel authoritarianism could be discerned. The Balearics, technically part of the same dominion, had somehow, he thought, spared themselves some of its worst features. So he persuaded Ruth that since they were starting again as a couple they should do so where he had lived first, in Majorca.

They rented a small apartment in Soller from one Doña Maria Mayol whose personal history confirmed many of Sillitoe's opinions about Spain. Before and during the Civil War she had been a Republican, a Socialist Deputy in Barcelona, and had seen many of her friends endure the horrors still hardly acknowledged for decades after Franco. Following Franco's victory she had fled to France – political association could result in death – and after the Second World War had returned to live in Majorca where her family owned several properties. She was reluctant, despite Sillitoe's tactful probing, to offer details of her past, and her silence bespoke, he thought, terrible memories. What was evident was that she had reclaimed a degree of contentment in a place where customs and habits which antedated the 1930s remained strong. She was also the first of the dozens of writers he met on his Mediterranean odyssey who came from the indigenous population. Her poems were written largely in the Mallorquin dialect, and Sillitoe felt a special affinity for them; he even translated some of them into English. They were unpublished – and they seemed to indicate a preference for the language and by implication the outlook of ordinary people over the sophisticated, tainted idiom of the literary establishment. Sillitoe had by now become fluent in Spanish, and Lucia Graves, Robert Graves's granddaughter, remarked to me on how 'Alan, more than any other expatriate, had a perfect command of the language, its accent, tempo and idiomatic peculiarities. On the mainland strangers took it for granted that he was from the Balearics. Even Mallorcans themselves mistook him for a native of the island.' When he taught himself Spanish he had been fully aware of the differences and he had chosen this allegiance deliberately.

It is doubtful that £4 7s 6d a week would have been sufficient to support even the most ascetic individual in England in 1954. In Majorca it paid the rent for Sillitoe and Ruth, kept them well supplied with logs for the stove on which they cooked and which heated the main room of the flat, and enabled them to live as well as anyone else in the district. They had enough for food and wine at home and could go out to bars and cafés regularly. They borrowed books from other expatriates, and had some sent on from friends and family, mostly Ruth's, in England.

As a couple they began where they had left off in Menton, committed to each other and dedicated individually to making their names as writers. In October 'The Match' finally appeared in *Carrefour*, and a few weeks after that Ruth had three poems published in the prestigious *Hudson Review*. This resumption of a relationship interrupted by heedless circumstances is dealt with by Sillitoe in *Life Without Armour*, but the omissions are glaring. For one thing he had become friends with an enormous number of people in her absence, a circuit to which she would now be introduced. The Tarrs were still in regular contact; Sillitoe had become a family friend of Beryl and Robert Graves; Mike Edmonds sometimes returned to the island. Also he had formed a close friendship – platonic and flirtatious – with the exotic Elizabeth Trocchi, who kept a flat in Soller. She co-edited with her husband Alex the Paris-based journal *Merlin*, recently containing new work by Samuel Beckett and Christopher Logue. There were still more people to meet, virtually all of them writers who regarded the Mediterranean as some kind of touchstone for their ambitions. Tony Buttita had previously made a comfortable living in the USA as a theatrical agent and had now treated himself to a sabbatical, taking a suite of rooms in a hotel in El Guia to pursue his ambitions as suitor to Elizabeth Trocchi – whose husband Alex had recently left the island – and as yet another contributor to that hallowed sub-genre, the Great American Novel. Sillitoe knew of at least three other such weighty blockbusters currently in progress – his cuckold's included; none would go into print. Mack Reynolds, also an American, had lived on the island for six years. He too had once had great ambitions to become the new Hemingway or Fitzgerald, but pragmatism, the need to make money, had intervened. Now he contributed regular pieces to downmarket science-fiction magazines and collected these into books which in the United States sold as well as Westerns – the country was warming up for the space race. Mack's Dalmatian was the largest dog Sillitoe had ever seen, a supine beast who devoted his time to noisy and unbearably noxious bouts of flatulence. Pointedly they had named him Story.

Looking back on this period, particularly 1955–7, the two years following Ruth's return, Sillitoe has no clear recollection of episodes being linked by anything resembling cause or purpose. When he had no other commitments he would write for ten hours a day, and at the end of 1955 he found a means of supplementing his pension by teaching. The professional classes in Soller were keen that their children should learn English. Signs indicated that Spain would soon begin, tentatively, to rejoin the rest of the world, a community dominated by America. Private tuition agencies were proliferating, but Sillitoe worked as a freelance. He was interested in the teaching and the money was useful. The following spring Ruth, now almost as proficient in Spanish, began work as the representative of an English company that let holiday apartments.

They lived in modest comfort, socialized regularly and would sometimes join their friends – particularly Mike Edmonds, Elizabeth Trocchi or the Reynoldses – for trips to other parts of the island or less frequently the mainland. Sillitoe and Ruth did their best with some success to get to know the locals, to assimilate, but most of their time was spent in the company of expatriates for the simple reason that nearly all of them shared a common purpose, the realization of creative ambition. Most people went there because it had a good climate, pleasant scenery, a casual lifestyle and a cost of living roughly a quarter that of the UK or the USA. Their backgrounds varied in that the majority were Americans, followed closely by Britons and other Europeans. Equally diversified was their artistic self-image; most thought themselves capable of making the nineteenth-century grand narrative available to the new agenda of the Cold War; a few saw it as their duty to keep the flame of modernism alight; others, like Reynolds, indulged bohemian fantasies while playing to the market. The common factor among them, however varied their schemes for escape or reinvention, was their middle-class background. A number enjoyed private incomes, a few such as the Graveses lived comfortably from literary success, most were only slightly better off than Sillitoe and Ruth, but prosperity or lack of it were of negligible significance compared with the formative factors that make such people who they are. The expatriates had different reasons for removing themselves from their previous lives, but unwittingly aspects of it came with them and remained alive at the lunches and dinners where they would meet to discuss their work and prospects.

Even though his new companions would certainly not have treated him as anything other than their equal – and he could prove himself to doubters – there was something about him that announced itself as unnervingly different. He never paraded nor apologized for his background, and his accent was inconspicuous, giving no indication of class or region. He had become the ultimate writer abroad. He had witnessed yet at the same time side-stepped the various conditions of social programming which entrap the vast majority of individuals and cause them to feel for much of their lives various levels of insecurity, unworthiness, heedless superiority or guilt.

His principal point of contact with his past was his brother Brian. In 1952 he had given him the manuscript of 'By What Road?' in exchange for a good suit. Brian is about five inches taller than Sillitoe but the cuffs and trousers were taken up. As far as the novel was concerned Brian thought it amusing but implausible; he would return it to Sillitoe in 1958. As the presence of Arthur Seaton began to make larger claims upon his imagination so he wrote more to Brian about this man. This was 1954–5, soon after Brian had finished National Service and become a panel beater in a local factory – he was at the time roughly the same age as Arthur in the book. Brian offered advice. You can't, he wrote, have a barman bring eight pints of beer, two gins and orange, a whisky and three packets of Woodbines to a table in a pub. First, Nottingham barmen don't do that sort of thing, and also 'he wouldn't be able to get all that on one tray' (BS to AS, 18 April 1954). Sillitoe recognized the problem and decided to shift most of the contents of the tray to Arthur's stomach, and thus the beginning of *Saturday Night and Sunday Morning*, the drunken descent, was born.

The progress of the novel is recorded in a haphazard but no less tantalizing manner in what remains of Sillitoe's diaries from his time in Spain during the 1950s. 'The Rats' would eventually be the title piece for his first book of verse, but the term originated in his notes for a novel about an individual, unnamed, who is the aggressive antithesis of everything that these rodents advocate and embody: standardized morality, a political and cultural status quo designed to reduce the masses to a state of supine indifference. '"The Rats" is to be a philosophical novel.' 'Autobiographical fragments will be brought in . . . the book starts in the trimming department of a plywood factory, the character is my age, but it goes back.'

'I want to destroy,' he affirms when young to a friend.

'Why?' the friend asks.

'Why?' he replies, surprised and hurt that his friend does not laugh with him and say that he would also like to destroy, that he even needs to ask him why. They were 14, about to leave school.

Sillitoe's notes reflect a dilemma. His central character is a cocktail of rage, energy and private recollections. He wants to write about such a figure but he feels that this impulse has set him adrift from any literary precedent.

The character of the book confesses that he would not carry out any nihilistic actions. I know this. He has to be believable, but by becoming believable will he be absorbed by the system he rebels against? What will be the plot of my novel? It *must* have some sort of plot. The reader of course will continually wonder: What is going to happen to this man? What will happen? If I knew that, planned that, it would ruin him. [Private notebook, 1955]

It testifies to Sillitoe's calibre as a writer that from a prototype who refused to comply or affiliate he forged as memorable a character as Arthur Seaton.

Arthur Seaton is, like all great literary presences, more an invention than a copy, but Brian unwittingly played a significant part in his genesis. I met Brian in 2006 in the bar of a Nottingham hotel. Michael, Sillitoe's other brother, was also due but Brian arrived first. Most people, when meeting a stranger in unfamiliar circumstances, become hesitant, cautious, overly polite; we rarely give much of ourselves away during first encounters. With Brian this routine was notable for its absence. Brian was certainly not arrogant but he seemed able to do without the protective rituals upon which most of us rely. Once Michael had arrived we began to talk of all manner of things – Nottingham after the war, family history, and Sillitoe of course. Both had stories to tell, but what intrigued me almost as much as the anecdotes was the way in which the manner of the two men disclosed something of their character. While Michael worked hard at accurate recollection Brian would come in with a brief coda that seemed at once perverse and appropriate. He was not attempting to outdo his brother – quite the opposite – but something about the way his mind worked was slightly at odds with ordinary customs of conversation. There was nothing pretentious or provocative about it but it bespoke a heedless singularity. There was something of Arthur Seaton in him, then aged seventy-three.

Sillitoe first became aware that some of the unfinished 'Nottingham' fragments were shaping themselves into a longer narrative in the summer of 1955. A few pieces would always be short stories, but others began to depend upon the presence of a single figure. He was a little younger than Sillitoe and his Nottingham was that of the present day, the mid-1950s, rather than the city of even five years before. In this respect Brian kept his brother up to date on what was happening. Most of the slums where they had grown up in Radford were still standing, but the same sort of people who had once had no choice about where and how they could live were now finding themselves places in new council and private estates, with bathrooms and modern kitchens. Some even had cars and televisions. As a conduit for up-to-date information Brian did his job well, but there was something else about the exchanges of letters between the brothers that in a less obvious way contributed to *Saturday Night and Sunday Morning*'s undercurrent of uniqueness. Sillitoe regularly informed Brian of his objective, he hoped his destiny; he was a writer who would eventually be recognized as such and published. Brian, presently a panel beater, kept his brother updated regarding his own trade. Neither made anything of or cared about what many would regard as the different status of their jobs. They had chosen what they wanted to do, and for the time being Sillitoe was having to live on a pittance.

There was a casual, unforced dynamic between them. Brian was as intelligent and sharp as his brother but he had no inclination to be a writer, and this for Sillitoe was invaluable. He had an ally in a world which those who wanted to write about it had always treated with detachment. Brian anchored Sillitoe to the real significance of the lives people lived, not just as their witness but as their witty embodiment, by equal degrees unpretentious and unnerving. In the novel Arthur forms an alliance with his narrator, by implication his author, that should not on the face of things seem viable or credible. Not once does he disclose an interest in anything vaguely literary or intellectual, yet at the same time there is a natural affinity between his state of mind and the tough eloquence of the narrative that surrounds it. No one in English fiction had ever achieved anything like this before, and again the diaries provide an alluring insight into his achievement. It is autumn 1956, Sillitoe has been reading travel books and is struck by how frequently their first-person narrators acquire a shroud of anonymity, '. . . a ghostly shape who moves like an omniscient eye and pen over mountain ranges, and along sea coasts, from street to street . . .' How, he wonders, can one achieve this blend of immediacy and obscurity in fiction?

> How to describe oneself is a problem. One hopes that the adventures, events, will delineate your character sufficiently at least psychologically to let people know what you are like, and this often happens, so that the ghost takes on a soul, but it still remains for the most part intangible for want of a direct physical description [notably lacking for Arthur in *Saturday Night and Sunday Morning*]. The only way I can see out of this embarrassing dilemma is to fictionalise myself, but only slightly, to use detail where necessary, be there but not quite there, let the character and the narrator switch roles. [Private notebook, 1955]

This is a perfect anticipation of what would happen in the novel.

In early summer 1955 Sillitoe invited Brian to come and visit them in Majorca, and he stayed for almost the entire month of August. Two weeks of his absence from work were unpaid but he still brought enough cash to enable Sillitoe and Ruth to live more lavishly than their standard income generally allowed. He was introduced to most of the expatriates with whom they socialized, something which could in other circumstances have amounted to a condescending social exercise, even an act of provocation at another person's expense. But Sillitoe knew there would be no unease. As far as Brian was concerned what these people wanted to do – writers, artists, academics et al. – was up to them, and he certainly did not make fun of them for it. Sillitoe remembers a long night with the Graveses – a barbecue – during which Robert tentatively enquired of Brian about life in Nottingham. He had seen some of his brother's work and could hardly believe that people lived and behaved so shamelessly. All Brian recalls are several decent dinners out with 'Robert and Beryl, a grand couple. Like Alan, writers.'

Saturday Night and Sunday Morning was now acquiring shape and direction but it was one among many of his ongoing projects and he certainly had no intuition that it would be more likely than the others to break the impasse. Rosica Colin had by 1955 complete drafts both of 'The General's Dilemma' and his fictionalized account of a serviceman's experiences in post-war Malaya, 'Letter from Malaya'; parts of the latter would eventually be distilled into *Key to the Door*. Rosica was a scrupulous, pragmatic reader. She knew how to judge the merits of a piece alongside its potential marketability and she was confident that a major mainstream publisher would go for one or both. She was in regular contact with commissioning editors who trusted her estimation of new talent, and she pressed Sillitoe's case with houses which had recently taken her clients, Gollancz, Chatto and Macmillan particularly. All agreed that the drafts were in their way worthy, and all turned her down.

The catalogue of disappointments seemed limitless. Aside from the full-length pieces being promoted by Rosica he continued to send short stories and poems to virtually every literary magazine in Britain. A number of the former – 'The Fishing Boat Picture', 'The Match' (in English) and 'Uncle Ernest' – are now justly treated as classics of the genre, and every month (Sillitoe would never send the same pieces simultaneously to different magazines) rejection slips for them arrived, some showing evidence that the editor had at least read them, others more standardized and requiring only a signature. All would eventually appear in *The Loneliness of the Long Distance Runner*, which can make some claim to uniqueness as the only major collection of short stories comprised of work in continuous circulation among publishers for the previous five years and deemed by every one as unworthy of publication. Did he, I asked Sillitoe, begin to feel not just dispirited but defeated? Few if any other writers have made such an exclusive commitment to their work, detached themselves from their home and any prospect of an alternative career with so little reward. Did he not feel after six, seven years like giving up? 'No. You just keep going. Several things kept me going. Industry, commitment certainly. No, I would never give up.'

Indeed not. Between early 1955 and mid-1956 he completed two more full-length novels, 'The Palisade' and 'Mr Allen's Island'. The latter was – or rather is, the typescript of 60,000 words being lodged with the Indiana Archive – an idiosyncratic piece of work. Mr Allen is a millionaire who makes use of his vast wealth to indulge what might either be a desire for omnipotence or a gargantuan taste for farce. For much of the narrative Allen manipulates his contacts in international politics and the media in order to create a public perception of something which does not exist. Despite there being no record, historical or geographical, of this small island in the Bering Straits it acquires incontestable status as the subject of public debate among everyone from the ordinary newspaper reader to Cold War politicians. As the novel closes it has become the cause of a dispute between the super-powers, both of whom lay claim to it as a site of political and military importance.

In this respect it is intriguing that the novel was so politically prescient. Imagine an island of little or no previous significance which within a year becomes the subject of tense exchanges between the superpowers, a nuclear-laden fleet heading to it from one direction and on the other nuclear missiles being primed in preparation for the fleet's arrival. This, roughly, is the con-clusion of the novel, leading to the beginning of the Third World War. In six years' time the world was plunged into the Cuban Missile Crisis.

'The Palisade' was less ambitious, being the story of a Lincolnshire farmer's son who, serving with the RAF, develops TB and is hospitalized. While recuperating he begins an affair with his nurse, leaves the hospital before his treatment is concluded and persuades her to give up her career and come with him to the South of France. Some of the early parts, based on his own time in hospital and his relationship with Hilary, would resur-face, little changed, as two chapters of *The Open Door*, but the novel as a whole was flawed because of a convergence of incompatible themes. At the time he was beginning to feel both haunted and frustrated by the reputa-tion of Lawrence. In Britain Lawrence's image as a rebellious scourge of orthodoxy had been sustained by what now seems the absurd ban on *Lady Chatterley's Lover*. While Sillitoe had little direct knowledge of this it was visited upon him at regular intervals. When he went through the standard ritual with other expatriates of establishing region and background the reflex on their part, though usually not malicious, was infuriating for him: obviously he was the new Lawrence, or trying to be. The problem with 'The Palisade' is that his desire to rid the piece of all potential Lawrentian echoes is heavy-handed; it eclipses his central purpose of telling an unpretentious story of love that ignites and, painfully, fades. He makes sure, for example, that his hero's family are prosperous landowners – how so unlike the Morrels or Brangwens, you can hear him whispering.

Again Rosica was impressed by both novels. He asked her to send 'The Palisade' to Chatto, having talked about it in July 1956 with a guest of the Reynoldses', one Anthony Brett-James. Major Brett-James had served with the 14th Army in Burma and his memoirs of the period (*Report My Signals*) had been published by Chatto, of which he was now an executive director. The draft of Sillitoe's novel was waiting for him on his return to London, and in his letter of rejection he stated that while the story was gripping and rich in naturalistic detail it was implausible. No nurse, in his opinion, would give up a secure career for a man who might suddenly expire. His objection seemed, to Sillitoe, perverse given that this moment was based on fact. His relationship had ended by mutual consent, but had it continued Hilary would have been willing to accompany him on his planned trip abroad. Was there, Sillitoe wondered, something else at work in Brett-James's decision? He had met Sillitoe and been fascinated by him as an individual – the energetic autodidact from nowhere – but Sillitoe's hero was not what he expected. He was like Sillitoe, yes, but this was Sillitoe taking his abrasive intellect up a rank or two into the landed gentry. The working-class writer was permissible, but the working-class writer as over-reacher? Perhaps the shock was too much for Brett-James. Alan comments, 'Perhaps you're being a little unjust to him. "Working class" didn't come into it. Brett-James had been a signals officer, and I'd told him I'd been a wireless operator, so it was a matter of rank rather than class.'

Rosica was equally enthusiastic about 'Mr Allen's Island'. Her problem, however, was convincing editors that there was a niche in the market for such a work. Writers who projected fundamental human issues into the sphere of the symbolic or apocalyptic were few and marginal; provocative realism was the order of the day. William Golding, Doris Lessing and Iris Murdoch, now celebrated as luminaries of the age, were at the time treated by their publishers as bankable curiosities. 'Mr Allen's Island' did the rounds – six publishers in total – and by the beginning of 1957 Sillitoe asked Rosica to give up on it.

There is in Kingsley Amis's *Memoirs* (1991) an account of Amis's meeting with Robert Graves in 1960. Amis presents him as someone luxuriating in his status, the established writer-in-exile and patrician host to novices who had trekked across Europe for an audience.

'Do you know Alan Sillitoe?' asked Robert, and half seriously, 'I invented him. He used to live in Soller in the Fifties, writing I don't know what you'd call them, fantasies about imaginary countries set in no particular period. I told him, "Alan, nobody wants that sort of stuff. Write about the life you know in Nottingham and so on." So he wrote *Saturday Night and Sunday Morning*.' [Amis, *Memoirs*, pp. 214–15]

Sillitoe's two documented versions of this concur to the extent that he states that Graves had indeed read one of his more adventurous pieces – in fact 'Mr Allen's Island' – and then suggested that he concentrate on 'a book set in Nottingham, which is something you know about' (*Mountains and Caverns*, p. 34); or 'Why don't you write something set in Nottingham? That's the place you know best' (*Life Without Armour*, p. 209).

Though there is little difference in substance between Amis's and Sillitoe's versions we encounter in the former an exchange in which club-bish condescension, offered by Graves like a secret handshake, prevails. To Sillitoe he seems to be advising a choice of subject, one among many, but with Amis something else is implied. 'I told him, "Alan, nobody wants that sort of stuff . . ."' or, as he does not have to tell Amis, the sort of writing that is the gift of Samuel Butler or Huxley. Or us.

Sillitoe liked Graves and enjoyed the company of his family, a friendship that has been mutual and durable, but surely, I asked him, he must have detected in Graves's suggestion a hint of snobbishness. 'Yes,' he answers. 'There was something of that in it. But it was unwitting, he couldn't help it, and I was at an advantage there. It was a reflex for him, but I knew about it.'

Graves's counsel, offered in spring 1956, marked for Sillitoe a transitional moment but not quite in the way one might expect. Though he did not dedicate his time exclusively to the work provisionally entitled 'The Adventures of Arthur Seaton' – he continued with the other 'sort of stuff' as well – when he did so it was with a new, energetic feeling that a novel could be written about the people he had grown up with, indeed the sort of person he still was, that might unnerve the generous patricians who felt it proper and liberating for the worthy class to contribute something of their own to a vocation from which they had too long been denied access. Graves enjoyed the mistaken belief that he had 'invented' Sillitoe, but in truth he had made a small and inadvertent contribution to a process that was cumulative, explosive, and Sillitoe's alone.

There are, on the face of things, few obvious parallels between the Suez Crisis, the Soviet suppression of the Hungarian uprising and the activities of an invented Nottingham lathe operator. Yet when in the summer of 1956 Sillitoe received news and formed opinions on the first two events an imprint would be left on the unique enigmatic presence of Arthur Seaton. Newspaper reports on Suez seemed skewed, partial and contradictory. The Spanish papers sided with the Egyptians and the Arab cause in general, while their, albeit in Majorca scarce, British counterparts seemed confused about whether this was evidence of post-Imperial desperation (*Manchester Guardian*) or a necessary and justified act of intervention. What was agreed upon, or so it seemed to Sillitoe, was that an allegiance had been formed between the last two European superpowers, Britain and France, and a state less than a decade old clinging precariously to an existence which every one of its neighbours wished to extinguish, Israel. Sillitoe supplemented these reports with those from more reliable sources, the people involved. He tuned into the dense fabric of radio traffic coming from the other end of the Mediterranean, and as the crisis turned into a humiliation, at least for Britain and France, he found himself fascinated by the situation of Israel. Anti-Israel propaganda for some time presented the country as a US puppet-state, and now it seemed more isolated than ever before.

Hungary, he thought, was in a similar though eventually more abject and hopeless situation, punished by its oppressors in the East and let down completely by its supposed sympathizers in the open, democratic West. He even devised a battle to save Hungary, drawing upon military transmissions for an up-to-date knowledge of tactics and armaments.

At the time he had no clear idea of where Arthur's adventures would lead him or how his as yet diffuse personality would inform the book as a whole, but a phrase attached itself to him, part mantra, part dictum. 'Yes,' he now observes, 'that year, 1956, with Hungary and Israel, something gelled; a sense of bitterness and frustration. And I would repeat the words to myself, especially when writing about Arthur, and even send them out by Morse to God knows where: "Don't let the bastards grind you down."'

In spring 1956 Ruth and Sillitoe got to know the Swedish actress Ulla Jacobsson and her husband, the artist Frank Lodeizen. She, still in her twenties, had won considerable critical acclaim in films such as *Smiles of a Summer Night*. In the UK and US film industry most actors were treated by studios as commodities, but directors and producers in Europe listened to their on-screen colleagues, and Ulla was intrigued by the plot of 'The Palisade', partly because it seemed so un-English. She suggested a compromise. Rewrite it as a film script with the central character, still English and consumptive, now settled with his wife on the Côte d'Azur and growing weary of the once exciting allure of the south. And then he meets a similarly disillusioned Scandinavian actress, to be played in the film by Ulla of course.

He wrote 'The Bandstand' in about two weeks, and Sillitoe now reflects that at least it would serve to remind him of what not to do when he came to adapt *Saturday Night and Sunday Morning* for the screen. In December Constantine Films of Stuttgart paid him £200 for the rights, which forced a decision upon Ruth and Sillitoe. For little more than that amount they could purchase a modest townhouse in Soller itself or a ramshackle farmstead with a little land on the outskirts. It was not that they were unable to afford the rent on decent habitable places but one of their own would signal long-term commitment to this magnetic idyll, which day by day seemed to enrol another set of artistically inclined expatriates. The alternative, which they had previously only discussed as an unaffordable hypothesis, would be to spend time in England, mainly London. They were not so naïve, or desperate, as to assume that personal visits to publishers would suddenly get them into print, but Sillitoe in particular thought that some direct knowledge of the world he was dealing with through Rosica might at least enable him to understand why it was so consistently unsympathetic to his work.

They decided that Majorca could wait, and in January 1957 the Graveses drove them to the ferry terminal in Palma and they set off on a lengthy uncomfortable train journey via Barcelona and Paris to Calais and the ferry to Dover. They stayed for a while with Ruth's parents in Hove – despite the fact that they were not married Alan was treated affectionately as their son-in-law – and then spent a week with his own relatives in Nottingham. Since his departure seven years earlier his sisters Peggy and Pearl had got married; Peggy had three children, Pearl one. Michael and Brian still lived at home. Brian, now twenty-four, was making a decent living as a panel beater in a local engineering works, and Michael, eighteen, had taken a job in the same factory to sponsor his ambition to become a musician, specifically a jazz drummer. His parents' marriage was not exactly blissful but it now involved the sort of congeniality that comes with weariness and age.

Something had changed but in a way that he found difficult, at least at the time, to fully comprehend. The people he had known pre-1950 were still at the bottom of the social scale but they now seemed to have more money to spend on things that appeased the dullness of lives that few if any enjoyed. Shop fronts were crammed with record players, radiograms and televisions, and there was now a commercial, popular, channel for the latter. Washing machines and spin dryers had replaced the sink, and everyone from the youth on the scooter to the family packed into the Morris Minor or Ford Prefect appeared to have their own means of transport. Did he feel, even slightly, as though he had missed out on something? 'Actually I probably did, but at the time I would not have admitted to it.' Evidently. In *Rats* one notes how frequently consumer goods – particularly televisions – are presented as a panacea offered by the eponymous ruling-class rodents to pacify the lower orders.

Back in London Sillitoe met Rosica in person for the first time, bringing with him six chapters of what he had now decided to call *Saturday Night and Sunday Morning*, just less than half of the draft he would complete over the following six months. They had lunch, and the following day Rosica telephoned him to say that she was confident this one would get him into print. He had heard this before, and while he trusted her sincerity he had also come to expect an unsympathetic judgement from publishers themselves. Having spent the 1950s in self-imposed exile, however, he was not aware of what had been happening within the mainstream of British writing over the previous seven years. There was something new abroad – by equal degrees iconoclastic, popular and profitable – and it had ignited Rosica's enthusiasm for Sillitoe's new project.

He met Rosica in mid-March, and over the previous three weeks reviewers had been marvelling at the raw audacity of John Braine's *Room at the Top*. The *Observer* compared its hero Joe Lampton with Kingsley Amis's Jim Dixon, but while Jim is 'saved by [his] amiability [Lampton] is a beast . . . He is a ruthless rather than an angry young man' (17 March 1957). The *Daily Express*, announcing that it had bought the rights to the novel and would henceforth be publishing extracts, saw Braine as the senior member of this club of youngish reprobates; apparently Amis and John Osborne now trailed in his wake and John Wain brought up the rear (13 April 1957).

The question of whether or not the alleged members of these new literary groupings – principally the Angry Young Men and the Movement – shared essential techniques and predispositions is still a matter of debate. But what is certain is that as far as the literary media and publishers were concerned effect was more valuable than substance. Rosica, very shrewdly, knew where to send Sillitoe's half-completed novel. Since the beginning of the year Tom Maschler, commissioning editor at MacGibbon and Kee, had been busily seeking contributors for a projected volume to be called *Declaration*. It would, he explained to his correspondents, be the collective manifesto for a new generation of writers. In the end the collection comprised a motley set of individuals desperately trying to follow Maschler's ordinance to offer radical opinions on anything. The volume also seemed slightly lopsided since Amis had refused to take part, Maschler himself had excluded Braine – due to some quixotic personal antipathy to his book, a somewhat ironic decision by an editor seemingly dedicated to individualism and unorthodoxy – and figures such as Kenneth Allsop and Lindsay Anderson had been brought in to make up the numbers. Rosica was aware of Maschler's plans and also alert to the fact that whatever the ostensible reason for the project his real objective was to project his employers into the centre of things (MacGibbon and Kee would publish *Declaration*). They were among the few mainstream houses to have missed out on commissioning one of the procession of new names. Maschler's determination to seek out anything controversial is reflected in his decision at the beginning of 1957 to contract Bill Hopkins to do a novel, his first, called *The Divine and the Decay*, a bizarre confection of naturalism and the grotesque which would eventually be pulped after early reviews accused it of being sympathetic to fascism. Maschler was an impresario who compensated for a suspect evaluative faculty with an instinct for the spectacular and controversial.

The heroes of the new wave of caustic realism were generally lower middle class, with a few exceptions such as Amis's working-class librarian John Lewis of *That Uncertain Feeling* (1955). All were reasonably well educated and made use of their intellectual resources to undermine the institutions and habits they would once have been expected to exemplify. Braine's Joe Lampton was slightly different in that he eschewed wit and scabrous unorthodoxy in favour of the ruthless pursuit of sex and money. Maschler, snobbishly aggrieved by Lampton's vulgarity, was fascinated by Arthur Seaton, or at least by the version of him he thought might emerge from the prototype. Initially he saw only two chapters. He sensed in Arthur a hint of Nietzschean anarchy, but not enough. In short he wanted Sillitoe to rewrite the novel according to his own prognosis of what it ought to be and do.

He treated Sillitoe like a promising if somewhat guileless pupil, as was his manner with those whose reputation did not earn them his fawning respect. In June he wrote to Sillitoe indicating how Arthur should become a more vigorous presence, alight with 'existential *hauteur*'; he should rise above the drabness that surrounded him rather than be swamped by it. In the RAF – the most classless of the services – Sillitoe had not come across such a peremptory assumption of superiority. That it was also so apparently heedless made it nearly laughable, but what turned his astonishment to anger was a letter from Rosica, blameless on her part, conveying a request from Maschler that Sillitoe should supply him with the complete original draft of the novel at the same time, July, that he (Maschler) expected the revised version. He would then, of course, have the opportunity to compare the amateurish first attempt with the one redesigned according to his own directives. He had been told, and apparently ignored the fact, that the six chapters were at present all that existed. This image of Maschler as a man whose perception of the world involved few concessions to the one shared by others was reinforced, for Sillitoe, by the spectacle of him scrutinizing page by page the improvements wrought by himself and inscribed by his grateful apprentice.

Maschler begins his letter to Sillitoe with the 'hope' that their talk about *Saturday Night and Sunday Morning* 'was helpful to you' and goes on to indicate how Sillitoe's otherwise 'authentic portrait of the anarchy of the factory worker' can be improved. Regarding Brenda:

> here you must establish clearly whether Arthur feels any real love for her, or merely physical gratification. I feel that your phrase 'wants to love' on p. 59 is a clear indication of the latter. It is in his inability to love that the book becomes a forceful exposure of this machine age of ours at its worst. [Tom Maschler to AS, 6 May 1957, from the files of Rosica Colin Ltd]

When Arthur says to Doreen, 'Everyone in the world is caught, somehow, one way or another,' Maschler perceives a 'hopeless resignation . . . the crux of the book . . . a prevalent attitude amongst working class people'. Curbing his first instinct to reply to Maschler in the manner of Arthur,

Sillitoe resolved to finish the book as he wished and then see what his new patron thought of it. In *Life Without Armour* Sillitoe refers to the episode with characteristic restraint.

> Maschler may have looked on the book as something worth influencing, but if so it was difficult for me to feel in any way flattered by such interest. I had not been working unrewarded for eight years, and learning to write the hard way, to be told by any editor how to revise my novel. [p. 235]

Almost five decades later I take the liberty of asking him if something more economic, less measured, might sum up his view of the man: smug arsehole? 'Yes. That's about right.' Maschler despite himself played an unwitting role in making *Saturday Night and Sunday Morning* the book it is. Arthur's refusal to conform to anything is in part borne out of a similar inclination provoked at the time in his creator.

A more blunt account of his state of mind as he returned to complete *Saturday Night and Sunday Morning* is found in one of the last fragments from his 1950s notebook.

> Whom do I hate? I don't honestly know. At a rough guess I would say everyone, hoping to qualify that statement to my satisfaction later. Those that accept these qualifications are with me; those that laugh or offer me advice are against me. There, I almost started to answer that question without realising. In future I will be more cautious. Since I possess no knowledge I must not be trapped by you . . .
>
> Why do I hate? Answer: because I am a writer. Another answer: because I have too much love. Hate protects me against an inhospitable world. I wish no ill upon others but hate is my driving force, the only weapon with which I can fight . . . Fighting is living, and living is my right, the only kind of justice that anyone can ever expect. So I write. [Private notebook, June 1957]

Before leaving for London he had contacted the BBC to see if they still wished to go ahead with the broadcast of his account of the ascent of Kedah Peak. They replied that they did and it went out at 9.30 a.m. on 10 April. The eighteen guineas fee ('Guineas!' he reflects. 'How gentlemanly they were.') came in handy, but what struck him most was that no one even suggested that his draft might be copy-edited, let alone improved. He could write decent prose. Just as significantly he was allowed to read the thing himself. No one remarked that he had an accent that was not BBC received pronunciation, his manner confident yet perplexingly unaffected.

Alan and Ruth stayed in England for roughly two and a half months, some of the time, when not with their families, renting a furnished room in West Kensington and in April accepting the offer from Ima Bayliss, whom they had got to know in Majorca, of her cottage near Bishop's Stortford.

They visited Howard Sergeant and his wife Jean, with whom they had been in contact for the previous two years from Majorca. Since the early 1950s Sergeant had edited, indeed largely financed, a series of booklets called *Outposts*, and before they left for England Sillitoe and Ruth had written to him proposing one for each of them, comprised exclusively of their poetry. Sergeant knew their work, having already published individual poems by each, and was impressed by their suggested collections. The print run, he explained, would be short, and of the 350 it would be their responsibility to sell 300 by subscription to cover costs. Friends in England and Spain responded enthusiastically and generously and the costs were met. Sillitoe's, called *Without Beer or Bread*, is notable for its preface in which he boils with rage against the idea that art, specifically poetry, might now benefit from state sponsorship. Patronage, he argued, was an insult both to the poet and to the ordinary reader, who should choose what he wanted to read and not be subject to other people's notions of what was good for him. The message was vivid if ideologically capricious. Today he revisits the moment: 'I am a writer, and fuck you, I'll write what I like.'

Ruth's parents bought them tickets to Osborne's *Look Back in Anger*, then playing in Brighton. What struck him was the fact that his own sense of excitement at the spectacle of Jimmy Porter – the hectoring nemesis of middle-class complacency – did not seem to register with the rest of the audience, who appeared confused and unsettled. As he now concedes there was a reason for this, to which at the time he was largely oblivious. Despite the play's subsequent status as a landmark in theatre history the vast majority of early reviewers treated it with puzzled disdain. On the one hand Porter seemed to belong to the new school of learned philistinism – patented by Jim Dixon and Charles Lumley – but unlike his predecessors he did not try to solicit mischievous sympathy from the reader or members of the audience. The latter often felt as unnerved by Porter as his fellow characters. Sillitoe liked him.

In Majorca Sillitoe had been provided with fragmentary accounts of what had been going on in the British literary world. Tony Buttita, for example, had brought extracts from newspapers and magazines and reported on how writers like Wain, Amis, Colin Wilson, Philip Larkin and Elizabeth Jennings were being talked about as embodying a new trend, though no one seemed able to agree on what this amounted to. As stylists they were solidly conservative, but their manner, their treatment of contemporaneity, made the avant-garde seem staid and complacent by comparison. Ruth's brother, Harry Fainlight, had visited in 1956, the year after he had gone up to Cambridge to read English, and he too had news of how the literary environment seemed in a state somewhere between transition and confusion. Sillitoe, as he now admits, paid little attention. It was only when he went back and talked with Rosica and Sergeant that he began to form a picture of what literary historians would refer to as the Angry Decade. It was Porter who left the sharpest impression. Sillitoe did not intend to copy Osborne because he did not have to. He had already invented someone even more unorthodox than Porter, someone who neither knew of nor cared about the sort of person who might read a novel or go to a play.

Sillitoe and Ruth returned to Soller in May and Sillitoe went straight to the sprawling notebooks on *Saturday Night and Sunday Morning* from which he had earlier extracted his six draft chapters. He explains in *Life Without Armour* how the mosaic of impressions from their England trip began to coalesce as he wrote.

> While completing the final version of the book I lived as if the England which I loved but did not especially like had little to offer. A miasma of falsity was spread by those who assumed that their opinions were the same as everyone else's – and therefore the only ones that mattered – such hypocrisy stifling every aspect of life. These purveyors of conformism did not know about the great majority of the people, and did not care to consider them as worthy of notice. When they did not fear or hate them, they wanted them to be in perpetual thrall to values which the complacent upper few per cent had decided, because they were their own, were the only ones worth living by. This included those socialists and left-wing commentators who also thought they knew how people ought to live, but would never live like it themselves. The country was dead from the neck up, and the body was buried in sand. [p. 235]

'The Decline and Fall of Frankie Buller' was written at the same time. It offers an oblique, illuminating perspective upon its author's state of mind, and it provided Sillitoe with a touchstone for *Saturday Night and Sunday Morning*, an opportunity to reflect on what exactly he was undertaking. In *Life Without Armour* he calls the story 'autobiographical', which is a mischievous half-truth. Certainly Sillitoe in his youth knew a few young men like Frankie who were social misfits, some as a result of an innate and unwitting aspect of their character, others by choice. Frankie is an assembly of such memories, and more; he is as vividly present and puzzling as the other person in the story, one Alan Sillitoe, his friend and narrator.

The story begins with Sillitoe describing his 'study', 'a room in the first floor flat of a ramshackle Majorcan house'. He imagines how a visitor might 'scrutinise the book jackets on his shelves – Shakespeare, *The Golden Bough*,

Euripides, Proust, Dostoevsky, Homer – and recognise him as one of the tribe'. These badges of erudition, he muses,

> have become part of me, foliage that has grown to conceal the bare stem of my real personality, what I was like before I ever saw these books, or any book at all come to that. Often I would like to rip them away from me one by one, extract their shadows out of my mouth and heart, cut them neatly with a scalpel from my jungle-brain. Impossible. You can't wind back the clock that sits grinning on the mantel shelf. You can't even smash its face in and forget it. [*The Loneliness of the Long Distance Runner*, p. 156]

A dilemma had beset Sillitoe from the first moment writing became his ambition. He knew that to achieve anything he had to know, appreciate, what others had done, and at the same time he felt an equally powerful impulse to resist what he admired. He knew that if he learned his trade even from those he respected most then he risked losing something he valued much more: the ability to preserve in words perceptions and ideas that were his and his alone. All artists are preoccupied with uniqueness. It is a condition of the trade, though its causes range through a spectrum between pure egotism and commitment to an aesthetic ideal. Sillitoe was, is, different. He did not see himself as a class warrior – that too would involve exchanging truth for patronizing abstractions – but he knew that he had shared a world, seen things, felt things that no one had ever written about before. As the beginning of the story makes poignantly, brutally clear, he is determined to wrestle into the tradecraft he has acquired a cast of characters, states of mind that are, perhaps always will be, alien to it. 'Impossible', he says, but a paragraph later he hears a cuckoo and the simple sound 'accomplished what a surgeon's knife could not. I was plunged back deep through the years into my natural state, without books and without the knowledge that I am supposed to have gained from them' (p. 157).

The rest of the story testifies to his success in having achieved what he thought was impossible. At its conclusion we know Frankie Buller very well indeed but in a way that no character had ever before in literature been introduced and held the reader's attention. Sillitoe brings him alive and at the same time protects him. We suspect much about Frankie from his behaviour. He is perhaps a little unusual; 'backward' was the heartless euphemism of those days. These at least are our suspicions, and Sillitoe makes sure that once we carry them out of the story we experience a collateral sense of guilt. He has never said anything about Frankie. He speaks to him, reports his speech, describes his actions, respects his independence as another character. The rest he leaves to us, and we feel like the kind of smug middle-class guest whom Sillitoe imagined in his room at the beginning, carrying our expectations into a story where we are welcomed politely and then made to feel very uncomfortable.

Embedded in the story is the question of whether he could extend its effects to something more expansive and challenging. Could he 'plunge back through the years into my natural state' and return with a novel?

FOURTEEN

Sillitoe and Ruth still cannot fix upon a single moment when they knew that their next trip to England would be more than a visit, nor can they identify a cause. But as the winter of 1957 approached both were aware that the magnetism of Majorca and the Mediterranean in general was losing its force. They travelled through other parts of Spain feigning enthusiasm for the attractions of different regions but in truth doing so listlessly, as if delaying the inevitable. Sillitoe, as was his routine, went to Gibraltar to register for another year of pension and thereafter the two of them sampled Granada, Ronda, Andalusia, Almeria and – reluctantly, Sillitoe never having liked them – Alicante and Malaga. He sums it up with brisk honesty: 'We had to shift, yet it seemed impossible to go back to Majorca, though we couldn't say why . . . Neither did we wish to go to any other place in Spain. The dream was over, and England the only destination' (*Life Without Armour*, p. 243). Once again one becomes aware of why Sillitoe's most trusted apophthegm, of Rabbi Akiba ben Joseph, seems to be a contradiction in terms, involving that curious alliance between fate and will.

By the end of the summer he had finished *Saturday Night and Sunday Morning*, at least to his own satisfaction. What he had not done was to follow Maschler's 'advice'. Sillitoe says now that 'it was up to him to judge it, but it was my novel'. It was returned from MacGibbon and Kee to Rosica in mid-August with a terse note stating that 'regrettably' they felt unable to offer him a contract. It would be another five years before Sillitoe told Rosica that he had in fact ignored Maschler's instructions. She was a generous, open-minded woman but she was also a pragmatist and he did not wish to try her patience. Instead he offered her a circuitously honest account:

> I personally think *Saturday Night and Sunday Morning* didn't fit into the preconceived romantic notions they [MacGibbon and Kee] had about the working class, and that there wasn't enough of the 'angry young man' in it: in other words it was too realistic and did not satisfy the [theory regarding the working class] that Maschler had instilled into them, and that, as far as I am concerned, had no foundation. I am convinced that *Saturday Night and Sunday Morning* is the study of a working-class youth that has not been done before. As far as the 'type' goes, in Arthur, I have broken new ground, and I only hope that some publisher will have the insight to see this. [AS to Rosica Colin, 7 December 1957, from the private files of Rosica Colin Ltd]

To anyone else he might have come across as arrogant and uncooperative but Rosica knew him well by now, and indeed respected his book, and treated this as resolute determination. As it turned out his rather ambitious claim to have achieved something unprecedented would prove to be true, but it would yet have to be scrutinized by several other purblind publishers. Between August and January 1958 five more mainstream houses rejected it. Three offered Rosica accounts of why they thought it unsatisfactory, and she, knowing him better than he thought, kept them to herself. She suspected that he would not in any event have altered the book and she did not want to prompt fury along with disappointment. Two – one was Gollancz – had shown it to supposedly sympathetic left-leaning readers, one of whom said that it was fraudulent, clearly an attempt by a writer with no experience of proletarian existence to make money by inciting contempt for decent working men. Another was unconvinced by the ending, which they found discordant and inconclusive, implying that obliqueness was fine in mainstream fiction while tales of ordinary folk required something like a homily.

The 'dream', as Sillitoe termed it, might have been over but he and Ruth were still reluctant to wake up to the unforgiving, cold light of Britain, and following their return to Spain one more farcical episode marked their despondent period of transition. During the summer of 1957 they had met Philip Martin and Helen Marshal, painters both, unmarried but parents of two children and rare prototypes for what ten years hence would customarily be termed hippydom. He appeared not to have cut or combed his hair for some time and his beard almost reached his chest. Trousers, once formal, and collarless shirts were draped carelessly across his tall thin frame, here and there secured with pieces of thread. He was about Sillitoe's age. Helen, twenty years his senior, favoured voluminous skirts and smocks punctuated by strings of beads. It goes without saying that both came from comfortable, middle-class English stock. Sillitoe remembers a visit by Philip's mother, widow of a Suffolk bank manager, who while indulging her son's tastes and inclinations also completed a hilarious medley. There was Sillitoe, sounding and appearing much as he had done since his youth, while Helen and Philip frequently drew the bemused attention of the indigenous Spanish – who despite being used to the eccentricities of artistic incomers had never quite come across anything like them. Helen's mother, meanwhile, resembled a character from Noël Coward's *Blithe Spirit*. She would take on an expression of genial puzzlement when Martin and Helen turned the conversation to their main enthusiasm, Indian mysticism – Krishnamurti and Sri Aurobindo specifically – while all three shared an accent straight out of the BBC World Service. Sillitoe would never go so far as to deride Helen and Martin and their beliefs – though he does permit himself a wry sympathetic reflection on how their daughter Serafina coped with her Christian name in later life – but they served to crystallize his burgeoning suspicion that the Mediterranean provided, for many, an opportunity for avoidance or self-gratification rather than, as he had sometimes believed, the mainspring for brave ambitions. None the less Sillitoe and Ruth went along with Martin's suggestion that they should pool their resources and share a large flat in Alicante. The arrangement lasted two months and contributed to Sillitoe's sense that they were merely delaying the inevitable.

Amazingly they seemed to have acquired little more than they set out with almost a decade earlier, and as they boarded the train for Madrid their worldly goods fitted comfortably into two large trunks and a few cases. Sillitoe's manuscripts – complete, half-finished and meandering – occupied more space in their luggage than his clothes and footwear. The morning of Saturday 22 March found them on the Dieppe to Newhaven ferry, a spring day of typically English character: dank, cloudy and not quite warm. That night they stayed with Ruth's parents in Hove, an open invitation given that both would need time to find sufficient income for somewhere to rent. Over the subsequent few weeks bad news accrued. *The General*, which Sillitoe had revised again just before leaving Spain, had been turned down, 'The Palisade' had now acquired seven rejection notes and *Saturday Night and Sunday Morning* eight. While maintaining her own enthusiasm for the latter Rosica indicated, tactfully, to Sillitoe that quite soon there would be no dependable houses left to send it to. Shrewdly, she had decided that since those who were closest to the centre of the fiction market seemed so unanimously set against it she would try W.H. Allen, who published novels but were better known for memoirs and books on theatre and film.

Jeffrey Simmons, who knew Rosica well, was the stepson of the managing director Mark Goulden and had been chief commissioning editor for two years. Jeffrey read it and sensed straight away that something unusual had come into his hands. He had some knowledge of trends in contemporary fiction but within a couple of days of receiving the typescript a casual encounter prompted him to entrust a more informed reading to Otto Strawson. As Jeffrey says, 'The industry, publishing, was far more relaxed and informal in those days. Otto had dropped in for a chat and a coffee. He worked mainly as a reader for Gollancz's fiction list but I told him that I had received this amazing piece from a completely unknown, unpublished author. Would he look at it?' He would, and less than a week later he called again at the offices in Essex Street to deliver his unequivocal verdict. It was, he told Jeffrey, 'just about the best first novel I've read, certainly the equal of Doris Lessing'. Strawson had been the reader who 'discovered' Lessing and recommended her to Gollancz in 1955.

What struck Simmons was that this was a book and an author – before meeting him Rosica had given him an account of Sillitoe's past – that broke new ground in a decade already reeling from an onslaught of unprecedented gestures. He explained to me: 'The post-war Labour government changed everything, or seemed to have done. This was little more than a decade later and the very idea of being "working class" didn't have the association of poverty and hopelessness of the pre-war years. In a way John Braine's *Room at the Top* fed on this. But Alan was different, far more shocking than Braine. He showed ordinary life in a way that no-one had done before.' He adds: 'Braine was a good writer but in other respects he was something of a fraud. He wasn't really working class. Writers like Alan had never previously been published for the simple reason that people genuinely of his background didn't write books.'

Simmons and Sillitoe first met on 15 April 1958. In *Life Without Armour* Sillitoe describes him as 'a tall somewhat saturnine man' (p. 246), then briskly sets this impression aside for an account of the technicalities of their exchange: how many further books they might expect if they contracted him for this one and so on. His relationship with Simmons matured into one of mutual respect and affability – at least as much as the inevitable tensions between authors and publishers would allow – but there was something about their early encounter that could have been a coda to the work that prompted it. Arthur Seaton takes command of his novel but it is difficult to imagine him seeking acceptance in a world where people talk about 'literature' and its various qualities. One suspects that his creator, though proudly erudite, was protective of Arthur's indifference to culture. This was not anti-intellectualism, more a sense that culture and social élitism were indistinguishable, that to properly acquire the former involved an exercise in social climbing sanctioned by its curators. Simmons: 'It was tangible from the beginning that he was suspicious. There was something about the firm that he did not trust. It was "them and us" and as far as he was concerned we were certainly "them". Eventually he came to see that we weren't out to exploit him. He became more friendly with everyone in the firm, especially Mark, my stepfather, and my mother.' Indeed, Sillitoe has affectionate memories of Mark Goulden, but it is intriguing that he recalls him more for his deeds and principles than as an individual. Before the war Goulden had edited the *Sunday Referee*, the first popular newspaper to present Nazism, and fascism in general, as intrinsically evil. Sillitoe had seen copies in Burton's kitchen in the 1930s and now he was introduced to its one-time editor, whose first words were: 'They tell me you've written a masterpiece.'

At this meeting nothing was signed or formally agreed, but it was evident that W.H. Allen wanted to publish the book, without alterations, and that a contract would be drawn up in consultation with Rosica. Sillitoe describes his feelings after he left the office in Essex Street and walked aimlessly along the Strand: 'steeped in a compound of gloom and optimism, it was hard to understand what I had let myself in for . . .' He thinks of Ruth, Rosica, the Graveses, Ruth's parents 'who were helping us so selflessly', her Aunt Ann in America who had sent food, clothes, sometimes money to Spain, and of his own family, a bit better off than twenty years before but still by anyone's standards poor; they too had sent things to him, when they could. He recalls also the moment in 1945 when he had passed the Air Crew Selection Board and, had the war not finished, could have ended up as a pilot officer in the Fleet Air Arm. That too had been potentially transitional, but fate, circumstances, even luck had sent him in another direction, and now he knew that his life would be changed for ever. It was one book, yet he knew that he could produce many more, had in fact already done so – at least three of his later publications were then in first draft form – so why, I ask him, does the passage in *Life Without Armour* in which he describes the hour or two after his meeting with Simmons carry traces of disappointment? 'I don't know,' he confesses. 'The mind plays tricks. My memory of the day is vivid certainly but maybe I carried into it other things that I felt subsequently.' Maybe.

Simmons's recollection of Sillitoe's manner at their first meeting, the 'them and us' attitude and the invidious sense of suspicion, is honest but tells only half of the story. Sillitoe felt that he was being swallowed up, marketed, as a curiosity: the writer with no formal education from the very bottom of the social scale. A paragraph from a letter Sillitoe wrote to Rosica in late 1958 is revealing. *Saturday Night and Sunday Morning* had been out about two months. Initial reviews had been good but word-of-mouth exchanges in the literary marketplace fuelled by interviews Sillitoe had done for the BBC and articles on his background for *Books and Bookmen* and the *Guardian* had generated a new wave of interest in both the novel and its author. Most of the letter concerns technical details regarding future contracts, but Sillitoe for a moment sets all that aside for a bout of vituperation:

> Now with regard to what W.H. Allen all too frequently insist they have done for me. To me this is so much guff. I could just as well shout about what I have done for them, except that I can't be bothered to waste my breath. The truth is that they have done no more for me than I have for them. After all, publishers are *obliged* to accept new authors otherwise they would all be soon out of jobs. W.H. Allen have been very lucky: they could have made nothing out of my book. They mustn't forget that though they may have initiated the publicity my book has received by sending out so many copies and pulling the odd string here and there, it was *I* who made it so successful in the end by my manner of impressing the journalists and interviewers. Fortunately they all found me in a good

mood, otherwise I could just have easily have kicked them down the stairs.
[18 November 1958]

Sillitoe wrestles with competing impulses: battered pride, thwarted independence, the sense of becoming a presence whose media-generated image is now beyond his control. The contrariness is revealing and engaging. He is, for example, obviously proud of having faced down the 'journalists and interviewers' hungry for details of this author with no formal education – all of this was included in W.H. Allen's publicity material – and angry. One suspects he is angry with himself but he turns his rage outwards in that last memorable sentence. Hello again, Arthur Seaton.

The contract was agreed at the end of April. Rosica took 10 per cent of the £200 advance – a generously small amount for an agent – leaving Sillitoe with £90 on signature and £90 on publication. Ruth found a job with the British Market Research Bureau and they rented what might now be described as a 'studio' on the third floor of a house in Camden Square; it had its own kitchen but the bathroom was shared. Sillitoe worked on short stories and poems, distractedly, as he awaited news of his book's publication schedule. On being informed that the proofs would be ready by the end of June he insisted on collecting them in person from Essex Street and he received his six complimentary copies in early September, dispatching one to Ruth's parents and three others to family in Nottingham. (One of these resurfaces in a letter from Brian to Sillitoe in 1996. The former had found it at the 'bottom of my wardrobe inside a brown paper bag. I'd put it there some 18 years ago for safe keeping and forgot all about it. I always thought someone had stolen it when I lived in Shropshire. It's in very good condition but the jacket's missing' (4 July 1996).

The official publication date was the weekend of 11–12 October and the first reviews were by Richard Mayne in the *Sunday Times* and John Wain in the *Observer*, both of 12 October. Mayne begins with an appraisal of Basil Davidson's *Lindy*, a Fieldingesque story of contemporary working-class East Anglia: raucous, condescending and 'too artful to be true'. Sillitoe's novel, however, is 'far more convincing': 'unassuming but very outspoken . . . its idiom has . . . authenticity, bolshie anarchism . . . Politicians of all parties please note.' Wain enthuses that Sillitoe has created in Arthur 'a rogue elephant . . . not . . . a displaced intellectual but a genuine working man, who doesn't hanker for a dimly glimpsed world of books and ideas, but differs from his mates only by being more rebellious'. Peter Green in the *Daily Telegraph*, the voice of Tory England, was rudely enthusiastic. It is, he declares, 'that rarest of all finds: a genuine, no-punches pulled, unromanticised working class novel, which makes "Room at the Top" look like a vicarage tea-party by comparison. Intellectual critics are always complaining about the lack of proletarian fiction: well here's the real thing, and I doubt very much indeed if they'll like it' (17 October 1958). As if in confirmation the affronted, anonymous *TLS* reviewer upbraids Mr Sillitoe for his 'moral attitude' in creating such a 'graceless' creature as Arthur, whose 'behaviour is by any standard reprehensible' (7 November 1958). The *Guardian*, home of the middle-class leftist conscience, detects 'an instinctive accuracy that never loses its touch. His book has a glow about it as though he had plugged into some basic source of the working-class spirit' (Roy Perrott, 4 November 1958). The 'as though' made Sillitoe laugh.

According to Jeffrey Simmons the piece that really launched the book, 'had people talking about it everywhere', was Robert Pitman's review article in the *Sunday Express* (16 November 1958). By implication Pitman in his racy page-length account shows that Sillitoe had bridged the divide between the highbrow literary market and the less pretentious reader. He was the first to compare Sillitoe with Lawrence, and he dismisses the latter as undeserving of his reputation as the artist of the ordinary. 'What are we to make of this new hero from Nottingham?' asks Pitman. Arthur 'is miles nearer the real thing than D.H. Lawrence's mystic, brooding working man ever came. For author Sillitoe has worked from life, from the people he knew . . . You may not like that life. You may not like Arthur Seaton . . . [but] Sillitoe has written a stunner.'

Enthusiasm abounded, but the reviewers had something else, unstated, in common. Evaluation generally demands comparison but none of them seemed able to find a precedent for the book. References to Braine and Lawrence smack of desperation, they being respectively the most recent and controversial and the most revered spokesmen for proletarian consciousness, but both are dismissed as having variously lost sight of or misrepresented their subjects. No one, it seemed, had done it quite like Sillitoe.

The critics' self-evident sense of disorientation testifies to the novel's uniqueness, something that has been overlooked in subsequent histories of the so-called Angry Decade which catalogue Sillitoe as latecomer to a jamboree of collective moods and techniques. Book-length studies of the period claim to find parallels between Arthur and Amis's Jim Dixon or John Lewis, Wain's Lumley or Osborne's Jimmy Porter. There were class differences obviously, the last four being lower-middle or educated-working, but these tend to be sidelined in the pursuit of that core of anarchic bitterness which historians claim to discern in all the notable writers of the period. What stunned the early reviewers and has never properly been appreciated is Sillitoe's triumphant radicalism. He hadn't simply uncovered a previously untouched vein of working-class life; he had rethought and refashioned the customary techniques of writing about ordinary people. Joyce and his like had thrown the conventions of classic realism out of the window but Sillitoe had shown that realism could do things previously inconceivable.

Almost a year after *Saturday Night and Sunday Morning* was published Sillitoe was commissioned by *Books and Bookmen* to do a lengthy article on the working-class novel. He respectfully acknowledged Tressell, who for all his shortcomings produced something that no one at that time had even attempted. Lawrence he dismisses as a fraud: 'when he ran out of material for working class characters' he turned to 'bloated . . . mysticism': 'before thirty a fine writer; after thirty a crank' (*Books and Bookmen*, August 1959, p. 13). Of his near contemporaries he is as impressed by the dramatists as the novelists, specifically Osborne, Hall, Delaney and Behan. He discovers some qualities in Len Doherty's *The Good Lions*, Philip Callow's *Common People*, Hastings's *The Game*, but the best newcomers to this uncultivated genre are John Petty (*Five Fags a Day*), Samuel Selvon (*The Lonely Londoners*) and Braine (*Room at the Top*). Each, he argues, does more than just write about the underprivileged; the manner of their writing, abjuring a 'middle-class milieu', dismantles complacent stereotypes of what being working class involves. Thereafter he shifts to what is in effect his personal manifesto:

Compared with the 'thirties the modern proletarian novel has a New Look. From a wail of the underprivileged it is evolving into a solid branch of literary art. The sociological is being submerged by the literary . . . Though proletarian novelists are read mostly by a middle-class audience they should also make themselves readable by the people they grew up with – not necessarily an impediment to good writing. In that way they may break the barrier of pulp magazines and trash novels which – for those millions of the working-class that read – are often the first things they are able to get their hands on. Factory workers enjoy reading about their own environment, and few books will allow them to do this.

This was the task, or to be more accurate the dilemma, he faced when writing *Saturday Night and Sunday Morning*. Since its invention in the eighteenth century the novel had by its nature been the preserve of the erudite middle classes. It did not matter if its author was an uneducated figure from the very lowest stratum of society (in truth none were, but the hypothesis stands); as soon as they wrote a novel they would be obliged to expunge any trace of their background and become, as a presence between the covers, indistinguishable from their more privileged, better-educated peers. The reason for this is simple and brutally ineluctable. The unifying, predominant feature of mainstream fiction is the narrator, and whether this person takes on the mask of third-person anonymity or tells their own story they are required to have a percipient command of language and an intellectual capacity to orchestrate the events which they effectively control. A novel-ist need not be middle class to accomplish this but in doing so they would sound as though they were.

Tressell in his salutary attempt to deromanticize the working class appoints Owen with the task of showing things as they really are; his mindset and elocutionary habits dominate the texture of the novel and he is self-evidently of different stock from the hapless proletarians he attempts to radicalize. John Braine's remedy for poverty – greedy opportunism in pursuit of hedonistic excess – differs somewhat from Tressell's but he is faced with the same techni-cal conundrum: how to reconcile the language of a genre with that of a class. Joe Lampton tells his own story, but his rough philistinism is unconvincing. His ultimate ambition might well amount to a 'three guinea linen shirt', an Aston Martin and a 'girl with a Riviera suntan', yet he records these thoughts in prose that rivals the measured authority of Evelyn Waugh. In *Saturday Night and Sunday Morning* Sillitoe achieved something that no one had previously deemed possible. Indeed the fact that no one had even attempted it testifies to an implicit consensus that it was inconceivable.

Narrators and main characters had formed double acts before, for various purposes and with different degrees of success, but the one between Arthur Seaton and the slippery presence who records his escapades and discloses his state of mind was unprecedented. For one thing the latter will sometimes continue to do his job while in all other respects ceasing to exist. Then when he reasserts himself he is magnificently chameleonesque; a dimension of Arthur that is exclusively his, and ours, and to everyone else in the novel the Arthur they have never encountered. Consider, for example, the passage following the departure of Fred from Arthur's bedside, as he recovers from the beating-up dealt him by the off-duty soldiers:

> Fred left, and closed the door. Arthur fell back into a half-sleep. What girl? It must have been Doreen that gave me the brandy when I conked out in the White Hoss, and walked me back later, propping me along Eddison Road, one step at a time. He remembered trying to talk to her and wondered . . .

'Arthur', 'me', 'I', 'He': the switches between first and third person are rapid, seamless, almost elegant. This itself is a fine technical achievement, but why is Sillitoe doing it? Soon another paragraph opens with:

> On the fourth day sun shone through the bedroom window and made a javelin point of light across his rumpled bed.

It is a memorable, clean conceit; one that is not so self-consciously rehearsed as to seem out of place in the novel. It is the narrator's, but by now we are finding it difficult to discern clear borders between the narrator and Arthur, and within this texture of blurred identities it could just as easily be Arthur's. It is certainly not the sort of language that Arthur uses on the shop floor or with Doreen, but we know that he could if he wanted to.

If the narrator had merely acted as custodian of Arthur's untapped or undisclosed literary talents the novel could be filed in the time-worn tradition of *Jude the Obscure*. Instead, Arthur and his unnamed other half cooperate to demolish expectations of how class, status and literary art inter-relate. As Sillitoe argues in his *Books and Bookmen* essay, the middle classes are patrons and executives of literary art and the ordinary people its occasional subjects; *Saturday Night and Sunday Morning* turns this formula on its head. Previously working-class people would read books about themselves and feel patronized – only the middle classes with their mannered refinement seemed capable of making sense of their lives – but now the middle-class reader felt unnerved by this alliance between a man who discloses no intellectual or artistic ambition and his doppelgänger, who is as unpretentious and talented as Hemingway. We know that Arthur could tell his own story, but for the time being he cannot be bothered; he has other things on his mind.

Public recognition of Sillitoe's achievement was slow. British reviewers knew that something unusual had occurred but seemed reluctant to articulate their evident sense of shock. It was left to Anthony West following the novel's US publication to aver that Sillitoe had redrafted the rules of fiction writing.

> There have been novels about working class life in England before, but they were always flawed by fatal defects. Either they were written by working class writers who in the process of acquiring the ambition to write and learning how to do it lost touch with their origins and unconsciously acquired the outlook and values of the middle class, or they were produced by good honest bourgeois projecting themselves downward in the social scale for the good of their guilt-ridden souls . . . For the first time English working class life is treated . . . as a normal aspect of the human condition and as the natural subject for a writer . . . even if [Sillitoe] never writes anything more he has assured himself a place in the history of the English novel. [*New Yorker*, 5 September 1959, p. 99]

Malcolm Bradbury in the *New York Times* argued that Sillitoe should not be mistaken as an addition to the decade's retinue of 'angries'. 'If the heroes of some recent English novels are angry young men, Mr Sillitoe is raging' (16 August 1959).

FIFTEEN

Within two weeks of the first British reviews the novel was attracting interest in the film industry. Over the summer Braine's *Room at the Top* had been adapted for the screen, with key episodes involving Laurence Harvey as Lampton shot in the back yards and tenements of Yorkshire towns that seemed little changed since the previous century. Negotiations were underway for a film version of Osborne's *Look Back in Anger* which would eventually be made by a company formed by Osborne himself and Tony Richardson. No one was quite sure, as yet, how effectively the literary qualities of these novels would translate to the screen, but a desire to break a deadlock that had inhibited British cinema since the war was evident. Since the mid-1940s films made by Britons about Britain had rivalled Hollywood imports in terms of home-grown interest and status. Any claims that they might have made towards realism were, however, risible. The war featured in many of them, and generally speaking historical fact was adhered to, but, like the novel, prominence was given to middle-class officers, variously heroic and tormented, while NCOs and other ranks did their bit bravely and in the vernacular before going home to their respectable, down-at-heel wives and families.

Contemporaneity and 'social issues' were guaranteed to raise a laugh, but it would be generous in the extreme to treat the Ealingesque presentations of Britain as satire. In *I'm All Right Jack* (1959), for example, knock about stereotyping ensured that the film's alleged subject, trade unionism, became farcically uncontroversial, while *Passport to Pimlico* (1949) presented the working classes of post-war London as cheeky but harmless types, an emasculated, heart-warming combination.

Jeffrey Simmons dealt with negotiations for film rights, and tells a fascinating story. A friend of his, a theatrical agent called Clarence Pagett, had bought the novel as soon as the early reviews appeared, and Pagett's neighbour was Roy Ward Baker who had directed *A Night to Remember*, the first film account of the sinking of the *Titanic*. 'Clarence said to Roy that "I've been reading this marvellous, astonishing novel. Buy the film rights." Baker was at the time working for J. Arthur Rank and had enough influence with his US employer, who had never heard of Sillitoe, to persuade them to make an immediate offer.' They did, for £2,000, which even with W.H. Allen's 10 per cent cut was a minor fortune at the time – roughly the equivalent of £100,000 today. Simmons telephoned Sillitoe and they met at his office. 'I said to him, "Look, we've got this outright offer for a film. £2,000. But you get no increments or royalties.' He answered, 'Jeffrey, I'm desperately short of money. Accept it.' They did, but about a week later Simmons received a transatlantic phone call from Rank himself. 'Mr Simmons,' he said, 'we've bought a book from you called *Saturday Night and Sunday Morning*. When we did so I hadn't read it. Now that I have I find that in any form it is not suitable for a family audience. Rank will not make a film that is not suitable for a family audience. We will let you keep the £2,000 but we will not make the film.'

Fine, thought Simmons, a fair compensation given that many other producers seemed desperate to buy the rights to this radical gem. Simmons went first to Joseph Jenry, an avant-garde Italian producer and director who was then in London. On 6 November 1958 Simmons accepted by letter Jenry's offer to buy the rights for £4,500, which involved a down payment of £750 with a six-month period to raise the remainder from sponsors. By Christmas Jenry knew that his arthouse set-up, VIC Films, would never have the pull of the bigger mainstream companies and arranged to sell the option to Harry Saltzman, a US show-business entrepreneur who, had he not been real, would not have seemed out of place in *The Producers*.

Simmons again: 'Saltzman came over and rented one of the biggest houses in Belgravia. When Rosica and I entered the place I was reminded of that scene in Chaplin's *The Great Dictator* with the autocrat seated at the massive desk. The carpet between the door we went through and Saltzman's desk was the length of a cricket pitch. Also he had at least four telephones in different colours – yellow, red, green, blue – and as we discussed the deal for the film we were regularly interrupted by one of these, with Saltzman enunciating his replies to make sure that we knew who was calling. "Hello, Lauren," he'd say, and whisper to us, "Lauren Bacall." Clark Gable, Marilyn Monroe, Greta Garbo, all seemed desperate for his attention during the hour or so we were there.'

Did this, I asked, not seem slightly implausible? He smiled. 'Well, I would certainly not accuse so exalted a figure as Saltzman of contriving the exercise.' Indeed not. And what time would it have been in, say, Los Angeles when you and Rosica were talking to him? 'About 4 a.m. I should think.'

Egotist and fantasist he might have been, but Saltzman had a shrewd eye for good work and after buying Jenry's option he approached Karel Reisz as potential director. Even though Simmons suspects that when they first met Saltzman's knowledge of the novel was second hand, once he did read it he insisted immediately that Sillitoe should write the screenplay. He recognized raw authenticity and he wanted to secure for its author a key role in the adaptation. Such deference to the literary source was rare and for a first-novel author unknown. Even Reisz had initial doubts, but when he met Sillitoe after Christmas 1958 they formed a solid working relationship which would soon germinate into a lifelong friendship.

The three-year period following W.H. Allen's acceptance of the novel was for Sillitoe like nothing he had previously experienced or would again. For a decade he had dedicated himself exclusively to writing, with no success, and now he had become the most hotly debated topic in transatlantic literary circles. Requests for interviews – which for him soon came to sound like demands – poured in from everywhere, from the Nottingham local papers to the BBC. Clarence Pagett, who promoted the novel for film adaptation, had first learned of it over lunch with his friend Jeffrey Simmons. Simmons: 'Despite the fact that Penguin had been around for twenty years or so the paperback bestseller was still a new, untested phenomenon. The big houses were only tentatively leasing out their reliable hardback interests to mass-production paperback subsidiaries. Anyway, at the time Clarence was the talent-spotter for the paperback newcomer Pan and before *Saturday Night* came out I recommended it to him. Once he had read it he did not hesitate. By the early 1960s it had become Pan's first one million bestseller.'

In May 1959 Sillitoe received a letter asking him to report to a hospital in Luton for what would, as the results confirmed, be his final TB check-up. He was not 'cured' – no one ever was – but he was deemed sufficiently fit to be able to survive without a remittance. If only they knew. Seven months earlier he had received two thirds of the £4,500 from Harry Saltzman's purchase of the film rights, plus the same percentage of the £2,000 from J. Arthur Rank. He would also receive 2 per cent of the producer's ongoing profits, and his up-front fee for the screenplay was £1,500. In June of that same year John Braine, taking on his Lampton persona, had in the *Evening Standard* boasted of receiving £5,000 for the film rights. Sillitoe's cramped eyrie in 36 Camden Square was proving to be a little more plush than Braine's room at the top.

Sillitoe and Ruth knew that for the time being thoughts of a return to Spain were unrealistic, but at the same time they felt uncomfortable in central London. They missed the relaxed pace of life in the country so they compromised and in February 1959 took a year's tenancy on a pretty furnished cottage in Whitwell, Hertfordshire, about thirty miles north of the capital. Sillitoe felt that from here he would feel more confident when dealing with his agent, his publishers and everyone else. He was contactable but not easily available; he could dictate the pace of negotiations. His primary concern, following the successful reception of *Saturday Night and Sunday Morning*, was what would be next.

He wanted Simmons to publish *The General*, to be followed shortly afterwards by *The Rats and Other Poems*. He was proud of *Saturday Night and Sunday Morning*, certainly, but at the same time irritated by the image occasioned by promotional material and perpetuated in articles that he was a proletarian autodidact who had dedicated years abroad exclusively to the production of his working-class novel. His correspondence with Rosica during late 1958 and early 1959 is revealing. There is evident determination, even anger, but its impetus seems split between his dedication to some self-contained ideal and suspicion that he was losing control of his destiny. On 25 August he tells her of a phone conversation with Simmons where the latter had said that it would not 'be a good idea to publish *The General* as my next book because it was so completely different from *Saturday Night and Sunday Morning*'. Sillitoe interpreted the subtext here as being, 'Stick to what you can do.' By November he had scrutinized the contract and noted that W.H. Allen had agreed to decide on whether to publish 'the next (or any) manuscript I give them within two months of its submission'. '*The General* was handed in to them by me on Thursday April 17th.' He goes on to argue that since no decision on their part had been made they were in breach of contract. 'If they insist on sticking to the letter of the law over the thirty per cent film subtraction, I will insist on us sticking to the letter of the law over this defection. I'm sure the Society of Authors would see my point were I to approach them' (Letter to Rosica Colin, 18 November 1958). As a fallback policy he suggests that they, W.H. Allen, should be told that 'I have enough short stories of the same genre as *Saturday Night and Sunday Morning* to fill a book.' If they refused this then a civil action would be taken over the film percentage (30 per cent seemed to Sillitoe to amount to theft, given that all they had done was to publish the book), but if they accepted it a clause must be inserted in the contract that they also accept his forth-coming volume of poems. 'By then I may even be popular enough for W.H. Allen to make money out of it. Even if they only cover the expenses it will give tone to the firm' (18 November 1958).

Some would argue that *The Loneliness of the Long Distance Runner* was a greater achievement than *Saturday Night and Sunday Morning*, and even more would be astonished to learn that the volume was more a result of expediency than design. The stories he had produced almost as a relief from an arduous decade of labour on five full-length novels took shape as the contents page of a book on a hurriedly handwritten addition to the letter to Rosica, with the right-hand column listing the number of pages for each piece and reading like a balance sheet.

The story behind the title piece is captivating. During his brief return to England in 1957 Sillitoe had spent time working on the poems that would eventually appear in *Rats*. His method was to try to synthesize the subject with the rhythmic character of his own speech. One day, sitting by the window in the cottage they had borrowed from Ima Bayliss, he witnessed a young man in a running vest and shorts trotting by apparently oblivious to the calm and silence of his surroundings. Sillitoe wrote down 'The Loneliness of the Long Distance Runner' as two loose alliterative lines of verse. The next time he came upon them he was hurriedly disposing of old papers in preparation for his final departure from Spain a year later. He was in the flat they shared briefly with the Martins in Alicante, an episode he remembers without affection not least because the ground floor of the building was occupied by a printing works. The strange parallel between the moment evoked by the lines and the rhythmic persistence of the printing press downstairs seemed more than coincidental. He stopped what he was doing and began to write in a way that he had never previously attempted, indeed never considered. He had some knowledge of stream of consciousness as a radical though now rather jaded invention, with its most famous practitioners, Joyce and Woolf, having been paraded as badges of smug bohemianism at the Nottingham Writers' Group meetings and during numerous similar exchanges in Majorca. There is even a passage in the typescript of 'Man Without a Home' where Cyril Hill recoils from yet another expatriate seeking his opinions on Virginia Woolf. Hill, and his creator, found her writing, like most Modernism, clubbish and élitist. Talking about it was not so much a sign of intelligence as a disclosure of cliquish recognition. Now, however, as Sillitoe sat in the noisy Alicante apartment he found himself evolving, inventing a technique which had no precedent.

In Joyce's famous concluding chapter of *Ulysses* the routine framework of language – grammar, punctuation, continuity – is set aside to allow us access to the pre-linguistic meanderings of Molly Bloom. It is an exercise in snobbishness disguised as art. Fascinated as we may be by Molly's thought processes, we reserve our admiration not so much for the subject as the genius who has made her available to us. Even dear old Leopold is less a character than a puppet for Joyce's intellectual exhibitionism. Woolf's voices exist at the other end of the social scale from the Blooms, and though their monologues might be innovative they are interior in a more conservative sense, being comprised of mental habitats from which ordinary types are as a rule denied access.

Colin Smith is different. He does not abandon sentences; throughout his story we become aware that his bitter, aggressive command of his destiny is tied to his control of his medium. His achievement, and it is a magnificent achievement, is to become a self-contained literary presence who pays no heed to the conventions of literary writing. His prose reflects his rebellious unpredictability, but at the same time it has a special eloquence. His thoughts become words not via someone else's avant-garde exercise but because he can control and manipulate a sentence in the same way that he calculates the effect of refusing to cross the finishing line.

Grudgingly Sillitoe acceded to W.H. Allen's request for a book that would feed the excitement generated by *Saturday Night and Sunday Morning*. In return they would publish *Rats* and, in due course, *The General*. He had finished the final draft of 'The Loneliness of the Long Distance Runner' in the Camden bedsit shortly after returning the proofs of *Saturday Night and Sunday Morning* and when Jeffrey Simmons read it six months later his first instinct, apart from exhilaration, was: 'The story, far more than the novel, came straight from Alan. I know that it was not in the strictest sense auto-biographical – he had not been to Borstal – but I'd known him for more than a year and reading Colin was like listening to Alan. It was not only its mood. The story itself had captured something of his own "run".' I know what he means, in that throughout the previous decade Sillitoe had been caught between pressures and instincts very similar to those that propel Colin through his monologue and, eventually, his race.

Sillitoe had made himself as familiar with the landmarks and habits of high culture as those for whom such familiarity was ingrained and customary, and the self-conscious awareness of having ignored what for others is given put him, paradoxically, at an advantage over them. He had come from, was indeed still part of, a different world, and now he could step between the two; he could recreate the mindset of Arthur or Colin as a familiar and then carry these personae with him into a literary landscape from which they had previously either been excluded or admitted as inauthentic reproductions. Similarly Colin Smith knows how the minds of the Governor and his ilk work far better than they can ever know of his. His run is his narrative. He controls both and the effect of both upon their perceivers.

The volume's reviewers appeared to have been reading different books. None accused Sillitoe of bad writing, and this in itself testifies to the qualities of the stories, particularly the title piece which received by far the most attention. He had touched something far more personal, more visceral, than critical discernment. 'Anon' of the *Times Literary Supplement* (2 October 1959) is evidently displeased by the company of Colin Smith but shows equal discomfort in choosing who to blame for this. Having conceded that Sillitoe's own working-class credentials are fully in order he goes on to assert that Colin's 'modified dialect [is] an uneasy compromise between speech and writing. [This] adopted persona rarely sits easily upon [Sillitoe], any more than it does upon other writers when they tend to be bluff stockbrokers and country solicitors.' So though Sillitoe is authentically working class the reviewer finds it difficult to accept that the rough working-class persona he has created is genuine. One suspects that the reviewer's incoherent bluster disguises an elementary core of bitterness: people like Smith should not be allowed to take charge of serious literary works, at least not until they have received a decent education. The unnamed *Times* commentator is more honest (8 October), beginning with the claim that the title story 'does not invite discussion in purely literary terms'. Why? Because 'what emerges' after reading it is that 'neutrality . . . is a sin'. He concedes that one might be tempted to note the 'fantastic differences' between Virginia Woolf's and Sillitoe's use of the interior monologue but this would amount to obfuscation, an avoidance of confronting something that members of the literati had never previously encountered: 'the [stories] are [so] graphic, tough, outspoken, informed . . . they leave the reader free to exclaim, "I don't believe you."' Why don't we believe him? Because we have never met characters like this before or at least never encountered them in literary writing.

Roy Perrott in the *Guardian* (25 September) commented that in *Saturday Night and Sunday Morning* Sillitoe had disclosed a 'special strength', so special that the reviewer's usual set of responsive registers were thrown out of synchronization. 'A reviewer could fumble with words like insight and sympathy, admiring Sillitoe's ability to see his people in the round, to live their lives without feeling that he (the reviewer) had got it quite right.' In short the standard critical lexicon was insufficient to tackle something so unusual. Now Sillitoe had gone even further, making his 'special gift . . . much clearer, and the best word for it is perhaps "vision"'. Sillitoe had taken literary writing into areas previously unexplored and in doing so altered standard perceptions of what literature is supposed to be and do. He had not simply catalogued the situation of his working-class subjects – sociologists could do that – but rather invited them into his writing as autonomous figures. Perrott: 'It is a slight but most artistic study of the outsider, the dissenter, the man apart.'

Being unpublished had carried the compensation of being able to set his own agenda, and in many ways the works that eventually brought him success were shaped by his lack of it. There are striking parallels between the sense of inconclusiveness that pervades both *Saturday Night and Sunday Morning* and stories of *The Loneliness of the Long Distance Runner* and the fact that as he wrote them his mood was suspensive, resignedly unfocused upon what might happen next in his own life. Now, however, he found that writing was becoming more like the kind of work he had abandoned over ten years earlier, with other people making demands on his time and plans. The concluding sentence of one of his letters to Rosica sums up his sense of frustration: 'I want to leave it more or less in your hands so that it won't be necessary for me to upset my working time and atmosphere [crossed out in original draft] by being consulted so often' (12 January 1959).

The early interviews which accompanied *Saturday Night and Sunday Morning* mutated into lengthier studies of this new figure. Roy Perrott's 'Life Through the Eyes of the Odd Man Out' (*Guardian*, 25 September 1959) was the first profile which presented Sillitoe as a writer, indeed a man, who was difficult to categorize; it concluded that this new arrival had left people caught between admiration and puzzlement. Most other journalists adopted the easy route of presenting him as a proletarian hero, spokesman for a specific ideology and a particular sub-order of human kind, which enraged him. The *Daily Worker* ('Writer with Roots', 'Profile of the Week', 29 October 1960) took the party line and celebrated the emergence of a self-educated radical. Sillitoe had written several pieces for *Books and Bookmen* (such as 'The Pen Was My Enemy', January 1959, and 'Proletarian Novelists', August 1959) in which he was honest enough about his background and at the same time made clear that he was essentially a writer; his politics were one thing, his writing was his profession. None the less his articles prompted purblind, knee-jerk responses from letter writers to the journal who treated him as more a sociological symptom than an individual. The exchange of letters in *Books and Bookmen* between Sillitoe and S.J. Gale in particular (in August to October 1959) bristles with antipathy and not because Gale had taken against Sillitoe's alleged affiliations. Sillitoe had simply become sick of being classified as a 'working class' writer. His feeling of rage was still present more than thirty years later in *Life Without Armour*:

> I had never thought of myself as being of the so-called 'working class', or any class at all. As a child the term would have been meaningless, since it was hard to imagine belonging even to my parents. In the factory I was judged by the amount of work I was expected to do, and looked on it as little more than a basic commercial transaction, and if any knowing lickspittle had in those days implied I was a member of the 'working class' he would have been told in the harshest terms to find a quiet corner and indulge in sexual intercourse with himself. [p. 264]

But fame did have its advantages. His poems, which had been consistently rejected by the mainstream outlets, now came with a name that literary editors recognized; they saw the cachet to be gained from publishing verse by this new, unforgiving novelist. 'Carthage' appeared in the *New Statesman* (23 July 1960), 'Picture of Loot' in the *Listener* (21 July 1960) and 'Say Sheffield' in *Stand* (4 April 1960).

On 22 April 1958 he had been awarded the Authors Club Prize for the Best First Novel of 1958 at a ceremony held at the club's imposing premises in central Whitehall. Sillitoe attended in his only suit, a stylish dark blue unit that had once belonged to Ruth's uncle in America, and a rather starchy individual from *The Times*, whose name he almost immediately forgot, interviewed him for the paper before the presentation. Sillitoe was pleased by all this, indeed flattered, but he had soon learned to counterbalance both with a helping of amused disdain.

As if to confirm that the life and world that had formed him were immune from this new mosaic of media images, he heard from Nottingham two days after the award that his father, already ill, now seemed close to death. Some months earlier he had been diagnosed with cancer of the mouth and throat and, though the NHS regularly used radiation treatment for cancer, Christopher, or so the family reported, was beyond help. Sillitoe, now with an income and an enviable bank balance, went immediately to his and Ruth's GP to find the names and addresses of private specialists. He had passed on details from Nottingham and was advised that money could not buy anything better than was available on the NHS. Christopher died on 28 May, aged fifty-six.

Six months earlier Sillitoe had experienced with him one of their few moments of transparent mutual affection. *Saturday Night and Sunday Morning* was just out and Sillitoe was visiting family to deliver complimentary copies. He had gone first to Dawley in Shropshire where Brian had recently settled with his wife, and then to Nottingham. Christopher inspected his copy with admiration. He never would, never could read it, but he was impressed. 'My God, our Alan,' he said, 'you've written a book! You'll never have to work again.' He still respects the compliment far more than anything offered by the panel at the Authors Club. There were six at the funeral: Sabina, Alan, Pearl, Peggy, Brian and Michael. Edgar was dead but at least three of the other brothers outlived Christopher. None bothered to send notes of sympathy, let alone turn up.

The most fascinating index to his thoughts during this period can be found in an unpublished manuscript in the Indiana Archive, provisionally entitled 'A Man's Life'. There are two drafts of this, both incomplete. In *Life Without Armour* he refers dismissively to continuing 'the story of Colin Smith . . . for want of something to do' (p. 249) while waiting for the publication of *Saturday Night and Sunday Morning*. In truth the project is far more revealing and significant than that, the second draft running to almost two hundred typed pages. Sillitoe is a fast worker but two versions of the same novel totalling almost 370 pages with careful longhand revisions and marginal additions show that the project occupied far more of his time and attention than he concedes. He claims today that he can't really remember much of the piece, and one can only accept his word on this. However, had he completed the novel to his own satisfaction the landscape of post-war writing would have been altered significantly. Colin Smith in 'A Man's Life' becomes a first-person presence like no other, and Sillitoe's intention, his animus, is evident early in the work. What, he asks himself, would Smith be like after Borstal, back in the world where people such as the Governor can be faced as equals? The notes which accompany the main text are engrossing.

> Life is a prison – we are thrown in at birth and are taken away when we die. For what crime? Who sentenced us to life? We don't even have the chance to shout and rave at the judge. 'I didn't do it your honour. I'm innocent. I'm innocent.'

It isn't enough to blame Smith's downfall on the fact that the affluent society is always screaming at him: get money!

Smith is an idealist, a primitive communist; put over the idea that he is a freedom fighter.

One of Sillitoe's principal problems involved style. The monologue of the story – still at this point the first section of a prospective novel – was well suited both to the self-contained narrative of the run and Colin's determination to build himself a private space where his thoughts and ideas would be immune from the Governor's regime. Sillitoe recognized that after Colin was released this rebellious dynamic could not be sustained in a world comprised also of his relatives, friends, lovers and so on. In order to take charge of a full-length novel Colin must become a more versatile literary presence. Following his release from Borstal he is sentenced to three years in jail for a post office robbery.

> In those odd legged jail years, that grow worse the more I think about them, the only good thing I did was read . . . Towards the end I finished my library allowance quickly and was left with hours to think about how the books I'd read had been written, and get to know ways of putting down words. They taught me to read and write at school, to use commas, full stops, and capital letters but until this gash time in clink I was never sure how to write down talking – conversation. Now, I know, or think I do, and it took me about five hundred reading books to get it into my thick skull. [p. 3, second draft, folder 'A Man's Life', Indiana Archive]

Sillitoe had never been to jail but the years during which he read everything available and, significantly, did so independently of the character-forming protocols of an education system bear a striking resemblance to Colin's regime. Colin is, self-consciously, becoming the author of his own narrative while also an embodiment of the more intemperate features of his own author's state of mind – and the postmodernists were supposed to have invented this kind of thing.

Colin the 'primitive communist' is an enthralling spectacle. He draws you into his story as his confidant and then displays a frightening unpredictability. Early in his account he meets a character referred to only as 'Smiler' who attempts to recruit him to the 'British Party'. The party, explains Smiler, is far more dynamic than the moribund Conservatives and more radical in that it claims to offer a voice for the neglected, indeed silenced, body politic of working-class Britishness. Its programme will involve indoctrination by association. Everyone fears the Soviet Union, and the horror of what a conflict between NATO and the Warsaw Pact would involve: nuclear war or, perhaps just as bad, communist takeover. And what else continually produces a knee-jerk reaction among the kind of people who have to live with political decisions made by others?

> ... people saying that nigs this and blackie that on buses and in post office queues, saying they were dirty, took our houses, snatched our women, ate kit-e-kat for breakfast and sold it to their pals with salmon labels stuck on it at half-a-crown a tin, caused our unemployment, owned prostitutes, and gave everybody black looks. [p. 256, second draft, Indiana Archive]

Colin loathes Smiler but he is certainly not Sillitoe's avatar for an alternative untainted ideology.

> My old man and his communist pals used to hold meetings in our parlour during the war and I suppose in a way they amounted to the same thing as those blue-eyed empty headed bastards [the British Party members].

Almost but not quite. At least his father's cronies

> ... talked about helping everyone, making us all brothers and equals, building up a better world. It may sound crazy but it was a better sort of craziness than old Smiler's.

Colin, like Sillitoe, loathes the prospect of being associated with any kind of political ideology; whatever enrichments these might offer the world at large are outweighed by their claim upon the thing that both men value most – the right of individuals to decide for themselves how to live their lives.

Colin throws a brick through the window of a British Party meeting, a gesture planned to draw members outside in search of him. He turns on one of his pursuers and tries to kill him by delivering an uppercut with his fist followed by another brick which will, he calculates, crack his skull. The passage in which Colin discloses his thoughts prior to breaking the window is magnificently unapologetic. At no point does he indulge rational or ethical arguments. He simply pulls us with him through his account. There is a dead cat next to the pavement:

> I saw it was a tom, felt sorry for the poor black bastard, because maybe it had just had its oats and was on its way home for its daily herring; and I supposed the Cat-God to be similar in temperament to the one human beings had landed themselves with – 'God gives with one hand and takes away with the other' was what people said about him, forgetting to add that this made him an ambidextrous double-crossing bastard. [p. 259, second draft, Indiana Archive]

First-person narrators are by their nature unreliable, given that their roles as choreographer and entertainer sit uncomfortably alongside their obligations to honesty and credulity. Compromise and obfuscation are always necessary, but Sillitoe disproves this nostrum. Whatever our temperament inclines us to feel about Colin we have difficulties in breaking away from his magnetic company. Some might loathe him, despise the fact that this anarchic presence has been let loose within such sacred territory as a literary text – and many at the end of the 1950s would have felt this way – but the border between revulsion and addiction is notoriously porous.

The typescript is by no means perfect. As Colin puts it, 'My story follows no straight line, is shaped by a battery of pig sticking pens . . .' and it sometimes becomes too random and unorthodox; it begins to sprawl. But within it is a potential masterpiece. Sadly Sillitoe never returned to it after 1959, nor did he show it to a publisher.

One wonders if his reluctance to proceed any further with it was based upon his dissatisfaction with its qualities, or whether something more personal caused him to set it aside. The interleaved notes are revealing. Close to the passage on Colin's reflections on the British Party, communism and his assault upon a member of the former is a handwritten draft of a letter to the *Spectator*, undated, but written several months after Castro had seized power in Cuba. The *Spectator*'s regular political commentators had published articles on the communist takeover and two of them, Robert Conquest and Bernard Levin, had lambasted the British liberal left as apologists for this dangerous new wave of revolutionary authoritarianism. Sillitoe, through no fault of his own, had become an easy target as the most recent literary leftist, and his name was mentioned. His letter – never published – is a rational, measured version of Colin's mixture of apathy and contempt for both ultra-right-wing politics and communism, with a small helping of begrudged sympathy for the latter.

> A political movement such as Castro's began out of compassion . . . Often into the vacuum of compassion comes the dead organisational eye of the theorist whose goal it is to protect the revolution, and make it work. To consolidate they murder. The amount of murder is often in proportion to the strength of the counter revolution which has always depended for its strength on outside interference. [Unnumbered page, second draft, Indiana Archive]

He neither offers unequivocal support for Castro nor does he condemn the USA as irredeemably unjust in its policies; he simply states that the two, locked into conflict, will guarantee an escalation in loss of life. He sounds like the version of Colin whom the educated classes might welcome into their sitting rooms, but sometimes the mask slips: 'I come not to rap Mr Conquest's knuckles, not to stand him against a wall and shoot him' or hit him with a brick.

More compelling is a note in which Sillitoe speculates on Colin's family life.

> Colin has a dream about his father. His mother told him his father was dying with cancer, and when he goes to the house his father is up and out of bed dressed normally; and the accepted fact is that he's been cured by some new wonder drug, even though he was eaten through by cancer and about to die. But his face is chalk white. Colin looks at the watch his mother had given him after his father had died; a watch that had belonged to his father, and the watch has no glass in it. [Unnumbered page, second draft, Indiana Archive]

Nothing resembling this occurs in the draft, but the fact that the note is attached to the page where Colin contemplates God as an 'ambidextrous, double-crossing bastard' is intriguing. It was written shortly after his father's death.

Perhaps Colin was becoming too much like his creator, too much a version of Sillitoe as he might have been had he not decided to become a writer; unprotected emotion and impulse, life without armour, has its drawbacks. I ask him now: Does he not regret taking the novel further? 'Perhaps. It's so long ago. But I did like Colin. Yet, of course, I had to let him go.'

What he fails to mention is that Colin provides an index to the street politics of north London, which Sillitoe witnessed at the end of the 1950s. A very real version of the British Party had formed around Oswald Mosley, who spent much of 1958 and 1959 provoking racism in Notting Hill, where in 1959 he also ran for Parliament. Sillitoe wrote to Brian. 'Mosley is back, here in London, and anyone who thought Fascism was dead in 1945 is a fool. He and his thugs are on the streets, organising meetings, stoking hatred. The police can't, or won't, act, but I know what I'd do to him' (AS to BS, 12 May 1959). And so does Colin.

SIXTEEN

Despite Harry Saltzman's self-cultivated image as a Hollywood exhibition-ist he soon began to make shrewd decisions on how to turn an unclassifiable novel into an equally unprecedented film. Within six months of buying the rights he had raised more than £95,000 from backers, mostly in the United States, which testifies to his powers of persuasion. Most of the financiers he approached turned him down immediately. The British film industry and its US counterpart were dedicated to escapism. The Second World War had ended barely fifteen years before, and the Cold War persistently reminded people that something much worse might occur very soon. The prospect of a film set in a visually unappealing provincial British city, with no discernible narrative let alone a happy ending, and based on the lives of people at the bottom of the social scale, was greeted with incredulity: Why was he even thinking about making it? But, somehow, he convinced a sufficient number of backers that they would see a profit, and, with a boldness verging upon the foolhardy, appointed as his director a man who had before only ever made documentaries. Karel Reisz had co-directed, with Tony Richardson, *Momma Don't Allow* (1958), a vivid and unrestrained picture of life in an Islington jazz club, and his only single-handed directorial project was *We Are the Lambeth Boys* (1959), one of the earliest Free Cinema experiments, an account of working-class youth set in and around a South London youth club.

One reason why Sillitoe and Karel immediately got on so well was that both had been in their chosen profession for more than ten years and largely beneath the surface. Things had suddenly changed for Sillitoe, and Karel had now been given a free hand on what would be his first attempt at a feature film. Soon after they met in summer 1959 Karel drove them to Nottinghamshire in his Morris van, piled with film equipment, to look at locations for a documentary he wanted to shoot alongside the adaptation of the novel. It would highlight the contrast between how coal miners spent their working lives in dangerous, unimaginably harsh conditions and their other worlds on the surface, drinking, playing and watching sport, looking after families, fishing. Sillitoe would write the commentary. It was eventu-ally released as a public information film – which Sillitoe has never seen and is now unobtainable – but planning it gave them the opportunity to discuss *Saturday Night and Sunday Morning*. Karel wanted to use actors who were unknown to the cinema-going public, his argument being that while they would have the skill to do the job, the film, like the novel, would seem to have come from outside the glamorized mainstream. For Arthur he had in mind a young actor whose screen career had so far comprised bit-parts but who had a considerable reputation in the theatre. Albert Finney was playing Edgar in *King Lear* at Stratford, and Karel took Sillitoe and Ruth to see a performance. Sillitoe tried his best to connect this impressive contribution to high tragedy with the compound of images that had brought Arthur to life, and almost laughed, but Karel had a mercurial capacity to convince and soon Sillitoe was supporting him in attempts to persuade the casting director, Miriam Brickman, that Finney was perfect for the job. Within a week Finney's agent had agreed a contract. For Brenda they wanted a woman whose screen presence would recreate the vulnerable sexuality of the book and chose Rachel Roberts. Shirley Ann Field, already being touted as Britain's answer to the Hollywood goddesses, seemed an unlikely candidate for Doreen, who was pretty but, compared with Brenda, slightly prim. 'Trust me,' said Karel. 'She's right.'

During the winter of 1959–60 Sillitoe worked consistently on the screenplay. He'd had experience, of a sort, with the commissioned but never used script for *The Bandstand*, but now he had to deal with coordinating dialogue, much of which he could borrow from the book, with the complex multi-dimensional demands of film editing, endurance of shot, camera perspective and soundtrack. His first draft was, said Karel, excellent, except that the film would be about six hours long. Teamwork was required and Sillitoe shortened and revised the screenplay with advice from Karel, the photographer Freddie Francis and Seth Holt the film editor, mostly at Shepperton studios where some of the interiors were due to be shot. Karel craved authenticity, and despite Saltzman's anxiety regarding the considerable, but not gigantic, budget insisted that most of the film should be made in Nottingham, if possible in the actual locations which had inspired the book. Sillitoe knew that any rough industrial landscape of factories, back-to-back terraces and glimpses of benighted countryside would be convincing enough for virtually everyone in the audience; Manchester, Bradford, Leeds and Sheffield could still provide hopelessly bleak vistas, perhaps more cheaply, but Karel ruled out comparative estimates. Sillitoe was at once amused and, he concedes, slightly moved by Karel's conviction that the novel's allegiance to place must be respected. As a result of this the film created its own sub-generic niche in the incipient British New Wave.

When I met Sillitoe's brothers in 2006 both recalled the making of the film with a mixture of amusement and admiration.

Brian: 'You know, most of the family are in the film. I appear twice – my wife's in it and Michael's in it, of course. Wasn't Anne [Michael's wife] in it as well, Mike?'

Michael: 'Yes, she was.'

Brian: 'My mother's in it, Peggy my sister's in it and Patrick my nephew, that's Peggy's son. And there must have been at least half a dozen of the neighbours we'd known for years who appeared. It was made in the same streets, in Radford, where we'd grown up. You remember the scenes with back yards and sculleries . . .'

Bradford: 'Yes, such as the one where the woman is shot by Arthur with the airgun . . .'

Brian: 'That one, yes. The window Albert used was in a house where we, the family, had actually lived.'

Michael: 'Do you remember at the beginning of the film when we see a house half demolished? The interior is exposed, particularly the stairwell where the wallpaper has been plastered over and stippled. Our dad did that. It was the last house where he lived, and I remember him doing his own DIY job on the walls.'

Bradford: 'Did Karel know this?'

Michael: 'To be honest, I've no idea. We did, though. Alan and Karel arranged for me to appear basically as myself, doing my job, as the jazz drummer in the pub scene. I also worked with Johnny Dankworth in Shepperton on the score. The pianist was Dudley Moore, who nobody had heard of then. Johnny left me and Dudley alone for much of the time, and when we weren't doing pieces for the film we'd just improvise, for hours.'

Bradford: 'So part of the score for the film is played by Dudley Moore?'

Michael: 'Yes. He would have appeared in it as well, as a member of the pub band – his first film – but he was committed to playing with Johnny's group on tour when the Nottingham parts were being shot.'

Brian: 'What about the pushchair?'

Michael: 'Oh God, yes. There's a part where Finney runs down the road after a lad who's stolen a fiver when a pushchair with a baby in it seems to come from an alley and he trips over it. It looks . . . symbolic, probably, but it was an accident. Our sister Peggy was pushing the chair – her son was in it – and lost control as Finney sprinted towards her. It looked so good that Karel kept it in.'

All of which makes the revered episode of the pram descending the stairs in *The Battleship Potemkin* seem rather affected by comparison.

Michael was also taken on as a go-between responsible for payments to the people whose homes the crew used and who themselves often appeared as extras. He was, he recalls, followed around by 'a man with a gigantic suitcase full of cash'. Arc lights would be set up in back yards and alleys, and amounts agreed for use as sets and payments made on the spot, both for appearances and for uses of property. 'I think some people managed to get paid about three times for the same thing.' But the man with the suitcase was an indulgent sort – Saltzman had employed him as a means of avoiding tax liabilities for registered employees – and everyone seemed to enjoy the bizarre experience of watching a film being made about the kind of lives they led while being paid, tax free, to appear in it.

Michael: 'Shirley Ann Field?'

Brian: 'Lovely, wasn't she? We used to wind her up, asking if it was true, about her and Frank Sinatra. I asked her once if she fancied going for a drink.'

Michael: 'You didn't?'

Brian: 'She wasn't interested.'

Karel was an astute professional, aware that the key tasks had to be undertaken by those trained to do them, yet he also made sure that the set of his first feature involved an atmosphere similar to that which had informed his Free Cinema documentaries. For all involved, from bit players through technicians to stars, the borderlines between the real-life provenance of *Saturday Night and Sunday Morning* and its execution in the film often seemed to fade.

Reviewers were enthralled, with Dilys Powell (*Sunday Times*, 30 October 1960) and C.A. Lejeune (*Observer*, 30 October) averring that the adaptation was as radical and incendiary as the novel. Jack Clayton's version of *Room at the Top*, out barely a year before, seemed by comparison to bathe the working classes in nostalgia.

When he saw the first rough cut of the film Sillitoe felt a mixture of emotions. The locations, indeed many of the people, he recognized; the accents seemed a motley collection and not really authentic, but would the accent he had grown up with – used by the Arthur of his imaginings – be intelligible to the average cinema-goer? Did the latter know of Nottingham or care about how its people spoke? As he explains, he felt as though something of his own had been hijacked.

> ... whereas I had total control of a novel, with a film there was, in spite of writing the script, not very much ... there was some comfort ... in knowing that the reader of fiction becomes his or her own film-maker, setting their particular and idiosyncratic cameras moving after the first word of a novel or story registers on the brain, thus completing the work of the writer. [*Life Without Armour*, p. 266]

Sillitoe's misgivings did not dampen his enthusiasm for film, and his collaboration with Karel cemented a close friendship that would endure until the latter's death in 2002. In January 1960 he and Ruth moved into the top-floor flat of Karel's house in Gayton Crescent, Hampstead, and the two men made plans for further projects.

Eventually Colin Smith would launch the career of Tom Courtenay, just as Arthur had done for Albert Finney, but initially it was another story from the same collection that captivated Karel: 'Uncle Ernest'. Sillitoe had never even considered its potential for adaptation; it was a vignette with a bitter, compressed narrative. But he and Karel talked through the possibilities, with the latter offering suggestions on how the episodes in the café which led to Ernest's persecution could make up a rolling storyline counterposed against retrospective glimpses of the events that had formed his character. Sillitoe was convinced, and throughout 1960 the two of them did their best to interest backers in a feature film or an hour-length TV version. On Boxing Day 1960 Karel wrote to Sillitoe about the progress of negotiations for an adaptation – at the time Sillitoe and Ruth were spending two months in Spain and Morocco. Tony Richardson was keen and Trevor Howard, to whom Karel had spoken directly – 'very briefly . . . neither yes or no; certainly some keen interest' – was being hunted as the eponymous lead. In the end the venture came to nothing, but what a fascinating subscript on Britain and Britain's perception of itself it might have made. The battle-scarred introverted veteran of the First World War – the sort of man who officially did not exist – would be played by the matinée idol of *Brief Encounter*, his harmless affinity to innocence interpreted by the authorities as paedophilia. If only.

Karel began the letter: 'Bulging full of turkey dripping and with the noise of five thousand children still ringing in my ears . . .' It was 1960, a good Christmas. Brian Sillitoe remembers another one, twenty-five years earlier, when the Sillitoes had nothing to eat. There was a knock on the door, and it was Eddie. No, he wouldn't stay but he'd brought them this. 'It's a bloody cat,' observed Sabina. 'No it's not,' said Eddie, 'it's a rabbit, and a big one.' 'He also stank rotten,' observes Sillitoe. They had a Christmas dinner that year. Poor, decent Eddie.

The letters between Alan and Karel of the 1960s disclose something that went beyond friendship. They saw in each other a depth of commitment, an artistic sincerity that was rare in its selflessness. Neither treated their genre as a vehicle for egotism; they simply wished to make good art. Unusually, both were able to pursue this vocation with a mixture of resolution and self-parody.

Tony Richardson is back from Hollywood and we have already met and quarrelled. He's starting *A Taste of Honey* in eight weeks time – the young girl will be played by Albert Finney, of course – and he's madly excited to make the long-distance runner. He really seems to mean it too. Though what he'll say tomorrow is anyone's guess.

Social news of the week. The marriage has been announced of Mr Wolf Mankowitz and Mr Harry Saltzman – they hope to have a large family of plays and films and we all, I'm sure, wish them well. Ah! Showbusiness! [26 December 1960]

Particularly revealing are Karel's comments on Sillitoe's first major collection of verse, *The Rats and Other Poems*, which had come out at the end of January 1960. Though the title poem made up just over half of the volume (60 of the 111 pages) most reviewers gave it exclusive scrutiny, their evaluations ranging from indulgent puzzlement to contempt.

At the end of a decade during which counter-modernism had prevailed it was not unusual to find yet another figure who followed Robert Conquest's famous stylistic mantra of the Introduction to *New Lines*: 'to be empirical in [their] attitude to all that comes' and to 'maintain a rational structure and comprehensible language'. But 'The Rats' for most reviewers was unendurably transparent. The *Times Literary Supplement* commentator, probably the most sympathetic, found it 'Loose and coarse in its rhetorical structure and texture . . . his title poem has nevertheless vigour and the ring of conviction about it' (*Times Literary Supplement*, 6 January 1961). Reviewers searched for a precedent among earlier connoisseurs of bitterness – Dryden, Pope and Churchill are mentioned – but confessed to failure. There had been nothing quite like this before. As the *Times Literary Supplement* put it, while Sillitoe's predecessors had tended to be 'cool and amused' in their malice the speaker of 'Rats' would 'perhaps like to cut our throats', and no one doubted that the speaker and the author were the same person.

The poem belongs within that sub-genre of works which defy attempts to find room for them in either the canon or its dissolute offshoots. If you dislike it, it is difficult to articulate or justify your revulsion. Certainly parts of it seem carelessly assembled, with raging syntax shoed uncomfortably into couplets, but just as we begin to treat this as an irritating routine the verse shifts into a more controlled, even elegiac mode. Why? It is impossible to say. All we know is that our expectations are being continually disrupted. While the resemblances are not immediately evident, its closest relatives will be found in the work of Blake, at least until the latter gave himself over to the occult impenetrability of his later pieces. As with Blake's *Songs of Innocence and Experience*, Sillitoe often allows anger to override cohesion. We feel that he is addressing us directly, often nudging the verse form aside as an irritation, much as a speaker would shout over hostile voices in the crowd.

What is 'The Rats' about? The eponymous rodents are, probably, the Establishment, while the 'Ogads' – literally backwards 'dagos' – could be almost anyone who exists in a state of supine victimhood. The latter are not blameless; they watch too much television, seem willing to sleepwalk through a life drained of significance and are disposed to cooperate with the Rats:

> You shall love the rats who take the hours
> From your clumsy hands, who guide you over roads
> And traffic islands, take the heavy loads

> From lighter brains, and give you paper flowers
> Of happiness . . .
> . . . transport you to a house
> And television set and Ogad wine. [ll. 22–9]

You will search in vain for a clear correspondence between the polemic of the poem and the politics of post-war Britain. Sillitoe seems to espouse revolution, but it is an individualistic, idiosyncratic brand: hard-line communists and middle-ground Labour supporters are battered indiscriminately. Karel loved it.

> I have read *The Rats* and fumed against the rotten bastards who have reviewed it. I think the notices are to be explained in two ways – partly that the content must have hurt; partly that the critics have no tradition of polemical poetry to measure it against. My own feelings (remember I'm illiterate and don't read or understand poetry, though!) were ones of great pleasure and recognition of the *temperament* of it all . . . [Reisz to AS, 15 February 1961, Indiana Archive]

Karel has his misgivings too. Perhaps the 'ideas and sentiments' of the poem are a 'little too raw', expressed 'a little too literally'. Yet he qualifies his concerns.

> But then this whole question of the wretched 'commitment' has been worrying me a little these last few months. I'm in a complete muddle about it all.

He needed to be able to reconcile his affiliation to 'Pure Art' with his 'commitment' to ideas. Each could rob the other of its essential quality:

> So many people have spoken of *Saturday Night* (they're fools of course) as if it were a pure political film that I am a little scared. Anyway we must talk about it.

They did. They talked a lot, sometimes about particular projects and issues and just as often about their lives. Karel, Jewish, had been on one of the last trains loaded with evacuees to leave Czechoslovakia in 1939. His elder brother was already in England, and his parents, who stayed behind, perished in the concentration camps. According to Betsy Blair, Karel's second wife, he became a chameleon. Already fluent in German and Czech, he learned English rapidly – he was sent to a private Quaker school on arrival in London – and 'when he spoke there was no suspicion, unless you knew him, that he was anything other than English upper-middle-class, ex-public schoolboy' (Betsy Blair, 8 March 2007). While Karel's background was far more tragic than Sillitoe's they recognized in each other a sense of dislocation. Both had a close affiliation to their past while knowing that they could never fully return to it; both had, in a manner partly premeditated, partly unwitting, reinvented themselves.

During this period Sillitoe was wrestling with numerous Nottingham questions. The place and his involvement with it had made him famous, but he loathed the idea of being forever designated by class or region. He was a writer, no more, no less. At the same time he felt that there was a strain of tough, non-religious nonconformity which attended his family – the very presence of Burton, his mother's willingness to hide a deserter, Eddie himself a deserter – that guaranteed his attachment to the area. Karel was a skewed mirror image of Sillitoe: a man recreated but with a heritage that was ever present, haunting and fatiguing. They talked much about making 'Uncle Ernest' into a film. The censors, the reviewers and the general public would be appalled. 'My feelings about our second project [Uncle Ernest] are equally confused. I am terrified and attracted by it . . .' (Reisz to Sillitoe, 15 February 1961). 'Terrified', as Sillitoe confirms, because he saw a parallel between the insidious conspiratorial hatred for Ernest and anti-Semitism.

Tony Richardson, who was to direct *The Loneliness of the Long Distance Runner*, had known and worked with Karel since the late 1940s, and temperamentally they were opposites. Karel was amusing, inspiring yet self-effacing, while Tony thrived upon unpredictability and bombast.

Tony and Sillitoe got on well enough – they first met in early 1961 – but often the latter felt that his contributions were being dealt with by someone who made decisions in advance and then changed his mind with resolute capriciousness. He had now experienced the complexities of film-making first hand and he saw the opportunity to regain some of the novelist's command of the narrative that he had surrendered with the *Saturday Night and Sunday Morning* film and began by making notes on how the inferred polemic of the novel would translate, perhaps be made more insistent, in film.

In the story the events outside Smith's mind are gathered into a torrent of anger and obduracy, and while he rarely offers anything so concrete as an opinion we join him on his run, listen to him and intuit a great deal. As Sillitoe was aware, this effect was untranslatable into film, so while as a writer he loathed the idea of characters becoming puppets for dogma he now found that he had little choice but to accentuate what in the original had been insinuated. There would be more calculation and premeditation in Smith's act of rebellion. The cinematographic version of Smith's monologue would involve the use of flashbacks to pre-Borstal episodes and brief narrative comments by the actor, Tom Courtenay. The camera would follow Smith through the run, recording his exertion and facial expressions while switching to perspectives which incorporated the Gunthorpe runners and the Governor's retinue of invited guests. Sillitoe offered an immensely detailed account of forty-seven camera sequences. For example:

He slows down and stops, within fifty yards of the tape. Immediately he stops, the governor knows what his intention is, even though he had no idea of it up to that second, and it registers in his face.

Exhortation comes from all sides.

Montage. While he is waiting: Copper questioning. Magistrate advising. TV commercial. Snowfall of money. This montage is accompanied by cheers and exhortations, and interspersed with the shots around sports field, and final narration of the long distance runner. [Indiana Archive, unnumbered]

Tony Richardson – not temperamentally the most indulgent individual – recognized that Sillitoe's plan for interspersed moments of narrative was daring. All he asked for was more variety:

The only big problem is I think the narration and the difficulty of finding a rich and expressive enough way of treating the repetition of the running as there will be a great danger of feeling that it is just repetition – as visually it just can't be varied enough. Can you examine each of these sequences in relation to the rest and think of what visually should be the dominant thing, feeling or mood. [Richardson to AS, 8 March 1961, Indiana Archive]

Sillitoe returned to his sequence of shots and strove to give each flashback and narrative interjection a sharper integrity:

Gunthorpe almost overtakes, but Smith sprints clear. Flashback to father dying. Money falling like snow.

The money-as-snow image was, thought Richardson, too heavy-handedly symbolic, but he kept the rest.

In the screenplay itself his alterations to the original dialogue are designed to accentuate a conflict between Smith and a hostile, repressive establishment. When in the screenplay the policeman calls at Smith's house to question him on the robbery the former is far more aggressive than his story-based counterpart, shifting routinely from verbal abuse ('You thieving young bastard') to the threat of violence with a hint of corruption.

Up to this point no one had dared question Jack Warner's PC Dixon as the epitome of the beloved British bobby, the embodiment of decency and avuncular probity. Richardson was impressed.

I am enclosing the Censor's comments on the script. I don't know whether you understand this, it means quite simply that the committee threaten that we will get an 'X' instead of an 'A' if we present the police and screws in this way. Naturally I have no intention of changing anything but this is a marvellous concrete example of the insidious and evasive way in which the film censor works. [Richardson to AS, 15 January 1962, Indiana Archive]

In truth Richardson's concluding remarks were an example of the posturing radicalism to which he was sometimes prone. Sillitoe found the report mildly amusing, particularly the lengthy passage covering 'an excess of what is sometimes called "language"'. 'Bogger' apparently was 'unacceptable' while the more obscure 'clatfart' caused puzzled unease. '"Bloody" or "bleedy" is used extensively – actually 32 times according to the reader whom I asked to count them.' This meticulous clerk of egregiousness also found that '"Bastard" is used 12 times.' Self-parody can often be all the more outstanding when unwitting and unavoidable.

John Trevelyan had been appointed Executive Secretary of the British Board of Film Censors in 1958. He was the most liberal and open-minded in the history of the institution but his indulgent inclinations were continually impeded by the regiment of local bodies, mostly outside the capital, who functioned as self-appointed arbiters of public decency, and *Saturday Night and Sunday Morning* had already created problems. Karel had reported to Sillitoe – then in Morocco – that 'the papers are full of cartoons about it [outraged provincial officialdom]; the Warwickshire County Council has banned it as immoral; the Nottingham MPs have attacked it (see enclosed reply from Michael Foot)' (Reisz to AS, 15 February 1961). Michael Sillitoe recalls that 'the Nottingham "Watch Committee" – God knows what they thought they were – were up in arms. It was mad. They wanted a film that was about Nottingham and made in Nottingham banned in Nottingham. They even claimed that Arthur's references to "Slab Square" [the familiar term used by virtually everyone in the city] were obscenities' (Interview with Michael and Brian Sillitoe, 2006).

Trevelyan's report might have struck Richardson as evidence of 'insidious' censorship but in fact the section which deals with the violence inflicted upon prisoners by police and 'screws' is almost apologetic: '[The] film is one which presents ideas [and] we have no wish to restrain the expression of ideas in films, particularly for adult audiences ... [but] there are some people who feel that these ideas are dangerous for the young ...' (Report from BBFC Secretary, John Trevelyan, to Michael Holden of Woodfall Films, 9 January 1962). In short, unless it is given an 'X' no one will ever get to see it outside London.

The film was unlike *Saturday Night and Sunday Morning* in that it was shot in Shepperton and in convenient locations in London and the surrounding countryside, everyone involved was a professional and while Karel had evolved a blend of relaxed authenticity and improvisation in the Nottingham-based project Richardson was far more focused and autocratic. Betsy Blair remembers the different ways in which each director dealt with Harry Saltzman, who had raised finance for both films. 'Harry liked to wander round the sets offering advice. Karel indulged him, without taking him too seriously, but Tony was more calculating. He would stop everything and say, "Harry, please make any suggestions you feel will help," and Harry would withdraw, embarrassed' (Interview with Betsy Blair, March 2007).

The so-called British 'New Wave' in film was a brief phenomenon and too heterogeneous to make a claim upon an integral purpose, but the adaptations of Sillitoe's two pieces of fiction were outstanding and ground-breaking. Never before had literary works that had undermined their own generic routines and conventions replicated their achievement in their film versions, nor had any literary author played so purposive and significant a role in making this possible.

Did he, I asked Sillitoe, have any sense of becoming a member of a club, a circuit of writers, publishers and directors whose involvement with a new vibrant culture brought them together socially? 'Not really, no. I'd heard of the "new generation" or whatever you wish to call it but I didn't meet any of the more celebrated figures until much later. Kingsley Amis: I think we met around 1969 and we bumped into one another at parties quite a few times. I found him a friendly, easy-going man. Actually before we met in person he wrote in 1962 to ask if I'd contribute something to a volume of specially commissioned science fiction short stories he was editing for Cape. I had a go but I was too busy to complete it. Ted [Hughes] and Sylvia [Plath]: we met at the 1962 Hawthornden Award, and we remained close friends after that. I think the first writer who we really got to know when we came back from Spain, and who we've always liked, was Christopher Logue.' Logue wrote to Sillitoe in 1960, barely a year after they had met, and the letter reveals something of why they got on so well.

> *The Rats* arrived yesterday: thank you for it. Of course I have not read it yet, but I noticed a pretentious review by that nauseous old schoolmarm John Press which makes me sure I will enjoy it.
>
> Don't be surprised if you read the 'you must stick to prose' lesson, just as you got the 'stick to Nottingham and what you know' lesson after *The General*. They do not mean stick to Nottingham, for I doubt if any of them have left Palmers Green since puberty; nor do they mean stick to what you know, but to what *we* know. After all, if you don't stick to what they know,

then reviewing your book is going to be difficult, will mean rethinking their adopted positions . . . and that, well! [Christopher Logue to AS, 18 December 1960, Indiana Archive]

This is a shrewd, prescient assessment of the problems that Sillitoe would face, despite his status as a celebrated newcomer. He would be acclaimed for his portraits of life at the bottom, yet when he went beyond that he would often be judged an over-reacher. He was allowed to write of things which middle-class mainstream authors and reviewers knew only vicariously, but when he went on to match their versatility in manner and subject, showing he could move across boundaries that to them were closed, this meant that he became, technically at least, their superior.

Sillitoe and Ruth met Shelagh Delaney when Tony Richardson was offering Sillitoe advice on the screenplay for *Saturday Night and Sunday Morning*. It had been written into Sillitoe's screenwriting contract – and he is still unsure who instigated this – that Richardson should play an 'advisory' role. Delaney, whose *A Taste of Honey* Richardson would go on to direct, wrote to Sillitoe and Ruth in late 1962.

I went to see your *Long Distance Runner* and didn't care much for it at all. It seems to have quite a different message (if you like to call it that) as a film than it has as a book. I think Tony goes from bad to worse as a film director. The most unforgivable thing about the *Runner* is the way he underestimates the intelligence of his audience. Points are made and underlined three times and asterisked with explanatory footnotes and marginal reminders. It's very aggravating. I'm prepared to believe that everyone isn't as intelligent as I am but on the other hand I just refuse to believe that they're all big blobs. The way he handled the run and the deliberate losing of the race is just laughable . . . I found the whole thing depressing. Even more so than *A Taste of Honey*. And that's saying something believe me. [Shelagh Delaney to AS and RF, 12 December 1962, Indiana Archive]

Sillitoe too was unhappy with Richardson's hijacking of his story. He knew that some effects must be altered when translated from one medium to the other, but Richardson was a proselytizer; his version of Smith, via a tormented performance by Tom Courtenay, was an exercise in political rhetoric and, as Delaney had pointed out, patronizing. Delaney, Sillitoe and Ruth would remain close friends.

John Braine wrote to him in 1962, out of the blue, saying, 'We haven't met but I very much admire your work' (21 January), and invited him and Ruth to a drinks party at his house in London. They got on well enough and their friendship was cemented in the 1970s through their support for Israel. The two of them are linked, habitually, in histories of post-war fiction, but Sillitoe met someone else at Braine's party to whom he found himself, temperamentally, better attuned. B.S. Johnson is presented by critics as a heroic curiosity, one of the last unyielding modernists, but what Sillitoe liked about him was his belief that technique was a matter of choice; personally he was preoccupied with the nature of storytelling, but more important was a novelist's commitment to personal experience. They became close friends, and maintained a mutual respect for each other's writing; indeed Sillitoe in the 1960s and early 1970s did his best via contacts in publishing and the media to assist Johnson in promoting his work, which during this period was deemed fascinating but unsellable.

PART IV
THE UNSETTLED RADICAL

SEVENTEEN

In November 1960 Sillitoe and Ruth left Britain for the Continent. He gives an indication in *Life Without Armour* of what prompted this largely unplanned departure: 'the gutter press was harassing me to know whether or not my mother would be getting a new fur coat now that I too was rich. Gutter language told them what they could do. Sick of the novel [*Saturday Night and Sunday Morning*], and of everything concerning the film, we left by train and boat for Paris, to stay a week at the Martins' place' (p. 270). They kept going on an improvised journey with no clear destination. Spain and Majorca were obvious choices – they had kept in touch with Robert and Beryl Graves and there was the temptation of returning to old locations and friends, with author-aspirant now an acclaimed novelist, and all in two years. But the country seemed too familiar and Sillitoe found himself less tolerant of its character. He tells of how on the train from Madrid he noted an uncommon stillness in two of his fellow travellers, who seemed determinedly preoccupied with matters other than the conversation he was having with Ruth. Later, when they introduced themselves as policemen and asked for his passport, he wondered if his comments regarding the Civil War made during a guided tour of Toledo the previous day had been noted and passed on to the authorities. Neurosis? Coincidence? It could, he now admits, have been a coincidence, yet he is certain that whatever prompted his unease was a condition of living in Spain. Two years later he wrote in a letter to Brian:

> No, we decided not to go to Spain and live after all. It is too much of a dead country, kept down too much by Franco and his army of police. I prefer . . . Morocco which at least is an independent African country, and likely to make some sort of progress. Spain will just keep going down, unless it loses its spirit completely, unless there is a radical change of government. [AS to BS, 21 January 1963]

Mike Edmonds, their friend from the Majorca years, had written a guide-book on Morocco and had spoken to them of the place, particularly its attraction for writers and artists who saw themselves as embodiments of the avant-garde. Members of the so-called Beat Generation of US poetry had passed through the country during the 1950s like pilgrims, and William Burroughs had written *The Naked Lunch*, amply assisted by cannabis and Spanish brandy, in an appropriately decrepit hotel in Tangier.

Sillitoe and Ruth arrived in Tangier on 12 November 1960, stayed briefly with Jeanette and Mack Reynolds, who had moved there a year earlier, and then took a flat in Calla Campoamor. Their closest neighbours, with apartments in the same building, were Paul and Jane Bowles. The Bowleses' relationship had been the *liaison célèbre* of the arts world since the 1930s. They had married in 1938, each fully aware of the other's bisexuality, and after the 1940s their mutual affection had grown, as each had established same-sex relationships with others. Paul lived in his flat with a Moroccan artist, Ahmed Yacoubi, while Jane shared hers on the floor below with Sherifa, a domineering Berber market-woman. Paul and Jane often socialized, held parties together – sometimes with their respective partners, other times not – and while making no pretence to being anything other than what they were they seemed to embody the middle-aged middle-class marital ideal.

News of their new neighbours soon reached Paul and Jane. They called on Sillitoe and Ruth to introduce themselves, and quite soon the four of them became guilelessly at ease in each other's company. The Bowles had over twenty years acquired a Delphic status for those seeking an alternative lifestyle and had politely indulged scores of visitors, but their friendship with Sillitoe and Ruth was different. It would last until the deaths of the former, and each of the quartet treated the others as equals.

While Paul's and Sillitoe's backgrounds could hardly have been more dissimilar – Paul coming from a middle-class New York family – they shared a preoccupation with self-determination. Both recognized that some facts were unalterable but neither treated acceptance as submission, and in this regard Tangier held a special attraction for them. It had until the end of the 1950s been an International Zone – incorporating a mosaic of tribal and religious traditions but in other respects chaotic, verging on the anarchic. Hence its allure for those whose taste for the unorthodox included their personal inclinations and habits along with their opinions on art. Paul saw Tangier, and to a lesser extent Morocco, as a crossroads of affinities, affiliations and beliefs which offered fascination without obligation. Sillitoe echoed his enthusiasm in a letter to Brian written within two weeks of his arrival.

> When it was international it was a great centre of smuggling . . . There is no such thing as the vote. The King [of Morocco] rules, or tries to – backed by the fanatics of the Moslem religion, which is one of the most backward in the world. All the Moslem women wear veils still! except for the Riff tribes . . . But [also] there are Spaniards, Italians, Jews, French, English etc . . . [AS to BS, 1 December 1960]

Paul and Sillitoe corresponded until the former's death in 1999, and a sense of their shared fascination with Tangier can be discerned in Paul's observations on Orwell's visit.

> He seemed to take it very hard that there was so little wildlife around, and put it down to widespread hunger. Clearly it didn't occur to him that Moroccans *like* to hunt, and prefer the flavour of game to that of slaughtered domestic animals ... His reactions to Morocco were almost indistinguishable from those of any liberal-minded tourist. [Paul Bowles to AS, 11 May 1975, Indiana Archive]

The subtext is clear enough: Western liberalism is fine until it blinds one to the primitive autonomy of those who elect to live beyond its ministrations, and it goes without saying that Paul knows that Sillitoe will empathize with this.

Sillitoe and Ruth's visit in 1960–61 would be for only four months, long enough to decide on whether the region appealed to them as a more permanent base. It did, but for the time being Sillitoe needed to return to London to make arrangements with his agent, publisher, accountant and solicitor for the efficient management of his interests during his time abroad. His first two books were now in paperback with Pan and at the end of 1961 the sales for the preceding year stood at 95,530 for *Saturday Night and Sunday Morning* and 73,341 for *The Loneliness of the Long Distance Runner*; as Jeffrey Simmons proudly states, the former would in two years become 'Pan's first one million bestseller'. Sillitoe's royalties for paperbacks alone for the third quarter of 1961 totalled £1,330. In comparison with our culture of inflated advances the amount seems derisory (indeed his 7 per cent royalties contract on paperback sales was iniquitous given that all Pan had to do was reprint and rely upon the books' self-generated tide of acclaim for promotion). But add to this his hardback royalties, small payments for articles and advances on the film rights, and the equivalent today would be around £70,000, which for a professional writer with no other source of income is an impressive token of success. At the end of 1959 Sillitoe had been advised by his accountants, Messrs Westbury, Schotness and Co. of High Holborn, that given his sudden ascent from near penury his tax returns would be closely scrutinized and he should make pre-emptive plans. Consequently on 19 September the First Meeting of Directors of Alan Sillitoe Ltd had taken place at the Old Cottage, Whitwell, Hertfordshire. The minutes record that 'Mr A. Sillitoe was appointed Chairman of the Meeting and he took the Chair', which caused wry amusement among the new board given that its only member, and only other person present, was the new Secretary of the Company, one R. Fainlight.

Sillitoe has never treated his financial matters with anything other than modest candour. He is aware that some, then and now, would discern a conflict of interest between his sudden emergence as an astute financial steward and his generally left-wing commitments. But, as he states, the former was simply a means to an end. He was determined that his family would have more security than had been available to him and virtually everyone he had known; moreover he and Ruth had married in November 1959 and planned to have children. As for his politics, these were less an ideological package than an unsteady blend of private impulses and media-generated, largely false public profiles. Sillitoe had written that the gutter press had prompted his departure for Tangier in 1960, but this tells only half of the story. He was particularly enraged by an article in the *Daily Express*, so much so that he had asked his solicitor Maurice Spector about threatening the paper with an action for libel with a view to forcing them into a formal retraction of alleged extracts from an interview that formed the bulk of the article. He had been quoted as stating that he had been 'a member of the Communist Party' and that all of his family had been communists. Spector requested that the *Express* produce the notes taken by Miss Lewis, who had interviewed Sillitoe on 18 November, and for several months an exchange between Sillitoe, Spector and the newspaper's lawyers took place regarding the question of whether Lewis's largely shambolic notes were an accurate account of Sillitoe's statement and the extent to which these had been further rewritten for the printed article.

Sillitoe's anger was by equal degrees impulsive and pragmatic. He had never joined any political party – he never would, an index of his compulsive loathing for the power of institutions – yet he had, when asked, made it clear that his sympathies were left-leaning and he had campaigned openly for the Labour candidate in Hitchin. Choices had to be made, and common sense indicated that Labour was the obvious option for the general good of the majority.

During 1960 Sillitoe and Ruth had got to know Ella Winter and the script writer Donald Ogden Stewart who had been obliged to abandon their film careers in Hollywood and leave the USA for London after refusing to testify at the McCarthy hearings of the late 1940s. Winter and Stewart held Sunday afternoon tea parties which Sillitoe and Ruth attended regularly, along with Ken Tynan, Sally Belfrage, Elaine Dundy, Christopher Logue, Clancy Segal, Michael Hastings and Arnold Wesker. These were, as one might expect, hives of outspoken radicalism and dissent, but amid this the hosts bore cautionary witness to the consequences of publicizing one's affiliations, particularly if these inferred an attachment to the Eastern Bloc. Ruth was half American, some of her family still lived there and though the neurotic frenzy of the McCarthy witch-hunts seemed to belong in the past there was in the USA a reluctance to welcome visitors openly sympathetic to communism. Aside from the possibility that Sillitoe himself might never be allowed entry – and he was determined that now he had the resources he would travel – Ruth, as his wife, might also be denied access to the country of her birth. Even the *Express*, then the most right-wing popular British newspaper, acknowledged that a problem existed: 'the editor [is] prepared', wrote Spector, 'as far as he was able, apart from repudiating the story, to assist you in avoiding difficulties which might arise in connection with entry into the USA' (Spector to AS, 6 December 1960). Sillitoe went so far as to ask Spector to seek the advice of a barrister, who reported that a decision would be based on whose account of the original interview was deemed more accurate and that, given the *Express*'s resources, a civil action could be suicidally expensive. The letter in which Spector refers to 'our conversation . . . when you informed me that you did not propose to pursue this matter any further' (the 'matter' centring upon Sillitoe's alleged commitment to communism) concludes with the solicitor's confirmation that Sillitoe's company was now officially filed at the Companies Registry under the new title of 'Alan Sillitoe (Investments) Ltd'. Eventually, in 1977, it would be registered in Zurich.

One begins to understand why Sillitoe had become so infuriated by the press speculation on whether Arthur Seaton's creator and, they suggested, *alter ego*, would now be buying his mother a fur coat. The implication was that to be both working class and a financially successful author was in some way a vulgar anomaly, even dishonest. Sillitoe did not dignify the issue by addressing it in public, but privately he was in full command of those aspects of his life that seemed, for others, discordant. There is a fascinating letter to Brian written during his first visit to Tangier in which the various strata of Alan Sillitoe are laid side by side. He judges a recent strike in Belgium to be 'fairly successful, because it may cause the economy to be reorganised a bit more on socialist lines. The TUC helped, which I was glad to see.' At home, 'I hear Raleigh is on short time. How long can the people in England go on voting time after time for the Tories? . . . It's crazy.' As for his literary career, 'As far as I know the paperback of "Saturday Night" has sold a million.' The letter concludes:

> 'The Rats' has had bad reviews nearly everywhere: nobody likes the book at all – which doesn't surprise me much. This will ensure though that not many copies will be sold. A book can be stamped on unofficially in England just as it can be officially in Russia if it doesn't go with the party line. But one can't complain about this, because every society has to try and protect itself, no matter how rotten. [AS to BS, 1 February 1961]

He treats the consequences of the poor reception of *The Rats* with sanguine resignation, indicating that he foresaw them. His comparison of the reflexive self-protective mechanisms of liberal democracy with the authoritarian censorship in the Soviet Union might seem calculatedly blind, but he was under no illusions about which was more endurable: in one you lost money while the other might deprive you of your freedom.

Sillitoe and Ruth planned to return to Tangier as soon as they had settled practical matters in London: among other things they had taken out a lease on a four-roomed flat at 24 Pembridge Crescent, W11, which they intended to use as their permanent London base, lending it out to family and friends during their periods overseas. Autumn 1961 seemed their likeliest time of departure, but Ruth became pregnant in late summer. She had already suffered two miscarriages and both knew that a familiar environment and reliable health service were necessities. David was born on 30 March 1962, and in May the three of them set off for Morocco in Sillitoe's new Austin A40. In July he provided Brian with a report of their chaotic, often hair-raising journey. Sillitoe, it should be noted, had taken and failed his driving test on three occasions but from his experience of Europe the police did not give a high priority to checking a driver's status in his home country. The clutch discs wore out halfway through Spain.

> We were on a mountain road when it happened, with a sheer drop over to the right of a few hundred feet. I was just changing gear into second to take the slope, when it wouldn't go at all. So the car started to slide back and, being in Spain, I was driving on the right side of the road. I just managed to get the footbrake and handbrake on; otherwise it would have been curtains, for the three of us.
>
> So we got the car repaired. The mechanic in the nearest village hadn't got the Austin spare part, of course, so he had to make one on the lathe. Anyway, this lasted us the last 300 miles to Tangier . . . [AS to BS, 20 July 1962]

The episode would provide the skeleton for one of his best short stories, 'Guzman Go Home' – the real mechanic, though not an ex-Nazi, was just as apologetically versatile as the one in the story – and the jaunty reference to 'curtains for the three of us' would register, hauntingly, in years to come when Sillitoe and Ruth travelled more frequently with young David by air: the rule would be that when the family flew abroad one parent would always take a different flight, earlier or later.

During their childhoods Brian and Michael had treated Sillitoe with the affectionate respect normally accorded to an uncle, even a parent, and some of this endured into adulthood. Sillitoe had happily agreed to speak on behalf of his youngest brother at a 1960 hearing which would assess Michael's claim as a conscientious objector to exemption from National

Service; he did this despite his unease at exploiting his new status as a public figure and his temperamental misgivings regarding pacifism. With Brian, however, a subtle change occurred when both men were in their twenties. Even during Sillitoe's long period of near oblivion in France and Spain Brian never questioned his commitment to what many in Nottingham saw as a hopeless ambition. In this regard Sillitoe's letters to Brian, particularly during the years after his first literary successes, are revealing. He is writing to a version of himself, the one who did not become addicted to reading books and in due course writing them; but there is never a hint that he perceives Brian's intelligence and intellectual acumen as different from his own; differently engaged and informed, perhaps, but certainly no better or worse. Often Brian becomes Sillitoe's conscience; not his confessor or confidant – neither men kept secrets from others close to them – rather an extension of the life he was living into one he might have lived. Small clues emerge; some that Brian would intuit as tokens of their special friendship, others less so. In the letter about the journey to Tangier, for example, Sillitoe writes of driving their 'jalopy . . . out from London loaded with luggage and baby Nimrod'. This was David but the nickname was the one Burton had, twenty-five years earlier, conferred on Sillitoe. It was a strange family legend with no real explanation but Sillitoe and Brian were its curators and the two-month-old baby its newest sharer. In Sillitoe's fourth novel, *Key to the Door*, published nearly twelve months earlier, Merton (Burton) names the young Brian Nimrod and Sillitoe's use of the name in the letter indicates his guileless acceptance of his brother into the world where private existence and imagination coexist. At the conclusion of the same letter he writes of a meeting of the National Socialists – a hangover from Mosley's Blackshirts and forerunner of the National Front and BNP: 'I hear that the meeting . . . got broken up the other week in Trafalgar Square. If I'd been in London I'd have been in there too. I believe in freedom of speech but not that sort' (AS to BS, 20 July 1962). This of course recalls Colin Smith's attack on the fascists in 'A Man's Life' and it reflects another aspect of the friendship between Sillitoe and Brian. The former remained unaffiliated politically, at least in the sense that he refused to actually join a party or protest group, yet his temperament drew him continually towards radicalism in its various manifestations. Brian shared his inclinations, but for him idealism and pragmatism were largely indistinguishable; the strength of the union in the factory where he worked – at this point he was employed by an engineering company in Dawley, Shropshire – would affect his weekly income and future prospects for a stable family life. He and his wife Yvonne would have a baby girl less than a year after the birth of David.

On 10 December 1961 Sillitoe wrote to Brian of the anti-nuclear demonstrations that had recently taken place in various parts of England.

I didn't go . . . because I didn't think there would be much point in it. It is impossible to get into one of those airbases, without violence. The Committee of One Hundred is opposed to violence, which means that the most they go to is sitting down on the ground when confronted by a line of police. Unless you can get the numbers enough to push out of the way it is impossible to do anything. And if the numbers can't be got then the best tactic would be to form small commando groups armed with wire-cutters to get in during darkness. The best thing of all would be to get the workers to move on a base, then no power could stop them swarming all over it. But that, at the moment, if not for ever, is impossible, as you must know. What do the people in Dawley and at your factory think of the demonstrations? Not that yesterday's sit-downs were a failure, because 800 were arrested out of 6,000 and that is good. But to get rid of atomic arms and foreign bases means no less than a complete revolution, and that can't be done unless the whole of the working people get into action. Such a move against the bases has somehow got to be linked with industrial unrest – a wave of strikes, or even a general strike in winter may set people moving in that direction, especially if the Communist Party get their agitators going, and if the Committee of 100 also join in. This is a lot of 'ifs' though – but the penny could flip in a very short time, or it could never flip. [AS to BS, 10 December 1961]

The competing factions that made up Sillitoe's political outlook are busily at odds in this letter. Within the neutral reportage one can discern a suspicion on his part that the anti-nuclear protests are a conscience-salving, ineffectual gesture by the left-leaning middle classes. In *Life Without Armour* he writes that 'My opinion was different from those who wore sackcloth and ashes over the use of the atomic bomb against Japan in August 1945' (p. 263). In the letter he implies that the 'sackcloth and ashes' contingent are political dilettantes. The only way that the government and the police can be caused to concede anything is by mass direct action; 'commando groups' using wire-cutters, 'industrial unrest', 'revolution'. One suspects, however, that he is committed more to the act of rebellion than its apparent objective, unilateral nuclear disarmament. Similarly his suggestion that the Communist Party would have to take the lead, with the Committee of 100 as a coat-trailing rearguard, was not a disclosure of political affiliation. The former would, he suggests, simply be more ruthless and proactive than the predominantly pacifist assembly of writers, artists and intellectuals that made up the Committee. Brian believed the Communist Party offered ordinary working people, like himself, a more straightforward programme for political change than Labour, which seemed to differ from the Tories largely in terms of nostalgia and charitable condescension. In their correspondence during this period Sillitoe sympathized, to the extent that he offered his brother advice

Portrait of Alan Sillitoe in 1968 wearing his signature collarless cotton shirt that was modelled on a nineteenth-century Majorcan style; by Horst Tappe (Camera Press)

Sillitoe and his sister Peggy – 'Me with a mouth organ that Peggy had given me to keep me quiet'

Sillitoe, aged seven or eight, with comments by his sister Peggy

Sillitoe's parents, Christopher and Sabina, Kent, 1950

Grandmother, Mary Ann Tokins, 1889

Grandad Burton (1866–1946)

Sillitoe in uniform, 1947, with
a wireless operator's badge

Sillitoe in the Butterworth
radio hut, Malaya, 1947

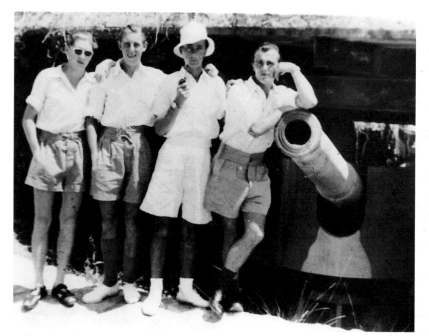

Sillitoe (with pipe), Fort Auchay, Penang, Malaya, September 1947

MALLORCA — Vista general de Sóller

MARCH 24th.

DEAR DAD,

HOW ARE YOU?
ALL RIGHT, I HOPE.
I THINK OF YOU
A LOT, SO BE
HAPPY.

YOUR LOVING
SON,
ALAN.

MR. CHRISTOPHER
SILLITOE
5 BEACONSFIELD
TERR,
SALISBURY ST
RADFORD, NOTTINGHAM
INGLATERRA.

Sillitoe's postcard to his father from Majorca, 1953

Ruth Fainlight and Sillitoe, Majorca, 1954

Ruth Fainlight (centre) and Sillitoe (right) with an unknown companion,
Majorca, 1954

Sillitoe, Hertfordshire, 1959

From left: Sillitoe, Harry Saltzman and Ruth Fainlight on the set of
Saturday Night and Sunday Morning, 1960

From left: Brian Sillitoe (the real Arthur Seaton?), Norman Rossington, Albert Finney, Michael Sillitoe and an unknown figure at the back on the set of *Saturday Night and Sunday Morning*, 1960

From left: Norman Rossington, Sillitoe's mother Sabina and Shirley Ann Field on the set of *Saturday Night and Sunday Morning*, 1960

Right: The Pan paperback edition of *Saturday Night and Sunday Morning*, regularly reprinted during 1960, the year of its publication

Centre: Sillitoe, Ruth Fainlight and David, Tangier, 1962

Bottom: Sillitoe and film director Karel Reisz, Pembridge Crescent, London, 1963

Sillitoe at Lake Baikal, Siberia, in 1963

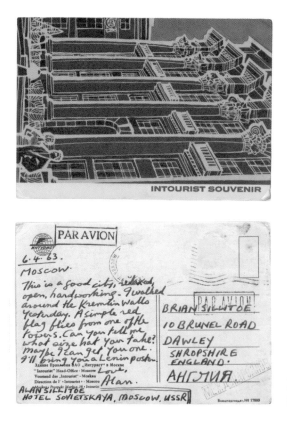

INTOURIST SOUVENIR

PAR AVION

6.4.63.
MOSCOW.

This is a good city, relaxed,
open, hardworking. I walked
around the Kremlin walls
yesterday. A simple red
flag flies from one of the
towers. Can you tell me
what size hat you take?
Maybe I can get you one.
I'll bring you a Lenin poster.
Love,
Alan.

ALAN SILLITOE
HOTEL SOVIETSKAYA, MOSCOW, USSR.

BRIAN SILLITOE
10 BRUNEL ROAD
DAWLEY
SHROPSHIRE
ENGLAND.
АНГЛИЯ.

Postcard to Brian Sillitoe
from Moscow, 1963

George Andjaparidze, Sillitoe's companion
on the road in the Soviet Union, June 1967

Outside the Moscow Writers' Club, 1967; Sillitoe is in the middle

Sillitoe at Wittersham, Kent, in the early 1970s, with David (front), Sue (left) and a neighbour's daughter

Sillitoe with producer Graham Benson at Ollerton Colliery, Nottinghamshire, 1976, the set for the BBC television adaptation of the short story 'Pit Strike'

Yehuda Amichai, Ruth Fainlight and Sillitoe, Israel, 1977

With Kingsley Amis at the Imperial War Museum, London, 1987

Left: A pause during a return visit with Ronald Schlachter in 1988 to the Malayan jungle, where Sillitoe would prepare notes for *Lost Loves*

Below: Sillitoe with Bernard 'Bunny' Sindall in France, October 1990

Portrait by David Sillitoe, 2000

my generation

SUNDAYS from 4th JUNE at 8.00 pm
BBC 2

Publicity card for a BBC 2 television series, broadcast in 2000 and presented
by Joan Bakewell, looking at various cultural figures – including Jonathan
Miller, Tariq Ali, Beryl Bainbridge and George Melly – who helped shape the
nation's destiny in post-war Britain. Sillitoe is bottom right.

Sillitoe in his London study with pipe
and *Sillitoe* by Bernard 'Bunny' Sindall

both on the party itself – Sillitoe knew some of the more active senior figures in London – and on what he should read. Gorky, he advised, would be far more engaging and instructive than Marx.

Had the correspondence been made available to a McCarthy-style committee, evidence would have been abundant for a profile of Sillitoe as a pro-Soviet activist.

> I thought last week that the balloon was going to go up over Cuba, and that we'd never meet again – not in this world anyway, and there isn't any other. I felt depressed, and full of rage at Kennedy and the Americans being just ready to start a war – and take the whole world with them. If I had been in London I would have been demonstrating at the American Embassy . . . At least Khrushchev has got the Americans to lay off Cuba, which was really all that he wanted. [AS to BS, 29 October 1962, from Tangier]

I ask him today, do the letters bear witness to his support at the time for Soviet Bloc communism? 'No. Like Brian I was disenchanted with Labour but I had no illusions about the claims of communism to be a remedy for the ills and injustices of the human condition. Life is too complicated for that. I admit, though, that as a threat to the smugness of the establishment, there were attractions.'

In the early 1960s Sillitoe formed a friendship with Helder Macedo and his wife Suzette that would endure to this day. Helder, scion of a distinguished Portuguese family, had, aged twenty-one, published a volume of poems which was unrestrained in its engagement with the country's shambolic authoritarian regime. He would eventually become the senior Professor of Portuguese at University College London, but when he and Sillitoe met he was an exile, mixing with similarly bohemian writers in London. He speaks now of Sillitoe as a figure at once diffident, enigmatic and mercurial.

'He was I suppose left wing but not in the conventional sense. He was critical of everything: the Soviet Union, Britain, the US . . . the list is endless. He has always had a streak of anarchy about him. He is a ferocious opponent of systems, systems of any kind . . . If he has an abiding principle it is that people should not be forced, coerced, even encouraged to conform . . . even if it is deemed to be for their own good. This is why he was ambivalent about socialism and communism. He loved the unorthodox spirit of both but he knew that they could quite easily become the orthodoxy. That, he hated.

'When I first got to know him in London in the early sixties we might be at parties with established, public figures – mostly from the arts, but sometimes politics. From them Alan would keep a cautionary distance. He did not provoke conflict but it was clearly his personal ordinance that he would never seek favour from the great and good. He was his own man, but at the same time he too had just entered the public spotlight and if younger writers asked him for advice or assistance he would be generous with his time. And he would do so modestly, privately. He genuinely wanted to help without seeming to be either condescending or superior.

'If he had a special affiliation it was with outsiders. That was how we first became friends. Our backgrounds were very different, but we were both, largely by choice, displaced.'

Arthur Seaton and Colin Smith had dominated his first two books, and the voice of 'Rats' resembled a combination of both who had invited himself to a literary soirée with trouble in mind. Brian Seaton of *Key to the Door* (1961) was a curious experiment, arguably the most authentically auto-biographical character in the history of fiction. Sillitoe here was not eschewing his obligations as a storyteller; quite the opposite. 'All truth is fiction, all fiction is truth' (*Raw Material*, p. 188). In *Key to the Door* he scrutinized this maxim and tested his capacities to verify it. He focused upon a life to which he uniquely had borne witness but recreated it from the outside, as if he were someone else.

Now, however, he sought a literary channel for the primitive impulses and tensions which fed his unfocused, often contradictory political beliefs. In the letters to Brian we can detect the genesis of a literary character, one who would take much longer to evolve than his previous creations. Throughout this period Brian's address in Shropshire was Dawley, and Frank Dawley would eventually emerge as the flawed idealist of *The Death of William Posters* (1965).

The delays in Dawley's genesis were due to two events that contributed significantly to his temperament and predispositions, the period spent in Tangier and Sillitoe's visit to the Soviet Union. Tamara Dragadza offers a fascinating account of the former. She was sixteen when Sillitoe and Ruth arrived with David for their extended stay; her mother and natural father were White Russian minor aristocrats and her Indian stepfather, with whom her mother had settled in Tangier, was a Cambridge-educated philosopher who held seminars on Saturdays for anyone inclined to attend. For most people her environment would seem ostentatiously bohemian but, as she reflects, it was not unlike that of most expatriates. 'Jane Bowles had become a sort of surrogate aunt to me. I spent a lot of time with her, and sometimes with Paul, and I remember her saying that "Oh there's this English couple coming over soon. Writers. I think you'll find them interesting." I would. Alan and Ruth rented a large house at the top of what the expatriates called Old Mountain. It, the house, dated from the nineteenth century and was equipped with balconies overlooking the rest of the town and offering views across the Straits to Gibraltar.

'Soon after Ruth and Alan arrived,' says Tamara, 'there was an influx of the new generation of eccentrics, mostly Americans. Gregory Corsa and Allen Ginsberg came – there had been others from what I suppose is called the Beat Generation in the fifties – and Burroughs had been there for four or five years.' Did Alan and Ruth get to know them, I ask? 'Oh yes, particularly after Harry Fainlight, Ruth's brother, came over to stay with them for a while. He already knew a few of the new American incomers and he made some introductions.' Despite Alan's companionable nature it is difficult to imagine him having much in common with Burroughs, Corso, Ginsberg et al. 'That's true, but young as I was it was immensely entertaining to witness their exchanges. Alan treated their ideas in a wry, sardonic way. They didn't notice he was doing this and his stance was the more effective for that. He made them sound pretentious.' Tamara avers that he didn't go so far as to satirize them but counterposed with their effusions his blunt candour seemed laudable.

'Apart from the younger expatriates Alan caused something of a stir with the established figures, well-connected bohemians from all over Europe and the States; some there by choice, others exiled or dispossessed. He was at the time very interested in Communist Russia and I remember that he would often infuriate my mother. He'd say that when he saw the red flag with its hammer and sickle or heard the "Internationale" his heart would jump. I don't honestly think he was being serious. There seemed to be more than a hint of self-caricature, but my mother never saw it.' Tamara has remained in contact with Sillitoe and Ruth, but her enduring memory is from Tangier. 'He was different from everyone else there, not because he outdid them by being more radical or idiosyncratic. The complete opposite. He had such a sense of self. His miserable childhood had provided him with something so solid that I almost envied him, and I think others there did also. He was grounded. The others in different ways were performers. I suppose the exceptions were the Bowleses. Despite their differences – Alan, Ruth and the Bowleses – they recognized in each other a shared respect for honesty.'

Tamara's comments on Sillitoe's aloof impatience with the expatriates and their affected nonconformity is echoed in his letters to Brian where one frequently comes upon disillusionment and a desire to find somewhere in North Africa that lives up to what he had expected of Tangier. 'During Christmas we went on a trip South, to Rabat, Casablanca, and Fez. Fez was wonderful, a dead European town (since they kicked the French out) and a vast Arab medina (walled city) of about 200,000. It is like Damascus, narrow crooked streets, covered with palm branches like in the Arabian Nights' (2 January 1961). 'This place is beginning to get me down though, and we are thinking of leaving . . . We've been thinking of going South with David to the Sahara Desert (or to an oasis on the edge of it)' (13 November 1962). Frank Dawley and his pregnant wife follow the same route that Sillitoe and Ruth had taken, first on their exploratory journey and next, with David, to their house in Tangier. Frank and Myra have no clear sense of a destination:

> 'I'd like to know where we're really going,' she said, 'I like travelling at the moment, and wouldn't mind if we never stopped, but where are we going right now?'
> Frank, as if tossing a coin, answers:
> 'We'll go to Tangier,' he said, his eyes fixed on row after row of orange trees flickering by, content again at the feel of a train under him. 'I've always wanted to go to Africa.' [p. 224]

But, like Sillitoe, he is disappointed at the smug, exclusive atmosphere of the place.

> Sitting on the harbour front was like being at the world's edge, and the only way he could move was on, across the world. To understand people, go to the desert, and do not come out until you understand yourself. [p. 232]

This echoes Sillitoe's comments to Brian, with the addition of some profound self-scrutiny, but Frank chooses a location more demanding than the desert. He leaves Myra in Tangier and joins a communist guerrilla group fighting the French in Algeria. One should not, however, see Sillitoe as here indulging an adventurist political fantasy or employing Frank as an inspiration for like-minded activists. Frank's embittered search for a cause triggers the story of *The Death of William Posters*, yet Sillitoe has him leave in its slipstream a suspicion that his idealism is misguided and fed partly by his ego. The novel ends without us knowing what the consequences of his act will be both in terms of his need to 'understand himself' and his relationship with Myra. Sillitoe has, however, left sufficient clues to indicate that when we encounter him again, and we will in *A Tree on Fire*, his revolutionary enthusiasms will have been compromised by raw experience.

Sillitoe too would make a journey after leaving Tangier, much less peremptory and hazardous than Frank's, but with comparable results. The dilemma they shared would be built into the two novels.

Tamara Dragadza: 'In Tangier Sillitoe's interest in Russia was based as much on pragmatism as ideology. He had received a preliminary enquiry from the Soviet Writers' Union, via London, asking if he'd accept an official invitation. Soon afterwards he started taking lessons in Russian from an elderly White Russian countess. I suspect he didn't provoke her quite as he had my mother.'

The formal invitation did indeed arrive when he was in Tangier but Sillitoe had been canvassed on the visit more discreetly in London before their departure for North Africa in May 1962. He and Ruth had been invited by the Soviet Ambassador to a reception at the embassy on 18 April, ostensibly to meet Mikhail Sholokhov. The Ambassador, Mr Soldatov, informed him during a private conversation that though the enquiry would come from the Moscow Writers' Union he was perceived by many others in the capital as unique among the current generation of Western novelists.

Alan, Ruth and David left Tangier by boat in late February 1963. The Austin A40 came too, and once back in England Sillitoe, still without a full licence, lent the car to Brian for the subsequent two months. They settled again in Pembridge Crescent and he made final arrangements for his Soviet visit; a visa from the embassy, details of his itinerary from the Writers' Union and flight bookings – he had asked for Aeroflot but BOAC proved more convenient. He left Heathrow for Moscow in April 1963.

Road to Volgograd (1964), his account of the visit, veers between candour, provocation and obfuscation. Often he appears to have become a willing spokesman for Soviet propaganda.

> Moscow is nearer the earth, and so are its people. The claws of God can no longer get at them: it feels strange to look over a city that has hardly any churches for people to worship God in. As a child I remember my grandmother regretting the fact that churches were being closed and turned into billiard halls. Here they are turned into museums, and I know she would have regretted this less.
>
> Without religion they are easy, casual, hardworking. The relaxed atmosphere in the city comes because they are striving for something in common, and not in competition with each other. The cut-throat flash of neon lights is absent . . . When I walk along the Kremlin walls my heart turns over at the sight of the red flag flying freely. [p. 16]

This is embarrassingly credulous, and when he witnesses the May Day parades in Moscow he seems seized by something close to idolatry:

> On, on, on the river of spring life. They've been going for less than an hour. Atoms for people, atoms for peace. Khrushchev and Castro are waving all the time, bear smiles that don't flag, arms that don't ache, unforced grins and smiles. [p. 165]

He would comment in a letter to Brian that 'the reviewers hate it, which is to be expected since I didn't follow the party line' (July 1964). One suspects that his refusal to do so – and by party line he means that then all but the most hard-line left-wing thinkers had conceded that the post-Stalin Soviet Union was still a totalitarian state – was founded as much upon a wish to infuriate everyone from the Tory establishment to the liberal middle classes as it was on political commitment.

In the opening pages he digresses upon his journey by liner from Tangier to London. The ship had come from Australia and 'Having a baby we decided to travel first class which was a pity because it turned out to be the deadest part of the ship' (p. 10). At dinner the colonial civil servants, directors and lawyers donned evening dress and grimaced at Sillitoe, who was more casually attired, and on the way back to his cabin after a night out with the beer-drinking Australians in third class he was stopped by a steward who informed him, 'This is first class here.' His monosyllabic reply contained neither 'I' nor 'know'.

In the parts of the book which deal with Russia itself there are curious, unexplained shifts from fascinated enthusiasm to disclosures which he does not attempt to deny or feel it necessary, or perhaps feel himself able, to excuse.

At a reading in Volgograd he asks his hosts why there seemed so much hostility to abstract art and avant-garde writing in the Soviet Union. Joyce and William Burroughs, he stated, were largely ignored in the West by the broader reading public but they enjoyed favour with a smaller clique, mostly of writers and academics, and were treated as no more than harmless egotists. It seemed, he argued, unnecessary to take an official line against artists who, as had been proved in the West, had a negligible effect upon mass culture.

> Were there I wanted to know any such writers in the Soviet Union?
>   Lednev smiled broadly. 'No,' he said, 'but if there were, they'd be in the lunatic asylum.' [p. 54]

Pointedly, Sillitoe leaves it up to the reader to decide whether this is a flippant critique of Modernism or a guarded reference to the grim consequences of promoting decadent art. There is also a puzzling sub-plot involving the poet Yevtushenko whom Sillitoe attempts to meet on several occasions, but his phone always rings out, or, as a helpful intermediary explains, he is unable to make their appointment 'due to unforeseen circumstances'. Eventually during his elated account of May Day he concedes what he had known all along. 'Yevtushenko is in the doghouse, so he won't be here' (p. 165).

The most fascinating, unsettling passage in the book is its conclusion, where he spends the evening of May Day at the flat of 'friends'. One of them, 'a thin-faced beautiful woman of about forty', tells him, almost distractedly, of how she had spent eight years in a prison camp. One morning police and security officials had arrived at her factory and arrested her and 250 other women who had just arrived for work. After perfunctory trials all were sentenced, for treason, to long periods in the camps. All just happened to be Jewish.

> Then, some time after Stalin died, she was allowed back in Moscow.
> There was no ill treatment, she said. Hardship, of course, but that existed in the rest of the Soviet Union. Perhaps the most difficult thing was having to live with three thousand other women. She seemed fragile and wistful, yet there was a strength in her face that belied this. Nevertheless I wanted some human reaction of rage and bitterness, a craving for revenge at having been put away eight years for nothing. But no. 'That's life,' she said. [p. 167]

She goes on to comment on how 'lucky' he'd been to attend the parades; she too hoped soon to be able to get to Red Square for the big day.

The book is supposed to be a transparent documentary report, but gradually, and at the end suddenly, the suspicion forms that Sillitoe has become a narrator as beguilingly untrustworthy as Dickens's Pip. Was his inflated enthusiasm his hedge against a sub-current of doubt that he does not allow to register personally but which becomes evident to the reader? Stories abound, particularly from the 1950s and 1960s, of individuals, predominantly middle-class intellectuals, for whom the selfless allure of the left became raddled by cynicism and empirical evidence. Most – Kingsley Amis, Paul Johnson and John Osborne, for example – treated their old affiliations as immature conceits and were unreserved in their contempt for those of the same generation who had not similarly matured. Sillitoe was different. In *Road to Volgograd*, at least in the published version, he made use of his novelist's skills to create a mosaic of interpretive dilemmas. His intemperate celebrations of how the communists had defeated the Nazis and heroically rebuilt a country from one more devastated than any other in the Second World War were designed to infuriate the class-based establishment. For those whose response would be less impulsive he, brilliantly, raised questions. The final one, of whether the woman from the camps impressed him with her resolution or horrified him, remains unanswered.

Or it would were it not for the unpublished diaries and notebooks. His diary, which is filed in Indiana with the first draft of *Road to Volgograd*, provides a fascinating subtext to the book, disclosing that his apparent commitment to this socialist nirvana was actually rooted in unillusioned rage and often attended by a knowledge of the regime's repressive underpinnings. Some of this material would be refashioned for the book, but more fascinating are the passages in which a personal struggle becomes evident between two immensely powerful impulses. There is a feeling of affinity prompted by the breathtaking achievements of ordinary people, much like the ones he had grown up with, who are now, apparently, in command of their collective destiny. Equally strong and nagging is his knowledge that the one thing which he personally values more than anything else, the inalienable right of the individual to be and do what he wishes, has been forcibly removed.

Between each paragraph of the original diary written in Moscow over the three nights before May Day he records the sounds outside his hotel window. 'The tanks are still moving past', 'the sound of the tanks is endless', 'the sound of the tanks is fading away', 'the tanks can still be heard riding away'. His persistent references to them testify to their emotive effect, and eventually he tries to make sense of what he is feeling.

> Robert's mother [a friend in Leningrad] had six brothers. All went to war, and only one came back. This is four million times multiplied in the Soviet Union. Red tanks went from Stalingrad to Berlin. Every year in Red Square tanks go through to remind people of that fact. Red tanks saved the world. [Unnumbered page of diary, 27 April 1963, Indiana Archive]

In the book Sillitoe rewrites this passage as the words of Robert himself. 'Red tanks saved the civilized world, a fact which no one can deny, and which many like to forget – or would like to, he added' (p. 147). But in truth the dialogue took place in Sillitoe's head, alone with his diary, and his struggle to persuade himself, indoctrinate himself even, is evident. His exhortatory prose seems an attempt to smother doubts, extinguish a suspicion that the tanks, the massive exhibition of strength, might be as much a reminder of the authoritarian power of the state as a celebration of a past history.

To follow him through the diary is like witnessing a man desperately searching for assurances that might overrule perplexity. God, for example:

> Death is blackness, the finish, which is what I have in common with the Soviet masses here in Leningrad – the capital of proletarian Europe. The communist man who has discovered how to live without God – that is an advance that those who still live with God cannot imagine.
>
> A communist can look into the blue sky without thinking of God. As the Siberian spaces are something to be crossed, so the blue sky (limitless though it might be) is something to be navigated and explored. [Unnumbered, undated page of notebook, Indiana Archive]

The logic is persuasive, all the more so because Sillitoe builds into it an opportunity for release from the oppressive anti-individualism of the still

God-fearing West. Look hard enough, he seems to be telling himself, and nuggets of freedom and opportunity will be found in the Soviet system. But, as with all conspicuously overwrought treatises, collapse can only be postponed. On a sheet torn from the notebook binder we find the following:

> I remember the man in Moscow at midnight on Gorki St, blind drunk sitting down and pressing himself into the wall of the building. He wore a long raincoat and fur hat, was tall and lean-faced, eyes looking ahead and seeing nothing. He was sitting with his legs stretched out straight, as if it wasn't any use lying down flat because he would be pulled on his feet or to this sitting position (again) after hardly any sleeping flat-out bliss. Yet he wanted to lie down, he didn't want to get up. People, however, were reasoning with him; trying to pull him upright.
>
> 'Leave me be,' he cried. 'Leave me alone,' he cried. 'Leave me alone.' And by the tone of his voice you knew he really wanted to be alone, but he couldn't be, that he knew also that he had no right to be.

The empathy of the passage seems like a release from the pressured mood of the rest of the notebook, and it recalls the moment in *Saturday Night and Sunday Morning* when Arthur, without reason or logic, defends the man who has smashed the undertaker's window. We are reminded also of family legends that Sillitoe valued so much: his two cousins, and on another occasion the complete stranger, deserters all, taken in by his mother with no questions asked. What mattered was keeping them out of the hands of an authoritarian system which would blindly enforce rules and extinguish the most valuable thing available to all human beings, choice, even if this meant only the right to lie down drunk in the street.

At the time Sillitoe kept his misgivings from his hosts, and the impression left among the cultural *apparatchiks* who supervised the visit and their political mentors was that he was their best catch since H.G. Wells and George Bernard Shaw had reported back on the Soviet achievements of the 1930s. In November 1963 he received an invitation from the Writers' Union of Prague to visit Czechoslovakia the following year, which he did and returned there in 1966. Budapest followed suit in 1965, as did Bucharest in 1966 and Moscow again in 1967. None of his hosts indicated that their enquiry had been prompted by anything other than interest, but Sillitoe knew that insidious calculation was abroad, and began to make his own heretical plans.

EIGHTEEN

Imagine if, say, some time in the late 1940s Evelyn Waugh had conceded that God was man's invention and the Roman Catholic Church a dangerous blend of autocracy and ritual. It is an unlikely hypothesis because Waugh was one of those figures for whom strength of belief buttressed their sense of superiority, and by the same token even if he had encountered personal doubt he would almost certainly have foreclosed such an option for his feckless readers.

For Sillitoe such matters were not so straightforward. Ideas on what sort of person Frank Dawley would eventually become had begun to form before his 1963 visit to the USSR. There are, for example, parallels between Dawley's realization that his beliefs are beginning to disintegrate and the mix of frustration and uncertainty disclosed by Sillitoe in the letters to Brian. When Sillitoe prepared *Road to Volgograd* from notes made during the journey it was a credit to him that he allowed into the draft for W.H. Allen at least a trace of the unsettling, implicitly totalitarian aspects of communism in action. Yet at the same time he offered them to the reader as moral conundrums; he did not explicitly condemn them. Instead the honest disclosure of his uncertainties remained in the unpublished notebooks. He began to revise the early, sprawling draft of *The Death of William Posters* almost immediately after completing *Road to Volgograd*, and many of the 170 or so typescript pages that were eventually cut contain portraits of Dawley in a state of equivocation. He had set out with Myra for Tangier with the apparent assumption that the frontier-style image of the place would lend some edge to his radical posturing. But once there the questions of how exactly he might contribute to an actual revolution and what its eventual benefits to mankind might be still seem like hypotheses swamped in drifting ideology. He has dragged himself physically away from the circumstances that had suffocated his idealism but he still feels politically ineffectual.

Sillitoe's visit to the USSR was comparable with Dawley's political odyssey to North Africa: both wanted to take ideas and frustrations that had matured in the claustrophobic environment of Britain to places where political change was a dynamic, tangible phenomenon. For Sillitoe the consequences were considerable; he began to feel foolish, naïve and hypocritical. The vast achievements of post-war rebuilding were, as he was continually being reminded by his guides, providing food, clothes and decent housing for a population which seventeen years earlier had been living in the remains of a battlefield, but what did this have to do with Britain in the early 1960s?

Notably in *Road to Volgograd* he offers unstinting praise of the monumental potency of the Soviet economy without ever once suggesting how something comparable might be implemented or even made relevant in the West. In the notes for the book he dutifully records the output of engineering works and collective farms, filling page after page with statistics on how many people are employed, the increase in output over the past five years, the average wage in 1962, and more of the same. His lack of comment speaks volumes. He was being bombarded with information by the guides at each magnificently presented unit he visited, and eventually he began to sense that these seamless accounts of efficiency were, even if they were accurate, disclosures as much of soullessness as abundance. After noting the impressive spectacle of a state piggery ('employing 840 people, kitchen has 3 floors and is mechanised. Steam boiled . . . in 1962 produced 3,600,000 kilos of meat') he allows himself a moment of private reflection: 'A far cry from my grandfather's sty.' Though he would never allow sentiment to obscure the harsh actuality of Burton's life he knew that given the option his grandfather would have favoured the sty.

Sillitoe had written to Brian five months before leaving for Moscow: 'I still haven't got a title for the new novel yet. I still really don't know how it is going to go on, nor what the ending will be, but I just keep writing, and I think the end will grow naturally out of the story' (29 October 1962). Significantly the end was postponed until after the completion of *Road to Volgograd*. Eventually Sillitoe went for an impetuous solution, and reduced most of the 170 directionless pages to a brief concluding chapter in which Dawley and fellow revolutionary, the American, Shelley, become combatants for the Algerian FLN. At the very end Shelley, once the more adventurous and capricious of the two, argues for pragmatism, a retreat from the overwhelmingly superior French forces. Dawley turns the Bren gun towards him and says they will fight on.

The attraction of the desert had been a running theme in Sillitoe's letters to Brian on life in Tangier. Throughout he had implied that the city disappointed him and that something more primitive might be found further south. Despite imagining himself with Ruth and David living alongside the nomadic tribes of the region – which he perceived as perhaps the last mid-twentieth-century cultures for which freedom was a state of mind rather than an abstraction – he took this ambition no further than occasional overnight excursions.

The concluding passage of the novel presents Frank in a more pointedly solipsistic manner than at any time previously. He leaves us with the impression that his personal odyssey has finally been stripped of any claims to political legitimacy, that it was all in truth about Frank, particularly his notion of an all-inclusive political philosophy. The conclusion is not quite autobiographical – Sillitoe himself still had a great many dilemmas of belief and affiliation to confront, let alone settle in the peremptory manner of Frank – but the creation and mutation of Frank provided something of an outlet for his author's ongoing catalogue of uncertainties.

In some parts of the unpublished notes for *Road to Volgograd* Sillitoe abandons the cohering thread of a diary format and instead jots down lists of unresolved apophthegms and conundrums. Beneath their apparent shapelessness one detects anomalies that had taxed Sillitoe since his teens. His preoccupations concerning Nazism and the baffling resilience of the English class system make regular entrances.

> Revolutions are bad for literature. The 40 years following the French Revolution are barren. (?) Inequality and injustice, on the other hand, make great writers. Here, many who write are generously rewarded while for others the telephone rings out. [Unnumbered page of notebook, Indiana Archive]

The subtext here was obviously Yevtushenko. Perhaps Sillitoe thought he might briefly allay his personal unease, even guilty sense of complicity, by filing this particular case under the broader category of historical inevitability.

> Communism is a collective ideal, in which every one is entitled to share in order to make the ideal into reality.

This seems a commendably precise account of a social arrangement to which only the obscenely rich could object. But he adds an intriguing coda:

> There is nothing comparable in the West.

Does he mean by this simply that in the West no political system resembles that of the Soviet Union – a naïve and obvious point – or that there is something about the West that renders the Soviet Union inappropriate? Tony, the thieving narrator of 'A Ragman's Daughter' (1963), had pondered a similar paradox.

> What I'd like, believe it or not, is to live in a country where I didn't like thieving and where I didn't want to thieve, a place where everybody felt the same way because they all had only the same as everybody else – even if it wasn't much. Jail is a place like this, though it's not the one I'd find agreeable because you aren't free there. The place that that fills my mind would be the same, but being free as well they wouldn't want to nick what bit each had got. I don't know what sort of system that would be called. [*New and Collected Stories*, p. 131]

Tony is confused, but contentedly so. The fact that his personal perception of freedom, involving all manner of antisocial activities, is incompatible with his vision of a fair society is not, as it would be for a political scientist, an anomaly. One senses that his creator envies his capacity to step outside the confining logic of ideology and reason, and one is reminded again of Sillitoe's painfully poignant account of the drunk in Gorki Street, begging to be allowed to do as he wishes irrespective of his duty to a collective ideal.

> The Russians are said to have defeated the Germans by superior courage. This is only partly true. They also beat the Nazis by superior know-how, improvisation, versatility. Communist organisation triumphed over the unreal inhuman blitzkrieg drive of the Germans.

This is taken from a lengthy passage in which Sillitoe again attempts to marshal conspicuously incompatible facts into something close to a formula. The question that attends his account of how the Russians defeated the Nazis is inferred but never quite made explicit. Did the system they had created make them better people, and therefore better able to overcome the most efficient blend of authoritarianism and capitalism to date? Several paragraphs later Sillitoe makes what is close to a confession:

> Stalin wasn't mentioned once in the documentary film [about the Battle of Stalingrad]. He haunts the place that once bore his name. His memory casts a shadow across the whole country and the people he led to victory fear him still. [Indiana Archive]

Sillitoe's first visit to the Soviet Union was so important for him as an individual and for his development as a writer because hypothesis and speculation were being assaulted by fact and observation. There were things he could no longer deny and many more that he could as yet hope to resolve. But he had, like Frank at the end of *The Death of William Posters*, pitched himself forward into circumstances from which he could not expect to return unchanged.

Frank was at this point becoming like Coleridge's albatross. Sillitoe couldn't, didn't, unshackle himself from his pervasive presence, and for the only time in his career as a writer he went immediately to what was effectively volume two of the same novel.

In *A Tree on Fire* (1967) he explores his own feelings of disillusionment and pessimism by sharing out aspects of it between three characters: Dawley himself, Albert Handley, who had appeared briefly in *The Death of William Posters*, and a new arrival, John Handley, Albert's brother.

Albert Handley and Frank grew up in similarly grim circumstances and the former is now a successful, wealthy painter. Apart from the fact that he has elected to paint rather than write, he bears an obvious resemblance to Sillitoe, a self-taught artist who suddenly went from obscurity to international prominence. In terms of temperament and disposition Handley and Frank are virtually identical: antagonistic towards any form of orthodoxy, prone to fix upon radical causes and then shift from zeal to empty pessimism. Frank as a political activist and guerrilla fighter is clearly a little further from his creator's lived experience, but Handley also involves a fair amount of exaggeration. It is as if Sillitoe has conducted an exercise in self-scrutiny and contrition, laid out the evidence of his idiosyncrasies in embarrassing detail, and then imagined the worst. Handley is Sillitoe as he might have been, had he allowed instinct to overrule reason. Myra, having waited several months in vain for the return of Frank from the desert war, returns to England and arranges to move in with Handley and his family at their rambling country house, 'The Gallery'. When he meets her at the docks Handley provokes customs officials, rails against bureaucracy as symptomatic of a moribund national obsession with order and regulation, and even demands to be deported by the dumbfounded officers. He is a recognizable if hyperbolic version of his author.

It had always been and has remained Sillitoe's undeviating view that human beings who act to enforce arbitrary regulations should be obstructed at all costs. Stories abound, most famously the visit of the census collector to the Sillitoe house in Kent during the early 1970s. On being informed that he was 'legally obliged' to answer questions on his age, profession, number of children, place and date of birth, etc., all to be eagerly and as he saw it pointlessly devoured by a faceless bureaucracy, Sillitoe advised the official of where he might 'stuff' the document. Almost two decades later he was taking lunch with Max, first husband of his daughter Susan, at the Savage Club of which his son-in-law was a member, and saw no reason – given that the meal looked likely to last most of the afternoon – not to light a cigar between courses. The butler, exuding authority and deference in equal measure, approached the table and whispered to Max that he 'should advise his guest that club regulations forbade smoking in the luncheon room before 2.00 p.m.' Not 1.30 or 3.30, you understand, or when all present had taken dessert; no, 2 p.m. Max knew Sillitoe well and for a moment was gripped by an expression of horrified anticipation, but this time Sillitoe opted for a statesmanlike response. He took off his watch, made sure that it was synchronized with the large clock on the wall and laid it on his side dish. In front of him he placed the unlit cigar and box of matches, folded his arms and, without saying a word, made it clear that no service would be required at their table until he had watched the minute hand make its slow progress to the top of the dial. Gradually the rest of the room became transfixed.

Handley turned his children into grotesque marionettes, versions of himself with the embarrassing delinquency of adolescent protest thrown in. His teenage son Richard's bedroom walls are adorned with military maps of the UK amended by father and son to include details of the location and nature of atomic weapons establishments and bases shared by the RAF and USAF. Together they plan a British revolution, 1917 updated to 1967, plus a subsequent civil war. One is struck by the resemblances between Sillitoe's egregious inventions and his own enthusiastic outpourings to his brother Brian, particularly when he wrote to him of how anti-nuclear protect could only succeed if there was a mass revolt by the working classes and the bases physically assaulted by 'guerrilla groups'. Literary authors sometimes opt for self-caricature, but this is almost always a disingenuous performance, offering the reader a glimpse of their capacity for humility and self-effacement. Sillitoe's exercise was unfeigned.

When he wrote the novel he and Ruth were living in their first purchased property, 97 Larkhill Rise, London SW4. Regularly during the mid-sixties they would spend two to three months in a house lent to them by the Graveses in Deyá, Majorca, and most summers would rent for at least a month near Aix-en-Provence a property from friends of Ilse Steinhoff. This peripatetic existence, which they maintained between 1963 and 1968, might have appeared heedlessly impulsive, but some calculation was involved, of the most unselfish kind. He wrote to Brian.

> Eventually, once David is at school, we will have to plan things more carefully, but we will continue for his benefit as much as ours to keep moving. If you grow up knowing only one place and little else your outlook becomes hidebound and bitter. I think that is what happened to dad. David even now is picking up French and Spanish as quickly as he understands English. He'll be a Nimrod who knows the world in all its colours. He loves it when we go to Robert and Beryl's house [the Graveses'] but he's just as happy knocking about with the kids in the village here [in France]. [AS to BS, 10 July 1966, from Provence]

This is the exact antithesis of Handley's world. He like his creator came from the bottom of the social scale and grew up despising arbitrary regulations but he has exchanged his past for an equally enclosed regime of bitterness and hedonism and his children have become indoctrinated as similarly insular pupils of his aggression.

Given that they would have to spend more time in Britain when David was attending school regularly Sillitoe began to look for an alternative to London, somewhere that would alleviate his fear of permanence. On two occasions when he visited Brian in Dawley in 1964 and 1965 he asked his brother in advance to check estate agents' lists for cottages or farmhouses to let or, if inexpensive and habitable, for sale in and around the Severn Valley. None proved suitable, but by 1966, inspired by his friendship with Ted Hughes, he started making journeys to Yorkshire. In a letter to Brian in January 1966 he reports: 'I haven't heard anything else about that farmhouse in Yorkshire – but I hope I do, because if it does stay at five bob a week I would take it' (11 January 1966). It was in the Dales and would, he planned, be used as a base to search for something more permanent in the region. Later in the same letter: 'I'm doing a lot of Handley in my new book [*A Tree on Fire*], but I don't know how it'll turn out.' As Sillitoe searched for his own quirky, isolated refuge from the metropolis, ideas for Handley's decadent principality, 'The Gallery', flourished. Eventually Alan and Ruth would buy the Old Rectory in Wittersham, Kent, about eighteen months after the novel was published.

Handley's closest literary antecedent is probably Mr Hyde. In creating him Sillitoe had looked back at his life over the previous ten years and asked: 'What would your tainted *alter ego* have been capable of doing?' For Handley the combination of circumstances that had made him a successful painter – he had first been acclaimed as a radical primitivist, disavowing the protocols even of the respectable avant-garde – has decomposed into a grim combination of inertia, self-caricature and unfocused loathing. When he speaks he seems possessed by hatred so inchoate and unmanageable that it verges upon the deranged:

> 'Grown-up mature people are ten-a-penny . . . They're all over the place, like flies in summer, strong-faced vacuous venomous pipe-smokers and happy savers and careful drivers. Don't talk to me about the lumpen living-dead. Put them in a room with a strong light and they'd start to confess.' [p. 77]

For the ordinary reader Handley is an enigma, and reviewers disliked him immensely, but for Sillitoe he was a means of saying goodbye to ten years of conflicting affiliations. There is an intriguing letter written to Brian from Soller in which Sillitoe states that he has been 'busy on my novel, which I will now call *A Tree on Fire* . . . I am about half way through . . . Parts of Handley remind me of myself but the more he develops as a character the more I dislike him' (22 July 1966). He was not as yet certain of the exact purpose of his morbid invention, but the rest of the letter indicates what he had in mind. 'What do you think about the Americans bombing Hanoi?' he asks his brother, and continues: 'The captured airmen are being put on trial by the N. Vietnamese as war criminals. I don't agree with this, and I'm beginning to wonder about the war itself. Like you I was against it but what will they be left with if or when the Americans get out? Communism by name, but it will not be the "greatest happiness for the greatest number".' How different this is from the tone and content of his letters of two or three years before. Then, when addressing political topics, his manner resembled Handley's: undeviating, bombastic and as much a symptom of personal disquiet as genuine commitment.

The rest of the letter exudes a sense of calm and equanimity. He tells of how they are staying in the house where the Cambridge don Robin Mariss had lived when Brian visited them in Majorca in the 1950s. It has no garden but they spend a good deal of time with the Graveses. '[Often] I drive David over to the Graves's places in Deyá where they have a marvellous big garden – like an oasis, with even a date tree.' The 'oasis' which once featured so frequently in his letters as a mythical location in the Sahara, his fantasy of primitive anarchy, has now it seems become domesticated.

There is an unpaginated sheet in the second draft of *A Tree on Fire*, not an obvious comment upon the book but revealing none the less. It is dated 1 August 1966, roughly a week after he wrote to Brian from Deyá.

> I see everything. London is garish and proud of itself. Everyone talks of 'freedom', even 'revolution' but it is ridiculous, a façade. Loathing the US and praising the Vietcong has become a reflex, as vacuous as a hairstyle. No one thinks. In Nottingham life goes on much as it has for decades. There is more money but few seem happier. In the villages of Provence no one cares too much, and the same can be said of the ordinary people of Majorca. The people of Russia are charismatic, but at what expense? I can live and go where I wish. I feel no guilt, only the certainty that systems and all embracing solutions will inhibit freedom.

The unrestrained iconoclast of the late 1950s and early 1960s is giving way to a more reflective figure, and this contrast between the two Sillitoes, of the recent past and the present, played a part in his creation of the embarrassing incongruities of Handley's life at 'The Gallery'. It is located in a prosperous, peaceful region of Lincolnshire, an elegant refuge from the demands of life faced by virtually everyone else. But it is here that Handley feels most inspired to create a late-twentieth-century version of Picasso's *Guernica*, with Vietnam the subject of his primitivist excesses and the USA taking over from the Nazis as specialists in mechanized genocide.

> The biggest colour began as green, fields, oases, valleys, seaweed and estuary, life perpetuation . . . [then] vile green effluvia falling from bomb canisters lobbed on paddy fields, lodged in ditches where green men were fighting or burning . . . A leg goes green, gangrene, dead green and livid, jealousy of green by those who are dead for the living flowers of people unconscious in

life but full of work and struggle in that humid green forest, blistering enmouldering green, emerald of defeat for the iron merchants and industrial strong whose chewing-gum tastes of spite and who try to belt down the guerrilla men and woman of the coming world. [pp. 100–101]

The prose cuts an uneasy path between the pitiable and the unendurable, the sort of writing that lends itself so easily to parody that only the cruellest would take up the offer. This is the characteristic of Handley, indeed the entire novel, that none of its reviewers nor subsequent critics seemed capable of recognizing: it is one of the most ruthless, tormented exercises in self-caricature ever produced.

Since *Key to the Door* (1961) reviewers had been divided on the nature of Sillitoe's work. The unqualified approval that followed *Saturday Night and Sunday Morning* and *The Loneliness of the Long Distance Runner* had been exchanged for puzzlement and irritation. Most seemed perturbed that his apparent attempt to engage with complex moral or existential questions had also involved a shift away from the stylistic rawness of his first two books. Typically Francis Hope, in an article in *Encounter* on *Key to the Door*, pronounced that 'when Mr Sillitoe tries to decorate his documentary, the metaphors tend to mix, the word order stumbles and the far-fetched adjectives pile up in a semantic log jam' (December 1961), and an anonymous *Times Literary Supplement* commentator chipped in, disapproving of 'Sillitoe's rash of double-barrelled adjectives'. Two years later Frank McGuinness summed up the court's assessment, barrister style, by pointing to the defendant's 'weakness for plush prose and imagery' (*London Magazine*, August 1965). Was he that bad? Consider the following:

> In the garden the birds that had sung erratically and spasmodically in the dawn on that tree, on that bush, now sang together in chorus, shrill and sharp . . . they swerved, all in one flight, when the black cat moved among the bushes, when the cook threw cinders on the ash heap . . . Also they sang tremulously in the clear morning air, swerving high over the elm tree, singing together as they chased each other, escaping, pursuing, pecking . . . then tiring of pursuit and flight, lovelily they came descending delicately declining, dropped down and sat silent on the tree.

One does begin to pity the ill-treated sentences, their backs creaking under the weight of such verbiage. And one sympathizes with the cruelly overworked thesaurus when it is forced to cough up quite so many adjectives:

> it was sharp, polished, dangerous, marvellously integrated and sweetly proportioned.

As for metaphors, they rarely come so mixed:

> . . . the world itself was bursting, bursting into black spouts of villages catapulted into space, with himself falling through it all, through the inconceivable pandemonium of a million tanks, through the blazing of ten million burning bodies, falling into a forest, falling . . .

These are, respectively, extracts from celebrated novels by Virginia Woolf, Iris Murdoch and Malcolm Lowry. None is any more or less stylistically egregious than the passages selected for scorn by Sillitoe's mid-1960s reviewers, and one does not even have to ask why the guardians of literary merit did not judge them with a similar harshness. This was the kind of writing that seemed to accord with the public status of the people who produced it; Sillitoe, however – and one must of course whisper this – was having ideas above his station.

Handley's account of his artistic vision is excruciatingly overwritten for two reasons. It is a verbal rendering of his pictorial technique, and it reflects his vainglorious egotism. More subtly it is a reply to those critics who had accused Sillitoe of stylistic intemperance. They implied that his flaws were the involuntary consequence of overambition, something that they in their wisdom could recognize while he as its perpetrator could not. This, he informs them, is gloriously bad writing and if I can create it as an index to my character's soaring ego I am fully capable of operating at the other end of the compositional spectrum.

One might expect that Handley and Dawley would have been sufficient for Sillitoe to uncloak, even purge those aspects of himself that caused him disquiet, but they were not. Albert's brother John Handley fought in Malaya in the Second World War and spent two years in a Japanese prisoner-of-war camp. There he founded a group dedicated to the subversion of both the Japanese authorities and the British class hierarchy which still obtained in the camp: had John featured in *The Bridge on the River Kwai* he would most likely have throttled Alec Guinness long before the bridge was begun. He edits and prints an illegal newspaper which promotes socialism and anti-militarism as compatible and necessary solutions to inequality, poverty and global conflict. Sillitoe makes this improbable scenario plausible by turning John Handley into a version of Conrad's Lord Jim, capable of mesmerizing both his fictional peers and the reader. He is a magnificent creation, so spellbinding that we need continually to remind ourselves that he is mad. Since the war he has lived in Albert's house largely as a recluse, making use of his skills as a radio operator to scan the globe for unrest, conflict and crisis. He has become a self-appointed diagnostician of mankind's ills and is unswerving in his conviction that the ultimate solution is mass revolution and international socialism, plans for which he lays out in his massive notebooks.

The image of John Handley, addicted to his Morse code receiver as a substitute for human contact and a private route to omniscience, is tragic and unsettling, the latter because he sometimes bears a close resemblance to his creator. Sillitoe of course was not deranged or reclusive, but during those private moments which many of us set aside for contemplation and reflection he would spend his time listening to the world and recording his findings in his notebooks. Sillitoe loved, loves, the idiosyncrasies and transformative potential of Morse, finding its primitive rhythm reassuring and its ability to transcend time, space and linguistic barriers compulsive.

Peggy's daughter, Sue, was adopted by Sillitoe and Ruth after her mother's death, and she tells of how in her early teens her bedroom had been next door to Sillitoe's study in the Notting Hill flat. The walls were thick enough for sounds to be dulled, but when Sillitoe could not sleep she could hear the rhythmic chatter of the Morse messages coming through; and then the pace and rhythm would shift. He would be typing what he had picked up. 'Weren't you irritated?' I asked her. 'On the contrary. It was soothing. The rhythm itself was pleasant; it would send me to sleep. And this was all part of Alan's routine. Comforting.'

Sillitoe picked through aspects of his own life and assembled in John Handley a terrible likeness, again raising questions about what sort of person he might have become had he endured experiences similar to John's. What would have happened, he asks himself, were he three, four years older and been able to realize his ambition of fighting in what he saw as a just war?

Apart from their all-consuming revolutionary fervour Dawley and the Handley brothers had another thing in common. For most of us commitment to our family and closest friends will override any idealistic calling, but for Sillitoe's trio dogma had in various ways undermined private emotion. It is difficult to determine if this was intended by Sillitoe as a paean to the sacrifices demanded by radical politics or an exposure of the latter as a perverse variant of egotism. What is certain, however, is that the selfless, or selfish, involvement of these figures in matters they deemed more important than those closest to them made them the antitheses of their creator.

In his notebook Sillitoe records:

A young man came to interview me this morning by the name of David Margolies, an American teaching at Essex university, wanting to talk to me for his magazine devoted to communism and literature.

It was a civilised good natured discussion, but we seemed to be talking about two very different sets of novels, me stating that the Wm. Posters trilogy was not a form of 'commitment' on my part but simply a reflection of the conflicting and often confused political fashions of the mid 20th century, and that rather than Frank Dawley being a 'proletarian hero' he was merely indulging a form of parasitism, latching on to a revolutionary cause as a substitute for facing his personal state of bitterness. I don't know what he made of all this but he seemed stricken by something like shock and disbelief. I'll wait to see what sort of article comes out of it. [Private notebook, May 1979]

Unsurprisingly, no article appeared.

In 1981, five years after completing the Handley trilogy, Sillitoe wrote Brian a quite extraordinary letter. It was, ostensibly, prompted by their exchange on when the last public execution had taken place in Nottingham (which Brian claimed to be on record as 10 August 1864). Sillitoe advised Brian:

In fact what the author of [that] book doesn't state and could not have known, is that the very last public execution took place outside 22 Garden Street on 8 September 1937 when a certain notorious Mr Handley (ably assisted by members of his large family) hanged an unfortunate man, sent from the Estate Agents Piggin and Day to collect what rents he could, in full view of the public . . . [AS to BS, April 1981]

Sillitoe continues the story, tongue resolutely in cheek, for another four pages, including details of how tables had been set up to sell whisky and lemonade to children in the audience and an account of the trial, presided over by Handley, which lasted less than ten minutes and concluded with him pronouncing sentence without his black cap, stolen by one of the intoxicated children. He concludes by admitting that the precise facts had over time been subject to competing recollections, one claiming that the condemned man had actually been reprieved 'because Mrs Handley had taken a fancy to him . . . and spent the next five years hunting him down'. He concludes:

You just don't know what to believe,
Love from us,
Alan

Brian remembers the letter as a faithful reproduction of the Handley stories that Alan had concocted to entertain his siblings when they were curled up together in bed as a respite from the parental warfare downstairs, a blend of the scary, the absurd and the fantastic so addictive to children. When he revived it in this letter it seemed an appropriate means of saying goodbye to the Handleys.

His letters to Brian throughout the 1960s disclose a composite of everything that Sillitoe was, is, and which his characters were not. Routinely there are enquiries about how effectively Brian's union is organizing strikes, broader commentaries on national and global politics – Cuba, Vietnam, the Cold War; all resolutely left wing – but then the subject and temper of the letter will change completely. They were brothers with families, and these commitments meant far more to Sillitoe than his raging diatribes on the fate of the North Vietnamese. On 7 February 1962 he asks, 'How did the strike go on Monday?', recommends *Ten Days That Shook the World* as a brilliant account of the Bolshevik revolution, and after that the prose decelerates.

> I expect I'll be seeing you on March the 3rd, when mam gets married. I'll have to go to Nott'm on a day trip, because Ruth is more than seven months pregnant now and I have to keep an eye on her.

Sabina was marrying Tom Knight, a decent, unassuming man, close to her age, and no one in the family saw any reason to do anything other than support her, and turn up; she'd loved Christopher, in her way, but he was gone. Later the same year Sillitoe wrote from Tangier and responded to his brother's enquiry. 'Yes I wrote that poem "Dead Man's Grave" after you Michael and myself went to Dad's grave that time up Bulwell. I wonder who goes to it now, whether Mam does or not?' (AS to BS, 13 November 1962). The poem, written in 1960, is one of Sillitoe's best.

> Three sons in silence by their father's grave
> Think of the live man
> Not yet split in three by blackness –

He goes on to tell of how the 'frost to prove the dead not dead' had 'Turned the water iron-white', a 'Swollen muscle garrotting the flowers/Till the vase exploded/By trying its own strength out on itself/Scattered petals to a dozen graves'.

> Three brothers stand in silence,
> Feel the strength the father lost.

The private registers shudder through the lines. They did not pity or censure Christopher for being who he was; rather they would make sure that the injustices that shaped him, assisted regularly by his own brothers, would never be visited upon those closest to them. Sillitoe's solidarity with his brothers was sincere and self-effacing. He was by now earning more than anyone else in the family could have ever remotely envisaged, but there was no envy, not even any comment and certainly no solicitations.

He and his relatives knew the difference between quiet sincerity and ostentation. Sabina and Tom lived modestly in a council flat, and Sillitoe wrote to her every week with a short note or card on how David was grow-ing and the state of the weather, wherever he happened to be at the time, plus £5 or £10 in the envelope. When he was away for long periods, at Deyá with the Graveses in 1963–4 and renting a house near Aix-en-Provence in 1967–8, he lent Brian his car, taxed and insured, and if either of his brothers wanted to use the London flat when he and Ruth were away they would have first option.

NINETEEN

Sillitoe's sister Peggy, two years his senior, had four children, Patrick, Jane, Gail and Susan, and had endured an unsuccessful marriage. In 1966 she fell ill with cancer and her three brothers – Sillitoe in particular, travelling regularly to Nottingham – tried to ensure that all possible treatments, eventually radiotherapy, were made available, but by the end of the year she was judged incurable. 'Peggy is at home now in Clifton, I hear, with Jane [then aged fifteen] looking after her. It's very sad that there's nothing my doctor can do for her' (AS to BS, 5 December 1966). For most of 1967 Sillitoe and Ruth had rented a house near Aix-en-Provence, not far from their first home as a couple almost fifteen years before – and though this meant that Sillitoe's visits to Nottingham were less frequent he compensated by asking both his brothers to keep him informed, by telegram if necessary, on the state of things. He continued to send money regularly to Peggy. Jane attempted heroically to look after her mother while Patrick, her elder brother, seemed intent on pursuing a life of his own. Sillitoe received a telegram in Aix from Michael on 2 January 1968. 'Peggy died. 4.30am 2nd January. Went Quietly But Fought Like Vietcong.' Michael too had absorbed Sillitoe's apparent enthusiasm for the Vietnamese insurgents.

For the next few months Sillitoe did his best, from half a continent away, to choreograph proceedings. His two brothers with families of their own could hardly be expected to ensure that a home now comprised exclusively of orphans could be rescued from catastrophe. The three older children, all teenagers, could just about look after themselves, but Susan was still only seven years old and the prospect of the social services stepping in filled each of her uncles, Sillitoe particularly, with horror.

> The Clifton place does seem to be splitting at the seams. I'm afraid Patrick isn't very clever and it's going to show more and more as he gets older. Even if Peggy had lived he would have been the same. As for that woman next door with the five kids – I saw her once and never liked her being in the house – she's the cause of all the trouble with Jane as well [and] obviously encouraged her to let that boyfriend sleep there.
>
> But what can we do?

In truth he had already decided.

Don't say anything about this: but we'll have Susan, and I shall pay to have
Gail put into a boarding school, where she will be quite happy, and will get
a decent education. [AS to BS, 16 May 1968]

By the end of June the house had indeed collapsed into chaos. 'I had a
telegram from Michael yesterday, saying *Patrick Gone Collect Susan*.' Sillitoe
booked a ticket on the next flight to London, from which he drafted the
letter the next day. 'Patrick and Jane can make their own way now. Gail I
hope will be ok . . . We'll have Susan – though I don't know how she'll take
to the gypsy life' (AS to BS, 20 June 1968).

As a seven-year-old neither did she, but as she puts it now, 'It wasn't
really that much of a shock – moving in with Alan and Ruth – because even
before my mother died I'd spent weeks and fortnights with them. With hindsight it's clear that they had decided to take me on long before matters came
to a head. That's the kind of man he is.' There is evidence that Sillitoe had
indeed been preparing, acclimatizing his niece for what was almost certain
to be her permanent environment.

She seems to like it very much here in Deyá [where they were staying for
Easter] running around with David – in the village and between here and
the Graves's. There was an Easter-egg hunt for them this morning in the
garden of Canellun, and I think they're stuffed with chocolate. I expect she'll
go back to Nottingham in a couple of weeks. [AS to BS, 14 April 1968]

The permanent arrival of Susan, who would be legally adopted by
Sillitoe and Ruth in 1969, hastened Sillitoe in his search for a place in
the country, and they bought the house in Wittersham, Kent, in April
1969. 'I'm mortgaged up to the hilt, and I don't like that feeling. I had to
borrow £4,500 to get [the house]. Still, what are a few debts to a Sillitoe?'
(AS to BS, 2 July 1969). As Sue recalls: 'The flat, or flats, in London and
the place in France seemed transitional but my enduring memory was
that great big Edwardian house. It had its own drive, a paddock, two and
a half acres of unkempt grounds and an orchard. Locally it was still known
as "The Old Rectory" but it had been empty for a couple of years and
before that it was a private hotel. Every bedroom had its own antique
washbasin. I'd never known anything like it. When we first arrived the
grass was so high that the two of us, David and myself, could get lost in
it, hide from each other.'

Physically the Wittersham rectory and Handley's grotesque fiefdom were
unnervingly similar, and for this reason, when he first looked at the Kent
property, it appealed to Sillitoe's sense of self-lacerating irony. It reminded
him immediately of a place and a state of mind he had created and grown

to mistrust. But while Handley embodied the worst kind of sanctimonious hypocrisy – zeal combined with a soaring ego – and collaterally influenced and damaged those closest to him, Sue provides an unsentimental yet affectionate picture of Sillitoe as his complete opposite.

'Most accounts suggest that being the child of a writer is a terrible fate, of how these unfortunate kids end up in a bubble – usually a horrible one – created by their parents. For David and me, our upbringing was very ordinary, and I don't mean uninteresting. At Wittersham where the two of us went to the local primary school Alan and Ruth would have designated roles. He was in charge of mornings – he was always up at a ridiculously early hour doing his exercises – and he'd have breakfast prepared in the dining room for the two of us. Cornflakes or porridge, toast and bacon and eggs. And he'd make sure that we were responsible for cleaning our shoes, with a brush and polish, so they shone when we left for school. Then he'd clear the breakfast table, wash up, and get on with his novel. I can say that now but then I had no proper idea what they, he and Ruth, did. Well I knew they were writers but life at home seemed to be the same as it was for everyone else I met.

'Anyway we'd get home for tea – that would more often be Ruth's job – and be left to ourselves while the two of them got on with some more work and prepared dinner. But we were never bored. I wasn't told to read books but there was something about the atmosphere of the place that made reading seem pleasant, natural, and I enjoyed it. And if I or David didn't want to read or stay in we had two acres of garden to ourselves. It was wonderful.'

David: 'At dinner times we would talk about anything and everything. We, the children, felt grown up because no subject was off-limits and Alan and Ruth would argue with us rather than talk down to us. Often Alan would wheel out the *Encyclopaedia Britannica* to settle disagreed facts.'

Susan remembers that too: 'We would be eating yet the table would also be covered with books. I know it sounds as though it was all some form of home-based education programme, but that's not the case. Alan and Ruth enjoyed talking and it rubbed off on us. At the same time we had fun. If they'd had people over for dinner, next day Alan would set up the empty wine bottles on sticks and the three of us, Alan, me and David, would spend hours shooting at them with .22 airguns.

'I remember once at the local fair I was shooting at targets at the airgun stall and Alan took me aside and said, "They always alter the sights. Aim direct at the target and watch where the pellet goes, above or below, left or right; then adjust your aim." I won the giant bowl and the stallholder looked very cheesed off. An eleven-year-old girl had outsmarted him.'

David's recollections of Wittersham are evocative of an unusual idyll, a blend of the orthodox and the quixotic. 'The church was just down the road but like most rural livings the rectory had been sold and the vicar now lived in a drab 1950s house next door. I think Alan enjoyed this. They got on well enough but there was some polite mockery in Alan's dealings with the vicar. The idiot ran over our cat, but I'm sure it wasn't deliberate.' The cat was less a cherished family pet than an irregular visitor whom Sillitoe indulged with leftovers and occasional sanctuary in bad weather.

Sillitoe reported to Brian soon after they had moved in: 'The house is the old vicarage but the parson now lives in a smaller house next door. I'm thinking of buying an air rifle' (AS to BS, 20 September 1969). Such droll *non sequiturs* aside, he followed this up with a less flippant report on how they perceived the charms of traditional village life.

> David and Susan go to the ordinary C of E school here in the village, which is god-ridden and not very good, but they get plenty of 'education' at home so I'm not too worried about it. Still, the sooner religion is taken out of English schools the better. Ruth puts it very well when she says that the kids around here are 'being groomed for serfdom'. [AS to BS, undated, 1970]

'That was my first impression of the place,' recalls Ruth. 'In fact we took them out of the village school after a few weeks – at most a term – and then sent them to an ordinary state school in the nearby small town of Tenterden.'

David's most enduring early memory of his mother is from their first year in Wittersham. She was preparing a chicken for dinner. 'It was midday and as she gutted the bird she came across three unformed eggs, took them straight out and fried them for my lunch . . . Also I remember many times walking down the lane from the house to the stream and Spedding's farm. Old Man Spedding would bring out a chicken, wring its neck and we'd take it back. Alan and I would go rabbit shooting and we'd gut, skin and cook those two.' While Ruth was more attuned temperamentally to life in the city she and Sillitoe shared an intuitive appreciation of the countryside's peace and largesse. In this respect Wittersham was a convenient compromise. It was an hour and a half from London and close to the Channel ports, which offered access to their properties they borrowed or rented in southern France and Majorca.

Their closest neighbours and friends in Wittersham were the Sindalls, Jeanetta and Bernard. Bernard was a sculptor, successful, respected within the art world, and a Fellow of the Royal Academy. Jeanetta Sindall: 'Despite being from different backgrounds – Bernard had gone to public school – they got on immediately. I don't know what it was about them. They were both very private men. I remember that Alan, when we would have people for dinner or go to dinner at their house, was not so much withdrawn as thoughtful and cautious. Others, especially with drink, would ramble on, but Alan listened before he spoke. Bernard too. Except when they were together, then they rarely stopped talking. There were similarities that they recognized, I suppose. Bernard dropped out of school, ran away, lied about his age and served in the Royal Navy in the war. As a sculptor he was largely self-taught. They were both mavericks.' Sindall's head of his friend, unerringly lifelike, stands on a chest in the sitting room of Sillitoe and Ruth's Notting Hill flat.

Did many people come down from London? I ask Sillitoe. 'We didn't have large dinner parties, but there were a few regular callers. Ted [Hughes] and Carol, when they could. Christopher Logue, who we'd known from the early sixties, enjoyed the place. Bill Daleski and Shirley . . . three times, I think. Let me see . . . Leonard Baskin and Lisa would come over. They had a manor house in Devon, close friends of Ted, and we also got to know John Bratby. He was based not far away, Hastings. For no obvious reason the place, and our lives for a while, seemed to involve the visual arts.' Sindall was the sculptor and John Bratby, also a Fellow of the Royal Academy, was a painter. His stunning portrait of Sillitoe hangs in the hall of Rosica Colin Ltd, his first and present agents. Baskin's letters to Sillitoe and Ruth disclose his all-embracing commitment to the recondite aspects of rabbinic lore – they are in their own right visual artefacts, with beautiful Hebrew calligraphy interweaved with the emblems and designs of the notepaper. He was a renowned sculptor and printmaker, noted for his association with Ted Hughes – Baskin's engravings of crows were inspired by Hughes's volume of the same name – but he also worked closely, as an illustrator, with Ruth, notably on *Sibyls and Others*. 'Oh yes,' Sillitoe remarks, 'I almost forgot about Doris. We'd known each other for years in London, but she liked Wittersham a lot.' This is Doris Lessing. 'I'd love to come down and stay the night, if I may. Perhaps in August? You said you were going to be there in August' (Doris Lessing to AS and RF, 17 July 1973, Indiana Archive). Lessing was entranced by the house's sprawling, aimless character. It seemed to have been built in an impromptu manner and it suited her temperament. Her letters to Sillitoe and Fainlight are minor classics, joining artless scattiness with watchful intelligence.

When are you coming back, if ever? See you then . . .

Peter is off with two other blokes, heading vaguely towards Sicily, but for all I know he'll turn up in Majorca, because I see no reason why not.

My typewriter doesn't work . . .

I'm going to sleep now. Life this evening is too much for me and I can't wait for the mellow mists and aftermaths and nuances of lovely Devon, or is it Kent, where nothing happens. [Doris Lessing to AS and RF, 10 August 1973, Indiana Archive]

The quirky rural aspect of Wittersham, its token as a gateway between urbanity and the wild regions of Continental Europe, is evoked deftly by Sillitoe during his first full summer there. 'I'm bone lazy these days . . . It's such good weather, and the grass grows up and up and I stare at it through the window. If I don't go out and mow it it'll come in and get me soon' (7 July 1970). Sillitoe could take for granted the blend of empathy and wry amusement that this image would summon for his correspondent, since he knew him well. He was Ted Hughes.

TWENTY

Sillitoe and Ruth had first met Ted Hughes and his wife Sylvia Plath in 1961. Sillitoe had won the Hawthornden Prize for *The Loneliness of the Long Distance Runner* in 1960 and it was the custom that the holder should hand on the award to the new recipient at the following year's ceremony. Hughes had won it in 1961 for *Lupercal* and after the event the two couples had gone for a drink and arranged to meet again. In time Ruth and Ted would form a close friendship, but at the beginning it was she and Sylvia and Sillitoe and Ted who discovered intriguing parallels in their respective backgrounds and affiliations. Ted came from a working-class Yorkshire family – his father was a shopkeeper – and while his life thereafter differed from Sillitoe's in its conventional trajectory of self-improvement – Mexborough Grammar School followed by Pembroke College, Cambridge – he had for much of his adult existence felt out of place. He certainly did not advertise his background as a special claim upon real life, nor did his largely middle-class peers at Cambridge and thereafter treat him with awe or condescension. He simply recognized that virtually everyone he met in the literary world was different, until he encountered Sillitoe.

Sillitoe recalls him now. 'He was an ordinary man, unpretentious and thoughtful. A brilliant poet, of course, but aside from that he was genuine. He was plagued by tragedy but he was not its cause. I liked him very much.' The feeling was mutual. Hughes's poetry is customarily presented as a welcome if somewhat overwritten release from the smug parochialism of 1950s British verse – Larkin, Conquest et al. Perhaps it was, but it certainly did not involve a conscious act of rebellion. Hughes wrote what he wanted to write, allowed his sometimes confused emotional registers to find whatever verbal shape suited them best, and in this respect he and Sillitoe, as poets, had a great deal in common. The non-human natural world functioned for both as a magnet and a sanctuary, and though it has been claimed that Hughes's alleged pre-occupation with the occult underpinned his passion for mute, ungovernable nature he and Sillitoe shared a more straightforward taste for the countryside and its opportunities. The letters exchanged between Wittersham and Court Green, Hughes's home in Devon, are unrehearsed and informal, mixing confidential matters with observations on everything from politics to a leaking roof. They bespeak a reciprocal sense of trust, and in reading them one feels both captivated and guilty, much as one would when overhearing an exchange between the closest of friends. Persistently the countryside and its opportunities, culinary and affective, signal their presence.

Thanks for the books . . . Well it's beautiful down here, completely frost covered, peach dawns, blue days, new moon, and a dead salmon 3 feet long in the river under the bridge. A land of dead plenty.

This reads almost as an abstract for a poem, and later in the same letter the impressions do indeed crystallize into verse:

> If a whore and a trout
>> Lie where you least expect
> And if Christ is a fish
>> Forked to heaven in a tree
>
> Then Christ might well shout –
>> And I might well suspect –
> 'O lady, O lady
>> Why are you eating me?'

[TH to AS, December 1970, Indiana Archive]

In February 1974 Ted wrote lamenting the months that had passed since their last meeting: 'This is to get you thinking in good time so you can plan a trip down here . . . If you say you will definitely come I'll save the best piece of VENISON plus little gamey long backed birds, to enrich the accompaniment.' Following an earlier weekend at Court Green at which Ted had made ample use of the farm's and the landscape's offerings Sillitoe thanked him: 'We had a good time the other night, meat 'n swilling. I felt I'd eaten and drunk half the county' (24 November 1971). Ted loved fishing – on one occasion reporting to Sillitoe in a letter from Newfoundland of a day salmon fishing alongside similarly engaged grizzly bears – and in Devon he had a river virtually in his back garden well stocked with brown trout and the odd salmon or sea trout. Despite being asked on virtually every visit to join him, Sillitoe never went fishing with Ted. He confesses today that his aversion to the pastime was irrational and admits also that the concluding paragraph of *Saturday Night and Sunday Morning* played some part; Arthur's solitary preoccupation had an air of defeatism or at least grim resignation about it. But he would join him for a day out with shotguns – partridge, pheasant, even the odd rabbit might find its inopportune way to the kitchen that night. Sue and Frieda, Ted's daughter from his marriage to Sylvia Plath, would go riding on the nearby moors and have remained close friends since those years.

David tells a story which discloses beguiling parallels and contrasts between his father and Ted. 'He [Alan] has always loved animals, though he doesn't mind shooting them for food. We were in Provence, the year Sue joined us, and one day Alan came across a wild cat in the garden. I mean genuinely wild – enormous and undomesticated – and it had just had kittens. One of them seemed unwell, Alan kept going back to keep an eye on it and eventually he was so concerned for the little thing that he reached into the cat's "nest" under the rough hedge – he wanted to look after the kitten himself or take it to the vet if necessary – but the cat reacted and tore an enormous hole in his hand. Over the next few days it became infected but Alan dislikes going to doctors so he bound it up with an improvised pack of plaster, bandage and antiseptic. Ruth was convinced that it would become gangrenous and he'd lose his hand but he still refused to go to the doctor. He was more concerned about the kitten. For Ted animals had a savage grandeur, maybe a reflection of his ego. Alan, more often than not, would just want to look after them.'

The following is from Sillitoe's poem 'Wild Cat':

> A wild cat savaged my hand
> Bit deep into the flesh and poisoned it.
> What reason had I to touch it
> And desecrate those gallstone eyes?
>
> Unlucky opals, they looked and waited
> As if my hand were a torch
> To burn the bush around it
> And smoke out its young.

The affectionate impulse that prompted his act is excised from the poem and replaced by a question. Ironically he has left out the more authentic, if poetically less serviceable, aspect of his temperament. Sue remembers: 'Alan was a caring dad but certainly not in the touchy-feely manner that is routine today. You knew how he felt without him having to tell you and he seemed to me all the more genuine and dependable for that. Ted, from the same generation, could be similarly reserved but he usually gave the impression that he was smothering passionate impulses. Ted was great fun but as I got older I began to suspect that he was, well, something of an actor.'

The details of Ted Hughes's private life have long been open to public, some might say prurient, scrutiny and a good deal of speculation in print. Following Sylvia Plath's suicide he continued his relationship with Assia Wevill. He and Plath had had two children, Frieda and Nick, and he fathered a daughter, Shura, with Wevill. In 1969 Wevill too committed suicide after killing their daughter. The following year Ted married Carol Orchard, who came from a Devon farming family. Biographies of Plath, Hughes or both abound (prominently Crall, Stevenson, Wagner-Martin and Feinstein) and while there is no exact consensus on the apportioning of blame Ted Hughes emerges always as a rather opaque, sinister figure, the subtext being that while it is horrifying that two outstanding independent women should kill themselves the fact both were married to the same man indicates cause. Feinstein, for example, deals with Hughes's life and everyone involved in it with dispassionate sympathy in that she never actually attempts to explain the sequence of tragedies (*Ted Hughes: The Life of a Poet*, 2001). She does, however, give inordinate attention to matters such as Hughes's interest in astrology, the occult and the more esoteric branches of Judaism. Whether she intended it or not, he emerges from her book as someone with a faint whiff of the demonic about him.

Alan and Ruth are given respectful, marginal coverage, especially by Feinstein, but little more, which is misleading regarding the nature of their friendship with Ted. One reason why in 1961 all four wanted to stay in contact following that brief introduction was that each couple was fascinated and amused by finding another so like themselves. There were differences, of course, but these were made all the more intriguing by the abundance of similarities. Ruth and Sylvia, both of Eastern US educated middle-class origin, had originally studied to be visual artists, gone on to nurture literary ambitions and had fallen in love with Englishmen who transcended national and cultural stereotypes; both men were unashamedly proud of their backgrounds and each in their writing refused to conform to any norm, be it reactionary or avant-garde. In the few years that she and Fainlight knew each other before Plath's suicide Plath came more and more to regard Ruth as a confidante and touchstone. Plath felt that her own poetry, which apart from *Colossus* (1960) was in the early 1960s relatively unknown, would always exist, perhaps shrivel, in the shadow cast by Hughes's rise to prominence. Ruth's situation was almost identical in that during the period when Sillitoe was rarely out of the public spotlight her poems were emerging gradually, albeit in the most prestigious broadsheets, weeklies and journals. In the letters Plath wrote to Fainlight and during their private exchanges she seemed to be seeking a discordant blend of assurance and fellow victimhood, but her perception of Ruth as her *alter ego* was self-deluding. Sillitoe became an overnight superstar with *Saturday Night and Sunday Morning*, yet neither he nor Ruth recalls that this in the slightest way altered their relationship. Before 1958 each of them knew that if and when recognition came they would not achieve it simultaneously. There is not the slightest hint when she speaks of this period today that Ruth felt envious or unsettled by Sillitoe's fame; pleased, perhaps, because he treated his income not as a personal stipend but as something from which he, Ruth, David, Sue and other members of the family could benefit. In this domesticated respect his socialist principles remain secure. Plath, then, was projecting her own fabric of despair and resignation on to her friend. Perhaps she felt that a woman similarly afflicted would offer some resolution for her own feelings of love as stolen hubris. If so she was wrong, and not because Ruth was an unsympathetic listener but because of her misreading of Sillitoe and Ruth's relationship.

Sillitoe, when I ask him about Plath, is dismissive of the accumulation of theories that surround her life and death: 'In the end it was horrible and simple. She was mentally ill, mad if you like. And Ted didn't cause that.' Ruth is less explicit but her actions spoke for themselves. She was, like everyone else, appalled and distressed by Plath's suicide and felt sympathy for Ted who, in the time the two couples had known each other, she had come to love and respect. Sillitoe and Ruth also formed a close attachment with Assia Wevill, and almost two decades later Ruth wrote an exquisite poem on her own friendship with Assia, called 'Romance':

> She seemed to gloat on oppression,
> as if it were the fuel and source
> of her obsession, and each passionate protest
> a further confirmation.
> My spirit shrivelled, like fingers
> from harsh soap and cold water,
> to hear this version of the same old story.
> Yet I could not doubt her.
> Fairy tales are very specific,
> almost domestic . . .

One suspects that she has in mind a particular source for this 'same old story' told and heard before.

> I'd gone down that road before,
> and knew its forks and sudden twists
> where one false step has mortal consequence.
> But I was luckier.

The words form a tracery around a subject too terrible for bluntness but demanding attention none the less. In truth the road 'gone down before' was not one she had taken herself but one she had watched Assia's predecessor follow. She, Ruth, was 'luckier' not because Sillitoe was a better husband than Ted but through the simple fact that she was not mad, depressive and suicidal.

If further proof is required that Ruth and Sillitoe regarded Ted as much the victim of his tragic relationships as their progenitor one need only examine the correspondence. Typically in 1976 Ruth wrote to thank him for a letter which was a continuation of their exchanges on the revivifying powers of writing:

> Yes indeed, writing is a most unnatural activity, and every cell screams out against it. But at the same time, the bridgehead must be enlarged, as you say, or as it presents itself more forcefully to me, the channel must be widened with the contrivance and cooperation of the conscious mind before the pressure behind gets too much and it smashes through out of control – or, even worse, before everything is petrified into a sea of stone. [RF to TH, 14 November 1973, Emory Archive]

Regarding Hughes's maleness – a condition which many these days treat as a pernicious liability – much has been alleged and inferred, but it is evident from this letter that for those who knew him best it was an irrelevance. For Ruth he was a valued friend and respected fellow writer.

I asked Ruth about Ted. 'I liked him, respected him, of course. Often I confided in him but at the same time . . . well, how can I put it? Ted expected the women he knew to be in awe of him, and attracted to him. That wasn't his fault entirely. It had become a routine. But I didn't respond in that way, and he sensed it. He didn't take it as a rebuke but there was always a feeling between us of . . . friction. Despite himself – and he was a good man – I don't know if he could cope with a woman who regarded herself as his equal.'

We are drinking tea in Sillitoe and Ruth's flat in Notting Hill, and after a while Sillitoe adds, 'Yes, you're right. He was a good friend, good man, but he had a bloody gigantic ego.'

Ted read Sillitoe's books as soon as they were published. He was an honest critic, sometimes scathing when he thought his friend had wasted his gifts, and Sillitoe valued his comments.

> Before I see any reviews I'm writing – I think *A Tree on Fire* is a terrific book, your best by about 5×. I began it at about 9 a.m. and finished it about 11 p.m. and for about four days I seemed to be thinking about your idiom, your phrases etc. It really goes from beginning to end with one bang. All the characters are first rate, not one dud, not one that isn't especially interesting.
>
> In *The Death of William Posters*, I wasn't sure that the inner framework of it worked – I felt it creaked, as if you were forcing a dimension on the book which it hadn't naturally grown of itself. In this one the whole inner design seems to me masterly – relationship of Frank, Albert and John + the painting + the desert trek etc., really comes off . . . [TH to AS, 2 February 1967, Indiana Archive]

Ted recognized in the novel 'something absolutely authentic' to the extent that 'the only thing I can compare it with is [Patrick White's] *Voss*'. Sillitoe's problem, in his view, had been 'the political streak – which always seemed to me the intractable streak in your writing, ready to spoil it . . . tilting your longer works in to self expression rather than autonomous creation'. But in *A Tree on Fire* 'the political business comes off . . . the whole thing flares up together'. This is a shrewd reading because Hughes senses that each of the characters is no longer being protected by their creator's ideological biases, that their ideals, like his, were being allowed to find their own self-abnegating destiny.

For Hughes, Sillitoe was a rarity; as a man phlegmatic and unassuming, as a writer undaunted by custom or fear of denunciation, and he confided in him on a number of matters. There is a moving passage in a letter written four years after Assia's suicide and involving his thoughts on life now in Court Green with Carol.

> We have some beautiful beasts. I'm getting quite involved in them. Impossible not to. They're giving me more than I give them. I was quite intently enmeshed in their world when I was an infant – but I felt I was losing it. Fishing isn't enough, but now this working on the land and these animals has given it all back again. I feel to be waking up for the first time in my life. [TH to AS, January 1974, Indiana Archive]

The letter tells us as much about Sillitoe as it does of Hughes. It could be a diary, carrying no trace of either self-consciousness or uncertainty; he knew and trusted his correspondent as well as he did himself. In this regard he valued Sillitoe as an anchor when the sly allegations began to inform accounts of his work and his relationships. This started with Alvarez's chapter on Plath in his book-length study of suicide (*The Savage God*, 1972). Sillitoe had written to him soon afterwards: 'I see there was an article on Sylvia in this morning's *Guardian* by Thomas Wiseman. Maybe this bandwagon will turn into a juggernaut and throw them all off' (AS to TH, 2 November 1971), and by the early 1990s the whispers of suspicion had reached a crescendo.

> Sylvia's biographies have taken their toll – loathsome things that they are. If hyenas are not after all truly what they were always thought to be biographies have taken their place in the predatory scheme.
>
> I'm having to read Anne Stevenson's efforts in the faint hope that I might be able to head off some other possible five years of feeding the lawyers because a biographer needed the advance.
>
> Strange natural life cycle – biographer gets idea (or first walked into a publishing house and walked out again with $130,000 advance), I have to

struggle with his/her fantasies and delusions for a year or two before finally throwing it up in disgust then find myself in court responsible for allowing the publication of some detail I'd overlooked . . .

The notion that S [Sylvia] can ever be anything but a mythological figure, adaptable to everybody's metaphysics, has long past . . .

But how can people who boast of their integrity have the effrontery to draw conclusions about the lives of people they never met – how can they float their assured statements on such an absolute lack of any sense of the truth! [TH to AS, January 1989, Indiana Archive]

Shortly afterwards in a letter to Ruth: 'I'm always being told what I'm supposed to think and feel – by that claque who have none of their own business to worry about' (TH to RF, 5 February 1990). The letter was to thank her for 'the poem', a pre-published draft of 'Romance – for Assia'.

In a notebook entry for June 1979 Sillitoe records a recent 'literary' party.

The place was full of familiar faces from the poetry and literary world – all old friends and acquaintances. Ted looked worried, harassed even, and we greeted each other affectionately, knowing we have a brotherly feeling towards each other, feeling we should see more of each other, yet not being able to because of our various preoccupations. His are different from mine – an association which he calls his 'folly', though some would treat it as tragedy – but which I suppose is, for him, unavoidable, his personal history. It plagues him, but he needs it to keep his blood flowing and to get out the lines of poetry. [Private notebook, June 1979]

It would be misleading to claim that Sillitoe, Ted and Ruth had locked themselves into an exclusive triumvirate. (However, it should be noted that the volume they published containing verse by the three of them was prompted by a sense that each channelled their personality into their work in a manner unlike any of their peers: *Poems* by Ruth Fainlight, Ted Hughes, Alan Sillitoe, Rainbow Press, London, 1971). What they did share was knowledge of the truth about Sylvia Plath. Hence the tone of Ted's letters: he knew that both could be trusted as touchstones to certainty, particularly in the mêlée of speculation that came with the biographies. Sue Sillitoe remembers Ted almost as part of her extended family. 'David enjoyed visits to Court Green. He would go shooting with the rest of them, Nick, Ted and Alan. I'd sometimes go riding with Frieda who is still a very close friend. Ted, well, he had presence. And for a teenager he was great, fanciable, but at the same time he was like an uncle.' For Sillitoe their friendship would follow a special trajectory, particularly during the 1970s and 1980s when, Gentiles both, they passionately espoused the cause of Zionism.

PART V
JUDAISM AND ISRAEL

TWENTY-ONE

During my nap today I had a dream – that I was inside a pen with an animal halfway between a tiger and a leopard . . . My hand was on the leopard's neck, which lay by my side. I suddenly realised it was a dangerous animal – or could become so – and thought of getting out of the pen. It seemed to sense my intention, and I sensed that perhaps I had better stop trying to get out. I was in a quandary, yet determined to get out. The animal seemed friendly yet I knew I could not test its friendship too far. I woke up before I knew whether or not I had escaped from the pen. [Private notebook, October 1968]

At the beginning of 1967 Sillitoe received a second invitation from the Soviet Writers' Union to visit Russia. *Key to the Door* had been translated into Russian soon after its publication in the UK and had been promoted throughout the Soviet Union as an even more significant exposure of the vile injustices of capitalism than his first two books. Since his initial trip Sillitoe had acquired a reasonable fluency in Russian but not sufficient, he thought, to be able to check on how well his translators had dealt with the stylistic nuances of the book, particularly the reported speech in which the Nottingham dialect featured prominently. But this, he found after this second visit, would have been the least of his concerns. Some parts of the book had effectively been rewritten, with Brian's life in the 1930s reconstituted in the Socialist Realist mode of Gorky's *The Mother* (1906–7). None the less the novel he had virtually written had become a bestseller; almost 2 million copies were sold in its first year. Prospect, the state-owned publishing house, would not release royalties in non-Soviet Bloc currency and Sillitoe's payment in roubles amounted to nothing except accommodation, travel and hospitality in the USSR available to him whenever he wished. This time he decided to go by car, and in June 1967 he set off from London in his Peugeot estate for the thousand-mile journey through Denmark and Sweden, and then by ferry to Finland and the Russian border.

He was met in Leningrad by George Andjaparidze, then employed by the Soviet Writers' Union as a guide for eminent visitors. The Writers' Union had explained to Sillitoe before he left that George's principal role would be to assist him with navigation and to act as an intermediary in any encounters with the traffic police. In reply Sillitoe had expressed his gratitude but made it clear that map-reading had been his hobby, almost his obsession, since childhood, and one of the reasons that he had chosen to bring his car was the attraction of finding his own way through their magnificent cities and landscapes, aided only by an up-to-date road map. As for the traffic police, he welcomed the opportunity to practise his Russian and would, if provided with details, familiarize himself fully with their equivalent of the Highway Code. The Writers' Union's response was peremptory and unequivocal; George was to be his guide and that was it.

As an undergraduate at Moscow University George had, he explained, written his dissertation on Oscar Wilde and gone on to do his doctoral thesis on the novels of Evelyn Waugh. 'So we'll have plenty to talk about, and learn from each other on our journey,' he added, having apparently imbibed some of his subjects' taste for the ironic *non sequitur*.

George took him for dinner to a Caucasian restaurant on Nevski Prospekt, a meal that Sillitoe recalls as equal to anything available in London. They also tried several types of Soviet wine, emptied an entire bottle of vodka and became far more candid. Sillitoe asked if all this *bonhomie* was hard work, since he had been given the job of 'chaperoning' an Englishman, a demanding and for all he knew an uncooperative sort, for two weeks. 'My dear fellow,' replied George like a character from Wilde, 'it will be a pleasure. They were queuing up to get this job and I was delighted when it came to me. You are a celebrity.' Sillitoe laughed, but George continued, 'Yes, you are. Everyone knows your work, and tomorrow morning you will be a rich man.'

The next day, 11 June, Sillitoe went with George to the bank where 1,300 roubles in banknotes awaited him. This, George said, was for instalments from *The Loneliness of the Long Distance Runner* and *Road to Volgograd* recently published in magazines. It would save him having to touch his book royalties, which were lodged in a different account, and would keep him going until Moscow. 'It is the equivalent of around three months' pay for the average labourer,' George informed him. Sillitoe did a quick calculation. By British standards he had around £400 in cash to last him three days.

Leningrad was, he recalls, a shifting mosaic of impressions and contradictions. 'It suffered more than any other Russian city during the war. Over a million people died, killed by German artillery bombardments and air raids, or they starved to death. Nearly half the civilian population. Every adult there in 1967 was a survivor or the son or daughter of one. Superficially the city seemed happy with itself, relaxed. I remember one evening in the Park a young man was lying on the grass with a tape machine playing the Beatles' "Yellow Submarine" and two Swedish mariners were trying to chat up a couple of Russian girls. The four of them laughed and kissed.

'No one went hungry and everybody had somewhere to live, however small, but they knew they were still carrying the burden of the war. They had resisted the Germans but another form of authoritarianism was the cost of their suffering. I could feel it and they knew I could, even George.'

Sillitoe spent three days in Leningrad calling upon friends he had made during his 1963 trip and visiting museums and parts of the city he had not previously had the time to see. He got on well with George, who seemed anything but an apparatchik, but Sillitoe was as yet uncertain of how he felt about being obliged to spend most of his adventure in the company of someone he hardly knew, a man affable enough but hound-like in his constancy. The road to Moscow seemed largely empty but for some lorries and tractors and the occasional horse and cart, at least until late afternoon about five hundred kilometres from the capital when they were overtaken by a small fleet of brightly painted cars, mainly Volkswagens and Mercedes with West German number plates. Both of them sat for a while in perplexed silence, but soon George gave a slight nod. 'Yes,' he explained, 'I had read of this. It is the Berlin–Moscow rally.' Something had passed between them, unspoken, and of the perfunctory exchanges which took place before they went to their rooms at the Intourist hotel that night Sillitoe remembers only one, unprompted, statement by George. 'I was brought up by my aunt and my mother. Perhaps I was spoilt. My father died before I knew him. He was in the infantry, killed early during the first German advance on Moscow.'

Next morning they set off early and Sillitoe asked his companion: 'George, do you know what today's date is?'

'I never ask myself such a thing.'

'Well, ask yourself now. What's the bloody date?'

'How should I know? I was told which day to meet you in Leningrad and now it does not matter. I'm in your hands. I have no interest in the calendar.'

'Well, it's the 21st June. Tomorrow will be the 22nd.'

George paused, but not for long. 'The Great Patriotic War began. Tomorrow.'

'Correct,' Sillitoe responded, 'and your father would have survived for how long? A few months?'

'Less,' said George. 'But why do you mention it?'

Sillitoe did not reply, and soon each was aware of the other's thoughts.

'Sheer coincidence,' ventured George. 'Nothing more.'

Sillitoe said, 'Perhaps. But you have to admit, there is something typically tactless about it. Twenty-six years ago to the day, and now those middle-aged men in their shiny cars will reach Moscow at last. After that they'll push on to Kharkov and Kiev, swapping yarns, standing on hills with their binoculars and old staff maps, maybe wondering about how easy it will be next time.'

'Were you joking?' I ask Sillitoe now.

'No.'

'Do you think George thought you were?'

'I'm not sure, but his next words were, "Catch them up!" I said I couldn't, given the start they had and the fact that I was driving an ordinary estate car, but he insisted. So soon we were rattling along at ninety and George was playing lookout, being closest to the middle of the road. When a lorry appeared ahead I would edge out, ask him "Clear?" and invariably he'd reply "*Davai! Go!*" I don't honestly think he looked because we overtook everything without slowing.'

By mid-afternoon they found themselves behind the rally cars on a winding stretch of road with no-overtaking signs, the highly tuned emblems of Teutonic prestige dutifully observing the regulation. Sillitoe, thinking it worth the risk, dropped to third gear and the Peugeot screamed past them all. It was a right-hand-drive car, so George had to lean across Sillitoe to stick out his tongue and offer the gaping rally drivers a sequence of universally recognized hand gestures. Sillitoe kept the accelerator to the floor and they reached Moscow apparently unpursued at about 8 p.m.

Two particular memories are summoned when he looks back to his days in the capital, and the first is of a girl he never actually met. Sillitoe had no schedule of meetings or readings for the day following his arrival, and since he already knew the city well enough persuaded George that he might as well visit his girlfriend – George was divorced but was currently seeing a woman in Moscow – and they would meet the following morning for breakfast. What would he do, he wondered, and as he looked from his bedroom window across an adjoining roof to the shiny domes of the Kremlin he suddenly found himself staring into the face of a young woman, sitting casually on the pitched roof smoking a cigarette. She was dressed in overalls, and her brightly coloured headscarf had slipped down to her neck. She caught his glance, smiled, waved, and then skipped a little further up the roof ladder to get on with her job. She was replacing tiles, and to Sillitoe she had the appearance of a creature joyously alive to her world. She danced around the roof like a bird and she was, Sillitoe recalls, 'bloody pretty'. He was entranced and held up an unopened packet of American cigarettes. She nodded. It was almost lunchtime, but before Sillitoe could continue his sign language flirtation the telephone rang asking if he would come down to the lobby to sign for a package: English copies of *Saturday Night and Sunday Morning* and *The Loneliness of the Long Distance Runner* which he had insisted be forwarded for his readings. When he returned the girl and her ladder were gone, as was the package of cigarettes he had left on the windowsill. She had awakened in Sillitoe memories of 1963, of a nation, a world, so utterly different from the West that the standard rhetoric of polarity seemed redundant. He knew there was oppression and fear abroad, but where else had he seen such an image of heedless freedom as the bird-like girl? It was a beautiful image, but it was buttressed by a fantasy that would dissolve as his journey continued.

Two days later a party in his honour was held at the flat of Valentina Ivasheva, one of the senior professors of English at Moscow University. Ivasheva, George informed him, had authored the standard undergraduate book on Western fiction, or at least on that which was deemed worthy of mention. Sillitoe featured prominently as the only 'genuine working-class British novelist' ever allowed into print. He was flattered and unsettled, even more so when George told him that 'this is why you are invited here; you are idolized', apparently for being working class, irrespective of the quality of his writing. George had been taught by Ivasheva. She was, he said, a matriarch, generous to her students and merciless in equal measure. By now he had come to treat her as a friend, and he added a personal observation. 'You know why she adores the foreign working classes so much? Because she doesn't have to fraternize with them here. She is a snob, as are many others . . . Factory workers, peasants – yes, they're still regarded as peasants – would be seen by most people in this room as inferior.'

Later, when Sillitoe talked with Ivasheva, she seemed preoccupied with *The General*, asking him why he had given himself up to this engagement with art and universalist themes – so nineteenth century and bourgeois – when clearly it was his duty and vocation to write for and about the proletariat? He cannot recall his reply but he remembers that he spent the rest of the evening listening to Ivasheva's husband, referred to by everyone as 'Uncle Dima'. He had been a fighter ace in the war, shot down several times, and was now in early retirement as a consequence of his wounds. He preferred telling stories to theorizing on them and amused an audience of undergraduates all night with confections of folk tales and war anecdotes, often with a farcical subtext. How, wondered Sillitoe, can two people so utterly different live together? A year later Dima would kill himself. There was, Sillitoe remembered, something about Dima that bespoke the tragedy of Sovietism, a society composed of incongruities that could never really be acknowledged. He remembered the woman from 1963, a veteran of 'internal exile' who had treated her horrible experience with sanguine resignation, and he spoke of this to George. For once, his companion was candid. 'I knew a couple, both had been in the camps in the 1950s. They married, were happy, but not for ten years did they tell each other of what they had been through.' Was Sillitoe surprised? In the notes to his 1963 visit in the margin alongside his account of the woman from the camps he had written. 'Hidden histories. Secret lives.'

On 26 June they were due to set off south, first for Orel, then Kursk and eventually Kiev. George arrived with several flasks of drinks and large paper bags of food which his aunt and mother had spent most of the night preparing, fearing they might be tempted by roadside *stolovaya* – the equivalent of working-men's cafés, and 'filthy' according to George's mother. George's girlfriend stood on the pavement weeping openly, and after he hugged her she beseeched him, 'Don't go. Last night I dreamed you'd be killed on the train coming back. Don't go!' George explained, seemingly not for the first time, that 'I'll be back in ten days, my love. It is little more than a holiday, with my friend here.' He nodded towards Sillitoe. Sillitoe was surprised, even slightly envious. It was clear that the young woman was genuinely distraught and as they drove out of the city Sillitoe asked if she always became so upset when he left Moscow. 'Russian women are like this. It is a legacy of the war, even for those who cannot remember it. So many said goodbye to husbands, lovers, sons, fathers that the act has become a horrid talisman. The majority did not come back.'

Their next encounter with a past seemingly embedded in the present came that afternoon when Sillitoe turned right off the main road and after a mile entered Tolstoy's estate of Yasnaya Polyana. They had expected attendants, guides, gatekeepers and an abundance of tourists, but the place was eerily deserted. The house itself was locked and they wandered through the avenues of elms and oaks to a clearing in the midst of which was an unmarked grass-covered mound, and to the side an ancient carefully preserved garden seat. Neither had been there before but both knew the legend of how Tolstoy had asked to be interred with no headstone next to the modest bench where he would sit during the summer. Silently and without introduction a tall, elegantly attired man had joined them. To Sillitoe he seemed at least eighty, though still of upright, almost graceful bearing; and he wore a suit, waistcoat and watch-chain of at least turn-of-the-century vintage. He introduced himself, in French, and to this day Sillitoe cannot recall his name. Later, in the car, Sillitoe said, 'Come on, you looked as amazed as I felt.' 'Yes,' said George, 'ghosts.' The gentleman eventually explained, without prompting, that he had been one of Tolstoy's last secretaries, had been attached in some way to the estate since his birth – he was now a guide – except during the war when the Germans had almost wrecked the place. 'Writers come here often,' he said, without enquiring of Sillitoe's or George's occupation, 'but there will never be anyone to compare with him.' He glanced at the mound, bade them a respectful goodbye and set off back towards the house.

An hour later they passed the turn for Spasskoya Litovinovo, Turgenev's estate. Sillitoe still insists that their timetable ruled out a visit, which he had planned, but admits that another encounter with a potentially less endearing spiritual emissary had crossed his mind as he accelerated away from the junction.

He and George were, Sillitoe reflects, forming the sort of friendship that is intuitive and undemanding; each could read signs in the other that required no explanation, and the unstated conventions of amusement and provocation rippled through their private idiom. But there was something implicit and burgeoning that both knew would eventually have to be addressed. It broke the surface the next day, shortly after they had been stopped by a militiaman and subjected to the routine litany of questions regarding the provenance of the car, the status of the driver, their destination and the purpose of their journey. This, at Sillitoe's estimation, was the eighth time it had occurred, which did not surprise him; he had no illusions about the neurotic, authoritarian character of Sovietism even when it fixed upon the mundane matter of driving a car. What did irritate him was the fact that George had, three times, secured respectful indulgence from the police – once even a salute – by introducing his companion as a major writer of 'proletarian fiction', a distinguished guest of the Writers' Union. Sillitoe told him that he felt like a specimen, a curiosity, and George replied, apparently without a hint of irony, 'I must tell you that I feel privileged in spending so much time with a real English proletarian writer.'

Sillitoe said, 'Don't insult me, George, though let me tell you that I'm equally happy to be in the company of a university graduate I can enjoy talking to.' Condescension, as Sillitoe showed, cuts just as deeply and becomes more conspicuous when its complacent agent is suddenly turned into its target.

George, chastened slightly, then made a confession. He was fascinated by Sillitoe's background because, bizarre as it might seem, he like Ivasheva had never met any real Russian workers. Class, in the British sense, had been abolished but replaced with other stratifications, just as rigid. He and most of the people Sillitoe associated with at readings had been born into the intelligentsia.

George confirmed what Sillitoe had long suspected, that the fervid culture of ideas on art and politics which embraced him during his visits to the Soviet Union was focused almost exclusively on the world beyond the Eastern Bloc. 'George,' he said, 'when I come across the term "proletarian writer" – and it's used in Britain as much as it is here – I get angry because it reeks of hypocrisy. It's an annex to "working class", an idea created by the conscience-stricken left-wing bourgeois to keep the ordinary people in their place.'

George seemed perplexed and confused. 'But we're told that people of your background want to overthrow the governing élite, our textbooks present your novels as radical, as reflections of a desire for revolution.'

Sillitoe laughed. 'The workers in Britain have straightforward ambitions. They want more money, and I don't blame them. If people can buy what they want they don't care about politics.'

'What about the trade unions?' said George, somewhat desperately. 'They're constantly active in Britain and they represent the collective interests of the workers.'

Most trade union activists were, Sillitoe informed him, petty dictators. The best known were just as ambitious as their supposed enemies, the entrepreneurs and bosses. 'All they want in the end is to get into Parliament or the House of Lords.'

George, now exhausted, asked him, 'So what are your politics? What are you?'

'I'm a writer,' Sillitoe replied.

They continued south, a day's journey to Kursk, where they spent the night before another day-long drive to Kiev. Few Westerners had shown an inclination to visit the Soviet provinces and none would have been permitted to do so unmonitored, but the fact that Sillitoe had been allowed, apparently without restrictions, to plan his own route and timetable suggested that the system regarded its guest as a harmless presence who in any event would not object to benign supervision. However, Sillitoe's seemingly aimless odyssey had a more specific objective, as he explained to George when they left Kiev for Chernovtsy near the Romanian border. He wanted to visit a village called Ulashkovtsy, some way off the main thoroughfares, and George became mildly confused, perhaps even perturbed. 'Why?' he asked. Such villages in the steppes were just that, villages, possessing nothing of historic or architectural interest. Maybe, said Sillitoe, but this one has a personal significance. He had been told of it by someone who had once lived there. She was still alive and he intended to provide her with a reminder of her past, his own impression of how it looked, if any of the people whose names she vaguely recalled were still there, and he wanted to take some photographs. George enquired in a polite, slightly tremulous manner of the nature of Sillitoe's friend. A friend, he replied, yes; but more than that. 'She is my mother-in-law, and she left the village sixty years ago,' adding: 'She knew it, still knows it, as Loshkovitz.' George, Sillitoe recalls, muttered something inconsequential, but he had certainly received the message. Loshkovitz was the Yiddish name for Ulashkovtsy.

Anti-Semitism in provincial nineteenth-century Russia was as rife and frequently more violent than racism in the American South. The Soviet regime had invested a good deal of effort in promoting itself as the only society which had successfully outlawed racial discrimination and promoted integration – Sillitoe had indeed remarked in *Road to Volgograd* on how refreshing it was to find people of African, Asian and South American descent mixing so easily with the predominantly Slav population of the cities; so unlike, it seemed, the London of the late 1950s and 1960s. In truth, as he now admits, he had been told of violent, racist incidents and had sensed in some a visceral antipathy to outsiders, but had left this out of the book. The only truth in the official propaganda was that the USSR pursued an open-door policy for visitors from Third World nations where it wished either to sustain or foment revolutionary regimes. Hostility to Judaism, however, remained one of those features of the Russian psyche capable of transcending the shift from neo-feudal Christianity to Bolshevism. Religion had not been outlawed, even under Stalin, but what remained of the Russian Orthodox Church existed on the periphery of an officially secular society; everyone was fully aware that religious observation was tantamount to professional and social suicide. But Jews were perceived, indeed most of them perceived themselves, as a group that could not be defined purely by race or religious affiliation. Unlike successful politicians, soldiers or bureaucrats who had eschewed their parents' or grandparents' Christianity, secular Soviet Jews were still Jews irrespective of whether they were committed to communism. They might have become atheists but they were atheists with a legacy, a sense of identity which overrode such matters as belief or ideological affiliation. George was aware of this, as Sillitoe knew, and the rest of their journey that day seemed charged with a degree, albeit slight, of mutual apprehension. Next morning George was jovially restored yet apologetic. Ulashkovtsy, he announced, was outside officially approved routes for visitors and the trip could not, unfortunately, take place. Sillitoe found himself boiling with questions. How had George acquired this information between their parting after the previous evening's dinner and today's breakfast? Why was the village forbidden territory? He knew, however, that it would be entirely pointless to address any of them to George.

Instead he suggested that they visit Berdichev, which for centuries had been the Jewish capital of Eastern Europe. Sillitoe, again to George's perturbation, produced Austrian maps of the region which included details of all the major pre-war roads, including those to Berdichev.

Berdichev had once been populated mainly by Jews and had accordingly established a reputation for proud cosmopolitanism; the majority perceived themselves as inheritors of a diasporic, dislocated legacy and felt no inclination to impose their way of life upon their neighbours or guests. Balzac had loved the place, and spent two years there. During the nineteenth century its size and relative self-sufficiently protected it from pogroms – it was then located in the Russian-annexed, Polish-speaking region of the Ukraine – but between 1941 and 1944 it was in Nazi hands. Sillitoe wondered if anything remained of its Jewish character.

Sillitoe never knew if George had been acting as something more than his guide. He certainly does not recall how his companion would have had the opportunity to communicate their new unplanned excursion to anyone else – having announced it to him at breakfast – but recollection differs considerably from vigilance. As they got within five kilometres of the city the pre-war road of Sillitoe's map changed in character and direction. They were joining a bypass, so Sillitoe took the first exit and looked forward to testing his map-reading skills against what was left of a network of byways that predated the Revolution. Soon on an otherwise empty track they came upon a roadblock. Militiamen flagged them down and went straight to George's window – perhaps they assumed it was a left-hand-drive car. He translated to Sillitoe the militiaman's statement. This, too, it seemed was a route, region, which lay outside those Intourist zones which allowed visits by foreigners. Sillitoe wondered whether a three-man militia unit was permanently stationed on the remote country road to advise reckless Englishmen in their Peugeot estates of this, but he did not bother to ask.

They set off again on their originally planned route to Chernovtsy, and George now seemed a little more relaxed, at least until midday when Sillitoe turned at a crossroads along an unsignposted road. 'Where are we going?' he asked, hopelessly trying to hide his agitation. 'To Loshkovitz,' answered Sillitoe without adding, 'Who'll care?' Someone would, because a small militia detachment, almost identical to the one they had encountered near Berdichev, pulled them over and put them through exactly the same routine.

Next day he and George parted on good terms, as anticipated, at Chernovtsy and Sillitoe was left to make his own way home through Romania. Sillitoe would meet George again on three occasions, once more in the Soviet Union, once in London, and finally when he and Ruth visited Russia in 2005. He eventually asked him if he had indeed been ordered to report on their activities and likely destinations. 'What do you think?' he answered. 'But what I can tell you is that I was summoned by a colonel – military, not intelligence – to explain the incidents around Berdichev. They accused me of cooperating with a spy, you, but I got off. My foolish manner was convincing.'

Sillitoe recalls the journey over the Carpathians to Belgrade and on to the Adriatic and Dalmatian coast with a mixture of bemusement and disbelief. Hardly another motor vehicle seemed to exist. There were a few lorries but beyond the urban areas these were outnumbered by horse-drawn carts. Crossing the border to Italy was like entering another continent and a different century. By the time he had driven through central France and boarded the ferry for Dover more enduring, problematic concerns had filled his mind.

By electing to motor around the Soviet Union without a rigid schedule he was both testing his own indulgent perceptions of this reformed post-Stalinist enterprise and baiting it. As a result he had encountered a polite manifestation of what most Soviet citizens regarded as the norm; every decision he made appeared to have been quietly monitored and if necessary pre-empted. There was something else which when he confronted it seemed illusory, a foolish conceit, but it endured and provoked him none the less. Why did it seem that his every attempt to connect with the history of Judaism in Russia, including even so innocuous a gesture as a visit to a remote village, had been systematically frustrated?

At the end of Chapter 6 of *Road to Volgograd* is a passage so unobtrusively poignant that it seems alien to the rest of the text, as if placed there by Sillitoe to remind himself of an image by various degrees peripheral, inexplicable and immensely troubling. He begins a paragraph, 'By the synagogue the mud was jet black, the residue of a winter's soot . . .' and one is struck by the sudden arrival of the definite article – *the* synagogue – given that the building has never before been mentioned. This is puzzling because throughout the book Sillitoe gives a good deal of attention to the interweaving of history with the minutiae of his immediate impressions of buildings or locations. But the synagogue comes without warning. We know nothing of its past, or of how Sillitoe has found himself standing before it. He comments now: 'I'd seen it marked on the city plan of St Petersburg in *Baedeker's Russia, 1914* which I had with me; I wanted to find out whether it still existed. It did.' It is, he tells us, 'enormous, big enough to hold several thousand people. I'd never seen such a large temple' (p. 80). He is transfixed, and as if to underline the inference that such a number will never fill it again we are introduced to two seemingly ghostly figures: 'A middle-aged man and a woman with a shopping basket were coming down the stairs. I asked if I could see the synagogue . . .' They explain that they are locking it up but if he returns that evening they will admit him, and then they disappear like cautious spectres into the surrounding alleyways. Sillitoe had accepted a theatre invitation for that evening and couldn't return. He does not mention the episode again, at least not specifically, but the following day as he leaves Leningrad he reflects on how his nomadic impulse always creates sadness: 'Each town visited I could stay in for the rest of my life – after only three days there. Maybe I crave to fix on one town for good but, having left the one I was born in through some unexplainable impulse (that became, through such a long desire, a reason), it has become impossible. What temple was destroyed inside me to turn me into a wandering Jew?' (pp. 80–1).

This is more than a momentary slip into self-mythologizing. He sees the connection between a tribe for whom displacement is a state of mind and the spectacle of the vast empty synagogue, looked after by two lonely reminders of something lost. The image contrasted so grievously with the collective energy of the rest of the country that it cut him in two. It was this, a growing sense of affinity with the history and temper of Judaism, that impelled the enormous changes in his outlook and writing during the late 1960s and early 1970s. He did not reinvent himself as a convert or zealot; he was more a fascinated, often sceptical fellow traveller.

TWENTY-THREE

Troubled by his experiences, Sillitoe applied for a visa to enter the Soviet Union as a tourist in 1967 and it was issued for early September. During the visit he was asked to give a lecture at the Gorki Literary Institute on his work, his life and his opinions on the duty of a writer to their calling. This was one of the most prestigious academic and literary establishments in the country, and to be honoured with an invitation to deliver a guest lecture there testified to the fact that Sillitoe was still perceived by the authorities as an ideological prize. They were in for a shock.

Before an audience of almost four hundred, including correspondents from *Pravda*, Soviet literary magazines and international news correspondents, he delivered an hour-long lecture on how writers were insignificant unless they shared with everyone else the freedom to express whatever views they wished either in their work or as private citizens. Observations on this topic might, with scrupulous editing, have been presented as consistent with the policies of a state which ostensibly valued emancipation and equality, at least as abstractions. But Sillitoe was very specific in his accusations. He named Daniel and Sinyavsky as two writers who for no other reason than they had written things unacceptable to the Party were presently under house arrest, awaiting possible prosecution for crimes against the state and facing imprisonment if found guilty.

The Reuters correspondent was dumbfounded and did his best to copy a rough version of this anti-Soviet diatribe, delivered at the behest of the Soviet authorities, to every international agency he could find, and a somewhat blurred, synoptic account of what Sillitoe had done was reported in broadsheets from the *New York Times* to the *Daily Telegraph*. Officials from the Writers' Union and from other state agencies were, to say the least, perplexed. They begged Sillitoe to in effect recant, to write an article for *Pravda* which 'clarified' his views on the intrinsic values of socialism. He refused, and when a version of his lecture appeared in *Pravda* as 'I Believe in an Awakening' (8 January 1968) he found himself reading something utterly different from what he had actually said. No names were mentioned, of course, and his savage, scarifying attack on the politics of his host country had been completely rewritten as a eulogy for socialism.

The following November Sillitoe and Ruth were invited to Moscow to celebrate the 150th anniversary of the birth of Turgenev. Sillitoe had been asked to give an appreciation of the great writer's life from the stage of the Bolshoi. His draft was first scrutinized by Writers' Union members, who informed him that his reference to the fact that when Turgenev was writing Russia, for all its faults, at least had open borders – that its citizens could leave – was unacceptable. His argument that, surely, historic facts could not in these more enlightened times be damaging to the regime was met with a blunt rejection. Such matters, he was informed, were of questionable relevance to the subject of his talk, which would be attended by none other than Leonid Brezhnev. Sillitoe remembers delivering his speech – his original, unrevised version – and glancing anxiously towards Comrade Brezhnev, seated in a box reserved for Politburo members, whose countenance exuded utter boredom and indifference.

Sillitoe's next encounter with the Soviet authorities was in spring 1969. The novelist Anatoly Kuznetsov had been allowed to visit London to give readings and talk to the press, a gesture which many regarded as an indication of the softening of the repressive inclinations of the regime. Sillitoe was informed of Kuznetsov's visit by George, his old minder. George would now be Kuznetsov's escort during his time in London and looked forward to meeting Sillitoe again, and Sillitoe is still uncertain whether all of this amounted to a bizarre coincidence or a case of institutional idiocy. Kuznetsov was well known for his novel *Babi Yar*, which had been suppressed in the Soviet Union. Why, Sillitoe wondered, had this loose cannon been sent Westwards with such an affable and unreliable watchman as George? It might have seemed farcical were it not for his suspicion that behind the comic scenario was a party machine made no less tolerable by its incompetence. George had always wanted to see London, not of course as the capital of an empire now well in decline but because so many of the stories that had preoccupied him for most of his adult life had been in some way connected with it; it was the cynosure of his literary world.

Sillitoe asked George to lunch at his house in Clapham on 1 August. His friend arrived at twelve-thirty to be greeted with wine and vodka and a generous range of foods. George and Sillitoe ate, drank and chatted until early evening, and they missed the brief news item on the BBC reporting that Anatoly Kuznetsov had at around 1 p.m. taken a taxi to the Fleet Street offices of the *Daily Telegraph*, entered the building with an unexpurgated version of *Babi Yar* – an incendiary text which presented anti-Semitism and Soviet governance as indistinguishable – and claimed political asylum.

Official statements by the Soviet government accused Sillitoe and Graham Greene of colluding with British Intelligence in a plot to encourage Kuznetsov to defect, and released a report to international news agencies claiming that during a search of Kuznetsov's Moscow apartment a cache of letters, hidden under the floorboards, had been found. A considerable number were, they stated, from Alan Sillitoe and Graham Greene and included detailed discussions of the most opportune time for the defection to occur, how exactly it would be executed and his prospects thereafter for a life in the West. This proved, they averred, that the two Englishmen were instrumental in cajoling the naïve and vulnerable writer into what amounted to an act of treason.

Sillitoe had formed a genuine friendship with George and now feared for his fate. No one suggested that he had been wittingly involved in the alleged plot, but he was Kuznetsov's minder and to spend the day in which his charge defected enjoying the decadent hospitality of a man who had publicly repudiated the USSR's claims to allow free speech would no doubt earn him some form of retribution. George was flown back to Moscow via the Soviet Embassy on the night of the incident, and Sillitoe, certain that his letter would be intercepted and scrutinized, wrote to him feigning the manner of the bumbling *ingénue* seemingly in a state of shock at how the two of them had become associated with these events and – a good point – reassuring him that once his discerning bosses had sorted fact from speculation he would have nothing to fear. George was sent for about six months to a backwater in the Urals to take over as principal editor of a publisher of children's books, hardly severe retribution by Soviet standards and without doubt a token gesture to buttress the story that George had been duped by Sillitoe. On his return to Moscow he was appointed Chief Editor of *Progress*, the Soviet Union's most prestigious imprint.

I ask now whether it was purely coincidental that Kuznetsov decided to defect on the day George elected – was invited – to spend with Sillitoe. 'Some people do not believe in coincidence,' he answers. 'We might not be the principal cause of something but we might equally play a role in a sequence of events prompted by someone else. Read the article I wrote for *The Times* in 1974: "Although it happened that I was not consciously enrolled in assisting Kuznetsov to escape . . . I am certainly happy to have been of some help, however it came about"' ('When will the Russians see that humanity is good for them?', *The Times*, 10 June 1974, p. 14). This appears straightforward enough, but one wonders none the less. In a letter written to his brother Michael several months after the incident, Sillitoe is as usual expansive and affable, offering details on their new house in Wittersham, on how David and Susan are getting on at their local school, interwoven with enquiries about Michael and his family. Then there is what amounts to an aberration:

> If I ever go to Russia again I'll get you a fur hat and some records – though it's doubtful I'll be welcome there after the Kuznetsov affair. The KGB seem to think I had something to do with his defection, which is ridiculous. None of my letters were found in his flat because I never wrote him any. [AS to MS, 20 September 1969]

It is uncommon for Sillitoe in his letters to friends and family to shift to so formal, even cumbersome a manner, and the passage is even more curious because it is superfluous. He had already spoken to Michael of these events, so why did he feel the need to offer this somewhat laboured case for the defence in a letter that was, as ever, dedicated to news about their respective families and what each of them had been up to since their last exchange? We will never know – Sillitoe claims that perhaps he had forgotten that Michael was already aware of his case – but anyone else who might have opened the letter between Kent and Nottingham might have read it as an authentic private disclosure to his brother.

No records survive of Sillitoe's visits to Czechoslovakia, Hungary and Romania which antedate his 1967 trip to the Soviet Union nor of his single post-Kuznetsov excursion to the Soviet-controlled bloc, Budapest in 1971, or at least there are no formal records. In 1972 he received a letter from the writer Josef Škvorecký, whom he had first met in Prague in 1964. Škvorecký was one of the few to have escaped soon after the Soviet invasion of 1968 and he wrote to Sillitoe from Toronto, where he had become an associate professor of English.

> I hope you remember when we met in Prague in 1964, you with your beautiful wife, in that wine cellar . . . You helped me and others so much. We are all pawns on the chessboard of history, and individuals don't seem to count anymore. You showed us that they did, by example. Thank you again. I have met others, some you know, people who survived the camps in the fifties and many are living on welfare in the States and Canada, crippled by the uranium they mined for the Soviets. Many send their good wishes and thanks to you. [J. Škvorecký to AS, 10 November 1972]

Sillitoe will not comment on why precisely such gratitude was forthcoming from a dissident refugee.

Given Sillitoe's interest in and regular visits to the Communist Bloc in the 1960s and then the Kuznetsov affair it would have been somewhat remiss of the security services not to have kept at least a few notes on his activities. The nature of these would be intriguing, since Sillitoe had in two years gone from being the prize exhibit of the Soviet Writers' Union to an alleged lackey of the imperialist intelligence agencies. Selected files from MI5 and MI6 have over the past few years been transferred, abridged, to the National Archive, but the Archive, after studious and lengthy trawls, informed me that they have received nothing that relates either tangentially or in its entirety to Alan Sillitoe. MI5, with commendable tact, advised me that it has been their policy to release 'very few' files prepared after 1957 into the public sphere and stated that unfortunately they would not be able to respond to my request even for a monosyllabic response to the question of whether Alan Sillitoe had prompted their attention. They wished me well with the progress of my research.

Sillitoe recalls a conversation with the late David Mercer, who following a cultural soirée at the Israeli Embassy somehow found himself at the bar of a Soho club with a man who had once served in the colonial police and finished his career in London with 'the Service'. Mercer asked, not entirely flippantly, whether he should have bothered to introduce himself, and his companion answered, 'Of course not, old boy. We have a file on you as long as your arm.' What, he asked, about his friend Alan Sillitoe? 'Good Lord, yes. Longer still.'

Gadfly in Russia (2007), diffident and urbane in its manner, is Sillitoe's memoir of his last encounters with the Soviet Union, and it is enthralling to read it alongside a novel he wrote at the time, *Travels in Nihilon* (1971). Reviewers were unsettled if not exactly enthused by the novel. Only Robert Nye was brave and intuitive enough to detect its magnificently unprecedented character. Imagine if that gargantuan monument to impenetrability, *Finnegans Wake*, were actually readable. Consider it as involving something like a story and as comprised of sentences that allow of coherence while retaining its air of self-possessed insouciance. This is admittedly a troubling hypothesis, but *Travels in Nihilon* embodies it. It invites comparisons with such classics as Orwell's *1984* and Huxley's *Brave New World* and then withdraws the overture. Nihilon is an appalling place, but at the same time too chaotic and ridiculous to be treated as genuinely oppressive or frightening. Political decrees are issued, rarely implemented, usually forgotten or treated with casual indifference by state representatives and everyone else. Riots take place, people are shot, but no one, including those involved, appears all that concerned. It is a political madhouse run by individuals just as feckless and irresponsible as their alleged subjects. The prose and dialogue are possessed of a beautifully unhinged circularity, seeming for a while to exhibit what might be logic and then, always, coming adrift from whatever route we might expect them to follow.

'You're a disgrace to Nihilon!' shouted the police chief.

'I know. But why can't it happen? What's wrong with it? If you both agreed, I could still have my dream.'

'It would ruin your life,' said the police chief.

'I want to be ruined,' pleaded the despondent stationmaster. 'It would clear the air. It would make my life simpler, to have just one dream come true, and to be ruined as well. I've got the moral fibre for it, I swear I have.'

'Stop it,' pleaded Jaquiline, bursting into tears.

'You see what you cause by your dreams?' said the police chief.

'Making someone shed tears is a capital offence in Nihilon.'
Her eyes dried immediately. 'Is it?' [p. 86]

Sillitoe maintains this charming, anarchic manner for 254 pages, yet astonishingly our patience and levels of endurance are not tested as they would be with a routinely postmodern experimental work. We want to read on because within the chaos we detect in the characters flickerings of genuine emotion, kindness and tragic empathy. It is a superb, unjustly overlooked piece of work, and one that catches perfectly his feelings about a country so addictive, horrible and inexplicable as to defy classification.

TWENTY-FOUR

There was no specific moment at which Sillitoe unreservedly forswore socialism and its manifestation in the Soviet Union and shifted his commitment
to Judaism, Zionism and Israel, but it is certain that the two operations were
reciprocal and interdependent.

His first public statement on the subject occurred in December 1969.
He had for the previous two years been on amicable terms with the founders
and editors of a new left-wing journal called *Black Dwarf* which was attempting to offer a quirky, radical alternative to the standard organs of the left
from the *Daily Worker* through *Tribune*, the *New Statesman*, the *Guardian*
and the *Daily Mirror*. He sympathized with its refusal to conform even to
supposedly nonconformist politics. However, during 1968 it began regularly
to publish articles and letters which gave full support to Palestinian terrorist groups and condoned their actions as a justifiable campaign of resistance
to a repressive colonial regime, Israel, and its Western sponsors. Sillitoe's
letter of 3 December 1969 boils with anger. He begins:

> I was one of the people who originally welcomed a journal such as the *Black
> Dwarf* promised to be. I saw it as having a useful purpose in the left-wing
> revolutionary life of this island. Lately, however, one thing has begun to
> worry me. I extend this worry to other newspapers and journals of the 'left'
> in this country. It concerns your attitude to Israel, and the activities of the
> so-called Palestine Liberation Movement.

Israel, he states, has a right to exist and those who falsely claim a moral
imperative for their terrorist atrocities are in truth 'tools of Arab imperialism'. The Western left has, in its support for the PLO and other
organizations, exposed its hypocritical, anti-Semitic leanings, given that
such groups are funded and sponsored by 'rotten, despotic medieval regimes
. . . feudal set-ups' just as set upon the annihilation of the Jewish people as
were the Nazis. Even worse is the claim in *Black Dwarf*'s recent articles and
editorials that there is a symbiotic alliance between socialist principles,
support for the Palestinian cause and the instinct for justice to be found in
the ordinary British working man. Here, avers Sillitoe, *Black Dwarf* shows
that there is a very narrow margin between middle-class socialists, intellectuals who manipulate popular opinion for their own private ends, and
their fascist counterparts:

... it appears to be part of your 'Socialist Legacy' to give free rein to the deeply ingrained anti-Semitism of your middle class Edwardian grandfathers. The *Black Dwarf*, by its support for the bomb-throwing, child-murdering, so-called liberation movements of the Middle East are aiding the effort to make a mass Jewish grave in the sea and thus create a socialist final solution which would be more final than any other.

During the next few years the very idea of what being Jewish involved became for Sillitoe as fascinating and hypnotic as reflections from fragments of a shattered mirror.

Since they had met, he and Karel Reisz had subjected each other to the type of mischievous exchanges that belie a deeper unspoken affection. Betsy Blair: 'Karel came over to England on the last of the Kindertransports, from Czechoslovakia in May 1939. His parents were supposed to come later, but they didn't. They were killed by the Germans. His uncle was already here and had looked after Karel's elder brother, who'd been here for a while. He, Karel's uncle, was Eton-educated upper middle class and to spare his nephews the nightmare of his own upbringing he sent them to Layton Park, a Quaker school in Reading – far more civilized than Eton in his view. None the less Karel by the time he was fourteen sounded like an upper-middle-class Englishman – but one who could, if he wished, switch to German or Czech. He was a magnificent chameleon. Professor Higgins would never have guessed his true origins. Anyway, he loved Alan greatly from the start, and the feeling was mutual. But there was always what seemed to be role-playing between them. Being an American and by inclination left-wing, class was something that had never really meant anything to me, until I came to England. Alan and Karel would play games, slipping into stereotypes that for the onlooker might seem their natural territory. But in truth they found in each other something very similar. It was intriguing because even when Alan began to lose faith in socialism Karel's performance as an English gentleman could be relied upon to revive in him the spectre of left-wing apologist. But sometimes the masks would slip, there would no longer be room for joking. Karel might say, "Alan, give it up," shake his head and add, "You've seen how they treat people and why the system can never work." You see, Karel had been back to Czechoslovakia after the war, when the communists were taking over. He knew that he, as a Jew, had escaped narrowly with his life and that the incoming regime would be little better. Alan knew this too. Felt it. For Karel – what would you call it – the whole European tragedy was part of his life, but if you didn't know him properly you'd assume he was from comfortable Home Counties stock. And – for different reasons – there was something of that about Alan too, I mean something that was essential to him but which he is reluctant, too thoughtful, to exhibit.'

Since Karel's life and indeed his personality were shaped by a simple fact – that he was Jewish at a time when an entire continent seemed intent on exterminating his kind – did she think that this played some part in the special nature of his and Sillitoe's friendship? 'Yes. Because Alan too was made up of a series of dislocations and displacements, mostly self-willed. But yes.'

Sillitoe and Ruth got to know Dannie and Joan Abse in the mid-1960s. Dannie Abse recalls Sillitoe as an enigma. Political opinion on the Middle East during the late 1960s and early 1970s was polarized between those with left-wing affiliations and those with Zionist sympathies; it was virtually impossible to be both, and those in the latter camp, even the more moderate accommodating types, tended to be Jewish themselves. 'Alan had very pro-Zionist sympathies and in this he was, as someone with no religious background whatsoever, unusual to say the least. The fact that Ruth was Jewish was incidental. She didn't influence him. In fact he was far more vociferous and committed than she was.' He reflects. 'It is odd, though, because I can't recall a particular moment when Alan actually tore into anyone on these issues. We would sometimes be at the same dinner parties and as the evening wore on and more drink was taken plenty of verbal ping-pong would be played across the table . . . on the fate of the Palestinians, the Six Day War, the Munich Olympics and so on. But Alan tended to listen. He might add the odd measured, thoughtful comment but for most of the time he would sit back and draw on his pipe. And listen. Yet he did not simply hold opinions on these matters, he was utterly absorbed by them. I remember in the early seventies I'd been invited to give a reading in Vilna in Lithuania and I met a women there who told me of how there were still a small number of Jews who had survived the war and just as significantly were descended from a sect that could trace its heritage back to the ninth or tenth century. You'll find details in Arthur Koestler's book *The Thirteenth Tribe*. A wonderful book by the way. During one of the many conflicts between Islam and Christianity, almost magically a Jewish kingdom was founded comprised of people from Persia and other parts of the Middle East. After I returned from Lithuania I was talking to Alan about this – I'd never come across it before – and I was astonished. He knew as much as Koestler about this moment in history and the subsequent dispersal of these people across Europe. It was not that he was exulting in his erudition. Quite the opposite, because the knowledge seemed precious to him, though he was happy to share it. That's what I mean about Alan being an enigma, a benign, hospitable enigma. He is a secret man, without being secretive.'

And where better to keep one's secrets – though not necessarily to hide them – than in a work of fiction? 'Pit Strike' (1973), one of his best-known short stories, is perceived by most as documentary realism, based as it is upon the miners' disputes of the early 1970s; the BBC had Sillitoe adapt it for their 'Play for Today' series in 1977. But look closely at the tale and one will find its engagement with contemporaneous politics shadowed by a far more timeless and quixotic presence. It is about Joshua, a middle-aged Nottingham miner who travels south with his fellow NUM members to shore up the picket lines of the Kent coalfields. With an unprompted, reckless act he causes a coal lorry to shed its load and block the road for other vehicles. Joshua's story sounds like a paean to working-class solidarity, yet he, and his author, would frustrate even the most determined and accomplished Marxist's search for another recruit to their compendium of archetypes. Joshua is indulged by his workmates as an eccentric. In most respects he lives an ordinary life: married for twenty-five years and settled in his modest three-bedroom semi. He is a big man, six feet four inches, who has boxed and played football and is inordinately strong even by the standards of coal-face workers. He is also given to quoting verbatim from the Bible, even able to redraft his own observations and pronouncements in the idiom of the King James version. He drinks and socializes at the miners' welfare, and most there know him as 'the Bible man', who can be relied upon to test the patience of anyone with a political outlook on the scale between solid Labour and communist. But Joshua does not believe in God and never has. He carries his old battered Bible with him everywhere but he is indifferent to the New Testament. The Old Testament he regards not as doctrine but rather as a fabric of dilemmas, questions and stories, a text as open and troubling as life itself. His peers might regard him as a curiosity, a throwback to the years when Nonconformist ministers were as active in the coalfields as shop stewards now, but none of them really knows him. If asked whether he believed in God he would have told the truth, but the question is never raised and Joshua is content with his own world and his beliefs, or lack of them. One is, of course, reminded of Sillitoe at dinner parties, sucking on his pipe while observing the 'verbal ping-pong', and indeed Dannie Abse's memorable phrase could just as easily refer to Joshua: 'a secret man, without being secretive'.

Joshua's only solid conviction is his refusal to be corralled by abstractions or doctrinal solutions, religious or political, yet equally he abjures indifference. Hence his almost suicidal attack on the lorry. The episode is described with magisterial brilliance in that we are given facts which particularize but never explain – notably the insistent reference to the Bible hidden in his pocket – and the rest is up to us. Sillitoe dares the reader to speculate, maybe even proselytize, on the ideological significance of the act, confident that Joshua will remain immune from such attempts. Versions of such readers occur in the story itself, as the husband and wife with whom Joshua is billeted during his time in Kent. She is a sociologist, he a university professor; middle-class, well-educated products of the 1960s with a predictable political outlook. The thought of putting up a real member of the radical working classes, maybe even a 'Party' member, adds a keen frisson to their fashionable commitments. Again, Sillitoe works entirely by inference, but the words 'patronizing' and 'condescension' could be etched in the margins of each page. While his workmates know little of the real Joshua, they at least have shared with him the dangers of working underground and lived on the same wage in the same location, but for Jack and Pam, his hosts, he provides a tantalizing, suitably brief experience of *Guardian* editorials made flesh. One should note that the story was written shortly after Sillitoe drafted his letter to *Black Dwarf*, in which he charges the middle-class left-wing intelligentsia with the worst kind of élitism, of claiming to speak on behalf of a class and in doing so implying that ordinary people lack the volition and independence to think and speak for themselves.

Joshua is Sillitoe to the extent that we intuit in him two characters: one reserved, almost reclusive, and another close to the surface and ready to explode.

Helder Macedo: 'At parties Alan would sometimes seem distracted; when people were half drunk and talking continuously he might politely detach himself and go to the bookshelf, become absorbed in a volume. That would happen in larger groups. If there were two, three, four of us he would sometimes be outspoken. His anger would not be directed against those present but its energy, especially involving Israel, is something you do not forget. Ruth would take the moderate view.'

Sillitoe did not go in for gladiatorial combat with coal lorries, but by the early 1970s when he wrote the story a similar gesture – in that it crystallized his private and public worlds – was imminent. He was planning to visit Israel. Before the *Black Dwarf* letter Sillitoe's emerging sense of attachment to the legacies of Judaism and the current situation in Israel was largely a private affair, something that he might share with close friends and family. Israel, however, had for some time shown an interest in him. *Saturday Night and Sunday Morning* had been translated into Hebrew in 1961, and *The Loneliness of the Long Distance Runner* a year later, and given that 85 per cent of the population was fluent in English this reflected something other than the economics and pragmatics of publishing. For many Israeli readers the books echoed far beyond their settings, blending the minutiae of daily life with emotional absolutes in the manner of Israel Joshua Singer, Sholem Ash and Lamed Shapiro. Hebrew editions were not so much translations as cultural welcomings.

Also, organizations based in Britain but with roots in Israel were beginning to take note of a new, vociferous ally. George Evnine, Vice Chair of the Herut Movement of Great Britain (a branch of the Zionist Revisionist

Organization), wrote on behalf of his group to express his thanks for Sillitoe's letter to the *Guardian* of 13 January 1972 in which he accused virtually all of the centre-to-left-inclined British press of purblind hypocrisy in their support of a ruthless terrorist organization whose single objective was the destruction of the only democratic regime in the region. 'In the present atmosphere, whipped up by the press, it would certainly have been far easier to remain silent,' wrote Evnine. 'To write as you did required a conviction and a moral courage which is greatly appreciated . . .' (G. Evnine to AS, Indiana Archive).

Sillitoe had begun corresponding with a number of Israeli writers, in particular Yehuda Amichai based in Jerusalem and Aharon Megged of Tel Aviv, and his first visit was arranged for early summer 1974. This would be a modestly publicized affair, at least outside Israel itself, involving readings and talks by Ruth and Sillitoe in Jerusalem and Tel Aviv. Sillitoe had also arranged private meetings with individuals and campaign groups concerned specifically with cases of Jews in the Soviet Union convicted and sentenced for spuriously concocted crimes against the state or denied the opportunity to join other members of their family in Israel. Word had spread, by various means, that the disillusionment which followed this outspoken Gentile's 1967 visit involved more than a recognition of the inherently wretched nature of communism. For Sillitoe the curious ability of the Soviet apparatus to anticipate and politely undermine his attempts even to locate towns where Jewish culture and lifestyle had once flourished was echoed furiously and unambiguously by events in the Middle East. Israel won the Six Day War of 1967 emphatically, but only by pre-empting a strike by a gigantic force assembled at its borders, principally by Egypt with assistance from Syria and Jordan, whose single aim was to wipe Israel out. Every piece of hardware from tanks through MiG fighters to Kalashnikov rifles had come directly from the USSR along with a considerable number of military advisors and instructors, some of them veterans of the Second World War. Sillitoe's son David was only six in 1967 but as he matured he became more mindful of that year's transformative effect upon his father. 'That was when he really acknowledged, recognized, the alliance between the USSR and the Arab states intent on destroying Israel. He didn't become a Conservative – God forbid, at home his instincts were still toward Labour – but he no longer trusted socialism as an ideological principle. In fact his trust in ideology of any sort, which was anyway qualified, disintegrated completely.'

The only printed records of Sillitoe's 1974 visit are 'First day in Israel' (*Transatlantic Review*, Autumn/Winter 1974, pp. 91–9) and 'My Israel' (*New Statesman*, 20 December 1974, pp. 810–12), and both were mined from a far more revealing document (entitled 'FIRST DAY IN ISRAEL', in Sillitoe

Archive, Indiana) to which I will refer. He flew out on an El Al 747 from Heathrow, and Ruth came the following day. Yet one has the impression that he is alone.

> Darkness outside. At half past seven GMT (Israeli time two hours later) the tune and the worlds of 'Scholem Aleichem' starts pounding out as our huge plane floats low over the coast of Israel with Tel Aviv to the right and left. It's a stirring tune, and must bring tears to the eyes of those who are going home for the first time after two thousand years of bitter exile, and even maybe to those who are only visiting. [Indiana Archive, p. 6]

A more evocative subclause is difficult to envisage. He would have been reminded of a moment almost twenty years earlier in Majorca, 1956, when 'I slung an aerial from the top of the house, part of my old trade, and tuned in on short wave to what I could get,' and one evening he heard this same 'melancholy – as I thought – tune coming over the ether . . . A few minutes later came the news in English from a station called Kol Zion La-Gola – the Voice of Jerusalem in Israel' (*Jewish Influences on My Writing*, University of Southampton, 1996). This lonely, insulated nation telling its story to the world stirred his sympathies, but in 1974 as the El Al 747 descended towards Tel Aviv airport sympathy had become affiliation. He felt like a version of the country he was visiting: resolute, self-determined and alone.

On his return to London Sillitoe wrote perhaps his most provocative, peremptory political article yet. He tells the story of two families whose dilemmas would, but for his article, have remained beyond the canvas of journalism and international diplomacy. Yurli Roitkov-Fodoryachick, a 26-year-old engineer, and Yuri Tartakovsky, twenty-five, plumber and refrigerator technician, are political prisoners separated from the rest of their families who have been allowed to leave the USSR for Israel. Sillitoe does not speculate on the Soviet government's apparently perverse motives for such decisions. This is left to the reader, who is faced with an ineluctable conclusion – it might seem gratuitous, even sadistic, to grant emigration rights to some members of a family while withholding them from others, but the spectacle and pain of being forever divided would certainly have a deterrent effect on those similarly inclined to leave. And even though these are ordinary people far from the spotlight of international controversy they belong to a community who regard somewhere else as their true home and who can be relied upon to have knowledge of each other's sufferings and ambitions: deterrence yet again. The calculated inhumanity of the policy becomes all the more graphic through Sillitoe's refusal to specify it; the facts are eloquent enough. He closes with a masterfully poignant statement.

The point I am making is that if my friends and others were allowed to leave and live elsewhere there is no reason to suppose they would not be friendly to the country which allowed them to go. A country would gain as much as it would lose by a more liberal policy of the movement of peoples. [*The Times*, 10 June 1974]

The article prompted an avalanche of letters, one of the most affecting of which was from Leslie H. Hardman, Minister of the Hendon Synagogue, who explains that he has read many pieces on the plight of the Jews in Soviet Russia. 'None, however, has moved me so deeply as yours in this morning's *Times*. I cannot explain it in any particular definitive manner, but it brought tears to my eyes, and impelled me to write even before I could begin my morning activities.' He confesses to knowing nothing of Sillitoe beyond his reputation as a writer, but on encountering Sillitoe's phrase, 'I am the sort of person who is unhappy when my friends suffer, and suffer when his friends are unhappy,' was 'stirred' by a sense of recognition. 'I do not know your religious affiliations, but if you are not Jewish, you are certainly one of those men whom our Rabbis describe as "the righteous among the Gentiles" and who is assured of eternal bliss. It might require a miracle to save all Soviet Jews who are desirous to leave Russia, but you can help in bringing it about' (Leslie H. Hardman to AS, 10 June 1974, Indiana Archive).

Sillitoe wrote back explaining that during his recent visit to Israel he had met the families mentioned in his article and others similarly tormented, adding that while he is by temperament, indeed profession, a novelist 'this [story] almost wrote itself because I simply had to do it'. 'I am not in fact Jewish, though I can think of many good reasons for being so. I certainly appreciate your blessing' (AS to L.H. Hardman, 17 June 1974).

Sillitoe's next visit to Israel was in 1977, and a journal exists in which he records the particulars of his travels, along with more personal observations. Its manner recalls *Road to Volgograd* and though it was originally intended for publication Sillitoe decided against even offering it to his publisher. Why? 'I thought I might try to get it published but it wasn't well written and it would take too long to get it up to my usual standard. I would probably have needed to rewrite it endlessly.' Even in its preparatory state it is an immensely revealing document, the nexus for the many channels of influence and experience that made up the preceding ten years.

This time he had decided not to fly but to drive across Europe and take the ferry from Greece. There was no practical or obvious rationale for this, given that while he and Ruth loved the adventure of travelling the idea of a 1,500-mile journey through the Continent in midsummer, early July, in their Peugeot estate packed with luggage and with fifteen-year-old David in the back seat seemed to err more towards the masochistic than the reckless.

There is, though, a curious and striking similarity between this gesture, and it was certainly Sillitoe's idea, and the one of 1967 when he drove to and through the Soviet Union; perhaps he knew that something transitional and immutable was again about to occur.

Sillitoe had made friends with a number of Israeli writers over the previous few years and had become particularly attached to Yehuda Amichai, by general consensus the country's finest living poet. Ruth Fainlight: 'We were first introduced to Yehuda by Ted Hughes at the 1967 Poetry International Festival. Ted was one of the founders of the event and that year he and Assia stayed with us for the week, and Yehuda came to dinner.' They would meet again on several occasions in London when Amichai gave readings and talks, but they got to know each other properly during the 1974 visit, and Yehuda and his wife Hannah stayed with Sillitoe and Ruth in Wittersham and in London later that year. Sillitoe's diary for 17 July when he arrived in Jerusalem is a listless, lethargic document, until the closing paragraph when the previously rambling sentences gather pace and find focus. 'A long day. Spent more of the evening unpacking. Drank many cups of tea. Phoned Yehuda and he will stroll over tomorrow afternoon. He lives only a few hundred yards away – our neighbour.'

Yehuda perceived his Jewishness rather as a legacy than a doctrinal code, and though Sillitoe could not, would not, make any claims upon his friend's genetic inheritance he had begun to feel that Judaism's intellectual landscape was something towards which he had always felt an intuitive affinity.

The following day his entries bristle with energy and expectation. 'Cast the mind back through the glory and finesse of Jerusalem. Slept marvellously, though not too long. Got up and made breakfast for us . . . Relaxed as in the old days. Rushed upstairs to my study and scribbled a few lines of a poem. Then we must go out, and who can resist it?' (Indiana Archive, pp. 23–4). He and Ruth and David walked across the city, through the Christian quarter, calling at various markets, and arrived, apparently without planning, at the Western Wall.

> I touch the wall – David does so inadvertently; he is contemptuous of all religion, which I can understand. I don't believe, but I respect the Jewish religion.
> We rejoined Ruth (who had said a prayer for her mother and father) and went up the steps at the South West corner of the square leading to the Jewish quarter. [Indiana Archive, p. 24]

A few days later he was interviewed for Israeli radio, and one inevitable question would, he knew, trouble him most. The interviewer took it for granted that he was a member of that valued community, the 'Friends of

Israel'. But why, she asked him, had he become a friend of her country? His answer is unrecorded, but that night in his diary he reflected on his unease. 'It's difficult to *say* that I love this country and its civilisation, all that it is trying to do, and all the values it is trying to preserve, and succeeding so nobly in preserving.' One should note that he finds it difficult to *express* his love for Israel, not to feel it. He continues, 'If I left England for good, this is the only country I could live in' (Indiana Archive, p. 47). He did not feel guilty about the intensity of his attachment, but he had now reached a precipitate point in his life, found a single focus for the disparate, conflicting impulses of his character. Coming to terms with it privately was a challenge, and he was certainly not ready to discuss it live on a radio broadcast.

The next day he was enjoying a dinner with the Amichais, Denis Silk – another poet, English by birth but settled in Israel – Arieh Sachs, head of the English Department at the Hebrew University of Jerusalem, and Sachs's wife Gaby. Gaby reprised the radio interviewer's question. 'Instinct,' he answered.

Also in Jerusalem he got to know Teddy Kollek, the inspirational, controversial mayor of the city. Kollek hosted one of Sillitoe's readings, and in the years following 1977 they forged a friendship based on a mutual recognition of tough pragmatism combined with hair-raising unpredictability.

His account of his drive through the scorched landscape towards the Gulf of Eilat bristles with exhilaration. 'Desolation was total and salty after Massada – salt pans and pyramids. Landscape eroded like flaky pastry – created by a cook gone mad.' It is bleak, but he loves it and even finds room for a dart of caustic humour. 'Wanted to stop at Sodom and send postcards, but we missed the place . . .' (Indiana Archive, p. 51). They spent the night at a campsite and Sillitoe was reluctant to exchange experience for sleep. 'Woke at five. Went into the sea . . . Got some tea going . . . I felt very good . . . euphoric in fact, better than for years' (p. 52).

Back in Jerusalem he found that the energy of the place had caused him to abandon his addictive routine of reading. Since the 1950s he had acquired a hunger for books similar to a hedonist's appetite for food and drink; he devoured anything voraciously, recklessly. Now, however, 'I can't read any of the books I brought with me to Israel. I simply can't open them – except, very occasionally, the Bible.' He explains: 'Jerusalem is all-powerful, overwhelming, a fusion of high and eternal tensions pounding the spirit into a kind of bent-backed agreeable admiration as one either looks at it or walks its streets both old and new' (Indiana Archive, p. 70). Later he was further astonished by the ability of this environment to disrupt his equilibrium. 'I've written four poems since I got here – but no fiction. That's fitting. Why write fiction in Jerusalem?' He knows the answer to this question. He had indeed addressed it in *Raw Material*, published four years earlier: 'to write books is not to have an aim in life. It is a camouflage under which a real aim can wither before it is even understood' (p. 164). This seems dismissive of writing as a substitute for something more elemental and elusive, but later he qualifies his doubts: 'Being a writer is the one great fact, my only love, a love which I had to feel before I could fall in love with anything or anyone else. It had to be there even before I could fall in love with myself' (p. 182).

He feels unsettled by the capacity of fiction to remake the world, yet he is aware that in being able to do this it has become the key, defining feature of who he is. Now in Jerusalem he is, albeit briefly, detached from his mission. He is not worried because he sees this as a transitional moment, not a crisis. What has occurred is the conscious recognition of shifts that had been occurring in his writing and his outlook – which as he stated are indivisible – over the previous five years.

The most revealing passage of the entire journal involves Sillitoe renouncing and treating with contempt each of the ideals that he had previously espoused.

There is no greater proof that someone from the working class has joined the ranks of the middle class as that he becomes a communist, for in communism he sees the perfect tool with which to keep the workers he has left in a more sure and perpetual state of subjugation than capitalism ever devised. Only communism can make him safe from them. If ever any of them catch him up it will only be on his terms.

Communists in 'Western Countries' are the last great narcissists of modern times. If they come to power, they choose death, for they surely will not survive the consolidation of the state that they had worked and hoped for. Their deaths, therefore, would individualise them more than their lives.

If they do not come to power, they live as martyrs to a useless idea. Their lives, therefore, individualise them more than their deaths.

There is no greater proof that someone from the middle class has consolidated and accepted his middleclassness than that he or she joins the ranks of the communist party – or any other party to the left of the social democrats – because he sees it as the perfect tool to keep the workers from getting at his throat, something to keep them in a state of slavery which even early capitalism hadn't the nerve to concoct.

In both cases it is a short-term policy for them personally because, as already said, they go to the wall, if, through chaos and misery it comes to power. It never does come, of course, except through chaos and misery. [Indiana Archive, pp. 86–7]

He avers in *Raw Material* that writing is his profession and his condition, indeed that his life is comprised largely of stories, and he goes on to ponder the concomitant question: What is truth? Is it something that we make or something we disclose? Through the 1960s each of his characters had involved him in an engagement with these questions; Arthur Seaton and Colin Smith respected the flux of life without seeking inner purpose, while Dawley and the Handleys went to the other extreme, attempting to remake the world according to dogma. In his own life he encountered a commensurate division between a commitment to freedom as the only real source of happiness and fulfilment and his awareness that the one opportunity so far available to ordinary man for release from poverty and exploitation, socialism, led in practice to another kind of imprisonment and political authoritarianism.

Now, in Israel, he had found a means of resolving this dilemma. The individuals he met from 1974 onwards embodied something he had previously been desperate to articulate as a writer, his problem being that what he felt privately refused to correspond with the way that people behaved in life and in books. There seemed a continuous irreconcilable friction between the impulse of his inner world and what, he knew, would be unacceptable as words on the page. Israel, however, seemed populated by narratives that were unique to the location, stories of men and women who had variously suffered, fled, escaped, fought and become part of this untidy fabric. Everything seemed acceptable and incorporate, from Orthodox rabbis to secularists who had created a casual version of socialism in a kibbutz.

The 1977 trip to Israel is a mosaic of tiny stories shot through with Sillitoe's own, and he draws upon their uncompromising poignancy. Typical is his unplanned meeting with Jerry Fishman. Sillitoe was due to meet the novelist Rachel Fishman, but before that he had become engrossed in a conversation with her husband. Jerry did not write, but Sillitoe was as fascinated by the story of his life as by anything intended for print. Born in 1922, he had left Poland in 1939, lied about his age and joined the Polish (Free) Army in London. There he had contacted the Polish Embassy in the hope of finding a similar route west for his parents and been met with studied indifference. Despite his country's occupation by the Nazis and Soviets, Polish anti-Semitism proved durable. There were very few Jews in the free Polish forces in Britain, and the uninhibited abuse and discrimination he experienced caused him to desert. When captured he was exempted from the most extreme sentence, death, only after his true age was disclosed. When he did reach eighteen he joined a British tank regiment, served in Northern Europe and was discharged in 1946, having reached the rank of sergeant. Less than a year after that he was arrested again, this time by the Special Branch, on suspicion of providing forged passports to Jews who had survived the camps in Europe and were trying to reach Palestine. There was insufficient evidence for a criminal charge, though he had been detained for six months while the authorities looked for some, and following his release he returned to his search for news of his parents. Miraculously and ingeniously they had survived, having found their way through the chaos of Russia in 1941 on forged German passports and spent the rest of the war gaining sanctuary through bribes and less frequently acts of sympathy first in Siberia and then in Shanghai. Even in the latter they witnessed the relentlessness of the Nazi pursuit of the final solution, with special detachments of the SS allowed by the occupying Japanese to conduct searches for small numbers of Jews who might have slipped through the net. Fishman was eventually reunited with his mother and father in the United States.

Fishman's story was, Sillitoe mused, almost too extraordinary for fiction, but in Israel it did not seem unusual. He mixed mostly with writers during his visit but tried as often as he could to effect random encounters with as many other individuals as possible, sometimes in cafés and markets and more frequently by offering lifts to soldiers and others with no obvious occupation. Some opened up to him about their background, and almost all disclosed a legacy that drew comparison with Fishman's, if not directly then from their parents' generation. What surprised and animated Sillitoe was the fact that, amid this state of collective identity, individuality obtained. That the Jewish people had been the targets of loathing from virtually every other community for more than two millennia, most recently with an awesome attempt to wipe them from the face of the earth, was a given, something which required no further comment. Improbably the Jews, arguably the most foully treated victims in recorded history, had eschewed victimhood, found it stultifying and alien to their new identity as a nation. Sillitoe observed:

> Personal identity is more important than national identity; the nationalistic features inherent in such extreme movements as communism and fascism seek to crush the identity of the individual, to destroy all possibility of him searching to find his own unique individual soul . . . the more a country can allow itself [to give latitude] to this the more that country's [Israel's] strength. [Indiana Archive, p. 113]

It is evident throughout the journal that Sillitoe is comparing otherwise unremarkable events with similar experiences from his periods in the Soviet Union, looking at how each epitomizes a collective state of mind or more accurately provides a measure for something he unhesitatingly admires. The bird-like woman flitting across the roof in Moscow comes to mind as we read this:

> While shopping at the supermarket I saw a stunning girl at the milk stall. She was very small, very dark, and wore an army uniform with two white stripes on her sleeve. She wasn't particularly pretty or beautiful, yet seemed absolutely unforgettable. She was totally absorbed in the decision as to what to choose. [Private journal, not lodged in Indiana, p. 4]

The experience in Moscow was, he knew, the end of an illusion, the fading of a private chimera, but the 'stunning', 'unforgettable' soldier at the milk stall embodied the guileless courage of a nation.

Israel was the means by which Sillitoe could overturn the hypocrisies and contradictions of his past. He was not so presumptuous to assume that he could actually be part of it, but it reflected back an image of himself that the tangled class structures and customs of Britain had previously obscured.

> Israel is like any other country, yet like no other country . . . I feel as if I've been here before, in an earlier life. There is a freedom, a diversity that I've always yearned for but never found. [Indiana Archive, unpaginated longhand fragment]

He watches children playing near Yamit, with

> its superb view of the date palms (and a glimpse of the Bedouin encampment, and patient camels) and the wonderful beach to run on and swim from, and shout to each other across . . . America at the beginning of the century was called the Melting Pot. Israel is a furnace; a fire of constant war-threats bakes the people . . . But the children are free . . . [Indiana Archive, p. 106]

The most conspicuous literary testimony to Israel's effect upon him is *Sun Before Departure 1974–1983* (1984), in my opinion his most exceptional single collection of poems. Helder Macedo has worked with Sillitoe on translations of his (Helder's) poems from Portuguese into English, and he commented to me on how his friend operates as a versifier: 'He and Ruth are very different as poets, not only in manner but in approach. Ruth is reflective, she circles and contemplates her subject. When Alan was translating he would plunge into the poem, absorb himself, launch into it, and very often he would come up with something close to the original. And this I think was his method in composing his own poems.' This last is a shrewd observation. Sometimes his technique would distil gems from the verbal material, sometimes not, and rarely has he achieved such a convergence of inchoate emotion and measured eloquence as in *Sun Before Departure*. In the diary of the 1977 visit he records that after a day (18 June) in Jerusalem he rushed back to the flat and 'began to compose lines of a poem' (Indiana Archive). This would eventually become 'On First Seeing Jerusalem'. Each loose three-line stanza rehearses the same quandary of how to describe, preserve the city's unique blend of timelessness and dynamism.

> One joins the multitude and grieves.
> Knows it from within.
> One does not know. Let me see you
>
> Everyday as if for the first time
> Then I'll know more:
> Which already has been said
>
> By wanderers who, coming home,
> Regret the loss of that first vision.
> The dust that knew it once is mute.

In the Indiana Archive the manuscript of this poem, revised at least five times, reflects a man in a state of sublime absorption. When the collection was published in 1984 Sillitoe's friends in Israel were entranced. For the first time an outsider had captured a mood they thought exclusive to them. Yehuda Amichai: 'Beautiful and astonishing. It is Hebrew written in English' (Amichai to AS, 12 December 1984). In a long letter Aharon Megged wrote: 'Reading and re-reading the poems I found in them a creation of an illuminating harmony between landscape, mood and personality . . . which casts a new, very personal light on things and views we [Israelis] live with day by day, and made me discern meaningful depth in the shallow sands of Tel Aviv under my shoes' (A. Megged to AS, 24 June 1984, Indiana Archive). Teddy Kollek took time off from his political brokerings between Palestinian envoys, the White House and Tel Aviv to read the volume in its entirety. 'Perhaps it was the result of psychic phenomena but in the hours after I sent off my recent letter to you, inviting you to Jerusalem, your exquisite book of poetry arrived. I was very moved to read your beautiful words on Jerusalem . . . and I am more convinced that you should come and spend more time [here]. I hope you will join us' (Teddy Kollek to AS, 11 February 1984, private correspondence).

As he puts it in his notebook, 'there is a freedom, a diversity [in Israel] that I've always yearned for but never found'. He talks now of his relationship with Judaism. 'I think that there was always something in my temperament that suited me to it. I was not searching for a faith – I have never believed in an afterlife – but Judaism is I think unique, an evolved code of ethics that has as much in common with post-Enlightenment ideals as religious dogma. Christianity I find wanting in this respect, Islam is an abomination – repressive and totalitarian.' Is there, I ask him, something of the Jews' experience as perpetual outcasts which encourages fellow feeling? 'There's something in that. I admire the cosmopolitanism of the Jewish state of mind. They can attend to a set of ideals and yet rejoice in dissent, perhaps as a consequence of the diaspora. When I write I have always attempted to stand outside; you can't be fixed at the centre of society if you are going to write about it. If you're on the outside you can see the wheel of society turning and then you can pick out what you want to write about, but you can't be inside it because that would prevent you from giving full expression to what you feel. Yes, I can see that there is something in what you say. Jewish writers are always in some way outsiders even when writing about people, events that they know intimately. I too feel something of that.'

TWENTY-FIVE

During the mid-1970s Sillitoe came as close as he ever would to exchanging the role of writer for that of political activist. His support for Israel against what seemed to him a preponderance in the Western media and intelligentsia of pro-Palestinian opinion consumed a considerable amount of his time and energy. In 1974 he became, by virtue of his industry, the predominant figure in the Committee for Israel and recruited to it amongst others: Kingsley Amis, Frederick Raphael, John Braine, David Mercer, Ted Hughes, Stephen Spender, Iris Murdoch, Lynn Reid Banks, Margaret Drabble and Bernice Rubens. The Committee would make unapologetic use of celebrity and influence to promote the cause of Israel. The following is from Sillitoe's 1975 diary.

> Left Wittersham at 0905 – Ruth, David and myself – and drove 250 miles through Haywards Heath, Petworth, Winchester, Salisbury, Chard and Exeter to North Tawton. Rain in the middle part of the journey.
> April 7th. Talked a long time with Ted about Zionism and the Committee for Israel. We decided to have a meeting with Spender, Binyamin Tammuz and Jaquetta Hawkes etc and decide what can be done. When I get back to London I'll contact Tammuz. How can anything be done to improve the defensive position of Israel when the slightest attempt to do so brings about the execrations of the world? Only the intention to relinquish territory gets approval, and that is grudging enough since it is never sufficient to satisfy and never will be until the country has relinquished itself into extinction, which Israel will never do, but there is a malign force loose in the world which has taken into its head that Israel must go – against all reason and common sense to the world itself. Israel cannot be expected to act otherwise than she has in bringing the Golan Heights under permanent jurisdiction. Anyone who has been there immediately realises that northern Galilee is untenable when the Heights are in hostile hands. Ted suggested that the only thing for Israel to do would be to push all Arabs beyond the Jordan.

This should dispel the idea that Hughes was interested only in the esoteric aspects of Judaism. He agreed with Sillitoe that Israel was the West's buttress against a totalitarian predatory culture, Islam.

In December 1974 Sillitoe wrote to those already recruited to the Committee, and others he thought might be sympathetic, to ask if they would each be willing contribute to a 2,000–3,000-word piece to a book-length symposium which would be the first collective statement of support for Israel against the insidious pro-Arab lobby. The following wrote back stating that they would in principle support the project: Lynne Reid Banks, Saul Bellow, Heinrich Böll, Winston S. Churchill MP, Dame Daphne du Maurier, Friedrich Durrenmatt, Lord Feather, Lady Antonia Fraser, Professor Arthur Goodhart, Joseph Gormley, Ted Hughes, Marghanita Laski, Yehudi Menuhin, David Mercer, Lord Olivier, Harold Pinter, Jacquetta Priestley, David Price-Jones, John-Paul Sartre, Lord Snow, Stephen Spender, Gwyn Thomas, the Rt Hon. Jeremy Thorpe MP and Lord Ted Willis. The problem which over the next two years would cause the projected book to be continually postponed and eventually abandoned was of how to reconcile the notion of a consensus with the individual's right to qualify or particularize their case. Each potential contributor concurred with Sillitoe's statement in his letter that 'You may have noticed that, in all branches of the media, the Arab case for the dismemberment and ultimate destruction of Israel is gaining enormous prominence. If this proves nothing else it shows . . . that the world wouldn't protest too much against [Israel's] demise.' All felt similarly frustrated, but so diverse were the suggestions and enquiries on what might actually be written the book seemed in danger of losing focus, becoming, Sillitoe feared, a chorus of delusional ideals. David Price-Jones wrote to commiserate after Sillitoe had informed him of the book's atrophied condition, stating that the politicians 'on the list [tend to] keep their necks in no position to stick out' (David Price-Jones to AS, 16 February 1975, Indiana Archive). A year later when the project had been all but abandoned John Braine blamed intellectuals who when faced with the pandemic of pro-Palestinian leftism 'retreat into [their] private world; but when people like us do that the bully-boys take over . . . if Israel perishes, the West perishes' (John Braine to AS, 30 April 1976, Indiana Archive).

Sillitoe pressed on, however, and persuaded Lord Ted Willis to convene and chair, in the House of Lords, a meeting of prominent writers 'to discuss the attitude of British men [*Observer*] of letters to the current defamation campaign against Israel and the Jewish People' (AS to Ted Willis, private correspondence). The meeting took place in April 1975, and was attended by the Israeli Ambassador to the UK, Gideon Raphael, whom Alan and Ruth knew, along with Amis, Hughes, Banks and Spender of the now defunct book project, plus Drabble, Murdoch, Rubens, Lord Snow, Melvyn Bragg and Tom Stoppard. The point on which all were united was their objection to a recent UN resolution (15 October 1974) which compared Zionism with the South African policy of apartheid.

Shortly afterwards Sillitoe contacted his friend Aharon Megged, whom he had known since his time as Cultural Attaché to the Israeli Embassy in London in the 1960s and had met again on his recent visit to Israel. Megged had become a prominent member of the International PEN group, through which writers campaigned against censorship, transgressions of human rights and other forms of state coercion. Together they devised a shrewd response to the UN resolution. PEN was respected worldwide for its commitment to the freedom of the individual, and when Megged released his statement to press agencies in late May 1975 he effectively forced the hand of every PEN member. He wrote directly to them.

> This unprecedented UN verdict on a historic ideology is the most shameful perversion of historic truth, humanism and morality in our time. It constitutes base disrespect for the memory of all victims of racialism through the ages, and in particular for those massacred in the Nazi 'Final Solution'. Zionism, from the end of the nineteenth century onwards, is the organized political expression of the longing of the Jewish people to return to their historic homeland . . . It is the only national liberation movement which set out to achieve its aims not by force or war but through labour, agricultural settlement and the fertilization of a desolate land . . . It is the only settlement movement which aspired not to displace the native inhabitants but to live side by side with them; not to exploit them but to help them advance; not to fight them but to find a way for peaceful co-existence. [From *Leket*, Cultural Affairs Bulletin, Embassy of Israel, London]

His letter was an ultimatum. Dissenting PEN members were by implication invited to fillet from Megged's statement those parts they agreed with and those they did not, a difficult task given that Megged had, brilliantly, sewn together the notions of 'humanism', 'morality' and 'peaceful co-existence' with the objectives of a nation born, horrifically, out of the Nazis' pursuit of the 'Final Solution'. Did Sillitoe influence him at all in this? He recalls that at the time they were in regular contact, mostly translating from Hebrew to English the poems of Avi Hazak, an Israeli *kibbutznik* killed in the Yom Kippur War. But there is a letter, or to be more accurate a condensed manifesto, which Sillitoe forwarded to Ted Hughes, David Mercer and several others from the Committee, asking for comments. He hoped that since the symposium book would not now be likely to appear this would at least offer a statement of commitment from an influential group of writers and politicians. The date on the Indiana transcript (January 1976) indicates that it was written at least three months before Megged drafted his letter, and the two pieces are almost identical.

In Sillitoe's view the general public in Britain and in most other Western European countries, or at least those who cared, were being fed systematically inaccurate accounts of both the state of the Middle East and the history of Israel. Tirelessly, he bombarded newspapers and BBC news editors with meticulous rejoinders to what were either deliberate obfuscations of the truth or lazy connivings in an anti-Semitic consensus. Typically in response to an article by Frank Giles in *The Times* Sillitoe wrote in to correct him on the cause of the 1948 conflict: 'in 1948 after the creation of the state of Israel (following the UN resolution of November 29, 1947) Lebanon, Syria, Jordan, Egypt and Iraq, all foreign armies, rushed to Israel for the kill as soon as the British pulled out' (AS to *The Times*, 8 July 1975).

In August Sillitoe and Stephen Spender flew to Paris at the invitation of a small group of French writers and spoke at a public meeting to protest against Israel having been voted off Unesco, and in February 1976 he appeared at a conference which Golda Meir also attended, a gathering focused specifically upon cases of Jewish 'prisoners of conscience' in Soviet Russia. Meir and others asked Sillitoe if he thought his long-established relationship with the Soviet Union, now albeit rather threadbare, might be useful in placing specific instances of human rights abuse in the international spotlight. He said that he would be happy to take on the private role of advocate, and over the next eighteen months, particularly during his visit to Israel in 1977, he was provided with details of individuals and their engagements with obdurate Soviet officialdom. During 1978 he wrote four letters to David Owen, Labour Foreign Secretary, asking him to act on behalf of Ida Nudel, who at the beginning of the year had been sent to Siberia for an indeterminate period and whose only 'crime' had been to campaign, peacefully, for individuals to be able to emigrate to Israel.

During the same period Sillitoe wrote a one-act play called *The Interview*, based on Nudel's treatment by the Soviet authorities. It was performed at St Martin's in the Fields in June 1978 with Janet Suzman as Nudel. The small production company, Inter-Action Productions, which included such eminent patrons and advisors as Vanessa Redgrave, Tom Stoppard, Joan Bakewell and Peter Sellers, was, Sillitoe found, somewhat splintered and factious in its dealings with his script. The company was from its inception a radical campaigning entity, and in the 1970s this inevitably involved a predictable left-wing agenda. As a consequence, while they could hardly deny that Nudel's case was a blatant example of human rights abuse, Sillitoe's presentation of anti-Semitism and Soviet totalitarianism as complicit and Israel as a refuge from both caused the kind of unease that is tangible but rarely addressed explicitly. Would the play be interpreted as pro-Zionist and, Marx forbid, the sort of thing approved by the USA? After lengthy correspondence with Ed Berman, the company's artistic director, Sillitoe arrived at a compromise. Dr Alexander Shtromas had in 1974 defected from the Soviet Union and now held a post in the Department of Peace Studies, University of Bradford. Prior to that he had been a senior academic in Soviet legislative history and practice, and he agreed to go through Sillitoe's script and advise on anything that did not accord with the letter of the law in the Soviet Union. Shtromas's comments to Sillitoe are meticulous in their attention to detail regarding Soviet legal practice, the constitution and even the prevailing idiom of interrogation and response – Shtromas himself had direct experience of this – but he did not take issue with Sillitoe's representation of how these procedures were systematically abused. It might be noted that subsequent to this Sillitoe, when writing on matters involving contentious and emotive historical fact, went about his background research with the meticulous caution normally expected of an academic (see for example *The Widower's Son*, discussed below).

In life, as in literature, he cared for those who by chance, volition or invention had become his charges. In 1979 he contacted the Home Office to support the application to remain in the UK of Mary Diniyva, a Russian poet whom he had met during his trips during the 1960s. She had earlier that year absconded from a state-sanctioned tour and sought political asylum; her case would eventually be successful. Twenty-four individual cases from between 1974 and the dissolution of the Soviet Union were championed by Sillitoe, and he even attempted to use whatever influence remained from his 1960s heyday in letters to the Soviet authorities themselves. He began a correspondence in 1978 with V.P. Ruben, Chairman of the Presidium of the Supreme Soviet, Riga, in the hope that Yurli, the son of Mrs Dina Roitkov-Fodoryachick, be allowed a visa to visit his seriously ill mother in Israel. His letters were answered in a characteristically blunt manner, and Mrs Roitkov-Fodoryachick died without being allowed to see her son.

Spring of 1983 involved the case of Iosif Begon, sentenced to five years' 'internal exile' on a charge of producing and distributing anti-Soviet literature (actually he had applied officially to go to Israel and had openly advertised and taught classes in Hebrew). These letters went to the Prosecutor General of the USSR, Alexander Mikhailovitch Rekunkov. Throughout the correspondence Sillitoe's mood is measured, restrained, as he drops hints that unlike others in the West he is not an enemy of the USSR. 'I am an English writer who has had many books published in the USSR [and] I also happen to be a socialist . . . All I want to say is that apart from socialism there is another concept by which [we] should try to live, and it is called Justice. It has always been my belief that socialism and justice are synonymous' (AS to Rekunkov, 29 August 1985, Indiana Archive). This is from a letter urging Rekunkov to at least reconsider the severity of the sentence – three years in a labour camp – handed down for sedition to Roald Zelichenok. He too had simply made public his desire to join members of his family in Israel. He would serve his full sentence.

At the end of the 1970s he heard from his friend Barbara Hardy, who had recently spent time in the Soviet Union and had picked up unguarded comments by members of the intelligentsia on their once-cosseted literary proletarian. Professor Ivasheva, at whose Moscow flat in 1967 Sillitoe had proclaimed his independence from any class or ideology, now routinely referred to him as 'a Zionist agent', recruited by Mossad to promote falsifications of both the situation in the Middle East and life in the Soviet Bloc. Similar charges had been laid against him in magazines, weeklies and radio broadcasts in other Warsaw Pact countries, according to a Hungarian expatriate – circa 1956 – who now worked for the BBC World Service.

In 1979 he went with Ruth and Ted Hughes to Yevtushenko's reading at the Commonwealth Institute. He remembers vividly the contrast between the poet's performance – outlandish, wildly improvisational, almost hectoring and capable of mesmerizing the audience – and his memory of him in 1963 as a man restrained by invisible fetters, mysteriously unable to receive phone calls or attend appointments. Later in a restaurant where a group had gone for supper Yevtushenko approached him in the lobby, embraced him Russian style, and whispered in his ear, 'Keep it up, about the Jews. Please keep it up.'

He records in his notebook a visit to a once close friend, whom he feels should remain anonymous.

Left at 12 to see — at St John's Wood, and stayed only half an hour. — tells me that all her friends now consider me a traitor, a right wing reactionary, mainly because of my views on Israel. It seems that the left wing intelligentsia (as well as the jackboot left) cling to any vestige of anti-Semitism they can get their hands on. She also said she'd been told that the Russians have it in for me. (Told by whom, I wondered? On her desk, conspicuously placed, was a copy of my 'Ida Nudel' play!) I answered that they had loathed me (the police and the authorities, that is) since Kuznetzov defected in 1970. They suspected me of being in on the plot. She nodded and said there was more to it than that. So be it. [Private notebook, February 1980]

Those who might suspect Sillitoe himself of a somewhat biased approach to human rights should note that he did not confine himself to the persecution of Jews. It was a fact, however, that in the cases where individuals had been accused of offences against the state following attempts to leave it via official channels of application the vast majority of those prosecuted were Jewish. Anti-Semitism, Sillitoe knew, was a special aspect of Soviet authoritarianism, resolute despite the fact that it antedated it. Sillitoe is not a writer who campaigns in order to promote his public image – outside their availability in the Indiana archive and those disclosed to me privately no one is aware of these letters to individuals and government bodies – nor is he so naïve as to believe that his own overtures will overturn official policy, but he has always held the opinion that esteem involves obligations. If writers engage in their work with absolutes and fundamental beliefs then it is, he holds, their duty to make use of whatever influence they have in the real world to uphold these principles. Aside from his campaigning on behalf of political prisoners he also badgered the government regarding miscarriages of justice in the UK. In the 1970s, for example, he wrote regularly to the Home Office in support of Jimmy Boyle. 'No one who has read his autobiography *A Sense of Freedom* can seriously doubt the decisive role of the Special Unit in helping one violent thug to become a responsible human being ... Boyle's continuing imprisonment is a political decision, in which he is hostage to an increasingly brutalising prison system which is maintained at the public expense and supposedly in the public interest. He is an indictment of that regime' (AS to Home Office, 21 January 1979).

Writers frequently air their opinions on anything from the quality of television programmes to the imminent collapse of the global ecosystem, but none, I would contend, has devoted as much as Sillitoe, privately and without seeking recognition, to so many miscarriages of justice and examples of political mendacity.

While *The Widower's Son* (1976) discloses no explicit connection with Sillitoe's private state of mind it is formed and driven by the same impulse that allied him to Judaism and Israel. The widower is Charlie, veteran of the Great War, and the book is about his son William who serves with distinction with the Royal Artillery in the Second World War, gains a commission, and two decades later opts for an unassuming civilian life, first as manager of an amusement arcade and then as a college lecturer. He marries twice, initially unhappily and then with mutual though somewhat resigned contentment. From the second marriage he has two children whom he loves unswervingly. The reviewers liked it mainly because he seemed to have abandoned the Posters trilogy dogma and returned to hard-edged realism, but none of them appreciated the book's unprepossessing uniqueness. William often nudges his narrator aside, apparently impatient with a world whose direction is in the hands of others. We organize our lives according to predictions of what is likely to occur in the near or distant future, and we base those on a blend of idiosyncratic impulse and mature second guessing. So the relationship between William and his narrator is only strange in the sense that rarely if ever will it be found in other novels; in the world it is commonplace. It replicates the constant tension between our wish to know and control our destiny and our obligation to everyday contingency. The novel's thematic signature occurs in Chapter 23, barely two and a half pages in length and involving a description of William's nervous breakdown. Briefly and once only Sillitoe switches to the first person:

A blank mind is the bliss of life, emptiness without sleep. If I *try* to push all words out, to attain the peace of emptiness, I can't do it. I sweat with exasperation because I'm a human being. The dawn breaks and the words flood in . . .

There, suddenly, the peace that I struggled for comes without effort. Words vanish. My mind is at peace . . .

[But] I never succeed in keeping my mind empty, because I am not in control. The only way to stop words swarming in would be to kill myself. [pp. 203–4]

At this point the novel reveals its fraught autobiographical nucleus. There is a remarkable similarity between this passage and moments in Sillitoe's diaries where he contemplates writing as a burden and a necessity. Without it he feels hopeless, unfocused, yet the effort that it involves makes him desperate for at least a moment of freedom from it. In October 1976 he wrote the following, less than a month after *The Widower's Son* had been published and before he had decided with any certainty on what his next major work would be:

[I feel] I'm wasting my time when I don't feel I have long to live. Can't say why I feel this. But if it's so I don't much care. Is it just a feeling between novels? When I'm not moving, writing, I feel tired enough to die. Sitting at my desk I only want to sleep. It's ten in the morning right now and I want to lie down and go to sleep. It's a beautiful autumn day, and I should be full of life. Even between such sentences as those I stare into space for minutes at a time. [29 October 1976, private diary]

The point when he, Sillitoe, is engrossed by the moment of linguistic absence 'between . . . sentences' is a poignant reproduction of William's dilemma. Sillitoe is contemplating an existential fact. Writing, for him, is indistinguishable from life. Certainly he can function as loving husband, parent, entertaining public speaker, guest at dinner parties, and do so genuinely, but he knows that all of this will, must be punctuated by his continued return to words and stories. In *The Widower's Son* this private state – for all Sillitoe knows unique, given that he had never spoken of it to other writers – is projected into the dependent relationship between William and his narrator. Without him William in the painful brief moments of Chapter 23 begins to disintegrate, and as he disclosed in his diary Sillitoe was writing from personal experience.

The Widower's Son should not, however, be treated simply as a contemplation upon the addictive capacities of writing. It extends into a much broader philosophical realm, because William's narrator offers him a refuge, brings him close to an acceptance of destiny as something more than a forlorn craving. William embodies Sillitoe's commitment to the ethos of Israel, which is reinforced by the fact that Judaism plays no explicit part in the story; it was a private pledge and all the more genuine for that.

Far more background research went into the book than for anything he had previously written. He corresponded regularly with Major R.G. Bartelot of the Royal Military Academy, Woolwich, home of the Royal Artillery, and with Brigadier Shelford Bidwell who had published several books on the history of the gunners at war and had served in the RA in the same campaigns as William. With each he debated everything from the minutiae of mess convention to the exact details of battles. There are more than thirty letters between them both in the Indiana Archive and in Sillitoe's personal files. He concedes that his meticulous attention to authenticity was fed by two impulses, predominantly a commitment to the memory of those who had served in the war and alongside that his feeling that Israel through much of its brief history had faced a threat similar to Britain's plight after 1940. He had experienced both, as an adolescent and now as a mature observer, and felt that for each only unalloyed, almost religious attendance to truth would suffice.

He became aware that he had achieved something unusual not simply because of the reviews, favourable though they were, but when almost a year later he received a letter from H.M. Daleski, Professor of English at the Hebrew University of Jerusalem. He knew that they would remain friends following their meeting in Jerusalem earlier that year, but this letter was Daleski's first detailed commentary on his work and Sillitoe had never before come across someone who could so deftly guess the impulse and intent that had brought the words to the page.

> [Its] strength . . . seems to me to lie in a remarkable sense of appropriate action, a capacity for isolating the revealing gesture or response, the sort of action which sums up a life.

He was impressed particularly by the way that the accounts of William's experience of combat seemed so authentically frightening: 'those war scenes are an astonishing reconstruction, and – since you told me you were too young to be in that war – simply make one marvel at the creative imagination'. With thanks of course to Brigadier Bidwell.

> But perhaps my strongest impression is being left with a sense of the utter, implacable mysteriousness of life. Here you've given us a life in all its fullness, and yet at the end it's quite impossible to sum it up, to reduce it to one or another formula . . . just when one thinks one is getting the book into some

sort of accommodating shape in one's mind [it] makes one see that . . . it's time to go back and start all over again. [BD to AS, 21 December 1977, Indiana Archive]

This is an immensely shrewd reading, particularly since Daleski did not as yet know Sillitoe that well as an individual. He catches perfectly the novel's ability to replicate the tension between life as determinate and incalculable. Daleski had fought in two conflicts, with the artillery in North Africa and Italy in the Second World War and in the Israeli War of Independence, and this caused him to wonder at how a novel which captured the elemental nature of conflict was not based on personal experience.

Aharon Megged, however, detected another echo. 'You said you might learn the old language [Hebrew] and reading this novel I feel you would be suited to it. Our language grew from destruction and torment and now of course it has returned to its roots. William's war becomes his life, his personality, and so it is with us' (Megged to AS, 10 January 1978). Four years earlier Sillitoe had told him that he would keep diaries from his visits to Israel and turn them into a book. 'How I envy you for writing a book on Israel . . . this land as seen afresh by one who comes from the outside, say a pilgrim, or a writer . . . Now, you have an idea how curious I am to read what you will write!' (Megged to AS, 28 July 1974). Sillitoe decided against a non-fictional account of Israel, but perhaps on reading *The Widower's Son* Megged had picked out the new home for that project's emotive register. In all of the many letters and articles that Sillitoe wrote defending Israeli military policy during the 1960s and 1970s the one analogy that features persistently is that of Britain in 1940.

TWENTY-SIX

Sillitoe began and finished his next novel, *The Storyteller*, with astonishing speed during his fiftieth year. He wrote to Brian: 'Half a century. Dad was gone at 56, but I'm feeling all right' (AS to BS, 1 April 1978), and three days later to Bill Daleski:

> I will be in the Lake District with David: I promised months ago to go there and do a reconnaissance with him.
> The first draft of my novel is finished. I call it *The Storyteller* – about a man telling a story about a man who tells stories in pubs, clubs, common rooms and cruise liners for a living. I don't think the chaos is inextricable – I'm working on further drafts, and will be so for the next few months. I have to blacksmith it into shape and sparsity, hoping it will come out all right in the end. [AS to BD, 4 April 1978]

Ernest Cotgrave is the storyteller, a man who earns a living through his addiction to spinning tales out of nothing; frequently they lack any kind of logic or continuity, unrolling like celebrations of the pointless and the commonplace. Most of *The Storyteller*'s chapters are frantic set pieces with Ernest arriving at the venues Sillitoe described to Daleski and presenting himself in a manner which appears to suit the location – after-dinner speaker, political agitator, stand-up comedian or whatever the occasion demanded. Yet in each instance there seems to be a mismatch between what he sets out to do and the expectations of his audience, who respond to most of his performances with bitterness and abuse. Ernest's manic self-destructive odyssey veers close to the suicidal, and there are moments when one cannot help but recognize parallels between his circuit of engagements – somewhere between a job and a masochistic compulsion – and the life of his creator. In Chapter 8 he is about to address a university students' union on a subject as yet unannounced and we are left with few doubts about his perception of his audience: 'Left-wing students gave him the feeling that he was going up in the world. He had made contact with the middle classes' (p. 102). He tells them of his own brief period as a factory worker, of the injustices routinely endured by himself, his friend Tom and virtually everyone else who faces the basic choice between going to work and having no money. What he refuses to do, however, is extrapolate these facts into a prognosis for radical change, socialism. Gradually, calculatedly, he baits them, playing upon their patronizing expectations that he will behave, and speak, as a stereotypical exemplar of proletarianism.

The chapter is in part a dramatized version of the private reflections in his Israel diary of 1977. The responses to his talks range from 'Bullshit!' through 'We know what to do with traitors like you!' and 'Capitalist lackey' to 'Kill him' and 'Fascist bastard'. Ernest dwells particularly upon 'that long "A" of the first syllable of bastard'; he had indeed made contact with the middle classes. Having whipped them into a collective state of enraged inverted snobbery he tells them what he thinks:

> You socialists are put out at the idea of me 'betraying the working class'. How nicely you fart boxes put it. If it existed I'd betray it, because let me assure you that no one among those you lump together as a 'class' would blame me one little bit.
>
> . . . when the revolution was over you'd make sure those who were left called themselves working class for the rest of their lives and kept their places so that they'd know exactly where they belonged . . . [pp. 129–30]

During the late 1960s and 1970s Sillitoe had regularly given readings and talks at universities and had come to notice in his audiences a blend dissatisfaction and puzzlement. Worse than that was a palpable sense of expectation that he should perform to type, something which reinforced his determination to do otherwise. Academic studies of his work routinely adopted a Marxist approach to it and he felt, he says today, as if he were being treated more as a diagnostic indicator than a novelist (see A. Swingewood, *The Myth of Mass Culture*, Macmillan, 1977; D. Smith, *Socialist Propaganda in the British Novel*, Macmillan, 1978; R.D. Vaverka, *Commitment as Art*, Uppsala, 1978). These analysts were disappointed and seemed to have joined the student barrackers in perceiving him as a 'capitalist lackey'.

One event in particular stayed in Sillitoe's mind as he wrote the chapter. It occurred in 1971 and was organized and advertised by the 'Progressive Intellectuals' Study Group', a faction comprised exclusively of academics, postgraduates and undergraduates from the University of London, dedicated to 'smash[ing] the already decaying superstructure of imperialism, which is growing more and more fascist in its ideology. The basis for unity is a serious and detailed investigation in all aspects of the superstructure – the arts, sciences, politics, education, mass media – not merely for the purpose of self cultivation and understanding of the world but in order to organise to change the world.' This quote is taken from a flier circulated within the University of London, in bookshops in the capital and anywhere else willing to offer it counter-space or a noticeboard. It advertised a special meeting of the group to which all members and anyone else interested were invited; it would be a show trial, entitled 'Alan Sillitoe and David Mercer. TRAITORS TO THE ENGLISH WORKING CLASS'. When Sillitoe first saw it he was caught between laughter and astonishment. It seemed like a curious inversion of McCarthyism, with the rider that a group of largely middle-class communists appeared to believe that they could overrule a 'working-class' writer's choice to think or write as he wished. Hilariously, or horrifically, the document reached the following verdict: 'Considering all these aspects, the inevitable conclusion is that these men [Sillitoe and Mercer] are traitors to the English working class.' Why, he wondered, should there be any need for a meeting if its 'conclusion' was already 'inevitable'? Even Stalin, he thought, would have dissembled better than that. No wonder, then, that he came to regard the hypothesis, fantastic as it was, of a British version of communism as the dictatorship of the condescending middle-class left.

There was something else about the poster which confirmed his suspicions regarding the left-leaning British bourgeoisie. Why had he and David Mercer alone been selected as class traitors? What about Braine, Storey, Waterhouse, Barstow et al.? They had hardly become spokesmen for fundamentalist Marxism, but neither had they been particularly outspoken in favour of Israel. Sillitoe and Mercer had; they had indeed become friends in the process, and spent time together during Sillitoe's visits to Israel in 1974 and 1977. Sillitoe had made clear in his Israel diary that post-Holocaust anti-Semitism was kept alive within Western democracies through a conspectus of radical causes. In Chapter 8 of *The Storyteller* Sillitoe has Ernest become similarly convinced that there is something far more sinister than post-adolescent radicalism behind the wall of hatred he faces in the student union. The people are, he feels, not rebels at all but a group united by intolerance, and one issue, Israel, seems to preoccupy them. He begins to refer to them, privately, as 'anti-Zionist brown shirts' (p. 123).

In a letter to Bill Daleski written when he was finishing *The Storyteller* he states:

It's always seemed to me that the 'dagger of Islam', being aimed at Israel, is really pointed at the heart of the Western World (call it Christendom if you like, though I have little enough time for *that*); but Islam . . . sees Israel as the bedrock and bridgehead of the West which it thinks it must break prior to destroying [the West] itself. The fools in 'the West' who are pro-Islam are in effect a fifth column of masochists. Israel's problems and the West's are the same – but it's a terrible irony that the Jewish people which has suffered so much at the hands of the so-called Christians should now find themselves cast in the part of being in the forward defences of the battle which the Arabs are waging to destroy Christendom, at a time when the Western World doesn't much care about Christianity. When the Arabs fulminate against Israel, they mean 'the West' though I wouldn't expect any Israeli to get much comfort from that. [AS to BD, 9 July 1979]

At the time many who commended themselves for their balanced, relativist view of the Middle East would have treated this as hysterical, verging upon the neurotic. Now, however, it reads as an extraordinarily shrewd prediction of a forthcoming global conflict. Prior to the Millennium, outrages such as 9/11 and the London Tube bombings were for the vast majority unimaginable, but not so for Sillitoe.

While *The Storyteller* is strewn with Sillitoe's preoccupations they are not exclusively its subject. There is something far more elemental which unites him with Ernest Cotgrave. For both of them storytelling and their working existence have become largely indistinguishable. This does not result, as one might expect, in an unenviable combination of fantasy and madness. Instead Ernest thrives upon the friction between his world of stories and their effect upon other people. He exists for much of his time in a hinterland between the necessary routines of living – eating, drinking, sleeping and so on, undertaken seemingly by reflex – and his stories, which offer him a tangible, ill-defined sense of purpose.

In Chapter 7 he meets an old man who is self-evidently a cynical, more experienced version of himself. This figure, never named, tells of his own career, an account laced with an abundance of detail from Sillitoe's life, which is particularly intriguing since it seems to have been selected so that only he, Sillitoe, or his closest friends and family will recognize it as such.

I also told stories in order to find out why I was alive, would I be able to go on telling stories? You'll understand my dilemma one day. I was as far from people as the moon is from the earth, yet at least I discovered that they were worth all the love and respect I could dredge out of myself. I'd pondered a lot in the insomniac shadows of full moon nights. I made each story my obituary, shaped into a statue of egg-timer sand. I had to query, in pain and weariness, why I was alive if I was not to kill myself one hot afternoon before a thunderstorm, or die one pint-of-bitter dusk without having much to say in the matter. [pp. 95–6]

Bill Daleski discerned the interweaving of Sillitoe the individual and Alan Sillitoe the writer more keenly than anyone, with the exception of course of Ruth, and his letter to his friend after reading the novel confirms that the old man speaks for his creator.

[As] 'storytelling' comes more and more to be associated with matters of life and death . . . I was irresistibly reminded of what you said to me when we were on our way home after the Kol Yisrael interview and you were telling me of your ten-year stint before *Saturday Night* . . . I remember asking how you managed to keep on writing after so much discouragement . . . and you answered: 'It was simple – I had to write – or die.' [BD to AS, 15 February 1980, Indiana Archive]

The novel concludes in a dexterously bizarre fashion. Ernest is on a cruise ship in the Mediterranean telling stories, or at least he appears to be. Often the narrative that contains him, the one outside his stories, is eroded by the suspicion that it too might disintegrate or untangle. Events swerve from the routine to the fantastic without warning, creating the impression that the ultimate storyteller, Ernest's inventor, has become restless and capricious.

In a long letter to Ted Hughes Sillitoe begins by setting the scene: 'Midnight seems as good a time as any to write to you. I'm in Wittersham, the hatches battened against the storm, a fire in my study, Morse tinkling in from ships in the Channel. I keep it on as a kind of background noise, and read what's being said.' This self-portrait of himself as the intermediary between what he creates and the jumble of signals from the real world is enthralling, and later in the letter he describes his ongoing novel as a living entity, demanding his attention:

We should cut a swathe through the dross, lop off the tentacles of novels or poems, and arrange to meet. I'm only too willing to drop my novel any time, though it's such a big quantity it'd probably break my foot. I typed it from the first handwritten draft and it came out to 720 pages. Now I've got to clip and drill my way into it, break it down and put it through more drafts, the same old process, but it gets harder and harder. Meanwhile it sits on my table, a big heap, and I look at it resentfully now and again. Every so often I kick it and it squeaks piteously, the poor bloody thing; it didn't ask to be brought into the world but then, who did? [AS to TH, 20 November 1986, Emory Archive]

His jocose manner belies an enduring belief in the novel as an organism with a life of its own which asks for his guidance, even his protection. Here he feels light-hearted, relieved at having at least got it through its first gestation. In an earlier letter to Bill Daleski he is more unsettled.

I seem to have come to an impasse . . . The tension or guts or whatever it is have gone out of it [the novel] or out of me . . . I sit looking at the bloody thing . . . I suddenly don't know where I'm going . . .

I often start a novel with a vague theme in mind, but no plan, and bank on the impetus of the characters to carry me through . . . At the same time I often reach the halfway point and don't know where to go, and nor do they [his characters] . . . I have my two people in a situation and can't get them out. I shall have to devise something violent – either for them or myself. [AS to BD, 31 March 1980]

The borders between 'them', 'me' and 'it' are porous and shifting. He is living the novel and feeling that its own intransigent sense of purpose is drawing life from him. In this letter and others he uses the term 'black dog' (a phrase patented by Winston Churchill as, in his case, a euphemism for his manic depression), a thing he hopes he can subdue but which seems capable of resisting him: 'the black dog that I keep praying will let go of me if I stare at the words and paper long enough . . .'

TWENTY-SEVEN

Apart from the indisputable fact that more than two decades had passed, Sillitoe and Ruth felt in the mid-1970s much as they did when as ambitious itinerant bohemians they'd camped out in various parts of the Mediterranean. They were not rich, but now there was enough money to make easily available what they had always valued. Middle age had come relatively painlessly. They could with requisite supplies of caution and resignation adapt themselves to the fact that they were getting older. Witnessing the transit of others across the spectrum of junctions separating infancy from oblivion was, however, much less straightforward. Sillitoe wrote in his diary on 17 February 1977: 'Time goes, never to be recovered. I find this fact intolerable.'

When Alan, Ruth and David visited Israel in 1977 David, then fifteen, pursued his interest in natural history. 'David was collecting insects from a specific location – Wadi Kelt – for the department of Entomology at the National History Museum. He delivered an excellent selection to them when we arrived back in London' (Ruth Fainlight). He was in that grey area between childhood and precocious adolescence. During the visit itself he would spend entire days scrambling over wild terrain, collecting species he had rarely heard of and certainly never encountered before, while remaining happily oblivious to his father's equal enthusiasm for the unfolding history of the region. On one occasion Sillitoe drove his wife and son through what appeared to be a raid by rocket-equipped Phantoms of the Israel Air Force somewhere close to the Lebanon border. Sillitoe is still unsure whether the fighter-bombers were engaged in actual combat or a training operation – rockets were certainly exploding – but while he and Ruth emerged with mixed sensations of exhilaration and pure terror David seemed to have immunized himself from the experience, appearing concerned more with zoological specimens than the enveloping conflict. Sillitoe didn't know how to interpret this: was it innocent indifference or the onset of obdurate and dangerous temerity? Had David been closer to twelve or eighteen his father would have known. But that was the problem; he was not quite either.

David was now attending City of London, an independent school with a proud heritage – though its best-known recent old boy, Kingsley Amis, still had a flavour of delinquency about him. Sillitoe had chosen City of London because it was still part of the meritocratic system, not quite in the snobbish public school league, more a highly selective grammar school. Naturally he wanted his son to make the best of his abilities, but in the process he recognized that he had to advise him to follow a different route from his own, saying as little as possible about the fact that his avoidance of conventional education had been the engine for his originality and success as a writer.

After visiting the school for a parent–teacher evening Sillitoe pondered the reports.

'He is supreme in biology, all right at chemistry, history and geography, but bad at maths and French. [In English apparently he was promising; this was the beginning of his two-year O-level programme involving at least eight subjects.] The verdict is surprisingly in tune from each teacher – that he doesn't really do his homework well enough, or concentrate enough. He could do very much better with more effort . . . Yesterday I took the TV set out of his room, ostensibly because we need it in Wittersham. Maybe the radio should come out next, though it'll be hard to find an excuse.' [Private diary, 8 February 1977]

David was clever but showed no interest in the arts, preferring the natural sciences in which he excelled. Helder Macedo recalls arriving for the weekend at Wittersham and being met in the hall by David. '"Helder!" he said. "May I have some of your blood?"' He was holding a hypodermic needle. That year he had set up his own laboratory. Allied with this he savoured any opportunity to spend time in the countryside, including regular exercises with the school Cadet Corps. 'David telephoned [from his Cadet Corps Exercise]. He seems well, learning ambush and evasion tactics, how to cross canals, make roadblocks, orienteering, shooting etc. I loved that sort of thing too, at his age. It's always useful stuff to know. Once you've learned it you don't easily forget it' (Private diary, 3 April 1977).

Sillitoe's approval, boosted by recognition of his son as a version of himself, also carried a hint of anxiety. The two of them shared a predilection for shooting. Airguns and shotguns were standard issue in Wittersham, and in London they were members of the Hendon Rifle Club which they would visit together most weekends to target shoot with .22 rifles. This, however, was masculine excitement domesticated. Sillitoe exhibited watchful fatherly concern when David was doing things in combat gear with rifles somewhere else. He wrote to Brian: 'He [David] was given a choice between Community Service work and the Cadet Force, and he chose the latter. I didn't particularly like it but at the same time I think that military service is always useful . . . I'm sure David won't go into the proper army' (AS to BS, 17 March 1976).

In a letter soon afterwards (February 1977) he offers Brian a misleadingly relaxed account of 'how well' his son is doing as a cadet. His sense of unease filters through a desperately facetious coda: 'they'll probably put him on a bus to Ulster next week'. He had previously mentioned that when he and Ruth had 'measured [David] up' for his Army uniform they had found that 'He's five feet eight tall now – my height' (10 March 1976). He did not need to comment.

He had been honest enough about his past, but he had never talked much to David about his private idiosyncrasies, which in any event he thought best unspoiled by explanation, particularly his fascination with being alone in the wild, beginning with his visits to the Burtons' and reaching an apex of sorts in the jungles of Malaysia. Now David was displaying exactly the same instincts. Sillitoe had first channelled his into what at the time seemed like a career in the armed forces, which involved the attraction of foreign travel. It also meant danger. Sillitoe had done as he wished, but such choices were less easy to indulge when undertaken by an only son, and Ruth was less equivocal. 'David has written a poem – good visually and good resonance. Ruth says I *must* lay off technical and military subjects and talk about more literary and cultural things. So after tea I told him the story of Xenophon's Anabasis – "the ten thousand". I'll have to bring a few of the "classics" up from Wittersham – Herodotus, Thucydides, Homer etc.' (Private diary, 2 February 1977).

One cannot help but wonder how many present-day teenagers, even those from decent, stable backgrounds, would take to afternoon crash courses in the classics. But for David these episodes did not seem like cramming sessions because Sillitoe would shift seamlessly from casual chatter to fables and adventures. 'He was, is, a great storyteller,' David reflects, 'and it was only later that it dawned on me he might have been trying to broaden my cultural horizons. Painlessly.'

On the same day that he was persuaded by Ruth to guide David towards the civilizing nostrums of arts and letters Alan and she went to see Bertolucci's film *The Spider's Stratagem*. He felt distracted, and when he left the cinema one image obscured his other impressions of the film: 'the Italian villas, so like Corbetta's place near Menton where we went in 1952. The heat and rain and smells came back, distinct enough to break the soul . . . It's a long way to go back, a far greater distance than to go forward' (Private diary, 2 February 1977). He does not explain why the memory of 1952 returned so painfully, but it is more than likely that witnessing in a cosy Notting Hill cinema Bertolucci's evocation of the Mediterranean caused him to remember the compulsive aspect of his temperament that made him act as he did a quarter of a century earlier. No one back then had guided him – indeed, had they done so he would have resented their attempts and ignored their advice; he made his own choices. These might have been capricious, reckless, but they were his, and now he faced a dilemma. He knew Ruth's advice was correct, was aware that a formal education would enable his son to make a better life for himself, but this was all so different from the regime that had made him who he was, a past still so tangible that 'smells came back, distinct enough to break the soul'.

I ask David for his own account of his relationship with his father. 'I remember that he half severed his finger sawing logs in St Pargoire in France and he broke several ribs when he fell out of an apple tree in Wittersham. On neither occasion did he feel it necessary to bother the doctor, though finally Ruth persuaded him that his ribs had to be X-rayed. That's how we knew they were cracked, two weeks after the event. You see I was aware, from as far back as I can recall, that he was unlike anyone else. Asking for help, becoming dependent on other people or institutions – he would never, ever do that. This might sound anarchistic or irresponsible but it was not, because he did not try to turn me into a model of himself. Certainly he allowed us to make up our own minds – Sue and I – but he made it clear that we must always take responsibility for our actions and decisions.'

Margaret Drabble testifies to the results of Sillitoe's regimen. 'I've known David since he was an infant. Unlike many other couples Alan and Ruth did not exclude their children from social events and David was wonderful. Polite, talkative, but not one of those abnormally precocious children who seem like adults trapped in the bodies of adolescents.'

From the age of sixteen onwards Sue would live for two thirds of each year in Nottingham with her elder sister Jane, now married. Sillitoe wrote to Brian, 'She can go to school in Nottingham and then get her "A" levels which will take her to a higher standard of education than we ever had – and good luck to her. She's worked hard, and deserves it' (AS to BS, 17 March 1976). This new arrangement seemed to those involved the result of an evolved consensus, but in truth Sillitoe had orchestrated its progress with the same affectionate Machiavellianism that went into his writing; he valued the independence both of those closest to him and of his characters, but he also felt an impulse towards respectful guidance.

Sue recalls her childhood as a happy one. 'They both, Alan and Ruth, treated me as their daughter, as David's sister, but they didn't pretend or keep from me the fact that Alan was originally my uncle. I was a kid. I didn't think about such things, and it was only later perhaps when I had children of my own that it occurred to me that the sudden arrival of a new child, eight years old, would have asked more of Ruth than Alan. Particularly since after David they had decided, for health reasons, one was enough.' In the mid-1970s, however, Alan thought that it would be beneficial for his daughter to have at least some experience of her original environment and family before she reached full adulthood. He was not so much returning her to her past as forestalling its irretrievable loss.

In March 1977 Sillitoe made one of his regular visits to Nottingham, staying two nights from the 2nd to the 4th. His diary entries for this period are revealing in that a mood of unease informs both his behaviour and his syntax. He was searching for a sense of fixity within the fluid mosaic of places and people of which his world now seemed comprised.

Before seeing or speaking to anyone he drove to Langar aerodrome, north of Nottingham, where he had served as an Air Traffic Control assistant in 1945-6. '[It] seems to be out of use, but a new windsock flutters. The control tower still stands though doors are broken and windows smashed. The farm where we used to buy delicious egg sandwiches is still there. I parked my car near the control tower and ate my sandwiches.' The passage tilts between his sense of the past as something both forever present and lost, and as if to steady himself he set off for his brother Michael's house in Carlton. Michael, the baby of the family who once looked upon Sillitoe as his alternative father, was now thirty-seven, played drums in a reasonably successful jazz band and taught music at Nottingham High School. 'He is very good and serious, though I suppose he and Ann [his wife] have their troubles.' He meant financial troubles; they had three teenage children. Ten, twenty years earlier he might have tactfully offered to help out, but now, he knew, such an offer was neither appropriate nor expected. He and Michael drove into Nottingham to a second-hand bookshop on Mansfield Road that both had visited regularly since the latter's childhood, and then on to visit their mother Sabina. She was distressed. Tom, her second husband, had collapsed the day before when changing the car battery and had been kept in hospital for tests. (It was in the end diagnosed as a combination of iron deficiency and exhaustion rather than a heart attack, as feared.) Sillitoe did his best to comfort his mother and assured her that he would personally stay in contact with the hospital and keep her informed of developments. Next came the encounter that caused him most anxiety: Susan. She looked, as he puts it, 'very smart' in a black dress sent her by Ruth, but 'she seems very unhappy about school and thinks she can make no further progress there. She says she wants to leave to be independent, and get a job . . . I was very non-committal about this, because I want her to stay on till 18 and do A-levels.' This appears a contradiction in terms, and prompts the question of why, if this was in his opinion the best route to a secure future, did he remain 'non-committal'. He goes on: 'She seems to think this [getting A-levels] is impossible, but I stayed aloof, that is to say listened sympathetically without pressing her.'

When I interviewed Sue neither she nor I had seen this diary, but she was, unprompted, drawn back to the same conversation as a transitional moment in her life and, as she would later reflect, a perfect indication of the sort of man that Sillitoe was and is. I will quote her verbatim: 'Alan is amazingly shrewd. I remember particularly when I was doing my A-levels in Nottingham I just wanted to drop out. Routine teenage angst and impatience, I suppose. I talked to Alan and he reacted completely differently from the way I had expected. He didn't bluster and try to persuade me that it was in my interests to stay on. He seemed mildly disappointed – though he didn't say so –

but he made it clear more by implication than statement that my life was my own. This completely threw me off balance. If he'd jumped in with the predictable parental arguments on why I ought to have gone on with A-levels I'd have become more resolute in my decision to pack them in. But now, strangely, after he'd allowed me to make my own choice I just changed my mind and went back to doing my exams. And you know, I think he planned it.' The diary confirms that he did.

The next day, the 2nd, he began again with a private pilgrimage: 'I slept but didn't seem to rest properly – the packed impressions of the day fighting with the big meal eaten for supper.' He went first to the cemetery of Old Lenton Church where the Burtons are buried, and Oliver's grave drew him; Oliver, who died in mysterious circumstances in the First World War, his skull apparently fractured by a horse-kick. 'Oliver's grave – it's more visible than last time – his father is buried there as well. A man was tidying the paths and verges, a very cheerful very old man, so I gave him ten bob for a drink.' Very cheerful, very old and very much perhaps an intermediary between Sillitoe and a world he had glimpsed as a child. His actual destination was Radford and the house of his aunt, his mother's sister Emily, and once there he seemed to alight upon a way of living not too far removed from that of the long-deceased Burtons. Emily shared the house with Arthur, widower of her sister Ivy.

Arthur was sitting by a huge coal fire (it was a warm day, but his hand was cold when I shook it – he's 79, his birthday a fortnight ago – but he's very lucid and sharp) having finished his first pipe full of Condor for the day. Emily came from upstairs, she's getting on for seventy, never married, a very pinched sort of face, deprived looking, but she's fought through this sense of deprivation for so many decades that there seems to be quite a bit of spite and malice behind it. The family says that she torments Arthur, and maligns him to everyone she meets. [Private diary, 3 March 1977]

The two of them, with some stylistic trimming, make an appearance in Sillitoe's novel, *A Man of His Time*, Chapter 32, and in *Alligator Playground* in the story 'Ivy'. He catches perfectly the flavour of coexistence as an unasked, directionless fate. But these were real people, and in his diary Sillitoe suspends his drift towards crisp depiction and steps back into the narrative:

I hope Emily goes to see my mother, which I asked her to do. She hadn't seen my mother for three years, and they only live a mile from each other. It's amazing how a family can be living in the same smallish city and never meet. As Arthur says: 'They're a strange lot' – and they are; lazy, feckless and mean – also unintelligent.

Did he mean it? I ask him now: 'No, not really. Impatience, I suppose.' Sillitoe never wanted to be seen as the successful head of the family, advisor and philanthropist to all comers. Privately he worried, continually, and his ruminations in *Raw Material* on the interweavings of stories invented and lives lived seem here particularly apposite. When he did mediate he did so almost secretly, like the quiet narrator whose presence the unmindful characters feel but never discern. Sue can testify to this.

It is surely no accident that at this time he also began a novel like no other he had previously attempted. Though he had always abjured planning and preferred to allow his characters and narratives to germinate, the notion of a book writing itself was he knew both entrancing and absurd. He always had to be there providing guidance, sustenance, credibility and the words themselves. None the less he was nagged by the challenge of making a character with real autonomy, even more so now that his relationships with people he had known so well and cared for so much were entering states of flux. He was characteristically phlegmatic in not resenting the changes that were occurring around him, but they sparked an impulse to recreate this effect in his relationship with a novel. He wanted a character capable of exercising *de facto* control over their life. He would make his characters but never completely know them, see the world through their eyes but not fully comprehend the nature of their actions and emotions. The choice suddenly seemed obvious. He would write about a woman. In his diary on 4 January 1977 he recorded: 'I managed to type nine pages on the electric typewriter which might begin a new novel, about a forty year old woman leaving home. You never know – things could happen. Ruth has often said that I have never had a convincing female character in one of my novels.'

The woman Sillitoe knew best seemed at this stage entirely unsuitable as the model for his character, even as the source for polite borrowings: autobiography involved indulgent editing and mischievous distortion, but underhand biography was theft. She did, however, offer him a clue as to how he might undertake this new exercise. As in her poem 'The Betrothal':

> They search
> Each other's eyes, but only find themselves, minute,
> Plunging through expanded pupils to nothing.
> Each iris complicated as a stellar map,
> Once embarked into that flecked immensity.

[In *The Region's Violence*, Hutchinson, 1973]

The more hopeless the attempt to locate the nature of the other person, the more obsessive the desire to continue the search. Ruth's vivid evocation of the dynamic of attraction was adopted by Sillitoe as his creative ordinance. He began to collect pieces of women's lives, anything from behavioural or conversational routines to fragments of biography. He knew that he could never assemble from this collage an exclusively female character for the simple reason that beyond most radical, separatist hypotheses of the women's movement such figures did not exist. Men and women were mutually dependent, even if the corollary of recognition was distrust or contempt, and the fact that Sillitoe's character would in part carry a trace of himself guaranteed her authenticity.

On Sunday 6 March 1977 Sillitoe and Ruth walked down to the Speddings' farm, ostensibly to buy eggs, but in truth to offer Mrs Spedding some company and whatever comfort they could think of beyond the routine mantras. Her husband Rob had died barely two weeks earlier. 'She seems', wrote Sillitoe that night, 'to doubt whether she'll get over it. She talks a great deal of her son Horace, a famous fighter pilot from the war, who hasn't had much to do with his parents for the last 25 years. It's shattered her life' (AS's private diary, 6 March 1977).

Mrs Spedding was a valued friend, and Sillitoe would not have considered making use of her personal tragedy as material for his new project. She did, however, set in train a sequence of prognoses. She reminded him of his mother. As individuals they had little in common but both came from a generation for whom marriage and widowhood were virtual obligations; you found a man, had children, and he in all probability would die first. For nearly all women outside the moneyed intelligentsia this was life, and choice played very little part in it.

A month later Sillitoe visited her again, and this time she offered him Rob's shotgun. It reminded her of her husband and their respective roles, and she could not cope with its continued presence in the house. 'She was almost in tears at this. We talked for about half an hour . . . she finds it difficult to understand the violence and disturbance of the modern world, and in some ways it frightens her, especially now that Rob is dead' (Private diary, 7 April 1977).

Would it, wondered Sillitoe, have been the same for Rob if she had died? It was possible but he doubted it, because men, though they might love their partners, rarely felt dependent upon them as protection against the chaos and nastiness of the world beyond their home. One woman whom he knew well was the proactive, strong-minded antithesis of Mrs Spedding, and he recalled a particular event earlier that year, memorable because it was his birthday, 4 March, the beginning of his forty-ninth year. They were in Wittersham and Sillitoe was helping to prepare dinner – he and Ruth had shared this task between them since their first days in Menton. Potatoes on the Aga, tomato and cucumber salad, plates of smoked mackerel, sausage and black bread. (Despite his divorce from Sovietism Sillitoe still maintains an affection for Russian-style cuisine.) Ruth joined him in the kitchen. 'David wore his military camouflage gear and Ruth accused me of being responsible for his interest in the army and warfare. Hence the opening sentence of this entry.' Which is: 'Two people can live together only so long as they are able to maintain a mutual and undiminished respect for each other. This is not really what I get in my situation' (Private diary, 4 March 1977). The peremptory, ominous manner is misleading. He and Ruth would argue, sometimes bitterly, but their quarrels were not symptomatic of a flawed relationship; quite the opposite.

David recalls how an exchange on anything from his school to Sillitoe's commitment to Zionism would frequently escalate into 'a verbal brawl. To be honest Ruth usually incited this, but Alan was happy to participate. It didn't worry me as it might have done other kids – their parents arguing – because it was neither unusual nor unnerving. There was nothing wrong with their relationship, they simply went head to head on issues.' The next day Sillitoe makes no reference in his diary to his exchange with Ruth. It was as if it had never happened. He has, he notes, decided to write a love poem for her called 'Surveying'.

It was the contrast between Ruth and Mrs Spedding that caused his speculations to crystallize into a character. She would be someone who incorporated elements of both of them, but her story would focus upon a decision to unshackle herself from the conventional, dependent regime of the former. He did not at that point begin writing, choosing to jot down impressions and unforced ideas and wait to see if life might offer something unusual to shift the project into gear. He was in any event trying to complete the final draft of *The Storyteller* and was approximately two thirds of his way through a sequence of poems to be called *Lucifer*. The latter is a superlative reworking of the Old Testament tale of the rebel angels. Sillitoe begins where Milton and Blake left off and creates from the eponymous archangel a chameleonesque presence, more a matrix for irreconcilable states and ideas than a central figure. Sillitoe's *Lucifer* is part God, part man, possessed of feelings and able to choose, yet subject to the demands of fate. He has knowledge of everything but he can explain nothing at all, a mythological projection of Ernest Cotgrave. Appropriately, *Snow on the North Side of Lucifer* was published on 8 October 1979, followed only two weeks later by *The Storyteller*.

The moment that reignited *Her Victory*, as his novel based on a woman's experience would eventually be entitled, came in 1979. Every Friday when they were at the Notting Hill flat he would do the shopping for meat and vegetables at the nearby Portobello market. He was standing in a queue at a fruit stall and, as he recalls, had the stallholder served him a minute earlier he would not have noticed the woman on the pavement behind the stall. She had 'a certain look in her eyes' that was arresting, and he found himself speculating on what lay behind her rather gaunt, distracted expression. Was she married? Happy or not? What was her educational background? Did she have a degree? A career? He knew nothing of her, probably never would, but her face bespoke a personal history, one that he could not help but subject to his own speculations.

The mysterious woman in Portobello market would draw energy from others better known. Pam, as she would become, leaves George, her husband, for the simple reason that she wants to. He is neither particularly charming nor unusually unpleasant but it becomes suddenly clear to her that her life with him involves little more than a shared ritual of futility. Settled in her bedsit, Pam now for the first time has personal autonomy. She is no longer answerable to anyone else, and her decision to commit suicide is prompted not by a sense of despair or failure but because this option is open to her and her alone. As she prepares her room, taping the windows, tidying her belongings and choosing what to wear, she hears from behind her locked door someone moving into the neighbouring flat. This is Tom, an ex-merchant seaman who also has decided to embark on another life. Before going to bed he finds he has no sugar for his tea, and when tapping on the door of his neighbour he smells the gas. She does not resent his intervention, instead treating the arrival of this complete stranger as an act of fate which must simply be accepted. Thereafter the focus shifts slightly towards Tom, an orphan pursuing his genealogical heritage. He discovers that his father, killed in the First World War, was Jewish. The book concludes with his letters from Israel to Pam – they have now formed a relationship and have a child – and the sense of elation and discovery that inform his account indicate that Sillitoe had taken it almost verbatim from his own private journal recording his impressions of Israel in 1977.

Sillitoe concedes now that the novel had mutated from a work about 'a woman' to one which considers how intermeshings of decision, circumstance and pure accident affect our lives. There are, obviously, parallels between his encounter with the woman in the market and Tom's arrival. 'Often,' Sillitoe reflects, 'when I was writing the book I would look for her again at the market. I've no idea what I would have done if I'd seen her. "Excuse me, I don't know your name but I'm writing a novel about you, would you mind if . . ." I'd have been locked up.' He adds, 'But it was not that I was interested only in *her* life. That encounter made me think about how chance plays such a crucial part in what happens to us. It reminded me of when I met Ruth in the bookshop in Nottingham. For both of us everything thereafter was different from what it would otherwise have been. And Ted would tell of how he met Sylvia. Very similar beginnings but with very different outcomes.' What, I ask him, about Pam's suicide attempt? 'Yes, of course, I wondered why Sylvia had killed herself, as did everyone involved. But in the end no one knew, and it is Pam's feeling of absolute control of her destiny, of not even having to explain what she does, that causes her to plan her own death.' During the period he wrote the novel Sillitoe kept Bill Daleski informed of its progress, but despite the fact that he wrote almost as regularly to Ted he never mentioned it to him. 'I told him eventually, and he read it. He said some parts of it, on Pam, were familiar.' Tom's discovery of his Jewishness is a roguish blending of truth and fiction. Alan became a ruthless advocate of Zionism while maintaining his commitment to atheism and secularism, to which Ruth, like Pam, bore witness with varying degrees of admiration, puzzlement and mortification. David remembers 'combat after dinner, particularly when it came to the policy of the Israeli Defence Forces. It was darkly amusing. My mother, Jewish, advocating compromise while Alan argued that aggression was the only means by which Israel could survive. It is a hilariously happy marriage.' As the novel shows, chance meetings can be the making of unlikely and enduring relationships.

When Bill Daleski finally saw the book he was impressed, stating that its 'language has been absolutely honed down to the bone, so that it has a bare purity about it'. Equally important was 'your handling of consciousness . . . the way you penetrate to the depths of, say, Pam's being, so that we are right there with her, seeing everything from the inside – and yet you manage to persuade us that even at those depths we are still utter mysteries to ourselves' (BD to AS, 16 October 1982, Indiana Archive). But 'you're going to hate me, Alan, when I reluctantly say that I must join those who have reservations about the end of the book . . . the Zionist twist seems to me to come across with less force than anything else . . . seeming to lack that final punch of rightness that characterize the main relationships'. Sillitoe replied, explaining that when he began as a novelist the effort of writing was lightened by what he recalls as 'the slapdash ease of Saturday Night and Sunday Morning [for example] – though that wasn't easy at the time'. A quarter of a century on, however, he feels a greater obligation 'to explain'. His 'last few novels [principally The Storyteller and Her Victory] come out of my deep guts . . . they are important to me, much more so than my early work'. 'Her Victory is certainly [important] because the conclusions take in life-long beliefs. I could have emphasised the Zionism much more than I did but I thought that to make it effective – almost subliminal in its effect – I would keep it the way I did. An earlier draft had it far more portentous' (AS to BD, 17 December 1982). The 'earlier draft' deposited in Indiana testifies to this last statement.

The key phrase in Sillitoe's reply – because it forces upon us a decision as to whether the novel is a flawed curiosity or a great work in its own right

– is 'life-long beliefs'. Personal experience, including the most impulsive or biased, underpins all literary writing, but only the best writers can distil from it a work which has a heartbeat, a capriciousness of its own. Sillitoe achieves this with *Her Victory*. Tom is Sillitoe, but we do not need to know this fact to become fascinated by his presence and consumed by his evolution as a character. When we read his letter to Pam from Israel we feel an initial sense of surprise which gradually segues into recognition. He sounds different from the rather undemonstrative figure who entered the novel 250 pages earlier, but Sillitoe's achievement here is considerable since he has recreated in verbal form the sense of unsettled familiarity that accompanies our encounter with someone we know well but who has in some unaccountable way changed. The temperamental characteristics that define him are largely unaltered, but his relationship with Pam and more significantly with Israel now provide these with more animus and articulation.

Candour had always been Sillitoe's watchword, he has never dissimulated, but none the less during the ten years leading up to the composition of Tom's letter he too had undergone a transformation. There is a remarkable fragment, a reflection, composed at around the time he began *Her Victory*.

A lazy day [he is, so the note records, in Wittersham]. Wrote a poem about being left handed. I write with my left hand. All my writing comes through it, the hand on the same side as the heart, the hand I send Morse code with (but I am not left handed in firing a rifle or eating – though I drink with my left!) I suppose the reason I don't type my stuff is that then the right hand would have an equal say in what I write! And the left hand wouldn't like it. So I must always use a pen, otherwise the stuff doesn't come out right. My left is my vital and vulnerable side. I got tuberculosis in my left lung, and whenever I get flu or a bad cold it is the left lung or side which feel full of nails. [Private notebook, 12 March 1979]

'Left Handed' would eventually be published in *Sun Before Departure*, the collection informed persistently by his thoughts on Israel and Judaism. The poem itself rehearses the predominant themes of his diary fragment:

> Left hand is fed by the heart
> Strategically engined
> Between brain and fingers . . .

But neither the fragment nor the finished poem discloses the true cause of his sudden preoccupation with the relation between physical idiosyncrasies and the mental universe of passions and ideas.

Sillitoe wrote to Bill Daleski on 19 June 1980 from France where he and Ruth had decided to spend a week's holiday. He had reached a transitional point in *Her Victory* and Ruth had just completed the proofs for her sequence of poems, *Sibyls and Others*. 'Other people are in the meadow . . . French families having their lunch . . . Beyond, on all sides, are wooded hills. There's a wind blowing but it's fairly warm and not disturbing, as long as I hold the paper down – otherwise peace.' The account has an air of passive ritual about it. 'This is a good way to get it [the novel] out of the system – though it's still with me to the extent of phrases suggesting themselves that might be used . . . I've cut, thrust and pulled it into shape [but] I'll not know [what it is like] till I come to type it.' This, as Bill would know, was a reference to Sillitoe's personal regime of crossing the border between early longhand drafts and typewritten versions. The latter, as his diary entry indicated, would have attained some independence from his emotional, almost visceral involvement. He adds, in the letter: 'Ruth sits at the same rustic table, both of us writing, with our left hand.' Bill was one of the few for whom this seemingly superfluous reference to Sillitoe's left hand would have carried a private resonance. He knew that Sillitoe was learning Hebrew and had seen a draft of his poem in which he describes how:

> I laboriously draw
> Each Hebrew letter
> Right to left
> And hook to foot,
> *Lamed* narrow at the top,
> The steel pen deftly thickening
> As it descends
> And turns three bends
> Into a black cascade of hair . . .

['Learning Hebrew', in *Sun Before Departure 1974–1982*]

Suddenly Sillitoe had begun to absorb himself in a culture where an apparent technicality – writing that progressed in the opposite direction from Western scripts – altered completely his intellectual and sensual relationship with language and meaning. It was as though his left, his 'vital and vulnerable side', had now become the destination of the message, and the home of its significance.

As he also states in the letter he has now moved to his typewriter and he is saying goodbye to 'writing [the novel] that came through it, the hand on the same side as the heart', a novel about love, commitment and Israel.

After Tom and his world were complete, were no longer an extension of

Sillitoe himself, there was a subtle but notable change in his letters to Bill Daleski. When Sillitoe was composing the longhand first draft he and Tom seemed bound together on a journey with no predictable focus or clear destination. Sillitoe's and Tom's elemental states of mind were coterminous and indistinguishable. It was a special process, exclusive to the two of them, and as a consequence Sillitoe was somewhat reticent in this letters, as though he felt it necessary to protect the private world he shared with his companion. After June 1980, however, once Tom had been typewritten out of his author's system, Sillitoe begins to let rip. He reports first on his own appearance at that year's Cheltenham Arts Festival. He had shared a session with Q.D. Leavis, who talked about 'The Englishness of the English Novel',

> which as a prolonged expression of crass intellectual chauvinism I found hard to beat. It was the critical equivalent of Kipling's imperialism but not half as subtle, intimating that the White Prose Burden of the English Novel has as its noble task the purpose of illuminating the darker areas of the rest of the world. I almost expected to see ARP wardens come up the gangways blowing whistles and handing out cups of tea . . . 350 stayed to hear my reading, but a further 50 walked out during the stronger meat . . . Make that 53 because a young colonel on the front row had an apoplectic fit and had to be assisted from the hall by two of his maiden aunts. [AS to BD, 10 October 1980]

And why were the sensibilities of so many influenced by Sillitoe's 'strong meat'? Partly because he had offered some choice extracts from *Raw Material*, supplementing these with comments on why exactly the English – or at least, he implied, those of the comfortable background combined with fashionably leftish credentials who attended Cheltenham – were such repulsive hypocrites, especially when it came to Israel.

A year later he was unashamedly ebullient about an Israeli attack on an Iraqi nuclear reactor. He was responding to Bill's confidential account ten days earlier of how he had heard from an 'insider' in Begin's military high command that the Prime Minister had deliberately misled the international community, particularly the Arabs, by indicating that he planned imminent diplomatic and perhaps military action against the installation of Syrian missile sites; 'he said, "I don't know what Begin is cooking up, but you can be sure that if he talks like that (about the missiles) it's because he's planning something else altogether. That's the way he works"' (BD to AS, 4 July 1981, Indiana Archive). Sillitoe replied:

> I was delighted . . . I'd been wondering for some time when the great event was to take place . . . One doesn't play around with things like that. I got a

letter off to the *Times* about it [knowing that the *Guardian* would not publish it] . . . I regretted not being seated in a basket chair about one mile from the reactor at the time that it happened, having just changed into some nicely laundered clothes and being served with a long iced drink – then leaning back to watch that dramatic ten-second demolition job. [AS to BD, 21 July 1981]

He was almost as delighted by the sanctimonious protests against this act of aggression by the British 'Pinkish Lib Labs'. The letter could have been written by Tom: 'While life is normal, one senses a faint electricity of danger in the air . . . Maybe it's a more than usual feeling of existence, an urgency, liveliness and tension coming from three million people back in their own land after having been denied it so long, and determined to survive in spite of all adversities' (*Her Victory*, p. 587). But Tom is now just a character in a book. Sillitoe has taken over, and on his return to Wittersham following his visit to Israel in early 1982 he wrote to Bill that 'most of my good and best friends are in Israel, and the sense of loss on getting back to this island is almost intolerable' (AS to BD, 26 January 1982). Later that year:

News from the Lebanon is the only news of any importance for us. The place here is awash from the pigswill of the gutter-press . . . They make no connection between the atrocities of the IRA and the PLO, unable to concede that the latter will now be prevented from giving training facilities to the former.

Apart from that, I was amazed and delighted at the news that Beaufort Castle had been captured – a great feat. I was hoping also, of course, that no halt would be called on the outskirts of Beirut, that since the IDF had gone that far, they might as well finish the PLO . . . [AS to BD, 25 July 1982]

In November 1983 Sillitoe and Ruth were invited to a party in London to promote Amos Oz's recent book on life in Israel. Sillitoe had first met him in 1977 and encountered him several times thereafter; he admired his work, respected him, yet disagreed with him on Israel's military and political policy. Sillitoe felt a degree of unease regarding this, for obvious reasons. Oz and Amichai were arguably Israel's most prominent literary writers, and they had spent their lives in the country. Sillitoe's commitment was genuine and limitless, but he was still strictly speaking an outsider. He wrote to Bill:

I enjoyed his [Oz's] book, if that is the word. [It was an assembly of interviews covering the spectrum of Israeli opinion from those who favoured mediation with the Palestinians to others who wanted all-out war against surrounding states.] Of course (and don't tell Shirley this. Well tell her then, if you must. I hope she won't stop loving me!) I did (oh dear) find myself responding favourably to the more 'extreme' people . . . I had to pull myself up naturally – but many good points were made. Together with all the nice liberal humane sentiments in the book they reflect a dynamism which cannot be gainsaid, and is a very central part of Israel's strength. [AS to BD, 4 October 1983]

The poet Shirley Kaufman, Daleski's wife, was a patriot in the sense that she was committed unreservedly to the survival of Israel, and she shared this principle with at least 99 per cent of its population, at least if they were Jewish. Opinions differed radically on how it should be maintained, and those who Sillitoe refers to as the 'extreme' people – himself included – believed that attack was the only reliable form of defence. Others such as Shirley and indeed Ruth favoured mediation, which involved concessions regarding the post-1967 and 1973 occupied territories. Sillitoe adds that it is 'hard for me to imagine such a book [as Oz's] being published in England in November 1940 when England was in similar peril. Israel is in that situation all the time . . .' The two couples quarrelled, but their friendship survived, and Sillitoe ends his tirade with, 'Forgive me, Shirley!'

PART VI
OLD HAUNTS

TWENTY-EIGHT

Sillitoe spent more time working on *Her Victory* than on any other of his novels. It was the focus of his attention from 1977 to its date of publication in 1982. Often he works on two or more books at the same time but during this period his other projects were largely distractions, relief from the more demanding matter at hand.

The Saxon Shore Way was written from experience. He traced, on foot, the pre-medieval pathways of Kent that had eventually mutated into roads or disappeared beneath woods or farmland. Every week or so he would take the car to where he had completed his previous trek and start again. It reminded him of when as a child, in the rural hinterlands of Nottingham, Burton's country, he had become addicted to the landscape both as a means of disappearing from the rest of the world and as a challenge to his navigational skills. Now his rucksack was laden with up-to-date Ordnance Survey maps, reproductions of medieval and eighteenth-century charts and archaeological guides to thoroughfares never previously documented. He did not bother with sandwiches, preferring to choreograph his treks with an arrival at a pub some time around midday. He recalls in October 1981 meeting two RAF officers who had lost their group of Air Cadet Corps trainees out on a ten-mile orienteering exercise. History seemed to be repeating itself, and after leaving the two disgruntled officers he returned to his world as a sixteen-year-old and decided to cross a flooded stream by climbing along overhanging branches.

As he brought *Her Victory* to a close he decided that his next piece of fiction should make fewer demands on him as guide and adjudicator, so he chose to write a sequel to *A Start in Life*. As one might expect, Sillitoe's contemporaneous version of the picaresque, *Life Goes On*, is not so much a continuation of its predecessor as a reminder that its story is perpetual and indefinite. That is what Sillitoe loved about the picaresque. Its spirit reminded him of his own habits and state of mind in the 1940s and 1950s, and as fictional genre it allowed him to exchange vexation for opportunism and irresponsibility. In 1981 in a letter to Bill Daleski he referred to his new project as a 'holiday', a 'literary soufflé'.

Sue had obtained four good A-levels and, with a resolve which impressed Sillitoe, bypassed university and began applying for cub-reporter posts at local newspapers. When in the 1970s she had said she wanted to become a journalist he had encouraged her but privately dismissed her ambition as a fantasy to which teenagers are prone. By 1981, however, she was a full-time reporter on the *Nottingham Evening Post*. The year after that she married Max Lehrain, moved with him to London where she became a freelance journalist and in early 1983 they were expecting their first child. Max was an entrepreneur, the kind of individual for whom Margaret Thatcher's dismantling of state control and encouragement of initiative were utopia realized. Sometimes his ambitious projects succeeded, sometimes not, and he, Sue and their growing family would move regularly from the more fashionable, expensive areas of London to those that better suited their budget, and then back again. Max and Sillitoe got on well. Max seemed to his father-in-law like a character, albeit a fairly respectable one, who could have walked out of *A Start in Life* or *Life Goes On*. He had Michael Cullen's indomitable energy, and in a period when calculated greed was de rigueur Max's careless optimism seemed rather endearing.

David did well with his O-levels and went on to a further education college for sixth form, soon exchanging his predilection for Cadet Corps exercises and the smaller species of wildlife for a more enduring passion, motorcycles. Sillitoe and Ruth were petrified, but compared with other individuals in their late teens David seemed inordinately mature and circumspect. He would own and regularly ride a motorbike for a further seventeen years, until his own first child was born, and he never had an accident, though Sillitoe recalls a winter night in 1984 when after a rueful phone call from David he drove the Peugeot estate from Wittersham more than a hundred miles up the M4 to collect leather-clad son, his friend, and the BMW bike, whose engine had decided to rebel against its prestigious lineage.

Since his late teens David had been bringing girlfriends home to introduce to his parents, and when they stayed over Ruth and Alan made no objection to their sharing a bedroom. His letters to Brian, Ted and Bill during this time read like a record of a rite of passage which pleased Sillitoe but which he still has difficulty in believing has occurred so soon. 'David goes by bus to Greece tomorrow evening – sets off that is – with tent, sleeping bag, and his girl friend (lucky devil!), and has been getting his equipment together. He expects to be away for about a month' (AS to BD, 31 March 1980).

Continually Sillitoe was confronted with a version of himself of about three decades earlier. David in his late teens and early twenties was made up of the same puzzling composition of anomalies as his father. He had from his early teenage years loved guns and shooting but like Sillitoe had treated the weapons as machines with deadly potential and certainly not as the means of rehearsing potent fantasies. For each the lure of travel came from the same impulse: routine exchanged for improvisation. Sillitoe, before he owned a car, was always desperate for the completion of the bus or train journey so that he could set off alone with maps, compass and Baedeker on routes of his own devising. For David the motorbike offered a comparable degree of freedom and he carried his own accommodation – tent and backpack – into whatever remote region took his fancy. In letters from 1979 onwards when Sillitoe reports on David's latest expedition to various parts of the UK and Europe he seems absorbed, as if watching a film of his own life, suitably updated yet faithful to the original sentiment.

On 22 June 1980 he wrote Ted Hughes a letter that was at once characteristic and extraordinary. As usual he extemporized and reported on everything from the inner turmoil of the artist to the overgrowth of ivy at Wittersham, but on this occasion his manner seems hurried and unsettled, as if he is attempting to gather in all the phenomena which time might otherwise sweep away. He and Ruth plan ten days of motoring in France later in the summer, stopping at Arras and Amiens for him to do some unspecified 'research'; he has finished with W.H. Allen – as he once did in the 1960s, when he moved to Macmillan and then back again – and signed up with Cape. He has changed his accountant, his agent, his doctor and his gardener; in January they will be in Israel – six weeks and two days precisely – and before that he intends to spend two weeks on his own, cycling in north-east France and Belgium. He is worried about his tomatoes, also his cabbages. David's girlfriend has gone to Australia to visit family; David is staying alone in the Notting Hill flat ('alone . . . one wonders?') but they intend to find a studio flat together in the autumn. He catalogues phenomena and plans events at a breathless pace, and on a couple of occasions he pauses to disclose something of his mood: 'getting my affairs on a good footing for the last 20 years . . . it sounds like . . . I've never worked so hard for so long . . . Maybe it's that as one gets older there seems as if there's going to be less time available to do all one wants to do.' He appears uncertain whether he is chasing time or trying to slow it down, and the first indication that this state of mind would begin to affect his writing comes in the title piece of his collection *The Second Chance* (1981).

Among other things the story reaffirms Sillitoe's mastery of this subgenre; it combines the complexity of a full-length novel with breathtaking economy. Major Baxter and his wife Helen have lived for thirty years in a state of shock and agony, suppressed and muted in a characteristically English manner. Their only, beloved, son Peter, a fighter pilot, died in the Second World War and since then their life has been hollow, routine, borne with polite heroism. One day Baxter encounters in a pub a young man who is a perfect replica of his son, roughly the same age as he had been when he died and in manner and habit apparently a reincarnation. The new Peter conceals his actual background – he has recently spent six months in prison – and joins Baxter and Helen in a macabre denial of fact and the passage of time. Eventually he becomes so much like Baxter – as sons are prone to do

– that the major kills himself. We leave Peter and Helen in a grotesque state of contentment, or madness; it is impossible to tell, and this is a reflection of the mood of horrifying inference that informs the story from beginning to end. We never learn anything specific of how plans form in Baxter's mind on how to persuade the stranger to pose as his long-dead son or indeed about how the process is enacted, nor do we have any clear perceptions of Peter's or Helen's feelings. It is as though we have background knowledge of these people but are allowed thereafter only to watch and listen to them. The rest is inference – sinister and spiralling.

It is a masterpiece, but when he wrote to Bill Daleski of its genesis he seemed puzzled, troubled by what had inspired it. '[It] was a devil to write . . . I had this rather outlandish idea to begin with, and it seemed hopeless after the first draft . . .' For a while he left it and worked on other pieces. Then 'Eventually the story of the Second Chance took me over.' He finished it, 'still not knowing entirely what I've done, or not done . . .' Perhaps Peter might have been 'destined to become the Major, but the Major only more so because he would be the son as well . . . though it may be that I shouldn't meddle in these kind of speculations'. He goes on to suggest, unconvincingly, that some form of political symbolism was abroad in his struggle with the story, 'an inclination that England never changes' (AS to BD, 7 January 1981), that the class system embodied in the likes of Baxter and Helen has indomitable, almost supernatural powers to sustain itself. Sillitoe seems to be clutching at straws, and one does not require the techniques and gibberish of psychoanalysis to recognize that what unsettles him most about the story corresponds to something so intimately connected with his life that at the time he paid it little conscious attention. Time unsynchronizes previous states and relationships, and despite ourselves there is nothing we can do about it. Unlike Baxter, Sillitoe had not lost anyone in a sudden tragic moment, but his own past seemed to be if not dying then at least mutating uncontrollably.

Since the death of his father and Peggy he had visited Nottingham and environs regularly and for reasons that combined nostalgia with avuncular concern for the less secure members of his family. From the late 1970s, however, he began also to set aside at least half a day during these trips for a personal reconnaissance, often undertaken on his own or occasionally with Brian or Michael if the latter were not at work. He would visit churchyards such as Lenton where the Burtons were buried, and sometimes he would tidy the adjacent graves of his father and sister and then drive on to spend an hour in the heights of Abraham near Matlock or perhaps to Sherwood Forest, at least what was left of it – all regions he had explored first on foot and then on bicycle more than thirty-five years earlier. Wollaton Hall was a particular attraction. It is one of the finest Renaissance buildings in England,

and Sillitoe 'discovered' it when he was about ten years old. Of course he knew nothing of architecture then, but he was aware that he had come upon a structure and environment extraordinarily different from anything he had experienced before; it seemed unlived in, and no one disturbed him as he wandered through its gardens and exotic terraces. Now the place was patrolled by warden-like characters, ensuring, or so Sillitoe later learned, that the regular influx of paying visitors did not depart with examples of the abundant stone carvings and steel mouldings that decorated the grounds. Beyond the gardens the Burtons had their cottage, but any trace of it had now disappeared beneath new housing developments. Link roads had erased the lane. He consulted an old Ordnance Survey map of the location and it seemed to him like the longhand diary of someone long dead and unre-membered.

Arthur Denny was Sillitoe's exact contemporary in the Air Training Corps, who had taken Sillitoe's job at Langar when he'd left to join the RAF. Arthur later joined the Air Force as a regular and retired as a wing comman-der. He had only met Sillitoe again on a couple of occasions before 1950, after which their lives and careers had taken very different courses. After retirement he invited Sillitoe to RAF Scampton in Lincolnshire where he had once served and where, he knew, Sillitoe had spent time as a cadet. At Syerston, close by, just after the war ended, Sillitoe had flown in a Lancaster, in the rear gunner's turret. At Scampton the station commander gave him and Denny lunch, and afterwards showed them around a Vulcan bomber, one of the last still in service. Sillitoe was fascinated, and thrilled, and had confessed in a letter to Bill Daleski (21 February 1981) prior to the visit that he would 'love a ride' in the plane 'though I know there's little chance of that'. There wasn't, of course, but Sillitoe's memories, along with the RAF men's meticulous and vivid accounts of what flying in a Vulcan was like, lit an imaginative fuse similar to the one ignited by the mysterious woman in Portobello market. Writing to Bill after the visit he reflected that Denny had 'stepped into my shoes at the same airfield as a replacement – and when he joined up stayed on as a career officer . . . very likely the sort of life I would have been glad to have had if I hadn't become a writer' (15 March 1981).

The novel that began in Lincolnshire on a windswept, snowy late February day would eventually be called *The Lost Flying Boat* (1983). Sillitoe himself dismissed the book as one of his light 'diversionary' projects, 'a broth' of popular sub-genres, principally the *Boy's Own* style adventure story. When he sent a copy to Bill he almost apologized for it. 'It's really a common, hack-neyed adventure novel, so I expect you to throw up your hands in horror' (AS to BD, 15 May 1983). Discerning reviewers, however, picked out flickers of a more enduring theme. According to Michael Wood it involves 'Adventure' both as a means of 'escape' and a confrontation with a harsher 'reality'. 'Feels a bit like Joseph Conrad transferred to the Air Force,' and there is certainly an air of *Apocalypse Now*, the then recent cinema adaptation of *Heart of Darkness*, about it (*Sunday Times*, 30 October 1983). In the *Observer* Valentine Cunningham was similarly alert to Sillitoe's use of a popular sub-genre for insidious purposes. 'The overt simplicities of Alan Sillitoe – this time a generous freight of boyish looking adventure stuff – can prove most deceptive . . . *Boy's Own* hero meets frustrated semiotician. It's a rather dazzling convergence' (30 October 1983). The former is Captain Bennett, who reassembles his Second World War air crew for a single, private mission in a Sunderland flying boat, a 2,000-mile journey from Africa and involving a cargo and purpose that are never disclosed. The frustrated 'semiotician' is Adcock, beguiled by the enterprise and its odd man out. He is the only one who was not in Bennett's wartime crew, and it is from his perspective that we observe the mission; we know no more than he and we share his puzzlement and fascination.

Chapter 17 has the crew drinking and reminiscing, each raising the question of which was the best aeroplane they had flown in combat. Their flamboyant use of such criteria as the destructive power of the Spitfire or how well the Lancaster could defend itself against fighters has an air of schoolboy fantasy about it, yet for every man present these were once personal indices to death or survival; except of course for Adcock. The story, concluding with the destruction of the flying boat with Adcock as the one survivor, blends convincing and thrilling detail with an air of dreamlike unreality. For Adcock, and us, the crew seem almost an assembly of ghosts, trapped by experiences which have an unrelenting cyclic hold upon their personalities, as if they are destined to relive them again and again.

Sillitoe's visit to Scampton had reminded him of the moment in his life when as a teenager he had decided against training for air crew and of the period little more than a year earlier when the war had ended. He was relieved that the killing was over and not so vainglorious as to assume that his participation would have altered anything, but he felt uneasy none the less that he would play no part in what he knew was a just conflict. Throughout the novel Adcock – Morse code and wireless specialist – remains uncertain about what lies behind the behavioural idiosyncrasies and shared verbal nuances of his fellow crewmen. He knows that their wartime experiences must have played some part but he can only guess at how. Similarly Sillitoe, prompted by his day at Scampton, began wondering what would have become of him had he been born eighteen months earlier or decided to train for air crew. This oscillation between speculation and a potentially horrible actuality informs the novel. It is also, in part, a respectful memorial to a generation. Wing Commander Denny and Sillitoe were in their early-to-mid-fifties as the book was being written but their immediate predecessors, the ones who had flown in the war, were at retirement age, that time when memories come to depend so much upon a sense of sharing and comradeship.

Shortly after his visit to Scampton he made notes for an early draft of a poem completed in 1984. 'Lancaster' begins with a portrait of the pilot who had invited him on board forty years earlier.

> At twenty-two he was an older man,
> Done sixty raids and dropped 500 tons on target
> Or near enough. Come for a ride son:

'Son,' Sillitoe reflects now. 'He was only four years older than me, but he might as well have been from a different generation.' The closing stanza crystallizes the emotions that flicker as nuances in the novel.

> Alone, far back, to face the vanishing horizon squarely on.
> Dim as it is, don't go, corrupted by haze
> Loving what I cannot reach. The theatre's oratory
> And madness missed . . .

He began *Down from the Hill* (1984) during the year he completed *The Lost Flying Boat*, and their family relationship is self-evident. For the first half of the story Paul Morton tells of his experiences in 1945–6 cycling around the countryside of the East Midlands. He is discovering the same landscape that his creator knew so intimately and his elation blends with a conviction that all of Britain will soon similarly rediscover itself. The post-war Labour government would, he believed, alter the nation irrevocably, for the good of everyone involved, and Sillitoe instils into Paul's account a sense that the energy and anticipation that drive him forward on his bike draw upon a communal mood, a sublime future for all just around the corner.

The second half of the novel has Paul return almost forty years later to the site of his odyssey of optimistic enchantment. Now he is a successful screen-writer, up from his London home, a middle-aged man far more cynical and pessimistic than his youthful predecessor might ever have envisaged. Has he changed or was the promise of 1945–6 a delusion, hijacked by the self-preserving establishment? The novel comes nowhere near to answering this question, and is the better for it; Paul wonders if anything can be relied upon as a measure of durable truth, and so do we. The novel is selectively auto-biographical in that Sillitoe's regular visits to Nottingham and district enabled him to recreate very accurately, from memory, journeys undertaken forty years earlier. Unlike Paul, however, Sillitoe knew exactly why, how and when his disillusionment with socialism had occurred.

In *Out of the Whirlpool* (1987) fourteen-year-old Peter Grant watches the demolition of the terraced houses where he grew up and experiences a random influx of emotions. 'The fall and crumble of each house didn't finally satisfy him. He craved to witness a spectacular annihilation more inspiring than what had gone before, a house pulled out by the roots so that not even rubble remained' (p. 14). At this point Peter is about to lose his mother to a terminal illness, and when he wrote these lines Sillitoe had just lost his. Sabina Knight, as she was then known, died at University Hospital, Nottingham, on 16 October 1985 from a heart attack. She was eighty-four. Brian had been at her bedside, telephoned his elder brother with the news, and then witnessed the death certificate. Six months earlier he had written to Sillitoe of how, when passing through the parts of west-central Nottingham so far not surrendered to high-rise bocks and ring roads he had watched the street where *Saturday Night and Sunday Morning* had been shot, and where as a family they had lived twenty years before that, being demolished.

Orphaned, Peter Grant grows up with his elderly grandmother, drops out of school and becomes a labourer in a furniture factory. Via a series of random events he finds himself aged eighteen keeping regular company with Eileen Farnfield, a middle-aged, middle-class widow; he eventually becomes her lover, and attempts to adapt himself to her habits and mannerisms. Time appears in the novel as a malevolent, fickle presence, disembodied but tangible none the less. Apparently routine occurrences become, for Peter, portentous, seemingly marked out for his distressed scrutiny. The watch given to him by Eileen for his nineteenth birthday reminds him, horribly, of the one his mother had promised him shortly before she died, at roughly the same age as the living Eileen. During a brief conversation with an ex-girlfriend they seem drawn, marionette-like, to one subject: Why hasn't he visited his old neighbourhood for so long? 'I don't get much time,' he answers. 'You'll have to find it then, won't you?' she responds coquettishly. And in the background the town hall clock is striking the hour. The novel ends with Peter blinded by a gunshot (his gun had backfired as he tried to take revenge on discovering Eileen with her much older lover) and content. Time passes, but now the sensation of its passage is private; he no longer has to look at it.

Out of the Whirlpool is an anarchic, dystopian perversion of how time usually registers as a sequence of images. Imagine a collection of memorabilia spanning perhaps forty years of a personal history; each item carries an association with family, friends and events. Shuffle them, and as you spread each one upon the table see if anything like continuity, even recognition, is maintained. This is the working principle of *Out of the Whirlpool*. It reminds one of the letter Sillitoe wrote to Ted in which he rehearses just such a chaotic assembly, and it takes its cue from events that were continuing to envelop his life at the time he wrote it.

In 1984 Sillitoe had signed a contract with Grafton Books to do an account of the regions of Nottingham and surrounding countryside he knew best. His co-signatory was David, who would take the photographs. After leaving school in 1981 David had taken a year out doing part-time jobs to fund his enthusiasm for motorbikes and to set himself up in a flat with his then girlfriend. After that he went to Goldsmiths College to read geography and sociology but dropped out after a year; intellectually he was fully capable of finishing the degree but he had no interest in the vocational opportunities it might offer and had found other ways of fulfilling himself. He had always enjoyed taking pictures and became determined, with no formal qualifications, to earn a living as a freelance photographer. By the time Sillitoe began discussions on the Grafton book, David was earning money from a list of private clients and making a reputation for himself with the national press; the *Guardian* had already used several of his pictures. No favouritism was shown or expected – Grafton saw David's portfolio before agreeing to take him on – but Sillitoe felt refreshed by the prospect of sharing with his son what he feared was becoming his own rather reclusive habit.

Sillitoe insisted that the book should be authentic in that though he could, at his desk, have written an evocative and plausible account of the region, he wanted to do with Nottinghamshire what a couple of years earlier he had achieved in *The Saxon Shore Way*: days on foot with rucksack and maps, making notes as he went and then preparing drafts in the evening. After the first day in May 1985, following the Trent from the north Nottinghamshire border, David, to Sillitoe's concealed amusement, retired with blisters and rejoined his father twenty-four hours later suitably bandaged and equipped with larger boots. Sillitoe asked Michael and Brian if, when they had time, they too fancied a day out, and on one occasion all three Sillitoe brothers were reunited in Radford where they had grown up. Most of it was barely recognizable from those days. All of the back-to-back terraces had been bulldozed away, and where the new estates had not yet been built there were landscapes 'even flatter than Hiroshima' (*Alan Sillitoe's Nottinghamshire*, Grafton, 1987, p. 1). To their relief the only prominent landmarks spared from obliteration were the Nottingham Arms, the White Horse and the Dover Castle; most of that day's trek was between table and bar.

The book itself is intriguing in that it is unlikely that any of its readers would be ignorant of Sillitoe's personal history yet we wait in vain for a specific recollection. Much, however, is very cleverly inferred. When, for example, he names parts of Radford that have been flattened by developers we intuit traces of both melancholy and stoicism, and throughout the book there is a deeply personal register that is all the more affecting for its reticence. David's photographs complement the text excellently, shifting between a nostalgic mood that is unapologetic and unsparingly honest portraits of the present state of the place and its people.

It was during this same period that Sillitoe's mother died. Less than a month earlier his younger sister Pearl had succumbed to cancer, and in a letter to Ted Hughes he offers a catalogue of the year's events.

I walked 80 miles up the Trent from where it enters the county just north of Gainsborough. It took just over four days and I enjoyed the stroll. David did the first day, then got sore feet! [Then] my sister died of cancer at 52. She felt too tired to go to work one day, and lay on the settee for three weeks, then died. A month later my mother died, at 84. [AS to TH, 2 December 1985]

His manner reminds one of someone in a state of shock, not quite able to distinguish between routine events and their tragic counterparts but listing them none the less. The disbelief which prompts him to give exact measures – eighty miles, four days, fifty-two years, three weeks, a month, eighty-four years – is pathos *in extremis*. Its manner would be echoed in *Out of the Whirlpool*. In his letters to Bill Daleski written during this same period he is similarly stricken by what seems to be an unforgiving cascade of events, with death apparently determined to overtake everything else.

We're going to Nottingham the day after tomorrow, because my sister Pearl died a couple of days ago, from rapid cancer. I saw her – the last to see her conscious in the hospital – and feel a horrible sense of loss. She was just over 50. There's not much more I can say at the moment . . . [21 July 1985]

I've been [up to Nottingham] going around with David . . . David has lots of wonderful photographs so I think it will make a good book . . . we heard news today that Robert Graves has died. He was 90 . . . I first met him in 1953 in Deyá. He was the same age then that I am now . . . Then I had an old friend come to see me here the other day, Eddie Allen. He's a painter of about 60. He was born in Radford in Nottingham, and went into the air force and became a radio operator like me . . . We first bumped into each other in Majorca in the 50s . . . It's peculiar . . . [7 December 1985]

Ruth's recent experiences had been strikingly similar. Her parents had died within two months of each other in 1976, followed a year after that by her Aunt Ann with whom she had lived in the USA for much of the war. Apart from Sillitoe and David her last close relative was Harry, her only brother. He lived almost hermit-style in a remote cottage about ten miles from Newtown, Powys. After graduating with a good second in English from Cambridge he had spent three years in the early 1960s in the USA. There and following his return to England he wrote poetry continuously, but his ruthlessly self-critical temperament caused him to shun publication.

In mid-September 1982 Ruth received a phone call from the Newtown police asking if she was the sister of Harry Fainlight. No one could be sure of the exact date of his death – the certificate said between 28 August and 11 September – but the cause was bronchial pneumonia. A couple of weeks later Sillitoe went down to clear the cottage. It was an episode he still remembers vividly. The remoteness of the place and his determination to complete the job in one go meant that he stayed overnight. The only water source was a stream which ran close by the front door and there was no electricity. It reminded him of his forays into the jungle in Malaya. He had brought along a .22 rifle which he used to dispatch an unnervingly large and presumptuous rat, but he remarked later in a letter to Ted Hughes that the most powerful impression was of Harry himself. 'You could certainly still feel his presence . . . the way the candles were reflected back from the spines of his book collection . . .' Sillitoe was principally concerned with Harry's papers, particularly his poems. He was only forty-seven when he died. A volume Ruth selected from his extant work was eventually published by Turret Books in 1987 – including a short piece by Allen Ginsberg, a poem by Ted Hughes and a preface by Ruth. Her letters of the period closely resemble Sillitoe's following the deaths of his mother and Pearl:

> Alan is working on a long short story . . . and so is amiably removed from this plane of existence. David has just set off with his girlfriend and motorbike for a tour of Switzerland and Austria. Susan is waxing – she's expecting a baby in a couple of months . . . I'm here with my notebooks and poem folders, the garden, Harry's papers . . . [RF to TH, 9 July 1983, Emory Archive]

A month later she wrote to Carol Hughes of how she felt embarrassed after their last meeting because 'I was so absorbed in talking about Harry's poems with Ted that I paid so little attention to [you],' and later in the same letter that 'I feel quite odd now – having handed over Harry's papers to be typed, and receiving my book [*Fifteen to Infinity*] on the same day; the board swept clean. So I must start a great project' (RF to CH and TH, 12 August 1983, Emory Archive).

She meant a book, but something unpremeditated would preoccupy her within four months of writing this, an invitation from Vanderbilt University, Nashville, to become their poet in residence for 1985. She would be expected to be there for a semester, fourteen weeks, full time. It would be the longest period that she and Sillitoe had spent apart for thirty years. Sillitoe and Ruth

arrived in the USA on 27 December to attend a special Modern Language Association symposium in Washington, DC, on Alan's work. They then took the train to Nashville (2 January), where Sillitoe helped her to settle in, and they finalized plans for later in the year involving trips through the Deep South and eventually to the Pacific Coast.

Between 1966 and 1983 Ruth had published six volumes of poetry and a collection of short stories. Acknowledgement of her qualities by the literary establishment was gradual and persistent, but the invitation from Vanderbilt, unprompted, made 1985 her year of attainment. It was one of the most prestigious universities in the USA, and within a month of receiving their letter she was contacted by Jeni Couzyn who had been commissioned by Bloodaxe to edit an anthology of the most significant contemporary women poets, with lengthy prefatory essays written by each. It went without saying, Couzyn informed her, that Ruth belonged in this select group, eleven in total, along with Sylvia Plath, Elizabeth Jennings, Stevie Smith and Fleur Adcock.

She wrote to Ted Hughes that unlike Sillitoe 'who has managed to plunge into his new project and *mesh* with the present, I still feel somewhat "displaced"... The semester at Vanderbilt was absorbing, but all my "success" and the gratification of being able to do the job and to manage there alone, is hard to relate to the here and now' (RF to TH, 15 July 1985, Emory Archive). Tokens of her 'success' as a writer seemed to be arriving in abundance, including, shortly before she left for the USA, an approach from Viking to ask if she would consider becoming Sylvia Plath's official biographer, subject to the agreement of the Plath Estate. She spoke of it to Ted more as a formality than an enquiry; each already knew that their friendship, including Sillitoe and Carol, was more important than the book, which she turned down. It eventually went to Anne Stevenson.

Sillitoe visited Nashville in mid-March in order to break up the almost four-month period of separation, staying for a week during which he and Ruth visited Alabama and New Orleans. He returned on 2 May at the close of the semester when they hired a car and set off for a mammoth 2,500-mile run across the country to the West Coast. Sillitoe had developed a taste for topping 90 m.p.h. on the M1 between London and Nottingham and found himself in utopia on the straight, empty US highways, despite the 55 m.p.h. limit. He was soon able to spot the kind of dead ground hides used habitually by traffic police, and after chatting to long-distance lorry drivers in a bar was informed that a double flash of the brake light indicated they had received a CB warning of cops ahead. He was caught only once, doing eighty-five in Nevada, and incurred a surprisingly lenient $15 fine.

They stayed briefly in Albuquerque and Santa Fe and went on to Taos, whose most famous, temporary, resident had been D.H. Lawrence. Sillitoe made the visit reluctantly and as a token of his friendship with Bill Daleski, a Lawrence devotee, to whom he wrote: '[a] good place to work, I should think [it reminded him physically of Israel], though not with somebody like Lawrence and his friends around' (AS to BD, 4 July 1985). His duty done, they set off for the Grand Canyon. So overwhelmed were they that they stayed for four nights. One day Sillitoe set off at 5.30 a.m. determined to cross it and the Colorado River on foot, completing this trek almost exactly twelve hours later.

Following this they spent three days in San Diego to see Elaine Feinstein, there with her husband Arnold teaching that year at the Scripps Institute, and afterwards drove up the legendary coast road to San Francisco where they stayed for a week, seeing the sights and old friends, including Millicent Dillon and her daughter Wendy Lesser, editor of the *Threepenny Review*.

Turning eastwards they took a different route back, through Wyoming, Salt Lake City, and into the Rockies, which again they were reluctant to leave. They completed the journey, totalling nearly eight thousand miles, in New York and stayed with Ruth's cousins before flying back to London.

The panorama of places and experiences was all-consuming, but neither at the time had had much cause or opportunity to reflect on the trip's potential as something other than an extended holiday. Yet as Ruth's letter to Ted written soon after their return to London indicates, the whole experience of the USA, not just teaching in Vanderbilt, had begun to register as a crossroads in her life. Shortly after they got back, following Sillitoe's odyssey of remembrance with David and the deaths of Pearl and his mother, he wrote to Ted:

> I think that regarding time – or lack of it – what I feel in myself more than anything is greed. I want all of it, and I want to travel all the time. But also I'm gripped by an obsession that there's nothing more worthwhile doing in life for me than writing. Everything clashes – so I have to stay put and get done what's queuing to get out. The worms in the brain have to be resisted – though at times it's not possible. [AS to TH, 5 December 1985, Emory Archive]

Ever since David had reached his early teens Sillitoe and Ruth had indulged their appetite for travel. Sillitoe, writing to Bill Daleski, called Israel his 'other home, perhaps my first' – and in the years just prior to 1985 their schedule had been exhaustingly cosmopolitan: Yugoslavia (1978), the Netherlands and Belgium (1979), Canada (1980), Germany and Switzerland (1981), India (1982), Greece (1983), Japan (1984). These were the longer visits lasting between three and six weeks and all involving a daunting timetable of readings arranged by literary and academic networks in the countries themselves or by the British Council. Shorter journeys were even more frequent, with Sillitoe being invited to various parts of France at least twice a year. For example, in 1973 Jacques Surel of the University of Bordeaux had set up a specialized third-year undergraduate course based exclusively upon the study of *Saturday Night and Sunday Morning*, granting it a status which British English departments would be reluctant to accord to *Paradise Lost* or *Ulysses*. The course involved eleven weekly lectures ranging from 'The Environment of *Saturday Night and Sunday Morning*' and '*Saturday Night and Sunday Morning* as a Working Class Novel' to 'The Symbolical Pattern of *Saturday Night and Sunday Morning*'. Programmes such as Surel's were not uncommon in France and Germany; Sillitoe was treated by the politically attuned literary dons of Continental Europe as a magnificent aberration, almost unique within the otherwise predictable orthodoxies of the English canon, and he was invited as honoured *auteur* to Bordeaux on three occasions during the decade after 1973. Helder Macedo: 'You see, although Alan has always sold well in Britain, no one seems willing or able to determine his cultural status. The lazy, patronizing view of him is as a working-class, regional novelist, which excludes much of his important work. But in Continental Europe he is seen as an international author, who addresses universal themes. There are parallels between the nomadic aspect of his temperment, the unharboured wanderer, and his literary cosmopolitanism.'

Typically, in 1983 Sillitoe attended literary festivals in Cheltenham, East Anglia and Nottingham. He wrote to Ted that 'I can't help but accept the invitations and then as the date becomes imminent I have to think of something new to say. God, it's hard work.' But he never cancelled once he had accepted an invitation and the sense of drudgery would begin to lift as soon as he planned his route by car or booked his air or rail tickets.

Shortly after arriving in Israel in 1977 he had scribbled a note on how travel itself was a vital and invigorating aspect of his life:

> I like to imagine myself, wherever I am, to be a fish in water, indistinct and unrecognisable from the people roundabout. Yet I also must be conscious of my own uniqueness. I never cease to relish individuality, and travelling brings out these dual but opposite feelings more than any other state, which is why I like travelling more than anything else. A feeling of reality and spiritual well being blend, float up from deeper levels. A desire for this combination has been with me from birth. [Note among private papers relating to 1977 journey to Israel]

He could just as easily be discussing his addiction to fiction writing. Each involved the twin impulses of an anonymous journey and an autonomous act, but as he disclosed to Ted the enchantments of both led to 'clashes'. It was impractical to set off too frequently on the sort of lengthy journey which enabled him at once to lose and find himself, while at the same time earning his living as a writer. For the latter he needed a base, but 1985 hinted at a compromise. After their return Sillitoe and Ruth soon began to talk of how in the USA the nomadic impetus had returned. Sillitoe had stayed up one night in Nashville and written eighty pages of what would become the sequel to *Key to the Door*, a novel he had begun in Spain in the late 1950s; its inspiration, its subject, had been the instinct that prompted him and Ruth to set off for Provence. Now they started to discuss the possibility of selling Wittersham and moving further south, back to the Mediterranean, and by spring 1986 they had begun contacting estate agents, and the house was sold at the beginning of 1987. They had driven to Tuscany in the summer of 1986, found a semi-renovated farmhouse that was big enough for family and guests and signed the appropriate forms for purchase. Shortly afterwards the transaction fell through – a characteristic case of feuding heirs – and they again crossed the Channel, this time in September, for southern France. Provence, where they had lived a generation earlier, was becoming almost as crowded as Spain and much more expensive, so they went south-west to Languedoc. The village of St Pargoire is not a magnet for tourists and second-home buyers, but that is the enigma of France because it was, is, an unassumingly beautiful spot. About fifteen kilometres from Béziers and a few more from the coast, it comprises a square, a main street and a church that Sillitoe described as 'the size of a cathedral'. Almost everyone earns their living from wine-making – superb reds loved by the French and treated with suspicion by connoisseurs elsewhere.

In a street which backed on to vineyards a house of the type called maison de maître was for sale. It had been built in the late nineteenth century by one of the local wine-makers and its ground floor had once been a cave for barrels of wine and the vast arched openings were big enough for cars. There was no central heating – the region swung from 40° C in midsummer to sub-zero in January and February – and there were no *salles de bain*, only an antiquated lavatory. Until a bath and shower could be installed in what had previously been a bedroom they made do with a tin version. But the place had a timeless aspect. The front balcony overlooked a scene and a routine that had not altered since long before living memory – Sillitoe remembers the first 'traffic jam' of the village as a convoy of tractors and carts filled with grapes; the tractors, in his estimation, were first generation. Before them there had been horses.

They agreed; it would be like Menton again, except that now they would own the big house, be hosts to their family and friends. For both the move from Wittersham was shot through with a mixture of expectation and regret. Ruth wrote to Ted in August 1987 shortly after they had moved and thanked him for his contribution to 'Harry's book'. She added:

Though 'comparisons are odious' (as my mother used to say) I was fascinated by the parallels between the effect on you of the ghastly Trial-trauma and the effect on me of our move from Wittersham, from which I am just beginning to recover. It has eaten up most of this year, was extremely exhausting, mentally and physically, and more agitating than I would ever have imagined possible. The fact that all my immediate family – except of course Alan and David, which must have put a lot of pressure on them, I realise now – had died while we lived in that house: Harry, my parents, my aunt (who was another and perhaps more important mother-figure than my actual mother); and that all the material memorabilia had washed up there, made packing up, and the continual necessity to *decide* what to do with each object, feel like the dismantling of my own life – as though I were the one who had died. [RF to TH, 18 August 1987, Emory Archive]

The 'Trial-trauma' was a $6 million libel action launched in the USA by Jane Anderson, Plath's contemporary at high school, who claimed that a recent film of *The Bell Jar* had presented her as a lesbian. It was unsuccessful, but Hughes, who played no part in the making of the film, had heroically put forward his entire estate, Court Green included, to defend the case. It seemed as though his personal history would refuse to leave him alone; hence Ruth's comparison between his recent experience and hers on leaving Wittersham. Both showed that it was impossible to draw a line between the irrecoverable past and the present.

Nine months earlier Sillitoe too had written to Carol and Ted. He had not yet left Wittersham, but departure was imminent, and it is one of the most emotionally charged letters he has ever written.

We've known each other a long time – since the creation one might say – and so many long absences generate an air of unreality, which is unjust to the fundamental friendship that exists between us. The occasional letter which I send is a very etiolated signal in the long time gap . . . Sometimes it's like fighting for breath – so much keeping us away from true old friends when time is running fast. We ought to meet more often than we do, or have done . . . In life the only two things of value are work and friendship, and I know that whenever we meet its been wonderful and memorable, as with members of the same family but with no family tensions. There's always been an alliance between us, but it needs to be celebrated by more personal contact. On our part there isn't anyone closer than you and Carol. I know its hard to meet, living so far apart and being plugged into our work with almost sacrificial dedication, but even so . . . [AS to TH, 20 November 1986, Emory Archive]

The urgent, heedless manner of the piece seems at first an extravagance – he was after all only moving house while keeping the flat in London – but the clue to Sillitoe's agitation can be found in his use of the term 'since the creation'. They had met at the point when both moved suddenly from obscurity to the spotlight of the literary and cultural world. In Sillitoe's perception of his life it had been one of the two most significant turning points, the first being his departure for Europe with Ruth in 1952. Now he seemed to be on the verge of the third. Like Ruth he was experiencing an obligatory, profligate encounter with recorded memories. Every object – letters particularly – in Wittersham seemed to carry a trace of his past and was capable of reviving a plethora of feelings for individuals alive and dead – David, Pearl, his father, Peggy, his mother, Sue, Brian, Michael. He had to sort them, touch and look at them, reach and remember; it seemed, he recalls, like that mythological moment just prior to death when the salient points of one's existence are replayed vividly and at speed.

TWENTY-NINE

Of all Sillitoe's comrades in Malaya the one with whom he had most in common was Ronald Schlachter, but it was not until much later that their temperamental affinities would gel into a story and a lasting friendship. 'The RAF suited both of us,' Schlachter recalls. 'It was the only service in which the differences between officers and other ranks meant little. Ultimately they gave the orders, of course, but it wasn't a microcosm of British society with its rituals of deference and so on. You just got on with your job. One time we were attached to a unit of New Zealanders who turned the whole thing into a running joke – their officers would salute us, the men. Alan and I both appreciated that.'

They returned to the UK on different ships but promised to keep in touch, which they next did in London in 1950–51. Schlachter and his then wife Mary had a small flat in north Kensington. Ronald was training as a chef but eventually went on to become a successful businessman. When Sillitoe and Ruth announced their intention to set off across Europe and to write full time, funded principally by Sillitoe's pension, Ronald thought it entirely consistent with the man he had got to know in Malaya. 'He wasn't an eccentric and certainly not an exhibitionist but there was something about him,' he pauses, 'a stubborn refusal to do things in a routine way.'

Ronald wrote to him in 1962 to congratulate him on his recent successes, and Sillitoe replied, from Tangier, 'It's amazing how a letter from out of the blue can knock flat a dozen years!' he begins, and after three pages detailing their Mediterranean adventures and then the birth of David adds: 'I remember when I first started writing, showing you my first MSS – a blow by blow account of Malaya, very raw, semi-literate . . . It certainly took me a long time to learn how to write, much longer than I thought it would . . .' (AS to RS, 6 August 1962, private correspondence of RS).

It would be almost twenty years before they resumed contact. 'We were both busy with our lives and perhaps I was nervous about seeming presumptuous, Alan being a celebrity. But my second wife Ann became impatient with me mentioning this man who was interviewed so often on TV and radio and reviewed in the papers. Perhaps he's in the phone book, she said. He was and he insisted that we should meet the next day.' That was in 1980, and since then Ronald and Sillitoe have had lunch together on a regular basis when Sillitoe is in London. 'We go somewhere central and old fashioned. Alan has eaten everything in his time but at home he still has a preference for traditional British food: chops, steak and kidney pie, a good roast. And we usually have a bottle of claret.' Ronald took Alan sailing on several occasions in his yacht off the Kent coast, and Ronald's other major pre-occupation, owning and riding motorbikes, ensured that he and David had a point of contact. Their friendship, Sillitoe's and Ronald's, is simply that, an enjoyment of the company of someone you respect and like, but for Sillitoe there has been the special adjunct of being able to talk with a man like himself – self-made, intelligent and successful – but from outside the literary circuit. Ronald is a discerning reader but since he is unaffiliated to the 'business' of writing, criticism and culture Sillitoe treats his opinions as trenchant and unbiased.

'At lunch I'll ask him how the novel is going, but he is always cagey until it's finished. It's like getting blood out of a stone, but once I remember asking him a basic question. "Well, who's in it?" He replied, "We're all in it." He has said to me that most of his major characters are based upon real people. Sometimes the disguise is flimsy and on other occasions he turns people into hybrids, versions of themselves. I'm supposed to be in a few. I'm certainly Baker in *Key to the Door*, or part of him at least, and it was when I complained about being killed off in that novel he said that in the next I'd survive and he'd die, to make up for it.'

This would be *Lost Loves* (1991). Whether the novel was inspired by that particular conversation is debatable but there was between them a growing sense of their personal history becoming more precarious as age unpicked it. For example, Sillitoe wrote to Ronald of how he had been pestering HMSO for an early edition of *Eastward: A History of the Royal Air Force in the Far East, 1945–1972* by Air Chief Marshal Sir David Lee. The book, when it arrived, triggered memories. Sillitoe doubted that the researchers had 'unearthed a bundle of Bandit Routine Orders [from] under hut five of RAF Butterworth . . . They would certainly alter the whole tone of the book. I remember you burying them (you could hardly stand: nor could I) in a small steel chest painted with black lacquer, at dead of night, just before we left' (AS to RS, 5 May 1984). They had done this at the time in case 'Bandits', that is communist guerrillas, overran the camp and gained access to detailed orders on how British military personnel should deal with insurgents. But as Sillitoe indicates in his letter ('they would certainly alter the whole tone of the book') the act had also been a token of the unusual nature of their friendship. Most of their fellow servicemen followed orders and left ethical questions to those who issued them, but Sillitoe and Ronald had talked a lot about what exactly they were doing there defending one of the last outposts of the Empire. Specifically they were unsettled by what the Bandit Routine Orders told them to do. Beneath orotund euphemisms concocted by High Command and the Foreign Office was a straightforward ordinance: anyone suspect of guerrilla activity must be shot.

In Malaya, Sillitoe and Ronald recognized in each other something uncommon; their backgrounds were very similar and, unselfconsciously, without promoting themselves as self-made intellectuals, they talked of life and art. In 1986 Sillitoe went to a party at Ronald's house in South London at which there were several other ex-RAF comrades. Sillitoe wrote to thank him. 'It was good reminiscing with you about the old Butterworth days, though we didn't tell them about all those long philosophical discussions we used to have in the NAAFI on the meaning of life! And about literature of course' (AS to RS, 21 October 1986).

Lost Loves was brought to life, unwittingly, by Ronald's wife Ann who in 1988 arranged club class flight tickets and booked hotels in Singapore and Penang. These would be, for both, sixtieth birthday presents and Ann had made the bookings in secret as a surprise, after cautiously researching their plans and ensuring that neither had commitments for fourteen days following 4 June.

Sillitoe's diary of the trip contains no great revelations but is an important document because it provides a rare record of how events and random thoughts mutate into a piece of fiction. Interleaved with the day-to-day entries on their trips to Raffles Hotel, to Kedah Peak and to the original Butterworth Camp (then a Malayan military base and guarded by heavily armed soldiers in full battle fatigues; they did not get to revisit the site and search for the lacquered box under hut five) are notes on the sort of characters that Sillitoe and Ronald would become in the novel along with passages of dialogue and third-person orchestration based on their actual conversations and experiences.

Sillitoe would be George, son of a Yorkshire Methodist lay preacher; a bookish ex-teacher on the point of retirement. His wife has left him and he lives alone in a modest one-bedroom flat, 'the walls lined with books' (Singapore–Malaysia diary 1988, Indiana Archive). Watching George evolve in these notes is fascinating. Sillitoe is paring down aspects of his life and personality and then, godlike, seeing what would have happened if circumstances had been slightly altered and choices differently taken. What if he had gone to university, like George, and channelled his enthusiasm for literature into teaching rather than writing it? And if he hadn't met Ruth he might have had a marriage like George's, not catastrophic but moribund and destined for gradual failure. In his notebook he is creating a version of himself, at the same age, but with a different past.

> The young leave their country because every activity is an adventure, every new sight and sound a tonic for the spirit. At sixty, George thought, you've had it . . . It's no use leaving your country . . . unless you are still intellectually curious, as well as enthusiastic and even naïve. Otherwise all

is effort and waste. Certainly never go back expecting to meet memories half way. [Indiana Archive, unpaginated]

George has lost touch with the inspirational dynamic of travel. (Unlike Sillitoe who, for example, moved to St Pargoire in Feburary 1988, did readings in Struga in August and September, spent ten days on a solo bicycle journey around Picardy in July, and visited the universities of Poitiers and Orléans in April.) As a consequence the Malaysia journey, for George, becomes virtually a memorial to a life wasted. He knows he can never again be the twenty-year-old who served there in the Emergency, and he carries with him a self-destructive air. In the notes Sillitoe has him kill himself, politely, by pretending to fall from a boat off Penang. In the novel his departure is muted, between chapters, via a heart attack.

Also in the notes we find: 'George seemed to be sending dozens of postcards – but all were to himself – "my diary". They'll be waiting for me when I get back' (Indiana Archive). Elsewhere there is a list of the names of the very real people to whom he, Sillitoe, has sent postcards; fifty-six in total. Ronald first becomes Raymond and later Bernard. 'A tall saturnine Englishman – publisher's rep. Salesman all his life. Lived in London. Womaniser. Drinker. Sold everything. Cigarettes, cars, books, hi-fi – it's all the same. You make sense of different things but you only sell one thing – yourself. At least you know who you are' (Indiana Archive, p. 55). His wife knows of his brief affairs but there's an agreement between them, of sorts. As usual, Sillitoe sails dangerously close to the truth and then veers into fabrication. The Bernard who grew from this embryo resembles Ronald, at least in manner and appearance: well-presented men and easy, confident conversationalists both. But a womanizer? 'No, no. That part of the book was pure invention,' he states, and then smiles.

Sillitoe and Ronald certainly did not meet Gloria, who boards the jumbo at Heathrow at the same time as George and Bernard. She too is reclaiming her past. She is now thirty-six. Her father had been governor of Penang prison during the worst period of the Emergency, of which she has no direct memories, only a patchwork of awful rumours. She and George have a brief affair, curtailed by his heart attack, and the novel ends with Gloria and Bernard flying back to London together. Both remember him and feel, differently, his absence. 'Forty years or a week,' he comments. 'I'm sure they felt the same for George' (p. 189).

For connoisseurs of that rarely witnessed phenomenon, the artist at work, the diary contains some precious moments. It begins on their day of departure, 4 June.

Car arrived at 6.45 with Ronald. A variable day for weather, but fine on way to airport – high cumulus. At the security desk they emptied my bag –

a woman who looked into everything. I had to open whisky flask, tobacco tin, rolls of film, binoculars, and the short wave radio was taken back and put again through the screener – separately. Finally I was allowed to go, a very suspicious person, the perfect terrorist, as Ronald said, who had nothing looked at. Maybe it was because I wore a good jacket. Rohan trousers, but no tie. A mercenary, perhaps?

As we're travelling Business Class we're allowed in the Courtesy Lounge. Free drinks.

Aboard by 9.30. Upstairs – the upper deck, a drink served, bed socks, hot flannels given out, as well as eye shades and headphones. 9.55 no sound of engines. Soft music on the Kipling Special, Club Class to Raffles. [Indiana Archive]

This is its fictional counterpart:

The woman at the security check emptied George's bag, nosed into everything, a stern-faced upholder of something or other, with right too plainly on her side. Maybe he would have felt better if she had been his aunt or sister. He was asked to open the whisky flask, cigar tin, rolls of film, and take the binoculars from their case. She poked into the battery compartment of his portable radio, and sent it through the screener twice.

Bernard, who waited on the other side till George was allowed through, surely didn't look less suspicious, in his pale blue Rohan trousers, open Jaeger shirt, Reebok shoes, and jacket overarm. 'She had your number.'

'The bloody old dragon.'

'Still, it's for our own good.'

The only reason that kept him unruffled. 'I know.'

'You should have told her how we fought the terrorists in Malaya, all those years ago.'

'Before she was born,' George said.

'Almost before we were born. But we did.' [p. 14]

The dialogue was written approximately six days later, given that a rough version of it appears in a sheet facing the events recorded for 10 June. So far it seems as though two very real men have walked virtually unchanged into a literary text, but where the diary entry for 4 June closes, with drinks in the courtesy lounge, Ronald's roguish *alter ego*, Bernard, takes over and the door between reality and invention closes. He spies Gloria, who existed only in Sillitoe's imagination.

Bernard, in his nonchalance, noticed her: light coat overarm, halfway down the queue for tourist class; a white Fair Isle sweater, an eight-pointed purple brooch with a tiny silver cross in the middle just under her subtly lined throat, fair greyish hair like a halo. She looked away as he and George were called forward. [pp. 13–14]

When I asked Ronald about his transformation into Bernard he corrected me. 'Well, when Alan said we're "both" in the book what he really meant was that we were dismantled and reassembled as Bernard and George; most of me in Bernard certainly, but parts of each of us are redistributed through both of them.' George carries traces of the Sillitoe of the 1960s, treating compassion for the plight of others as the almost exclusive preserve of the left, while Bernard, the unillusioned free marketeer, bears a closer resemblance to his creator at the time the book was written. They take their differences no further than banter, but it is significant that Bernard is the one who survives beyond the final page. Ronald: 'I was out of touch with Alan during the 1960s, but by the time we got back into regular contact we seemed to agree on most things, politically. He thought the pit closures following the 1980s dispute were a catastrophe yet he blamed Scargill as much as Thatcher. She, Margaret Thatcher, he admired mainly because she came down hard on Irish terrorism – he saw the IRA and the Palestinian terrorists as two sides of the same coin – and for her leadership during the Falklands War.' Sillitoe wrote to Ted Hughes in February 1981 that 'I'm beginning to regret the disappearance of the Empire. God, what am I coming to?' There is some self-caricature here, certainly, but an equal amount of candour.

Sillitoe and Ronald were on the periphery of the campaign against the Malayan insurgents, but in the novel Bernard and George are in the Army, not the RAF. They have to implement the Bandit Routine Orders, and Sillitoe explores a private dilemma. As a radio direction-finding operator he had sent information to the Lincoln pilots who were carpet-bombing the jungle. What would he have done, he wondered, had he been involved in an exchange of fire on the ground? Bernard and George kill six poorly armed guerrillas and are neither proud of nor regret their actions. Would Sillitoe and Ronald have done the same? Sillitoe: 'Of course we would. Talking about principles of war is one thing, but all that goes out of the window if someone is shooting at you.'

Sillitoe wrote to Ronald Schlachter on 8 July 1989: 'I'm back at work on the novel I dropped to get the Malayan notion off my back.' This is true, strictly speaking, but both projects, *Lost Loves* and *The Open Door*, drew upon the same source – Sillitoe's experiences in the late 1940s and early 1950s. The latter would go into print first, in 1989, and is the sequel to *Key to the Door*, written thirty years earlier. These two and *Lost Loves* are his most autobiographical novels in the sense that chronology and facts are only tampered with rather than altered. When I asked him why at this point in his life he had again become preoccupied with a relatively brief period in his distant past he was, as he can sometimes be, honest and costive. 'It is impossible to say. I don't plan projects in advance. It is as though they have been waiting and when the time comes I tackle them.'

The longhand first draft of *The Open Door* contains, near the beginning, a loose sheet on which he has written, 'It's taken me nearly 40 years to be able to write this novel.' He cannot mean it was only the passage of so many years that enabled him to endure a return to this period – even in its lengthy first draft form there are no terrible disclosures – and one detects an air of gnostic resignation in the sentence. Only with the benefit of four decades' hindsight was he able to properly understand the enduring memories of that time. In this respect *The Open Door* is not simply a continuation of its predecessor. It is a book by someone who now perceives his past as most certainly a different country.

The narrative incorporates most of the occurrences between Sillitoe's return to Britain from Malaya and his departure for France. Some characters are recognizably versions of their actual counterparts and a few others are pure invention, most significantly Nora to whom Brian/Sillitoe is, briefly, married. Rachel, the nurse he meets when he is being treated for TB, is based partly on Hilary Bussey. Hilary, after a difficult first marriage, eventually found happiness with her second husband, a lieutenant-commander in the Royal Navy, now deceased.

'I switched on the television and there was a BBC2 Arts programme being shown,' she told me in March 2007. 'They were interviewing a writer in the garden of his large house in Kent – we were in Canterbury at that time – and I suddenly realized who it was.' It was Sillitoe at Wittersham in 1986, being interviewed for one of a series of programmes that the BBC's Alec Reid had commissioned on the Angry Generation of the 1950s. 'I was astonished. Of course I knew that Alan had become famous, renowned as a writer, but actually seeing him again, if only on television, was, well, a shock. Partly because he was literally only a few miles away.'

Three years later something similar occurred. 'I was in our new house in Whitstable – we'd moved from Canterbury – just standing in the kitchen, peeling carrots actually – the radio was on, Radio 4, and there he was again. I hadn't really noticed on the TV programme but his voice had changed. He still had something of a, well, Nottingham accent but the last time I'd actually spoken to him was forty years before. And his voice from the 1940s had stayed with me.' This was 1989 and Sillitoe was being interviewed on Radio 4 about his most recent novel, *The Open Door*, though it was not until some time later that Hilary would read the novel, recognize herself, and come to reflect upon the peculiar coincidence of hearing him again, suddenly, in her kitchen. When I interviewed her there were further striking, and unwitting, similarities between her random recollections and Sillitoe's early drafts of the novel, which Hilary has never seen. 'There were', she said, 'I think twelve beds in the ward, and in one was a man who seemed, I don't know, different from the rest. He looked lonely, I suppose, not in a sad or taciturn way. Just alone.'

Sillitoe begins Chapter 1, Part 2 of the Indiana manuscript as follows:

When he woke up he counted the beds. Numbers were important and there were few times when more than one of the twelve beds were unoccupied. All his life he had wanted to be alone, and now he was. But he'd never cared for being lonely, and that he was not. [p. 1]

The parallels are fascinating in that both focus upon the details that to each seem to characterize Sillitoe's state of mind at the time they met. Hilary continues: 'We started to have regular conversations and discovered we shared many interests. Alan loved classical music – there was none available in the ward – and so did I, had done since childhood. My father was a classical violinist.' Both of them were also interested in books, everything from literary classics to the standard works of philosophy. 'The NAAFI book trolley was practically all trashy fiction, and I asked Alan if he'd like me to bring him back from home, when I went on leave, some volumes from my father's library. I wasn't sure what to take so I went for the indisputably highbrow – Tolstoy, Dostoevsky, *The Golden Bough*, some Jung and, oh Lord [she laughs], Kant's *Critique of Pure Reason*. I don't think either of us understood it but, straight-faced, we tried.'

All this features in Sillitoe's account of the relationship between Rachel and Brian, with Kant respectfully thumbed by both. Sillitoe and Hilary were almost the same age, but in the book Rachel is made more mature, roughly twelve years older than Brian. Sillitoe is unable to explain fully the reasoning behind this, except that, 'Well she, Hilary, was different from any woman I'd met before. It was not a matter of class, simply that none of the women I'd previously known – and in fact hardly any of the men – were interested in the same things as me. We didn't see ourselves as particularly clever, just people with similar preoccupations – which is why we started talking to each other in the first place.'

Hilary: 'He stated unhesitatingly that he wanted to be a writer. So I encouraged him to write about his recent experiences in Malaya, which is how the story of the Gunang Barat came about. He sent it to the *Geographical* magazine and I remember – there were three posts a day – I'd be at the mail room for every delivery. They'd say, "Oh it's you again. Someone special writing to you?" or something like that. It took about six weeks and they rejected it with encouraging comments. But Alan took it well. He was determined, you could see that. Ten, eleven years later, when *Saturday Night and Sunday Morning* had made him an overnight star, I was overjoyed. He'd done it.'

Why, I asked, did they part? She hesitates before answering.

'When I went home I would gradually drop hints to my mother about a man who meant a lot to me. She was interested, and I answered her questions about Alan . . . I can't, won't, tell you exactly what happened, but at that time my mother dominated my life. After that I made it as clear as I could to Alan that things were over. We no longer met outside the ward. I remember the last time I saw him at Wroughton. I'd just left the train and was walking to the camp. He was coming towards me, in uniform, along the lane. We stopped and I told him how sorry I was that everything had ended. He simply stared at me, not angrily; just sad and surprised.'

In the book Sillitoe assigns no particular cause to the end of Brian and Rachel's relationship, treating it as a consequence of fate to be endured with resignation, and this offers a clue to his rationale for the novel as a whole. He was now in his early sixties and encountering the paradox of accumulated memory. He kept notebooks – rarely reflective diaries – which were made up of records of what he had read, where he had been living and the particulars of his day-by-day activities. These facts anchored a private tissue of emotions, vividly preserved but anaesthetized by the passage of time. He could take himself back, re-experience memories, but do so as someone largely uninvolved, able to assess more clinically the reasons, causes and consequences of his existence without being overpowered by them.

Two other characters in *The Open Door* based on real people are Percy and Chuck. Both are staunch communists, Labour men by proxy but biding their time until the whole system is ready to be replaced by a structure based on that of the Soviet Union, which they admire without reservation. They pursue Brian through the later part of the novel like evangelists or travelling salesmen, and it is surprising that he continues to indulge their presence. In private, to the reader, he confides his loathing for Stalin's speeches, lent to him by Chuck, and argues with both of them about what exactly constitutes 'working-class' literature.

Ruth's role in this literary rite of passage is intriguing. She features as Anne Jones, the most fascinating and enigmatic woman in the book.

In the unpublished manuscript there are two conclusions, a scenario that connoisseurs of the postmodern and other brands of self-indulgence would treasure, but in Sillitoe's case the dilemma arose from a very real fabric of memories and emotions. In one draft Sillitoe remains faithful to the truth. Brian and Anne, in bed, are talking of his plan to go to France.

'What if I asked you not to go,' she said. He knew there must be a long pause, but he certainly needed it. 'I wouldn't go.' She seemed to be asleep. He wasn't far off himself. Then he heard her say, 'What if I asked to go with you?' The pause was somewhat shorter. 'Come with me.' [Indiana Archive, p. 265]

Following this version the manuscript ends with them together on the train nearing their destination in Provence:

> . . . along the coast were villas with red roofs, patches of carnations, lemon and orange trees. 'We've done it,' he said, meaning: I've done it. I've done what I've always longed to do. 'Whatever happens from now on, I'll never forget this.' The door, he said to himself, is open. 'Nor me,' she said. [Indiana Archive, p. 270]

The uncomfortable shifts between their shared perspective and Brian's intimation of a private experience hold the clue to Sillitoe's decision to abandon this ending. Anne's presence in the novel is an understated testament to the depth of Sillitoe's feelings for Ruth, undiminished by the passage of four decades. She exists on the margins of a narrative dominated by Brian's search for himself and his determination to become a writer. But this in no way diminishes her stature; quite the opposite. She is the only character, aside from Brian himself, who remains independent of authorial insight or intervention. Paradoxically, had he remained faithful to their real story her individuality would have been compromised. Brian leaves a slipstream of energy and the departing image is of a man who has seized control of his future. Anne, leaving the final page with him, would forever be inscribed as his companion rather than the author of her own fate.

In the novel, Anne's question, 'Why don't we go together?' is left unanswered. We never know what Brian might have said because before he has the opportunity to respond she takes the initiative. '"Oh well," she said, "I'll have to find someone else"' (p. 346), and we are left with the memorable passage in which he is accompanied to the train by Arthur, who in ten years' time would launch Sillitoe's literary career.

Both drafts include variations upon the phrase 'the open door' and both carry an identical, attached sentence scribbled on the blank page beneath the end of the story and never intended for publication: 'The struggle had begun.'

THIRTY

In the six years between 1987 and 1993 Sillitoe produced five full-length novels, a travel book to Nottinghamshire, a volume of poems and two collections of short stories, this during the period that for most people involves a gradual slowing of pace towards retirement at sixty-five, his age in 1993. His increased rate of production and powers of endurance strengthened his qualities as a writer. In a period when a new generation of novelists – Martin Amis, Julian Barnes, Ian McEwan and Salman Rushdie in particular – were the glamorous subjects of public acclaim Sillitoe was one of two of the 1950s generation who could still claim to be a serious writer with popular appeal; the other was Kingsley Amis.

For example, the publicity departments of mainstream publishers have a standard list of media outlets – predominantly TV and radio – which they will target for pre-launch publicity, to create an air of anticipation and ensure that review copies are given priority in the broadsheets. Competition for attention at this first stage is fierce, but when Grafton began to trawl the usual targets for interest in *The Open Door* little persuasion was required. The *Sunday Times* wanted a full-length interview to be conducted by Harry Ritchie, not only on the forthcoming novel but involving his career and outlook (which took place in the Notting Hill flat on 10 February 1989 and was published on the 19th). Three days later the *Sunday Times* did a photographic session to accompanying the article. On Monday 20 February he was interviewed live for BBC Radio 4's *Start the Week*, and later the same day he did a recorded interview, this time for almost twenty minutes, for *Kaleidoscope* (the repeat on the afternoon of Tuesday the 21st was heard by Hilary Bussey as she peeled her carrots). That Monday Sillitoe spent the entire afternoon at Broadcasting House doing interviews for BBC Radio Oxford and the BBC World Service's *World of Books* programme. Next he was rushed by taxi to speak to the *Manchester Evening News* at the Waldorf Hotel.

On Tuesday a hired car and driver whisked him to Broadcasting House again for a 10 a.m. session with Radio Wales, and the LBC claimed him for a live exchange at eleven o'clock. Then he was at Bush House for another recording for the World Service, this time for their *Meridian* programme, and on to the Press Association for a syndicated talk at St George's Hotel. At 2.15 p.m. he was back again at Broadcasting House talking to BBC Scotland's *Tuesday Review*. Thursday began yet again with a visit to Broadcasting House for a live chat on Radio 2's *John Dunn Show*, though one doubts that many Radio 2 listeners of the time were zealous fans of, say, Martin Amis or Salman Rushdie.

Friday the 24th was spent in Manchester, with Sillitoe leaving Euston at
7.15 a.m. and getting back to Notting Hill at about 8 p.m. In between he
had talked with interviewers and indeed listeners/viewers for *Key 102*,
Piccadilly Radio; Greater Manchester Radio; Granada TV's *The Week in
View* (syndicated throughout the ITV network) and ITV's specialist arts
programme *The Other Side of Midnight.*
The following week, Wednesday 8 March, Radio 2 again asked him to
do a half-hour session for their *Round Midnight* programme.
Articles on him, and his life, were commissioned by the *Sunday Times*,
Publishing News, the *Guardian*, the *Observer* and *Woman's Own*. The reviews
themselves, appearing over the next two weeks, were unreservedly enthusiastic, with the *Sunday Times*, *The Times*, the *Observer*, the *Daily Mail*, the
Sunday Independent, the *Telegraph* and *The Economist* affirming that the book
reinforced the general perception of him as a writer who appealed to every
kind of reader, a modern Dickens. The *Times Literary Supplement* stated that
it 'confirms his standing as one of Britain's most powerful and sophisticated
fiction writers'.
A similar schedule accompanied the appearance of *Out of the Whirlpool*
(1987), *Lost Loves* (1990), *Leonard's War* (1991) and *Snowstop* (1993). All
were published by major fiction houses (variously Hutchinson, Grafton and
HarperCollins) whose promotion departments would only invest so much
time and expense in novels that they knew were guaranteed to attract wide-
spread publicity, reviews and, crucially, readers. The paperback edition of *The
Open Door* sold 10,275 copies in 1991–2 alongside a respectable 5,380 for *Lost
Loves*. Very few writers could guarantee continued profitable sales for their
debut works more than thirty years after publication, but that same year
2,083 people bought paperback copies of *Saturday Night and Sunday Morning*,
and *The Loneliness of the Long Distance Runner* sold at almost 100 a day: 3,498.
In 1993 Francesca d'Arcangeli of HarperCollins's International Sales
Division did a survey of English writers who featured most frequently as set
texts in French *lycées* and universities. Shakespeare was doing quite well, it
seemed, but the overwhelming leader among living English-language writers
was Sillitoe, with *Saturday Night and Sunday Morning* and *The Loneliness of
the Long Distance Runner* outranking any other single work as mandatory
reading in the universities of Bordeaux, Paris, Lyon, Poitiers, Nantes and
Tours. On the strength of her research she had no difficulty in persuading
her employers to fund an exhausting tour, beginning on 31 January 1994 at
Nantes and over the next seven days incorporating Toulouse, Lyon,
Versailles, Tours, Bordeaux and Paris. The average audience, including
academics, university students, senior *lycée* pupils and teachers and members
of the public, was 300, sometimes running to more than 350. Following
each talk – which included question-and-answer sessions and lasted up to

two hours – representatives of the local media were booked for interviews, almost always conducted in French. D'Arcangeli reported afterwards that at a conservative estimate the interest generated by the tour would justify a supplementary print run of five thousand for each of his early classics. He was, as she put it in the report, perceived by the French as 'the most influential post-war British writer', adding that he had been 'an absolute pleasure to be with' (Letter from Francesca d'Arcangeli to Ray Potts, 14 February 1994, copied to AS and in Indiana Archive).

Patricia Parkin was his editor at HarperCollins during the 1990s and one of the few people from the publishing industry he regarded as a true friend. 'Alan was, is, unique,' she observes. 'He was one of the biggest and most reliable sellers on HarperCollins's list, and most authors of that rank are difficult individuals. They can be reclusive or soaring egotists but consistent in their exploitation of status to make demands. Not Alan. For launches and readings he was meticulous in keeping to the timetable, he never complained. And he always performed brilliantly. It was, as he saw it, part of the job. The only time he would cause unrest was if he saw himself being treated as a product rather than a writer. That is, he never, ever permitted editorial interference. And again this was not because he saw himself as the perfect artist, but he had written the book and if there was anything wrong with it he would face the consequences.'

Despite his success and undoubted quality as a writer the literary establishment treated him more with indulgent respect than anything resembling adulation. Not all reviewers celebrated his work – and he has never once complained about that – but a consistent and considerable number recognized its importance. Yet he was never shortlisted for a literary prize after the Hawthornden in 1961. Sillitoe: 'I told my publisher never, but never, put me in for the Booker – and they didn't.' He was never really admitted to the elevated pantheon of 'significant' post-war novelists which included such figures as William Golding, Iris Murdoch, John Fowles, Doris Lessing and even, begrudgingly, Kingsley Amis. Did he, I ask Patricia Parkin, ever resent this? 'Certainly not. Alan is the only writer I ever met with no enemies. Let me correct that. There were some people who didn't like his work, and said so in reviews and elsewhere, but he feels no antagonism towards them. In his view they had a right to hold and express any opinion they wished, and good luck to them. I've never met anyone like him in publishing.

'At launch parties and literary get-togethers the competitive egocentric aspect of writers comes to the surface. They swallow the flattery and oleaginous drivel that we, publishers, are programmed to feed to them. That wasn't for Alan. He hates being flattered and he treats you as an equal, a colleague. When other writers – I won't mention names – were enjoying the, entirely false, adulation of editors and promotions gurus, Alan would retire to a corner with people he trusted and liked. Talk, have a drink, light his pipe, and probably suggest that we bugger off to a pub. He might flirt sometimes, and every woman I've known has found him – I don't know – beguiling; he is transparent and charming at the same time. But it is no more than that. He is devoted to Ruth.'

Sillitoe sees writing as a job, albeit a special kind of job undertaken successfully by relatively few who might on occasion produce a work of art. But along with maintaining one's aesthetic principles a living has to be made. His work rate is astonishing. On average each of his novels goes through three, four or five drafts. The first is in longhand, the subsequent versions typed on his 1970s typewriter (he once in late 1993 experimented with a word processor, for approximately two days). He does not work in the conventional manner. Instead each new draft is completely covered with inked corrections, and then retyped into another clean copy, which in its turn is smothered in alterations, additions or cuttings out, until no more can be done to any advantage. He will also practise economy, with the final draft usually being much shorter than the first. *The Open Door*, for example, began as 748 pages in longhand (approximately 200,000 words) and was reduced via four separate drafts to the final 120,000-word piece. In total, he wrote and typed approximately 650,000 words. Given that he frequently works on two books at the same time – particularly during his immensely productive 1987–93 period – it is not surprising that he often comments on how it is impossible to separate the narrative from his lived existence. He spends so much of his time in the world occupied by his characters that the border between his and theirs became porous. His average day – provided he had not committed himself to some other event, social or professional – would have him out of bed by 7.30 a.m. First he will do fifteen minutes of rigorous exercises learned in the RAF, using his study so as not to wake other members of the household. Next he will prepare breakfast, for everyone in the house if they have guests, or for the four of them when the children lived at home, then open his mail and spend at least an hour answering letters. He works until lunch, which he and Ruth prepare. After more work in the afternoon, he sleeps for an hour until teatime. He might take a walk before dinner, depending on whether or not they are in the country, and the meal will be accompanied either by wine or, as he often prefers, three shots of Russian vodka. Before going to bed after midnight he usually fits in at least three more hours of work. Typically he began a letter to Ted Hughes by setting the scene. He was in Wittersham. 'It's a stormy night and we're battened down. The radio is picking up Morse signals. I've just finished working on the novel and it seems a good time to write a letter. It is 1.00 a.m.'

I offer this portrait of Sillitoe entering the last decade of the twentieth century because the essentials of his character and temperament have not changed over fifty years. Most writers, by sixty, become either caricatures, exaggerations or antitheses of their former selves. The anarchic and hideously vituperative aspect of Kingsley Amis that he had balanced against his more charitable and generous side in his early years roamed free during the last decade of his life. Similarly John Osborne's raddled nihilism was at first an inspiration for his writing but later it took control of his temperament, and the flickers of optimism that Philip Larkin cautiously allowed into his world during the 1940s and 1950s had by the 1980s been extinguished by a ceremony of self-loathing. Not Sillitoe. Certainly his political affiliations had changed during the 1970s, but this was not symptomatic of a more fundamental modification in his character. He had not altered; he had simply had more time to think and to revise his mistakes. He had not changed but, as he was increasingly reminded, much else had.

In 1987 Channel Four approached him with an offer for the film rights for *The Lost Flying Boat*. The channel was then promoting itself as a radical alternative to independent television, and the BBC and several producers thought the novel would translate well into an idiosyncratic British version of *Apocalypse Now*. In early 1988 Channel Four paid Sillitoe £3,000 for the rights and as an advance to do the screenplay. Three years later the project was still at the planning stage and Sillitoe was sent a further £1,000 to guarantee his commitment to it. In the intervening years, 1989 specifically, he had contacted Albert Finney and suggested that they renew their working relationship. Finney, Sillitoe suggested, would play the enigmatic captain, and at first he was interested, but further delays by Channel Four meant that he withdrew to work on other more profitable films. Sillitoe, throughout this, expressed not the slightest hint of bitterness, frustration or impatience. Instead his enduring, prized memory is of when he was invited to spend time with the real star of the film, the last working Sunderland flying boat, then kept at Chatham Dockyard. Channel Four hired the plane and two pilots for a day and Sillitoe and five, as he described them, 'cultural executives' from the channel spent two hours over the English Channel in this magnificent leviathan of an aircraft getting a flavour of what they hoped would be the talisman of the project. Sillitoe's favourite moment was unforeseen. Before touching down on the Thames one of its Pratt and Whitney engines began to misfire and the propeller had to be feathered. Sillitoe, from experience, knew that they were safe enough but the men from Channel Four suddenly lost interest in their colloquy of projections and spent the rest of the flight in a state of mute hopelessness. Sillitoe did not gloat, but later came to treat the episode as a fitting memorial to a project that seemed comprised more of grandiloquent ideas than practical imperatives. How different things had been with Karel Reisz, he mused. The past, embodied in an aircraft that had served its time guarding Atlantic convoys, seemed to be commenting rather caustically upon the present.

This sense of former times as something both more dependable and exciting than the present informs a letter he wrote to Bill Daleski shortly after moving from Wittersham to St Pargoire:

> It can't of course replace Wittersham, as you surmise, but speaking at any rate for myself I was never so glad to get out of a place in my life – not the actual house, though it was far too big for us – but out of England, and into France. I feel more myself here if there is such a being, but better able to write, not necessarily to write better, but freer in spirit, which helps somehow to make it easier. Well, we'll see, but I was never more happy at having made a move. [AS to BD, 3 October 1988]

The passage bears a remarkable resemblance to the closing paragraph of *The Open Door*: 'Having lived so long, he felt young and inexperienced, fresh to life, eyes opening at last. He had done what he longed to do . . .' (p. 358). Excitement is present in both, but in the book it is unalloyed while in the letter one suspects that he is searching for something more dependable, a rationale, to accompany his enthusiasm. The phrase 'speaking at any rate for myself' is intriguing. Earlier in the letter he had written that 'I suppose, as Ruth says, the house is a smaller version of Wittersham,' a statement of fact rather than opinion, one assumes. Sillitoe thereafter begins to sound like a counsel for the defence, pointing out how friendly the locals were, and how neighbours, unprompted, would knock on the door 'and give us boxes of delicious grapes', and describing, estate-agent style, the grand 'cave' where wine barrels were still stacked. The wonderful mountains, the Cévennes and then the Corbières, with their Cathar castles, are 'only half an hour' away, he enthused.

Six months later Ruth wrote to Ted Hughes:

> We left London four weeks ago today – it seems like four years. It's amazing how totally we shrug off, and take on, the two situations . . . The place has the advantages, and disadvantages of a village . . . the vintage, I learned last year, is extremely noisy – after the first hundred tractors have rumbled past the charm of the situation diminishes. [RF to TH, Emory Archive]

Elsewhere she commends the house and the location but, for Ruth, unlike Sillitoe, enchantment was tempered by pragmatism.

'There were, though,' says Ruth, 'some good times down there. Usually the two of us spend so much time working that we fail to appreciate what an area has to offer. But sometimes we would get into the car and just drive. I remember once, late summer 1991 I think, we were on a road through the foothills of the Cévennes. We felt suddenly an enormous increase in temperature and we heard this terrible roaring sound. The forest, dry as a bone, was on fire. Alan turned the car around, drove back a couple of kilometres and blocked the road. A firestorm would have killed us if we'd continued, and anyone following us. Alan sent back one of the drivers whom we'd stopped who summoned the *pompiers*. It was rather exhilarating.' Sillitoe smiles and adds, 'We spent the rest of the afternoon celebrating.' In a bar, I ask? 'Eventually,' explains Ruth with a smile.

The remoteness of the area, plus its Catalan allegiances, seemed to revive the 1950s spirit of adventure. In the summer of 1990 they decided to drive into Spain, Barcelona specifically, to renew Ruth's passport and to see the new Dalí exhibition. Halfway across the Pyrenees they postponed this itinerary and just drove, staying at whatever hotels were open or habitable. The reckless, carefree odyssey ceased abruptly when their car was burgled. They lost chequebooks and credit cards, and when Alan reported this to the local Spanish police he was met with what seemed like calculated fecklessness. They listened, made notes but obviously did not care. Their luggage had been ransacked and the only items missing were their personal diaries and address books, not the sort of things that would interest the average car thief. It all seemed bizarre, ominous yet oddly predictable, recalling the incidents experienced a generation earlier under the Franco regime.

The previous year they had attended a literary festival in Struga, and yet again the present seemed to be caricaturing memory. Yugoslavia would soon collapse into various states of tribal loathing and concomitant slaughter, but at the time of the Struga festival it was still a confection of heedless communism and old European charm. 'There was,' recalls Alan, 'something timeless about the chaotic nature of the event – I remember we all gathered on a bridge, half drunk, and the writer who had won the festival's "prize" was crowned. He stood there – he was an Australian – resembling an extra from a pantomime. There were a few soldiers around, but no one cared too much and they, the soldiers, just sat there drinking and talking with the rest of us. It was rather like the Soviet Union as the most deluded optimist might have imagined it.' They drove back to St Pargoire through Montenegro. 'A magnificent journey, the roads empty, the countryside breathtaking, spectacular. It was as though we were suspended in time.'

Vanderbilt University, impressed by Ruth's first visit, invited her to serve again as poet in residence, which she agreed to do for the spring semester of 1990. As before, Sillitoe would meet her in the USA after teaching ended, but this time he spent most of the period prior to that alone in St Pargoire. It was at this point that he properly began to appreciate how different it was from Wittersham. In Kent the Sindalls were almost next door, friends called in from London regularly – it was barely ninety minutes by car – and if either he or Ruth wanted or needed the metropolis Notting Hill was always close and available. The only person they socialized with regularly in St Pargoire was the schoolmaster. Family and friends would visit, but a great deal of planning and effort were required. The Daleskis came in 1990, and Michael and Brian and their families stayed in the house for a week each summer between 1991 and 1993 when Sillitoe and Ruth were away at readings, with an overlap of a few days for get-togethers. Sue and Max drove down virtually every summer, and David, when he could, enjoyed trying out different routes on his motorbike through France from the Channel to the Mediterranean and back. By 1990, however, his work commitments meant that his trips became less frequent. He had been employed by the *Guardian* as a staff photographer.

Sillitoe remained convinced that their decision to move was the right one. He wrote to Ted and Carol Hughes when Ruth was away in Vanderbilt.

I'm quite enjoying the solitude – going for a walk through the vineyards or a drive across the garrique, exploring Visigothic tombs which no one cares about (or they just leave them alone) or sawing wood or weeding in the garden. I cook myself a meal every evening, after an English breakfast and a scratch lunch. I've done a lot of work on my novel since getting here. [AS to TH and CH, 1 January 1990, Emory Archive]

He enjoyed being alone in the house but lamented the absence of Ruth. He had written to Bill eighteen months earlier: 'Ruth . . . comes back tomorrow [from a week at conferences in Paris and the UK] – thank God. There's no one I miss more . . . I float in limbo when she's not close' (AS to BD, 22 May 1988). The limbo he refers to was productive but emotionally draining. Ruth spent more time away from St Pargoire than he did and this was the first time since Spain in the early 1950s that he had experienced such lengthy periods alone; hence his prolific output during their time there.

He completed several works following the move, notably *The Open Door* and *Lost Loves*, and began others that would only properly mature after they left in 1994. The two full-length novels that germinated and were brought to a conclusion in France indicate, differently but with equal obliquity, the effect of the place on their author.

Leonard's War (1991) is about the experiences of Leonard Frankland during the Second World War. He is a middle-aged widower, a First World War veteran with one son, who becomes involved and falls in love with Sophie whom he meets at bingo. Having left her husband she works occasionally as a prostitute. Their commitment to each other is passionate, genuine and doomed, and the novel's brilliance derives from Sillitoe's delicacy of touch. The story of Leonard and Sophie is harshly realistic but Sillitoe's use of period and context promotes their tale to near-classic status. The war is a continuously present feature in the lives of everyone in the book. It affects them – Leonard's son, for example, signs up and is severely wounded – yet at the same time the dreadfulness of the conflict does not suddenly transform pre-1939 individuals into citizens-at-war. Their own lives involve continuities and commitments that to them are more important than the invasion of Czechoslovakia. Readers who recalled that period, even as children, admired the book greatly, and those born later were fascinated by a perspective on the war years completely different from the one routinely offered. This novel was about the way ordinary people lived, people who were not directly involved in the struggle to determine the future of humanity. The reviews were good, *The Times*, the *Sunday Telegraph*, the *Mail on Sunday* and the *Times Literary Supplement* coming in with unequivocal praise for his ability to capture a period so well. Sillitoe was equally pleased by private letters such as that from Barbara Hardy of Birkbeck, University of London, whom he and Ruth had known since the late 1960s:

> I love the way it tells a love story without aesthetics, or without charm. Most love stories try to get the reader to fall in love with the object of desire, but no fear of that with your story. Also it's about compulsion but untragically, uncompulsively, making the stuff both strange and yet ordinary. As a history of self and the public world it is brilliant, and yet it seems effortlessly done – long labour but seeming clear as a bell and no stitches showing and no self-preening and no trendy tricks. And the great Sillitoe sense of – I don't know how to put this – a kind of angular and yearning authenticity – to do with that refusal to charm and solicit and show off, but also coming from the language, in ways I can't quite put my finger on. [Barbara Hardy to AS, 5 September 1991, Indiana Archive]

Paul Fussell, writer, academic and Second World War veteran, had got to know Sillitoe and Ruth during their period in the USA in 1985. He greatly admired Sillitoe's ability to recreate the war years as something other than a vortex of military events.

> I've just finished reading it – virtually in one sitting: *you can narrate!* . . . and I hasten to register my admiration.
> Leonard and Sophie, not to mention Ted, are infinitely more real than most of the so-called people I know. But that's the nature of art isn't it? You are a master of it, and I congratulate you on this newest book. [PF to AS, 16 August 1991, Indiana Archive]

Most novelists treat the past with the quasi-religious respect that a restorer feels for a painting or a piece of furniture, and offer the reader a tour of meticulously reproduced settings and idioms. As a consequence cautious, respectful reconstruction begins to eclipse the characters themselves as real, unpredictable human beings. *Leonard's War* is informed with a sense of unreconstructed immediacy. Leonard, Sophie and their associates are possessed of special vitality, often fed by their struggle against various states of despair. They seem too pitiable and ordinary to belong in the standard web of mythologies that the Second World War had become for most people after 1990. Yet we never doubt that their story and its concomitant baggage of unresolved questions are most certainly not of our time. Sillitoe's recollections of the war were made up variously of his own memories and the experiences of people he knew, supplemented by an abundance of carefully acquired historical details. In France, in those lengthy periods of 'limbo', these began to coalesce while remaining largely untouched by the bothersome features of the present.

Bill Daleski was unreserved in his praise.

His [Leonard's] war is wonderfully done, as much a war with himself as with Sophie. I think you catch very movingly the kind of passion which persists despite everything, and certainly despite rational promptings . . . And the writing . . . is first rate . . . so bare and honed, a body without a single ounce of flesh. [BD to AS, 27 October 1991, Indiana Archive]

He was, however, slightly puzzled by Sillitoe's use of 'the short bits' in which the narrator slips out of the third-person mode and speaks to us prior to the beginning and after the close of the story. 'I didn't get the point of bringing in scenes from France,' he added.

The narrator begins with an unhurried account of how as a child he had witnessed wounded soldiers billeted near Nottingham after Dunkirk and then brings us to the present, a market in the French town of Bedarieux. The casual manner of the introduction is misleading because Sillitoe sews into it an enormous amount of detail – meeting a photographer friend at the market, the colour of his knapsack and his map-case – that only those most intimately acquainted with him, in this instance Ruth who was there also, would recognize as drawn without doubt from very real events experienced by Sillitoe himself; it is the verbal equivalent of a fingerprint. Halfway through his stroll around Bedarieux market he is interrupted by 'the serious forlorn face of Leonard Frankland, a life long shunter on the railway [who] appeared as if he had actually followed me to Southern France and expected me to greet him with: "Hello Leonard, how have you been all these years?"' The 'as if' seems to guarantee Leonard's status as an imaginary figment, but

Sillitoe then begins to speak of him as someone he knew well, of what made him laugh, his favourite shows during the 1930s and so on. 'At the table I scribbled a few lines – at the risk of offending our hosts – as a reminder to write his book.' Surely it is, one assumes, Sillitoe's book as much as 'his', but the very brief, closing chapter indicates otherwise. In this Ted, Leonard's friend, tells of his final years and eventual death, and it is not until the last sentence that the identity of Ted's listener is disclosed. 'So Ted told *me* when I met him on the street five years after the war – convincing me, if ever I needed it, that Fate rules everything' (p. 237).

In response to Bill's query Sillitoe was both apologetic and elliptical. For much of the letter he berates the 'tricks of the trade' formalism currently 'in fashion in so many books these days which are more novelty than a novel' (AS to BD, 7 November 1991, private correspondence). But while he distances himself from metafictional reflexivity he cautiously avoids any explanation of why he allowed these curious authorial intrusions into a solidly realist novel. The reason is far more guileless and extraordinary than anything that the postmodernists could come up with. In 1990 he had driven to north-east France, met up with his son-in-law Max, and the two of them had set off on foot – Sillitoe with numerous military maps and books – to trace the route taken by the British regiments forced to retreat to Mons in 1916. Aside from an unwitting instance of authenticity when Sillitoe was forced to spend a day in hospital having his blistered, bleeding feet bandaged, he also sensed that there were more than the two of them on the walk. Leonard had introduced himself, and later particularly during those periods he spent alone inn St Pargoire, working, cooking or walking through the vineyards, Leonard, Sophie and Ted really were there alongside him, telling him their stories.

THIRTY-ONE

In letters to Bill Daleski Sillitoe is drawn frequently to the subject of terrorism, mainly but certainly not exclusively the Palestinian brand. Typically:

> Certainly Margaret Thatcher had (and has) the right idea [particularly regarding the IRA], much more so I'm afraid than the Labour Party who, I think, will not get back into power in the next general election . . . Her [Thatcher's] actions and statements over terrorism are more popular than you might think, and if her popularity is increasing (which it is) that may well be the reason. The Labour Party is totally unconvincing on the matter. I also believe that Chirac isn't popular either, in France, on his belly crawling towards the terrorists. There is a gut feeling in Europe that the third world war has started, and it is against terrorism, mostly Islamic terrorism, but the so-called media hardly seems aware of it, due partly to the fact that they are cut off from such primal issues, and the fact anyway that, being mostly students out of the sixties, they are still half in love with the so-called romance of terrorism. The Tory party (again) are right in saying that the BBC is biased. [AS to BD, 12 November 1986]

It hardly needs pointing out how prescient this is, the so-called war against terrorism having become as familiar and persistent a feature of public discourse as the state of the weather. The letter – and there are dozens like it – reflects Sillitoe's preoccupation with violent fanaticism, and he once commented to Ted Hughes that he was 'thinking about' a novel 'involving a terrorist' (AS to TH, 20 April 1986). His problem was how to reconcile his beliefs and opinions with his artistic principles. He was determined that he would never produce a didactic literary work. He certainly allowed personal idiosyncrasies, sometimes prejudices and affiliations, to manifest themselves – such were the inevitable and necessary preconditions for all writing – but he abhorred instructive homilies disguised as art. *Snowstop* evolved from the dilemma.

The characters – twelve potential victims and one terrorist – are presented with Sillitoe's ruthless attention to naturalistic detail. They are all credible but in equal measure odious. The terrorist, Daniel, has been diverted from his mission by the snowstorm and parks his van, crammed with high explosives, next to the wall of the hotel in which the rest of the characters are sheltering. Daniel is English, a schoolteacher. His mother shaped his childhood according to Roman Catholic doctrine, a faith she inherited from her Irish mother and returned to as a zealot after the failure of her marriage. Psychologically he is probably the most complex figure in the book, committed to 'the Cause', Irish Republicanism, but driven by something far more deeply, grotesquely embedded in his personality. Sillitoe: 'I confess that I had rather a liking, but no sympathy, for him. I may be a somewhat more complicated person than you imagine, or even as I let on to others through my letters and when face to face with them.' Daniel prompts comparison with figures such as John Stevenson, who as Seán Mac Stiofáin exhibited a murderous contempt for Britain – where he and his parents had grown up – far surpassing that of his Ireland-based compatriots. Sillitoe saw a complicity – sometimes proactive, more often smug – between much of the post-1960s intelligentsia and the more prominent terrorist groups. Daniel then is a dangerous manifestation of a broader intellectual consensus; activists, such as him, often seek out a cause in order to justify and animate their otherwise unfocused feelings of contempt and victimhood. Others, more supine, comfort themselves with a recipe of middle-class leftish shibboleths such as a collective sense of guilt for their colonial past or, as Sillitoe put it, 'the so-called romance of terrorism'. It is for this reason that Sillitoe, cleverly, creates in each of the potential victims characteristics that are at once familiar and repugnant. We get to know them well enough to fear for their safety, but feel a concomitant level of relief; they are after all not very agreeable individuals. He is leading us along an emotional and moral cul-de-sac where eventually we are obliged to examine our own implicit sense of superiority over people we have judged expendable.

Sillitoe stops short of turning the novel into a dystopian sermon, but we leave *Snowstop* with a feeling that everyone in it is in some way responsible for what seems about to happen to them. Almost a decade earlier, in a letter to Bill Daleski, there is a passage that could serve as the book's rambling epitaph.

The Arab and Hibernian bomb-butchers seem to be having a field day. You'd think that Israel in its tribulations would get more sympathy from bloody Albion these days. The whole world in fact faces the same terrorist problems, not to mention militant Islam which sooner or later will have to be dealt with and not only by Israel. But there's a kind of supine masochism in the West . . . [AS to BD, 25 December 1983]

His use of a snowstorm to bring lamentable figures together in a remote Peak District hotel seems to be a nod towards the improbability of fable, but the idea arose from a combination of singularity and perverse logic. He has always been fascinated by snow but rather erratic and inconsistent in pinpointing the nature of his fixation. During his visits to the Russian steppes in the 1960s he marvelled at how an entire continent seemed comprised of one element – so different from the Western European Christmas card image – yet at the same time snow reminded him of how malignancy could be addictive and all-controlling; it looked beautiful but it treated us with cruel indifference. He reported to Bill Daleski in 1981 'I didn't stay long in Nottingham – there was too much snow around, and I hate snow. I have a prejudice against the stuff. Even the beer in Yates's didn't compensate' (AS to BD, 15 March 1986, private correspondence). This was more than a quirky twist upon the pathetic fallacy. He could never fully dissociate the emotional and ideological aspects of his Soviet experiences from their visual correlates. Snow had become an actual and figurative trigger for notions of entrapment. (At a more mundane level he also recalls an incident in the Lake District when he and David, on a hiking weekend in 1979, had been 'snowtrapped' in a remote inhospitable hotel – 'bloody infuriating'.)

It rarely snowed in the lowlands of Languedoc where the novel was conceived and completed, but there was something about the isolation of the place, particularly when Ruth was away, that fed the novel's quixotic, unorthodox character. His study offered him a view of a largely flat, rocky landscape, punctuated by farmhouses and criss-crossed by small vineyards through which he would walk when he needed to relax or think. The place reminded him of Israel, and on his study wall he had pinned an enormous map of his 'other home'.

In February 1992 Sillitoe set out on his second tour of readings in Germany. His first visit in 1990 had involved events in Munich, Frankfurt and Hamburg, but in 1992 he went further east, doing readings in what had recently been communist East Berlin and Dresden. In the 1960s he had received the occasional invitation to visit both West and East Germany, and turned all of them down. In his letters to Brian during this period he discloses that he could not reconcile his knowledge of what the Nazis had done with participating in polite, equable exchanges on cultural issues near the places where evil had thrived barely two decades earlier. On 26 August 1963 he explained to his brother that despite the fact that 'I hate giving talks', of the two invitations to do so that month, from Germany and Denmark, he had accepted the latter. 'Denmark is a special case. During the war . . . the Danish people got nearly everyone [of the Jewish population] away, overnight, to neutral Sweden. That didn't happen in any other country' (AS to BS, 26 August 1963, private correspondence). Two years later he had been invited to attend the first night of a stage adaptation of *Saturday Night and Sunday Morning* in Berlin. Again he declined and reported later to Brian: 'I hear that it was a "scandal" with all the Germans walking out. That makes me happy: I'd hate to entertain those pigs' (AS to BS, 10 December 1965, private correspondence). In 1962 he had argued that Britain should never join the Common Market. Nazism, he contended, was still an intrinsic feature of some European societies, part of a legacy of nationalism and anti-Semitism. 'Germany would dominate any Common Market and be very tolerant of them [the fascists]. The Common Market will become an alliance against Bolshevism – with Germany dominating, restoring ideas they had been forced to bury in 1945, and just longing to go East again and get back the land from Poland and Russia' (AS to BS, 20 August 1962, private correspondence). Sillitoe was suspicious of the apparent transformation of Germany into a liberal democracy. The people who had given almost unanimous support to Hitler's regime still, in the early 1960s, made up at least half of the adult population. How, he asked himself, could individuals who colluded in something so intrinsically vile be changed by a system devised and put into practice by others?

His perception of the country over the next quarter of a century was altered gradually by encounters with a new generation who were at once detached from and willing to confront the truths of the 1930s and the war. Moreover, Sillitoe had been impressed by a number of individuals he had met in Israel, some of whom had lost close relatives in the Holocaust, who argued that pretending that Germany did not exist was a perverse, self-lacerating variant upon Holocaust denial. The Germans he got to know he judged simply according to their human qualities. For example, in November 1972 he received a letter, unprompted, from Heinrich Böll, who had recently won the Nobel Prize, offering 'belated' praise for 'one of the most outstanding novels in English of this century' (*Saturday Night and Sunday Morning*). Sillitoe knew of Böll's 1950s novels which addressed the various states of guilt – unutterably feigned and hypocritical – which informed German consciousness after the war, and was impressed but not entirely convinced that they spoke for a consensus. Böll also invited Sillitoe to a conference in Cologne against the Olympic Games of that year. The hall was full, but none of the delegates asked to speak mentioned the murders of the Israeli athletes – except Sillitoe, to much applause.

To claim that after fifty Sillitoe exchanged his left-wing sympathies for positions in the centre and on the right is a misrepresentation of a man who valued individuality, with all its contradictions, far above allegiance to an all-consuming ideal. He became certain that the ideology of the left involved more than an affiliation to a recipe of conjectures and policies. It incorporated a state of mind that was as pervasive and inflexible as religious faith; believers were imbued with a commitment to a system that allowed of no alternatives.

In 1993 the Poetry Society wrote to him about its new database, which would contain biographical and other details on major contemporary poets to be made available to publishers and organizers of conferences, readings and literary festivals. They asked him to fill in a form, which he was happy to do until he encountered question 6. In his reply to the information officer, Andrew Lindesay, he stated that 'I will never fill in any form which requires details of my ethnic origin. If I did so I would not consider myself to be a poet – a statistician, perhaps, but not an individual. If you receive more than a dozen unprotesting responses to this macabre questionnaire poetry in this country is doomed' (AS to Andrew Lindesay, Poetry Society, 21 November 1993, Indiana Archive). Sillitoe was fully aware of why in 1993 question 6 existed. The quality or otherwise of a poet's work must now be considered alongside the more significant fact that English verse had for several centuries been the preserve of the white, male, middle and upper classes. In Sillitoe's view the question was a benign, patronizing symptom of leftist dogmatism and sham contrition.

Three years earlier Peter Florence, director of the Hay-on-Wye Festival of Literature, had invited him to give a talk. Other participants would include 'Umberto Eco, Martin Amis, Paul Theroux, Edna O'Brien, Melvyn Bragg, Billy Bragg, Andrew Davies, Sue Townsend, Denis Healey...' (Peter Florence to AS, 10 December 1989, Indiana Archive). 'We would', wrote Florence, 'be honoured and delighted to have you,' and most writers would indeed have felt honoured and delighted to appear alongside such luminaries. But Sillitoe had been allocated a special role. 'Please will you come and take part in a discussion about writing about the working classes in different media, with Alan Bleasdale and a young Welsh poet and novelist Chris Meredith (whose work I will happily send you if you wish).' Sillitoe did not know whether to laugh or fulminate. He surmised that not one of the stars of the festival, or indeed the audience, would ever vote or admit to voting Conservative, but at the same time he was being asked there not really as a writer but to speak on behalf of his 'class'. How generous and indulgent, he thought; rather like allowing servants to the drawing room to recite their poems at Christmas. He replied:

While much appreciating the honour of being asked to attend the Hay on Wye Literary Festival I am sorry to say that I will not be able to take part in a discussion on writing about the working classes. From the beginning I have only ever written about people as individuals and never as members of any 'class'. If I had ever had such a project in mind I would never have written at all. [AS to Peter Florence, 20 December 1989, Indiana Archive]

Would there, he wondered, be a marquee where representatives of the oppressed could talk of their dreadful backgrounds? Thatcherism, it seemed to him, had made virtually everyone in the media and arts sectors of the economy better off financially, but also provided them with a means of salving their consciences and perpetrating the fashion for designer radicalism that he hoped had died out at the end of the 1970s.

He was amused by the frenzy that greeted the publication of Anthony Thwaite's edition of Philip Larkin's letters in 1992. The *Guardian* became a symposium for those who had long perceived Larkin as the cynosure of everything a good left-winger had been taught to loathe – he had now been exposed not just as a white, male, middle-class poet who produced verse that people could understand, but also as a self-confessed misogynist who on several occasions had used the term 'wog'. Even those who wrote to defend him did so apologetically, as if he were a talented elderly relative with personal habits best not talked about. None of this shocked Sillitoe particularly. He knew that the regiments of self-styled Marxists comfortably ensconced in academia and the media relished the opportunity to indulge their taste for revolutionary Puritanism. He was, however, unsettled by letters from Terry Eagleton and Lisa Jardine, the latter affirming that she would excise Larkin from the curriculum of Queen Mary College, University of London, where she was Professor of English. He believed this would set a precedent for the type of official censorship he had last witnessed in the Soviet Union in the 1960s. He wrote to the *Guardian* on 8 December, the day that Jardine's piece was published, deploring a policy which would allow those in power 'to deny access to, and analysis of, excellent plays, novels and poems which (never mind the private letters of their dead authors) do not pass the vetting of narrow-minded apostles of political correctness'.

Sillitoe felt that beliefs and principles based upon unyielding abstractions were both lazy and potentially totalitarian. He formed opinions on matters strictly according to his own notions of efficacy, justice and common sense. Interviewed by Sally Vincent of the *Guardian* (3 July 1995), for example, he offered his views on the privatization of the railways. He objected, but not because he disliked private enterprise. In his judgement the dividing up of a system whose parts were by their nature interdependent would guarantee chaos. His belief was not, he reassured Vincent, founded upon ideological principle; it came from his experiences of travelling in France, Italy, Switzerland and Germany.

In 1993 the Swiss newspaper *Tages-Anzeiger* commissioned him to visit and write about what seemed to be the final stand of the coal-mining communities against the policy of closures that followed the NUM's defeat by Mrs Thatcher in 1984. The picket lines in the coalfields of South Yorkshire were composed mainly of individuals who had never worked underground: the wives, mothers, daughters and sisters of the miners themselves. He was moved and sympathized with their plight – the Nottinghamshire coalfields had already all but disappeared – but at the same time he detected that their resolution was fed in part by a nostalgic longing for a time when trade unions, tribal and unaccountable, regulated the activities of the elected government. It was published in German by *Tages-Anzeiger*. The *Guardian*, however, rejected Sillitoe's abridged English version without hesitation.

A few years earlier he had reported to Brian of how the police had arrived at the Notting Hill flat at 7.15 a.m. They 'were after David'. David had been commissioned by the *Mail on Sunday* to cover the Wapping dispute 'and the cops wanted his photos'. When Sillitoe asked them why, and if some crime had been committed, the police refused to offer an explanation, leading him to suspect that the pictures they thought David might have taken included ones of police violence against pickets.

> As he [David] says, you never give anything like that to the police in case they use it against the strikers. He was in the front line, and got some astonishing stuff. The *Observer* and the *Mail on Sunday* also refused to hand [his] photos over. The Northamptonshire police are conducting an enquiry into police violence at Wapping, and say they only want to see the photographs as evidence – but even so, David's very firm in not letting them go. [AS to BS, 17 November 1987]

Sillitoe seems reluctant to disclose his own opinions on the dispute itself, but what comes through in the letter, implicitly, is his sense of pride in David's act of principle, as a photojournalist, to risk prosecution – the police threatened him with a writ – rather than turn over material which might be altered or manipulated as evidence. In truth Sillitoe's loathing for the Rupert Murdoch media empire, which seemed to him like a vulgar capitalist version of *Pravda*, was almost equalled by the contempt he felt for the chic left-wingers who seemed so keen to perform on camera at what was becoming a fashion show for the anti-Thatcherites. A dispute involving newspapers and only a taxi ride from the West End seemed far more *beau monde* than trouble at a provincial car plant. He had not renounced his affection for the old Labour Party, the one that installed the social welfare system and the NHS. Sillitoe: 'Well, let's say I still voted for it, or what was left of it, but reluctantly.' But by the end of the 1980s the left seemed to him to be comprised either of grandstanding extremists, in love with some purist brand of radicalism but blind to the fact that less than 1 per cent of the electorate would ever endorse their fantasies, or a more numerous, apparently intelligent and articulate group which dominated the cultural and literary worlds and whose attitude to anything remotely associated with Conservatism was smug and predictable. He perceived Arthur Scargill as typical of the former, and though he wished that the pits were still open his enduring impression from his time in South Yorkshire was of a group of people clinging desperately to a lost ideal, still idolizing figures such as Scargill whose determination to overturn the elected government had done as much to ensure the miners' defeat as the Conservatives themselves. He wrote to Bill Daleski of his visit. 'Not all the pits are closing in England, but most. Quite soon there'll be about twelve left, and some privately run ones. Lawrence would be happy, but the miners aren't' (AS to BD, 24 April 1993). The facts spoke for themselves and could not be altered. He felt no inclination to comment, except for an oblique suggestion that the writer whose visionary mission grew out of a hatred for his home and its primary industry had been granted his wish, via economics.

THIRTY-TWO

Sillitoe has neither in private nor in print explained what prompted him in 1991 to begin writing his memoirs. Neither vanity nor a desire to set the record straight played any part. He is one of a small number of authors never to have been affected by the former, and as far as others' perceptions of him are concerned he has always been of the view that people have every right to judge him as they wish; and in any event he does not care too much about what they think. Having questioned him on this matter – an experience not unlike attempting to play a game of chess without first learning the rules – I have resorted to intuiting reasons from the available evidence.

Throughout his correspondence with close friends, particularly his letters to Bill Daleski, he returns continually to the image of his fiction as something that absorbs his waking existence. After thirty-three years of making his living primarily as a novelist he would, understandably, begin to wonder about what would happen if he reversed the formula and worked on a book with a lengthy narrative and an abundantly varied and complex cast of characters which was verifiably true: his life until 1958 told as it was and not his imagined variant upon it. The result, published in 1995 as *Life Without Armour*, is meticulously honest and unintentionally misleading. He wrote to Bill Daleski and offered what comes closest to an explanation for writing the book.

> So why did I do it? Well, I suddenly saw a 'Theme' which was: how did a little ragged-arsed cabbage-headed slum brat turn into a novelist and writer? Perhaps in other words, I looked on it as a novel, but in the process, charting every move and jink of the way, stuck absolutely to facts as far as I remembered or had proof. Therefore the reason for ending when I did seemed perfectly logical to me – I'd got there. [AS to BD, 18 September 1995]

This does indeed seem logical; *Life Without Armour* tells the story of how he became a writer. But there is also an intriguing subtext which surfaces later in the same letter.

> But you might say I tackled the project as fiction, using fiction as a machine tool to keep me on the track of truth, truth as you know being a very slippery commodity indeed, verging on quicksilver.

He explains to his friend that he did not alter facts – aside from two instances in which names were changed to protect the privacy of those involved – but the question remains of what exactly he means by tackling 'the project as fiction' and 'using fiction as a machine tool'. If you wished to present an account of your activities during a year of your life three decades previously you might, if by nature a businesslike sort, produce a file of bank statements, air and train tickets, tax returns and, best of all, a diary. Supplement this with photographs and a microfiche of newspapers as an index to what was going on elsewhere, and you will have a reliable buttress of detail to shore up the principal source of the tale, memory. This is how Sillitoe set about assembling information from which he then distilled events he thought worth preserving for the book. He entered those in a three-column notebook. He explains, 'Listing events chronologically is fine except that to reduce experience to a sequence of successive occurrences distorts it. I wanted a plan of my memories, not a list.' Some of the notebook is preserved alongside the first draft of *Life Without Armour* in the Indiana Archive. For example:

Jim Donovan	Margaret and Peter Emmerich	
Tarrs		
Elizabeth	3.6.55	20.6.55
Colette	15.5.55	
Mike	18.4.55	
5.2.55 Novel sent		
Harry after 16 March		
Iko etc.		
	Mack and Jeanette	
Brian July		
Bullfight at Inca with Robin Maris		20.8.55
Ruth, Brian and myself invited to Graves's 60th birthday party		

As Sillitoe commented, truth 'is a very slippery commodity indeed', especially when one is attempting to create for the reader an honest account not just of what happened but also of the private fabric of impressions and emotions which absorbs these events. Sillitoe, to his eventual regret, was too honest. He could, without distorting the truth, have been selective in his representations of his past, refining and modifying memories about which, half a century on, his feelings were still divided. Instead he employed the 'machine tool of fiction' to create for the reader the same sense of irresolution that accompanied his private recollections. His father, particularly, remained with him as a collage of often disparate and incongruous images: sometimes the taciturn misanthrope who either had nothing significant to say or kept his troubled thoughts to himself, and on other occasions a man who had made the best of a horrible life and nursed a primitive affection for his family. Consequently the opening page of Chapter 1 involved a storm of sensations and sketches: 'The mind of a ten year old in the body of a brute'; 'short legged and megacephalic'; 'He often hit my mother, and an early memory is of her bending over the bucket so that blood from her cut head would not run on to the carpet.' These, uncensored, were his worst memories but he tempered them with others: 'he had a self-centred kindness which brutes are said to possess'; 'His way of atonement was to be helpful in a sentimental sort of way.' These contrasts prefigure what would become far more measured, if still not certain, accounts of this unsettling yet complex man. Sillitoe cannot, for example, disguise his feeling of affection for a figure for whom his own first book generated genuine unalloyed pride, a book he held and gazed at with awe and which he would never be able to read.

Problems arose, however, when HarperCollins negotiated a deal with the *Daily Mail* to serialize extracts. As is their custom, the *Mail* employed hacks to scour the book for passages that would guarantee the attention of a readership hungry for offence and shock. Consequently Sillitoe's mosaic of perspectives was pared down to a single dimension. The headlines above the first extract read: 'His Mother Worked as a Prostitute'; 'His Father Was a Violent Drunkard'. The text itself was not in the strict sense of the term rewritten, but it was abridged to meet the promise of the headlines.

The day after this first extract appeared he received a letter from his cousin, Richard Richardson, grandson of Burton and a retired Kent coalminer whom he had last met when he had stayed for a few weeks with his aunt in 1950. He was, he wrote, 'surprised' that Sillitoe's work had appeared in the *Mail*, 'which is a paper I would not relegate to my shit house as it has done immense damage to the working class movement, and in particular we coal-miners; if ever there was a gutter press this is it at its worst'. This was bad enough, but 'let me say that I regard your words as devastating and offensive in the manner in which you castigate your Mother and Father (my Aunt and Uncle) . . . I feel you are scraping the bottom of the barrel . . . when you stoop to denigrate your family. No one had a harder life than my family but I would never reveal what you have revealed' (Richard Richardson to AS, 26 June 1995, Indiana Archive).

Sillitoe contacted HarperCollins that same day to demand that they write to the *Daily Mail* expressing their dissatisfaction at the paper's treatment of *Life Without Armour*. Sophie Brewer then wrote to Jane Mays of the *Mail* expressing their 'disappointment of your handling of the serialisation' and conveying Sillitoe's particular 'distress' at the headlines. 'Both those statements are untrue and there is nothing in the book to suggest otherwise' (Sophie Brewer to Jane Mays, 28 June 1995, Indiana Archive). The *Daily Mail*, familiar with complaints such as this, consulted their lawyers, and the managing editor, Lawrence Sears, replied two weeks later, stating that 'The trailers are clearly substantiated in the author's text and I am afraid that we are unable to offer an apology or retraction in these circumstances' (Lawrence Sears to Sophie Brewer, 14 July 1995, Indiana Archive). He enclosed photocopies of pages of the original book, highlighting sentences in which Christopher was indeed referred to as being 'drunk' and 'violent', albeit eighty pages apart, and, where the word 'prostitute' appeared in the same paragraph as 'Sabina'. Sillitoe wrote back refusing to accept the *Mail*'s explanation.

> The facts are, firstly, that my father was referred to as a drunkard, when in the text this impression was nowhere given. Only on one occasion was he said to have been drunk, and that was on VE Day – when nearly everyone else was.
>
> As for my mother having been a 'working prostitute', that simply can't be allowed to stand, because in the text the only reference from which this outrageous statement might be construed was when she was said to have gone out for a few evenings and accepted money from men, whereas the *Daily Mail* stated that she was a 'working prostitute', as if she was that for her whole life. The word prostitute only came up in the text because my father used it. He was an enraged illiterate, and I can't understand why the *Daily Mail* followed so eagerly in his footsteps, especially when it resulted in a clear violation of the truth. [AS to Sophie Brewer, 3 August 1995, Indiana Archive]

HarperCollins sympathized, but advised him, on behalf of their lawyers, that the *Mail* was well practised at distilling subtlety into shocking gobbets without transgressing laws covering copyright or misrepresentation.

In his letter Sillitoe's embittered cousin had wondered 'what your brothers Michael and Brian think of you now'. In fact neither was unsettled or surprised by Sillitoe's account of his early years; it merely confirmed what they knew. Michael: 'He told the truth about the circumstances in which we grew up. I don't recall every incident precisely – I was too young for some – but they became part of family lore. Our parents were no better and no worse than anyone else at the bottom of the ladder, and I mean right at the bottom. If anything he, Alan, was too modest, because although he was only a few years older than Brian and myself he was often like a second father.'

All of this took place while Sillitoe was in the midst of a schedule of promotional activity – his *Collected Stories* came out at the same time – beginning on 20 June with lengthy interviews for the *Daily Telegraph*, the *Guardian* and *Kaleidoscope* and lasting until 17 July when he spoke to the BBC live at the Central Library, Nottingham. In the interim he had contributed to a half-hour special, devoted exclusively to him, for BBC Radio Scotland, and had appeared on Classic FM, London News, Talk Radio, Radio Oxford, Radio North, Radio West Midlands, Radio 2's *John Dunn* programme, Sky TV's *Sky Books*, BBC Greater London and played along with Sheridan Morley's arch fascination at his past in BBC Radio 2's *Arts Programme*. Just before the promotional schedule began Sillitoe wrote to Brian:

> We got back to West Chinnock at half past two this afternoon, after a very energetic week getting ourselves installed. It all went well – but a few things seemed to be missing out of the stuff brought from France, unless we just haven't found them yet. Anyway the place is very nice and I'll be going there again next Sunday for a few days because there are still a lot of bits and bobs to be done. [AS to BS, 15 May 1995]

'The place' was 47–51 Higher Street, West Chinnock, Crewkerne, Somerset, the numbers indicating a charmingly untidy legacy of four tiny cottages, dating from the fifteenth century, having become a spacious asymmetrical house – part half-timbered, part stone. They had sold the St Pargoire property almost a year earlier, a decision that Sillitoe begrudged rather more than Ruth but had finally accepted as inevitable. Sillitoe's letters from France over the six years between 1988 and 1994 contain mixed, sometimes antithetical versions of life there. To Brian, in 1991, for example:

> I'd love to be down there [but] to tell the truth, I sometimes find it too hot (and noisy) at the height of the summer. Also, Ruth and I have appointments, so it won't be possible to get there till sometime in October, and then only for a few weeks, till it gets cold. Believe it or not it gets pretty raw in the winter. You get a few good days, when it's warm outside, but cold as soon as you come into the house . . . Anyway, I like the place, and we go when we can. [AS to BS, 8 July 1991]

Similarly, to Bill Daleski he reports on the house as 'too dark' (7 November 1991), 'too hot' (27 July 1993), complains about its 'state' after being uninhabited for five months (24 April 1993) and of 'problems with travel' shortly before the decision to sell (21 January 1994). On each occasion he qualifies the lament with a desperate affirmation of his 'love' for the place or how 'free' or 'inspired' he feels once there.

Sillitoe had come to accept reluctantly what Ruth had for some time tactfully pointed out. The pioneering spirit of their 1950s years had now mutated into endurance. Their family and professional lives were tied to the UK, and travel between Languedoc and London was time consuming and exhausting. Alan usually drove, a journey of approximately 1,500 miles.

Sometimes, if he was travelling via other parts of France for readings, he might take the train, and in 1993 he composed an unintentionally hilarious letter to the manager, British Rail International. His ostensible complaint was about the disappearance of smoking carriages during the Folkestone to London stage of his journey ('the French seem to have more tolerance') but beneath the surface bubbles a general feeling of impatience and rage ('the windows . . . were dirty, the toilets were blocked') (AS to Manager, British Rail International, Victoria Station, 9 September 1993, Indiana Archive). The journeys, sometimes of almost two thousand miles, had begun to weary him.

West Chinnock seemed a fair compromise, remote enough from London for Sillitoe to indulge his taste for getting away from a place he felt was busily self-obsessed – while Ruth craved its crowded anonymity – but not too far from everything which mattered. Notting Hill was three hours by car and Nottingham two and a half beyond that. David was to be married in 1995 and would be based in Hertfordshire. He was still working for the *Guardian*'s London picture desk but would a year later become staff photographer for the Midlands. The Hugheses were only forty miles away. Ted and Carol had kept in touch but had never stayed with them in France; now both couples hoped that more regular visits could be resumed.

The move had been pragmatic, prompted by no conscious motive on Sillitoe's part for a return home. Yet it coincided with a discernible shift in focus which would affect his writing for the subsequent ten years. His family, his past and his sense of how these had formed him as an individual and a writer now became the predominant influences upon his work. Self-absorption can of course be damaging, but Sillitoe's preoccupation with material that was intimate and continually more revealing enabled him to produce some of his best fiction.

Sillitoe and Brian had often talked of Burton, particularly after he had featured so prominently in *Raw Material*. They perceived their mother's side of the family as the branch which embodied a refusal to conform. As early as 1989 Brian was writing to his brother of how he intended to assemble an authentic family history. He wanted to sort through the accumulation of myths and rumours, and he concentrated first on the death in 1914 of Oliver, Burton's son, obtaining a copy of the original death certificate. 'Fracture of the base of the skull and lacerations of the brain following injuries accidentally received while following his calling.' Brian and Sillitoe thought this an ambiguous description of the cause of death, perhaps calculatedly so. What did 'following his calling' mean? His trade was farrier, he was employed as a soldier, and the horse which had, allegedly, killed him was not mentioned in the death certificate. Brian obtained a copy of the *Nottingham Evening Post* for 21 November 1914 in which the death and burial of Oliver Burton were reported in detail, with photographs of his uncle prominently displayed.

Why, Brian wondered, did the paper give such attention to him being 'kicked by a horse' when the death certificate contained no mention of this? How did they know? He also obtained an extraordinary photograph of Oliver's burial, attended by thirty-five members of his regiment, the South Nottinghamshire Hussars, involving a thirteen-rifleman salute over the grave and with two clergymen, one the Army chaplain, present. ('Why thirteen?' Brian wrote to Sillitoe on 14 April 1990. The number had obvious superstitious connotations.) All this for a man kicked by a horse? Were there, perhaps, extant records with the Ministry of Defence which might explain how the newspaper had obtained the story of the horse? Sillitoe enquired and received a polite, apologetic reply from the MoD stating that they could locate no record of Oliver's death; it had either been lost or destroyed in the Blitz. 'I enclose a letter from the Ministry of Defence about Oliver Burton,' he wrote to Brian. 'It seems we've come to a dead end, unless you can find out something from the Hussars TA Centre on Triumph Road' (AS to BS, 10 August 1982). Brian tried, but the Hussars did not have any record of the death either.

The more 'dead ends' the brothers encountered – and Michael often joined them in their hunt – the more intrigued they became by a group of figures who had obtained the ethereal power of legend. Their collective research would eventually become *A Man of His Time* (2004), but in the early 1990s Sillitoe began to sew together facts and speculation for a radio play to be called *Burton*. Radio 4 showed an interest when he contacted them in 1993, but instead of pressing forward with a contract they, as media corporations tend to do, turned his proposal into something else. Would he, they asked, leave aside *Burton* for a while and write a two-hour adaptation of *Saturday Night and Sunday Morning* to be directed by Pete Atkin? After lengthy and costly demands by Mentorn Films, who had held the adaptation rights since 1960, Sillitoe's version was broadcast in 1995. The BBC's suggestion was prompted by the simple fact that none of the individuals then responsible for commissioning and making programmes had any direct memory of the late 1950s. For them the world of Arthur Seaton held a recondite fascination; did people of their parents' generation, though probably not their class, really live like that, they wondered? A similar impulse to retrieve something from a recent yet rapidly receding past that seemed by degrees horrible and exciting played a part in what from the end of the 1980s was Sillitoe's promotion to cultural icon of the East Midlands.

During the 1960s officialdom in Nottingham and the surrounding region had, when it bothered to acknowledge Sillitoe at all, treated him with outraged disgust. One Nottingham councillor – Labour Party – had campaigned unsuccessfully to have *Saturday Night and Sunday Morning* banned from local libraries. Thirty years hence, however, civic pride had become far more tolerant and interested in creating a profile that would attract visitors and tourists.

The universities of the area led the way, with Nottingham naming one of its new halls of residence 'Sillitoe Court' in 1990. Nottingham Polytechnic, as it then was, awarded Sillitoe an honorary doctorate in the same year, and in 1993, as Nottingham Trent University, it elected him as an honorary fellow. Leicester De Montfort University appointed him as visiting professor from 1992 to 1997 to do two-week intensive courses each semester on 'How to Write a Novel'. 'Basically, students would bring me their work and I would advise them on it. It was demanding because I didn't wish to cause offence. The work varied in quality but the one thing that was most difficult to teach, and most vital for any writer, was self-scrutiny. If you can't evaluate literature – and unfortunately students are not encouraged to do that – you can't judge and go on to improve or rewrite what you yourself have produced.' De Montfort awarded him an honorary doctorate in 1998, and in 2007 he was appointed visiting professor in English at the University of Ulster.

Like their BBC counterparts, Midlands theatre producers suddenly took an interest in ground-breaking fiction of the recent past that had rooted itself provocatively in the local language and environment. In 1998 the Derby Playhouse ran a version of *Saturday Night and Sunday Morning*, based on Sillitoe's film screenplay, and Nottingham followed suit in 1993. Sillitoe wrote to Brian:

> I agree with you absolutely about the accents in the play of 'Saturday Night and Sunday Morning'. Ever since the old days, when the film was made, etc., I've cringed with embarrassment on hearing the idiotic attempts to produce the Nottingham accents. I've often mentioned it to the actors, but it's made no difference. They just won't get it into their heads. If they sat half an hour in a Nottingham pub they'd know what I meant – or so you'd think. It's not all that difficult, actually, to say 'note' instead of 'knout'. In the film it didn't make too much difference, but on the stage in Nottingham, to a local audience, it sounds awful – as you say. I don't know what the solution is – maybe I'd have to spend a couple of weeks at rehearsals, and that would work, but I don't have the time. I should have put them on to you, of course, but I didn't think of that ... [AS to BS, 11 November 1992]

The Nottingham Players put on a version of *The Loneliness of the Long Distance Runner*, adapted by Paul Brennan and Stephen Jameson, in October 1996. Sillitoe, with Brian, Michael and their families, attended and found the accents less cringe-making.

In 1994 Nottingham University, Lawrence's *alma mater*, awarded him an honorary doctorate. At the graduation ceremony on 14 July he alone was invited to deliver a speech. He extolled the benefits of higher education but remarked that unlike everyone else who received degrees that day he had avoided the years of toil and 'entered through the roof like a burglar to collect

[his] doctorate'. He admitted also that he felt genuinely honoured and proud, quoting Dr Johnson: 'Every man has a lurking wish to appear considerable in his native place.' Brian and June, Michael and Anne were at the reception and in reserved seats in the hall. Brian wrote to him later:

I thought the speech you made was terrific. I think everyone else did too. I felt very proud of you, seeing you on the stage talking to a vast audience like that. I started thinking of when we were kids all huddled to you in bed, and you telling us stories about the Handleys.

I wish the rest of the family could have seen you. [BS to AS, 22 July 1994, Indiana Archive]

The three brothers had never been out of contact with each other for long, but during the 1990s they became inclined not only to socialize but to talk of what their pasts, shared and respective, meant to them. Hence Brian's account of how his elder brother, holding the attention of the vast audience, had prompted his poignant recollection of the storyteller of their childhood. The Handleys were, of course, the family, not unlike the Sillitoes, invented by Sillitoe when he was about eight or nine years old for the entertainment of his brothers and sisters.

His most generous advance of that period came from Macmillan for a book that he would not actually have to write. *Leading the Blind* (1995) is an anthology of extracts from travel guides and travellers' diaries from the eighteenth century onwards. Sillitoe worked hard on the collection, but the annotations presented no great difficulties since he had been assiduously collecting and researching books such as these for the previous forty years.

That aside, he has since the mid-1990s been less prolific than before, but by ordinary standards his output is still outstanding: *Alligator Playground* (1997), *The Broken Chariot* (1998), *The German Numbers Woman* (1999), *Birthday* (2001), *A Man of His Time* (2004) and the non-fiction *Gadfly in Russia* (2007). At the time of writing the final volume of his picaresque trilogy, provisionally entitled 'Moggerhanger', is still being revised and he is hard at work on a very different novel, the nature of which, as is his custom, he refuses to disclose before completion.

The fiction in print is extraordinarily good; quixotic, magnetic and unimprovable. The book of short stories, *Alligator Playground*, reminds us again that Sillitoe can lay claim to being the most accomplished practitioner in this genre of the last fifty years. These are the literary equivalent of seventeenth-century Dutch paintings; their transparency is deceptive because the closer you look the more you become aware that complex, half-disguised substrata and states of mind underpin the unsparing honesty. The title comes from a code signal that he picked up during the preparations for the first Gulf War:

for the RAF 'Alligator Playground' meant an imminent encounter with hostile aircraft or ground-launched missiles. The story carrying that title is a distillation of everything repulsive he had encountered in the literary and cultural circuits of London over the previous three decades. It is impossible to fix upon the most loathsome or hypocritical character because everyone – even if they at first seem reassuringly equable – proves to be equally foul.

Sillitoe judges people on their merits, as individuals, and though the story offers a somewhat dystopian picture of the British intelligentsia it does not reflect a corresponding state of misanthropy on its author's part. Over the previous forty years, however, he had come across abundant cases of intellectualism as the filter for various shades of temperamental bias and malice. Hence his use of the RAF call sign as the story's title; the world of writers and thinkers demanded as much caution as hostile air space.

'Ivy' is a beautifully oblique piece. Ivy herself competes for attention with another figure who arrives unexpectedly following a few pages of anonymous narration. 'Ivy was my aunt, and I recollect everything vividly from those days' (p. 129). Ivy was indeed Sillitoe's aunt, daughter of Burton, and in a letter to Brian written after the story was published she appears again:

> It's always hard to get to the heart of a person, and there's always more there than you think – and Burton was no exception. I agree with all you say. Nobody is an angel, and nor was Ivy. When she took his food to Wollaton Pit late at night, and he said she shouldn't have bothered, he could have been thinking about the days of her going down there in the dark, and really meant she should not have done that. She still had to go back, and he used a gruff tone so as not to frighten her, and because of everything else she took it the wrong way. It's easy to imagine. All Burton's daughters had short tempers as well, and were an unruly and at times scatty lot . . . I expect he was glad when they each got married. Ivy never did, while he was alive, so had to stay at home. [AS to BS, 29 January 1997]

Read alongside the story the letter provides a fascinating insight into Sillitoe's *modus operandi*. He was certainly not borrowing from family history as a substitute for invention. The Burtons were more troubling, intimate versions of the woman sighted in Portobello market. He and Brian had recovered facts, some from records and others from family legend, but the more of these they accumulated the more the questions multiplied; truth began to fragment and draw them into further speculation. As he put it in the letter, 'It's always hard to get to the heart of a person, and there's always more than you think . . . It's easy to imagine.' 'Ivy' is as much about its narrator as its eponymous subject. She resembles Sillitoe's aunt almost exactly, except that aged sixty she marries Albert, a noisome opportunist. At least we think he is because this is the impression left by the narrator as he visits one last time her father's house, just before the 'mangonels of synthetic modernisation' are due to demolish it. 'High rise hen coops were deemed to be the order of the day by those who would never have to live in them but had decided that that was how the "working classes" ought to want to live' (p. 137). Leaving, he notices a screwed-up piece of paper on the floor, their marriage certificate, and the image forms in his mind of Albert discarding it 'like a piece of rubbish' (p. 131), reinforcing his contempt for a man he never met. The story is brief – eleven pages – and blends ellipsis with candour quite wonderfully. The narrator speaks as he finds yet discloses his own desperate wish to wrench some truth from the myths he is in part responsible for making. When he was working on *Life Without Armour* Sillitoe had written to Bill Daleski that 'this wrestling with the so-called truth stymies me . . . Wondering whether anything's true or not distorts the imagination' (AS to BD, 6 March 1993). What troubled him was separating feelings – so preciously unreliable – from a package of facts in order that the latter would predominate. *Life Without Armour* was the result, but 'Ivy' is a brilliant representation of the struggle.

His belated recognition by the East Midlands' establishment as their greatest living writer involved him in some events that his former self would have treated with mordant disbelief.

This weekend I'm to be the after dinner speaker at the Nottingham Police officers' annual do. *That* will amuse you, I know. It does me. On Friday evening a police car (with flashing blue lights, I hope) is to pick me up at my brother's council house in Nottingham, and take me to the place. If they ever let me go, for what I tell them about my early life, I'll be surprised. But don't worry, I'll arrange to get bail for July [when he would visit Israel]! [AS to BD, 21 February 1996]

Despite Sillitoe's regular complaints to friends about having committed himself to yet another demanding reading or lecture he has probably performed in public on more occasions than any other living writer – his average during the 1990s was thirty per year – and he is a great speaker. He brings to a live audience the same shrewd respect that the reader encounters in his fiction. He disarms listeners with his transparency – he has no secrets – while drawing them into stories and anecdotes that leave key questions open. The policemen gave him a standing ovation. He was honest regarding his sympathies with Colin Smith, coy about autobiographical parallels, and he left no one in any doubt that these days Colin would more likely join the force than accept the condescending ideology of victimhood. He received a letter from C.F. Bailey, Chief Constable of

Nottingham Constabulary, thanking him for the signed copy of *Life Without Armour* and informing him of the enormous number of 'complimentary remarks about your address'. 'You have', he assured him 'many "fans" within Nottinghamshire' (C.F. Bailey to AS, 25 March 1996, Indiana Archive).

THIRTY-THREE

The image of a 1990s Colin Smith prompted more involving speculations. Are there, he asked himself, individuals who endure, whose defining characteristics resist the mutations of history; or are we all, at least in part, the products of circumstance? This was the kernel for the first draft of what would become *The Broken Chariot* (1998). The novel was also inspired by Sillitoe's ruminations on his friendship with Bernard 'Bunny' Sindall, his neighbour in Wittersham.

Their backgrounds, one might assume, would have guaranteed at least mutual suspicion with potential for hostility. Bunny was from a wealthy upper-middle-class family, which sent him, aged five, to preparatory school and then to King's School, Canterbury, which insisted its boys wore a uniform that looked garishly exclusive and anachronistic even when it was first designed in the 1880s. Bunny's accent, mannerisms and robust presence brought to mind James Robertson Justice, who was custom-made to play judges, minor aristocracy and consultant surgeons in British films of the 1950s. But from the moment they met Sillitoe and Bunny recognized in each other versions of themselves. At fifteen Bunny had run away from Kings and, lying about his age, joined the Royal Navy in which he would serve in the Atlantic convoys during the Second World War. After the war he decided to become a sculptor, and though over the next few decades he acquired a gargantuan knowledge of art history he was as an artist largely self-taught; he abhorred anything that required the sanction of orthodoxy or officialdom. Jeanetta Sindall, Bunny's widow, recalls their time in Wittersham. 'Alan and Bunny hit it off immediately. Superficially you would think they'd have nothing in common but temperamentally they were a perfect match. I remember during the Falklands campaign they were glued to reports on the progress of the Task Force. Bunny of course had a naval background, but what both of them admired most of all was the determination of Thatcher not to be swayed by the view, and not just from the left, that we, Britain, were past it, that we should now be supine, even apologetic.' A flavour of their friendship can be gleaned from Bunny's letters after Sillitoe had left Wittersham.

Your book *Lost Loves* was marvellous, but I wanted more and was sad when it ended. Well done Alan.

What about that election? The *Guardian* went scribbling on about Neil's entry into No. 10. Glenys sent out dozens of address cards. That triumphalism on Labour's behalf sickened me. And that wet Major became the only alternative to the Welsh windbag. We hated and loved the affair!!! [Bernard Sindall to AS, October 1992, Indiana Archive]

By its nature correspondence incorporates the mutually agreed subtexts and assumptions that underpin a friendship, and Bunny in this letter knows that Sillitoe will share most of his opinions about the state of British politics in 1992.

Planning *The Broken Chariot* Sillitoe pondered these letters, and from them emerged Herbert Thurgarton Strang, an upper-middle-class boarding-school boy who absconds aged seventeen and goes to Nottingham to become Bert, lathe worker, boozer, womanizer and street fighter with an authentic East Midlands accent. Throughout the novel Sillitoe scatters traces of his own history, fictional and actual. Episodes from *Saturday Night and Sunday Morning* resurface, part disguised, part desperate for exposure, as do fragments of *Life Without Armour*. The novel originated in questions that Sillitoe asked himself about his past and present, but in it he offers a unique account of social mobility in reverse. Changing status in British society involves only one route, upwards. If you come from the middle or upper classes you might scrutinize and report upon what the masses had to endure – as did Orwell – but you would always be a visitor to this region; an observer, and never a resident. Sillitoe's Bert/Herbert is a magnificent chameleon in that no one he meets in Nottingham suspects that he is not one of them. Though the material for the novel came from experience and observation it was driven by anger. In Sillitoe's view the 'working classes' had since the 1940s exchanged one form of inferiority for another. Prior to the post-war Labour government and the imperious growth of trade unionism they had been ruthlessly exploited, and now they were categorized, patronized and subjected to the same tough instructive charity that reformist clergymen once visited upon delinquent members of their flock. They had more money and more to eat than their predecessors, but other people determined the exact nature of what was best for them. As Sillitoe had put it in 'Ivy', improvements were bought in return for allowing others to 'decide that that was how the "working classes" ought to want to live'. So Sillitoe created Herbert, a quixotic, sometimes unpleasant individual, who does something outstanding. He becomes part of the class 'below' him, not as a scrutineer, anthropologist, philanthropist or social reformer but because he wants to. Nowhere do Herbert or his author provide an explanation for his actions, a strategy which will either infuriate or enthral the reader depending upon their disposition. He is certainly not slumming or seeking a rough brand of gratification – we know quite soon that he is a person who will satisfy his appetite for misbehaviour and sex irrespective of his environment. Nor is he a lens for Sillitoe's vision of the social landscape; he is too unpredictable and obtuse for that. If he does serve some purpose beyond his vivid 300-page tenancy in the book it is to illustrate the predominance of self-hood over the hidebound routines of classification and prediction that, for Sillitoe, now seemed to dominate the ways in which society viewed and organized itself. Margaret Drabble: 'The novel that reminds me most of Alan himself is *The Broken Chariot*. He, Alan, often seems like someone with two personalities. It is not that he dissimulates or deceives, just that like Bert he refuses to conform to a known stereotype.'

His shortened Christian name is a running jibe at Nottingham's most famous 'Bert' (D.H. Lawrence), who had taken the other route to become idolized by his bourgeois fans and patrons as a magnificent example of how clever the working classes could be.

The German Numbers Woman (1999) is the story of Howard, blinded when serving with the RAF and now in retirement. He spends his days and indeed his nights – the distinction is of little significance to him – picking up Morse signals on his radio equipment. It was, Sillitoe wrote to Bill Daleski

> a funny sort of book. I enjoyed being a blind man for a while, as if I'm not blind half the time anyway, underwater and underground, like any novelist work-ing, I imagine, and not noticing the other half of what goes on in the real world around him. But it must be hard, or unusual, to do both. And even when you are seeing the real world you're not seeing it as other people see it, but missing half and yet seeing it as they can never see it. [AS to BD, 14 December 1999]

Fascinating as this is, it provides only a partial account of the novel's personal significance. Howard's existence, with his patient, dedicated wife Laura, is a picture of the contented routine of Home Counties England, at least until he begins an exchange in Morse with Richard, who will eventu-ally involve him in international drug smuggling and a search for the real presence behind the enchanting disembodied voice of the 'numbers woman'. In theory such a transition should cause any novel, no matter how well executed, to buckle under the strain of plausibility. This one survives because Sillitoe is so successful in bringing the reader into Howard's world. Given that most readers will be sighted this should have been difficult, but as he indicates in his letter to Bill there are parallels between blindness and fiction. The panorama that unfolds on the page is created exclusively via dead signs; its complexity, its life, depends both upon how well the writer deploys them and how we decode and match them with our private store of images. As Sillitoe said, tantalizingly, 'even when you are seeing the real world you're not seeing it as other people see it', and this dependence upon subjectivity and partiality is multiplied as each separate reader creates an image of their own from the printed words of the novel. Howard becomes the equivalent of a novelist who is unable to return from the 'underwater', 'underground' state of writing to the real world around him. His universe is composed almost exclusively of words, and the language of Morse offers him a super-human capacity to transcend time and space. When he listens clandestinely to people from a thousand miles away they are as tangible as the man he has spoken to in the newsagent's. Therefore during his first contacts with Richard – and their exchange in the novel is of course recorded as ordinary spoken dialogue and not Morse – there is no suspicion that his life is about to be altered for ever. He seems to be talking to a man in the same room, and Sillitoe has led us, as readers, across the frontier from the commonplace to the fantastic without our realizing it. It hardly needs pointing out that Sillitoe's own addiction to Morse – to which he was particularly attracted when night fell and the rest of the world seemed to disappear beneath the horizon of this impersonal language – was the inspiration and impetus for the novel.

Ted Hughes's death in 1998 upset him but did not greatly surprise him. He had last seen him in November 1997 when Hughes and Roy Davids had called on Sillitoe at West Chinnock. They were returning from London to Court Green. No reason in particular was offered for their visit, which was not unusual given their friendship, but Sillitoe detected something in Ted's manner – casual yet distant, as if he were committing the detail of the meet-ing to memory – that hinted at finality. Sillitoe's moving article on his friend for the *Guardian* (reprinted in *A Flight of Arrows*) gives an account of the funeral, but he is more candid in his letter to Bill Daleski: 'The proceedings', he reported, 'were inverse', with the hundred or so 'guests (or should I say mourners?)' first wandering around the house where copious amounts of food and drink were available and then being ushered a short way up the lane to the church 'for an hour's service, a tedious experience for me, except that Seamus Heaney spoke well. By half past three it was all over: Ted's body in a rather big box near the altar was carried out on half a dozen stalwart shoulders (they had to be) to a waiting hearse...' (AS to BD, 10 November 1998, private correspondence). Sillitoe suspected that the itinerary had been planned by Ted, a droll comment on the usual order of things. At the house people at first felt slightly uncomfortable, until the drink began to flow; and then they had to listen to the vicar.

It reminded him of Armistice Day three years earlier. He and Ruth had been invited to Deyá for Robert Graves's centenary commemoration, and Sillitoe himself, at the request of the family, read three of Graves's First World War poems at the lectern in the small church and announced the two minutes' silence. Outside a wreath of Flanders poppies from Graves's regiment, the Royal Welch Fusiliers, was laid on his grave. 'A sudden wind blew it away (Robert would have liked that) and someone had to scramble down a few terraces to bring it back' (AS to BD, 7 January 1996, private correspondence). 'Beryl', he reported, 'thought that Robert, wherever he was, must have had a hand in the wreath's whirligig escapade, to amuse himself at our expense.'

Sillitoe has always been, and will he insists remain, an atheist. It is beyond the territories of Christianity that the sureness of his disbelief begins to fray. In 1995 Bill Daleski suffered a heart attack and later underwent bypass surgery, and in his correspondence throughout this period Sillitoe invokes 'God' as a benefactor in Bill's return to good health. This was not, he insists, an empty reflex or a concession to his friend's belief in an eternal authority. The God of Israel and Judaism was now something more than the Old Testament figure; He was custodian of natural justice in the face of terrible suffering, as real to the religious atheist as to the orthodox believer. As for fate, that was something we must accept and, if we can, improve.

In 1997, a year after the death of her husband, Hilary Bussey wrote to Sillitoe, via his agent, simply to tell him something of her life and of how greatly she admired his achievements. She apologized for seeming to make a claim upon his time – she even wondered if he remembered her given that in *The Open Door* and *Life Without Armour* she was discreetly disguised and renamed – and assured him he should not feel bound to reply. He did, explaining that the delay was due mainly to his having spent many of the recent months in Nottingham.

> My brother's wife died of cancer five months ago, so I have been going there to cheer him up a bit – impossible of course, but I like to think my presence helps, and we have always been close. There are three of us brothers. There were two sisters but both died of cancer in their forties. Our father died of it as well, in his fifties. [AS to Hilary Bussey, 28 May 1999]

Sillitoe once visited Hilary in Kent. She has returned to what had been her vocation before she became a nurse, painting, and did a portrait of Alan from a photograph which he admires greatly. His letters to her are intriguing and unique. Only once before, with Ronald Schlachter, had someone significant from his distant past returned, but the two comrades were then still in their fifties, lived in the same city and gave accounts of their missing years mostly over lunch and at dinner. Sillitoe's letters to Hilary, however, remind one of a private memoir. He discloses no terrible secrets – there were none to disclose – and the correspondence was certainly not confidential. From the time Hilary first wrote to him he informed Ruth of who she was. Yet as he writes to her the protective manner of *Life Without Armour*, in which he dispensed truth with few collateral emotions, is replaced by a wistful, contemplative manner. He concludes the letter quoted above: 'You were an angel to me when I was young and in despair! They were wonderful days at Wroughton, which changed my life.' Later that same year he reflects on

> all that we meant to each other in the old times at Wroughton. Happy days is what I often tell myself – and they were, no doubt about that. What I thought of as the worst thing that ever happened to me – getting TB – in fact turned out to be the best, and changed my life. You were part of that change. I'd be daft and dishonest if I didn't say so. [AS to Hilary Bussey, 2 November 1999]

Sillitoe's temperamental mien can be best described as mordant optimism, and he knew that its resilience would soon be tested more and more. It was Brian's wife, June, who had died from cancer, and though, as he informed Hilary, he had spent many of the subsequent months 'there to cheer him up a bit' he had also begun to feel a stronger allegiance to the place that had formed him.

THIRTY-FOUR

In his letters to Bill Daleski of this period there are frequent reports on the antics of 'the Sillitoe brothers'. Brian's research into the family history, always diligent and enthusiastic, now became also a distraction from his terrible sense of loss. In 1999, with Sillitoe driving, the three brothers set off on a week-long journey into the past, specifically the years that Burton is thought to have spent in the Severn valley and across the border in Wales. Dannie Abse and his wife Joan knew the region well and supplied Sillitoe with an account of how the population had altered in the late nineteenth century, with itinerant navvies and miners and journeyman smiths like Burton finding temporary jobs in newly industrialized areas. They also offered advice on agreeable pubs and small hotels. It was the first time the brothers had been alone together for this length of time for more than fifty years, and though nothing much happened they remember it as a special experience. They stuck dutifully to their itinerary of checking records in town halls and extant tenants' registers and witnessing the places that had become part of their grandfather's legend. Though it was not obvious at the time they also became aware that each seemed to the other much the same as they had been in the 1940s, yet subtly changed. The paradox, such as it was, did not trouble them but it convinced Sillitoe that a novel he had begun a year earlier should be returned to with vigour and confidence.

Birthday (2001) concerned Sillitoe at its inception because he had begun to suspect himself of relying too much on familiar territory at the expense of new ideas. It is about three brothers, Brian, Arthur and Derek Seaton, veterans of Sillitoe's earlier work who assemble in Nottingham for the seventieth birthday of Jenny. I have met Jenny, a woman whose modest, unassuming manner belies her role as chimerical talisman in Sillitoe's fiction. She is called Doreen Haslam. Her maiden name was Greatorex and she was the model for Doreen Greatton of *Saturday Night and Sunday Morning*. 'Well, that's what Pearl, Sillitoe's sister, always told me. When we were both married she, Pearl, lived in the same street as us, and when the book came out, and then the film, she always said to me, "It's you, Doreen. He based her on you."' What do you think, I asked her? 'I don't know,' she replies with a knowing laugh. But isn't she also Jenny in *Birthday*? 'Oh yes, *Birthday*. That was my novel. I was coming up to my seventieth and my son told me he'd take me out for dinner. He said, "Come on, Mum, get your glad rags on." "Who's going?" I said. "Just us." But when we got there, well it was a surprise. A floor of the restaurant was booked. Alan was there, and Brian and Michael. All my family as well. It was a lovely night.' Did Alan plan it? 'He had a hand in it, but I think Brian was behind most of it. As I say, our families have always been close. Their mother, Sabina, she used to come round here to us, with Tom, every Thursday for dinner. I've known the brothers since they were kids, Brian particularly.'

In 1972 Sillitoe wrote to Brian of how he had been asked by Sisson and Parker's, Nottingham's largest bookshop, to spend a morning signing copies of his most recent novels, particularly the new paperback edition of *A Start in Life*.

> I enjoyed being in Nottingham, wandering around the old streets in the middle of town. I saw mam, of course, and also Ivy and Em. While I was signing in the bookshop . . . one of my old girlfriends popped up in front of my eyes, Doreen, so I gave her a copy too. That was the least I could do. She's married to a collier now and got five kids, but her husband was injured in the pit four years ago and hasn't worked since. [AS to BS, 25 April 1972]

Brian knew of Doreen's husband's accident, which had left him partially disabled, and of how she had looked after him and brought up the children without complaint. In the novel an early passage takes us back twenty-five years, to around 1972. The other Brian, successful screenwriter and of course Sillitoe's fictional confrère, is up from London, and at the station he sees a face from the past.

> 'Hello! Don't you know me?' As if the likelihood of his not doing so would devastate her. Though the distress in her features wasn't due to his changed appearance. 'It's me, Jenny.' [p. 15]

Jenny is about to catch the train for Sheffield where her husband had just been rushed by ambulance to be treated by specialists. That same day he had suffered a terrible back injury at the foundry where he worked. He, like Doreen's husband, would never work again.

Doreen's namesake from *Saturday Night and Sunday Morning* does not appear in *Birthday* – as she explains to me, 'I can't be two people at once now, can I?' – but we learn of her history with Arthur. They married, but it did not last, and Arthur is now with Avril. Sillitoe's apparent game of musical chairs with his characters and their real-life counterparts has a more profound purpose. The Doreen Greatton of his first novel had become one of those migratory figures whose appearance on screen would forever eclipse their elusive presence behind the words. Just as the Arthur of the book would always be a version of Albert Finney, so Doreen Greatton could never again be detached from Shirley Ann Field's brilliant but not entirely accurate performance as a Machiavellian virgin. Sillitoe had been reminded of this in 1998 when BBC2 did a series of profiles of writers of the 1950s; there were quotations from his work, but he along with Finney, Field and Tom Courtenay seemed to have become fixtures in cinema's predominant hold on recent cultural history. *Birthday* was about the present day, so Doreen became Jenny. Kingsley Amis in *The Old Devils* had turned an assembly of his earlier creations into pensioners and proved – to refashion a line from his closest friend Larkin – that what will survive of us is rough. Sillitoe's lot are not without bitterness, but most of this is directed against a society pledged to the ideals of transience, selfishness and hypocrisy; Tony Blair receives an ample share of invective. For all their imperfections the brothers, their partners and Jenny are united in a visceral recognition of the difference between right and wrong, manifesting itself particularly in a duty to others, especially the ones to whom they have committed themselves. The brave, uncomplicated Jenny gets her birthday party, as did Doreen. Brian, being a reflection of his author, is presented least sympathetically, but before suspecting Sillitoe of false modesty we should note that he works as a foil for everyone else.

The most memorable aspect of the book is Sillitoe's presentation of the relationship between Arthur and Avril. Love, unreserved and unalloyed, is notoriously resistant to representation in words, mainly because of its uniqueness to those who experience it in life. Written about, no matter how skilfully, it becomes garishly public. When Arthur and Avril are alone Sillitoe achieves something quite extraordinary, to the extent that these passages alone confirm his status as one of the outstanding prose fiction writers of the last half-century. Chapter 8 is set in Arthur and Avril's kitchen where they sit peeling apples from the garden. Nothing else happens, but the shared task provides the rhythm for their conversation.

'I can't imagine our Brian sitting at a table, and slicing apples hour after hour.'

Her smaller and more perfect apple was soon finished. 'I expect he'd do it if he had to.'

'If somebody tried to make him he'd get out of it. Can you see him sitting all nice and quiet like me as he worked? He's far too canny to get sergeant-majored into this.'

She reached for another. 'You mean you don't like to do it? I can read you like a book.'

'And what page are you on now, sharpshit?'

'I can see you aren't doing very well.'

'That's because you pick all the little 'uns, and leave the monsters to me.' He slicked the completed apple into the bowl. 'I love doing this, you know I do.'

'Tell me another.'

'Have I ever complained?'

'No, but I can tell by the look on your face that you don't exactly enjoy it.'

'Do you expect me to look as if I've just opened the newspaper to page three? I'm concentrating. I love cutting up apples. The first thing I said when I learned to talk was to ask mam if she'd got any apples that wanted cutting up. When she said no I cried so loud people in Derby thought there was another riot in Nottingham.' [p. 105]

Neither of them has cause to reflect on the meaning of their lives or on issues of profound significance for mankind, but we know by the end of the chapter that we have encountered something deeper and more enduring than would be found in an exchange where such issues are addressed ostentatiously. They are the most unpretentious witnesses to the most invaluable aspects of the human condition, and we leave the chapter with mixed feelings. Optimism and enchantment vie with a touch of shame because Sillitoe convinces us that these people deserve their privacy.

The quality of the writing testifies to Sillitoe's skill, but it would be wrong to assume that Arthur, Avril and the others embody an optimistic fantasy. Avril, like Brian's wife June, has been diagnosed with cancer, and the enduring tenderness which informs the book was drawn from what Sillitoe had witnessed, not imagined.

I asked Doreen Haslam if she thought there was more of Brian than Alan in the original Arthur Seaton. Was Brian more of a Jack the Lad than his brother, the author? Her laugh was long and affectionate. 'Brian? Well, I couldn't say, could I? I didn't know him that well when he was Arthur Seaton's age. But I'll tell you this, he's a good man.' Well said, Doreen.

By the end of 2002 the burdens and obligations of the West Chinnock house seemed to equal those which prompted the sale of St Pargoire. Records dated part of it from the early fifteenth century and Sillitoe often joked that someone much worse than Falstaff had paid for it with loot from Agincourt and employed cowboy builders. The Daleskis, prior to their visit in 1998, were warned that they would have to negotiate scaffolding to get to the front door. The stone chimney had been on the point of collapse for years and now catastrophe had to be averted at great expense. The entire roof sometimes appeared about to follow suit, with warped A-frames causing the tiled surface to resemble the surrounding undulating landscape. Full replacement, Sillitoe was advised, would cost close to a third of the market value of the house. On 15 December 1991 he wrote to Ronald Schlachter of how they had spent the previous two days waiting for a heating engineer – the system, dating from the 1960s, was persistently unreliable – and were spending most of their time keeping 'the two fires blazing away'.

Given that they spent less than a fifth of the year there, the place was proving to be the single most expensive aspect of their lives. In 2002 Alan's diary read: 'Chinnock 67 days. 14 talks and readings. 22 press, radio and television interviews, all elsewhere.'

We spent August in West Chinnock, but it meant a lot of work, especially in the garden, which had had no attention for a couple of months. Anyway, we've decided to sell up, put it on the market, either not have a second place at all, or buy a very small cottage close to David so that we can see more of the children. [AS to BD, 3 September 2003]

David and Julia's first child, Jed (full name Jedediah Ethan), was born in 1995, and they have since had two more children. Until 2003 they lived in Buntingford, Hertfordshire, close enough to London and not too inconvenient for visits to West Chinnock. David still worked for the *Guardian*, and though Julia decided to give precedence over her career to the children she had from the mid-1990s worked with Sillitoe on the preparation of his final drafts. He still used a manual typewriter but HarperCollins insisted on submission by disk or electronic transfer and Julia typed his hard copy into her word processor. In 2003 she and David moved to Diseworth in Leicestershire, and a year after selling West Chinnock Sillitoe and Ruth bought a cottage across the lane. It was little more than twenty minutes from the centre of Nottingham, and Sillitoe, inevitably, felt at home.

I'm very happy here – it's a fine landscape, with often good sunsets from our back windows . . . My brothers in Nottingham haven't called yet, but they've been entertained by David [reporting on the move], who likes having them so close . . .

We're only a mile south of East Midlands' airport so there's noise from planes, which I don't mind at all – in fact as I see them gracefully drifting in to the runways like birds with gaudy plumage at the tail I'm reminded of when I was working in air traffic control myself, talking the kites down after giving them the green light. Heady days, for a seventeen year old, and a good job after three years in the factories. [AS to BD, 28 December 2004]

The wistful hint that their life had become more tranquil, even inactive, is misleading. In April and May 1998 they had spent almost two months in Peru, Argentina and Uruguay giving readings and lectures, and in November of the same year they set off at the invitation of the British Council on a week-long tour of Italy. February 1999 involved three weeks in France, giving talks in Boulogne, Bordeaux, Lyon and at the Sorbonne, and they spent most of June in Israel, again to do lectures, readings and interviews. Two trips to France and one to Italy made up in total six weeks of 2000, and 2001 took them to Paris, Gothenburg, Sicily and Majorca. Typically 2004, the year of their move to Diseworth, began:

Jan.	2nd	Ruth to Mexico
	4th	Me to West Chinnock
	7th	To Nottingham – Brian's
	10th	To London, via Buntingford
	17th	Ruth back from Mexico
	26th	Beryl Graves Memorial Service (Deyá)
	31st	Great Haseley
Feb.	2nd	To London
	4th	Me to Berlin
	5th	To Dresden
	7th	Via Berlin to London

[Private diary]

The year 2005 proved particularly zestful. For three weeks in November they toured Mexico; Ruth's poetry both in English and translation had established for her a large enthusiastic base of admirers in Latin America. It was, they recall, rather like becoming part of a Hollywood version of life south of the border. Ruth: 'They were very generous but from time to time I wondered if they'd mistaken us for political emissaries. Men, apparently from the Ministry of Culture, would rush us from hotels in large cars, and then we'd go by helicopter or private jet to the next appointment. Often we'd be accompanied by men in uniform. What were they protecting us from? Hostile critics? How so unlike readings in Camden Town.' 'Exciting, though, wasn't it?' adds Sillitoe.

Their relationship, unlike so many involving writers, has endured enviably:

Listened to the second half of Tchaikovsky's 1st Violin Concerto – played in Moscow, one of the old records I brought back from my 1960s trips – God forbid. I think this is probably his best work – marvellous virtuoso stuff – because he has the discipline and concentration of a single instrument . . . Also, listening to this, I think that the violin is what unites Ruth and me. When we've sat together, not speaking but listening, something has passed between us that is far more powerful than a declaration. I told her this, she smiled and said it was only the four vodkas talking. Oh dear, only four! [Private notebook, January 2000]

Early in May they had spent a week in Moscow. Sillitoe, out of favour since the late 1960s, had received an official invitation by the British Council to give readings, and see something of the sixtieth anniversary of the end of the Second World War. He reported to Brian:

It was very moving to see so many old veteran Soviet soldiers walking the street with all their medals on their chests. President Bush and other world leaders were there – all, that is, except Blair, who couldn't be bothered to come. Many Russians were shocked at his absence, and so was I. He sent Prescott instead, who got pushed into the background on Red Square. It's hard to imagine Blair not going to such an event . . .

I spoke for about half an hour to a room full of Russians, who appreciated it when I condemned Blair for not being there during that historic week. TV and press were there, and I hope they reported my words. So was the British Ambassador, and I don't care what he thought. [AS to BS, 16 May 2005]

He met George again, for the first time in more than thirty years. His old friend was sanguine about the Kuznetsov affair. He had survived; his only sadness was that the anxiety regarding what might happen to him had, he was convinced, hastened his mother's death. 'But,' he said, 'under Stalin I would have been shot. Let's drink.' And they did, for quite a while.

Sillitoe and Brian had never talked at length about his, Sillitoe's, change in political outlook. For one thing they respected each other too much to challenge or question their respective opinions, but Brian none the less was intrigued by Sillitoe's preoccupation with Judaism and Israel. In 1994 for instance Brian read *Schindler's Ark*, obtained the video version *Schindler's List* and began reading more about the history of Jews in Europe. Sillitoe lent him his copy of Martin Gilbert's *The Holocaust*. Sillitoe had become friendly with Gilbert in the 1980s and assured his brother that this bare, unemotional account was the best available. In his letters to Brian from the late 1980s onwards his commitment to Israel features as prominently as his reports on the Soviet Union had in the mid-1960s.

Israel is a great country, and will survive [he had earlier mentioned a terrorist car bomb]. You feel a strength there, and a sense of purpose, that you feel in no other country in the world. We spent all the time . . . seeing friends – mostly novelists and poets, though we went to a Kibbutz for a day (having friends there as well) and had a good lunch in the dining room. It was half way between Jerusalem and Tel Aviv, a beautifully green and cultivated settlement called Nachson. [AS to BS, 7 March 1994]

Neither here nor in any other of his letters to Brian does Sillitoe proselytize. They were close, and he simply wished to tell his brother about his life and intuitions, yet one can't help detect a hint of pride, alongside fellow feeling, in his report to Bill Daleski:

> As for the trouble in Israel, I was in Nottingham recently and my brother Brian, quite unsolicited, on hearing on the news about the mad bus driver who killed eight Israelis, said that Israel should make an all out war and settle the matter. I've always thought there was no other way . . . [AS to BD, 18 February 2001]

At Brian's request Sillitoe forwarded to him monthly circulars of the '35s Women's Campaign for Jews of the Former Soviet Union' which monitored the revival of anti-Semitism throughout the former Communist Bloc.

THIRTY-FIVE

The brothers' research into their family history was far more than a hobby or distraction. They wanted to recover something of a heritage that no one else would ever care about; they were the ordinary people, consumed and exploited by the forces of history but ignored by historical record. As early as 1992 when the project was in its infancy Sillitoe had written to Brian about the unanswered, probably unanswerable questions that surrounded their paternal grandfather.

> I've always supposed that Grandfather Sillitoe came to Nottingham because he thought he'd get more work. But people in those days often left their town because of debt or bankruptcy. Or maybe he met his future wife, and she wouldn't leave Nottingham. I suppose Dad would have told us these things if we'd thought to ask him. The trouble is . . . it's too late. [AS to BS, 24 April 1992]

By the end of the decade they were making up for lost time. Sillitoe had abandoned his original plan to turn this research on Burton's life into a radio play. Eventually it would become the source material for his novel *A Man of His Time*. 'I'm up to where he and Mary-Ann get married,' he reported to Brian, 'with the reception at the White Hart.' 'I see that on the marriage certificate Mary Ann was about the only one to sign her name. Next time I get to Lenton I must get into Lenton church, and look at the births, marriages and deaths' (AS to BS, 14 December 2000). He did, and in the novel we find a faithful adherence to known fact.

Little more than a month later he thanked Brian for photocopies of the *Evening Post* of 1887. 'They'll be very useful researching prices etc. of the time, good and essential information for me to have and give authenticity to the story.' He adds that 'at some time during the summer, or when the nights are shorter, I'll retrace some of the route Oliver's regiment took after he left Nottingham. He went first to Diss in Norfolk for a couple of weeks, then by train as well to Reading. From then on to Hungerford he would be on a horse' (AS to BS, 17 January 2001). Sillitoe drove and sometimes walked along the roads and, if they were still operating, took the trains that their research had disclosed were used by Oliver before his fatal injury. Then with maps, logic and a small allowance of imagination he followed what he believed would be the route back through central England taken by the cart carrying his semi-conscious uncle. For the first time ever in his life as a writer he showed his work in progress to someone other than Ruth and discussed it with them. Brian received two typescript copies of the passage describing Oliver's injury and eventual death and funeral. They talked of how this matched with their background research, and more significantly Sillitoe asked his brother if he thought the description felt right, corresponded to the emotional register that both had attached to Burton's son.

During the round of interviews that preceded the book's launch he made some acknowledgement of its grounding in family history – he could hardly deny to anyone who had read *Raw Material* or *Life Without Armour* that Burton was indeed his grandfather – but said nothing of how he, Brian and Michael had been obsessively concerned with a search for the essence and lifeblood of its characters. Which of course raises the question of the effect of all this upon the book itself. Do we need to know of its, albeit fascinating, background to appreciate its essential qualities? We do not, but the prose is possessed of a remorseless, fatalistic energy that makes the work far more convincing, indeed compulsive, than novels, historical or otherwise, which adopt a spare, realist mode. We can sense, without having to be told, that the energy of the novel is sourced by something more mercurial than imagination. The characters' actions are never reduced to the standard formulae of explanation and analysis; each of them is instilled with a vibrancy usually obtained only by actors. Burton himself is enigmatic in that we are never quite certain whether to judge him morally or just make do with attenuated feelings of dread, fixation and anger similar to those he wills upon everyone else in the story. It is a superb achievement, and unique because the fascination shared by Sillitoe and his brothers informs its texture.

The novel ends in the present with Burton's three grandsons, Brian, Arthur and Derek, in Lenton churchyard. It is the fiftieth anniversary of his death and they have brought a bottle of chilled Moët et Chandon to toast him at his grave. Brian (the real one): 'Yes, 1996. Alan brought the champagne, chilled. It was a dismal day and somebody, could have been Alan, said, "Don't drop the bottle, else the old sod will rise up and belt us!"' In the novel: 'Brian carried flowers, and champagne in a plastic bag. "Don't drop it," Arthur said, "or Burton will jump out of his grave and thump you."' (p. 374).

As usual Sillitoe redistributes characteristics of the three real brothers among their fictional counterparts, but here direct parallels are much more evident. Brian, for example: 'Warm in his countryman's three quarter woollen overcoat with poacher's pockets, he wore a navy blue suit, a white collarless Jermyn Street silk shirt buttoned to the neck' (p. 373). Patricia Parkin: 'I'm sure you'll have seen photographs of Alan from the sixties and early seventies in his signature collarless cotton shirt, Russian peasant style. They're misleading because he has always had a connoisseur's taste for high-class clothes. Never anything garish or extravagant, but made from the best material by good London tailors. I remember when I went with him to Nottingham before *A Man of His Time* was launched we went out on the town with his brothers and I must say I teased him. "Alan," I said, "you have the dress sense of a peacock." In fact he loved understated quality.' Ruth Fainlight comments: 'Those shirts – nothing to do with Russian peasants. The originals were modelled on nineteenth-century Majorcan shirts, and were made by my Majorcan dressmaker, in the 1960s. Alan was wearing this style years before it became the trend. When it did, he stopped wearing them! Some of them were silk.' Later in the chapter Brian tells his brothers that the other night Burton appeared to him in a dream, that he has a constant sense of his presence (pp. 375–6). Sillitoe wrote to Bill Daleski of how, when preparing the novel,

I very strongly felt the tall appraising figure of Burton standing nearby, ready to upbraid me more mercifully than he ever did his sons if I put a word wrong. By then maybe he'd picked up enough of his letters in hell [being illiterate in life], sufficient to give him knowledge as to whether I was too far out in my description. All I heard was a grunt of appreciation as his ghost faded away. [AS to BD, 25 July 2004]

His ghost had been around for some time. To Brian in 1993:

I dreamed about him last night – the first time for twenty-odd years. I was putting some earphones on him so that he could listen to some wonderful music from the radio, and he seemed quite pleased to hear it. He wore a suit and had the same shorn white hair. [AS to BS, 23 November 1993]

Derek, more introspective and reserved, balances his two brothers' exuberance, and is certainly Michael. The dynamic between the men in the novel reflects the three actual brothers' enjoyment of their differences. 'I got back about five o'clock this afternoon. I had a wonderful time in Nottingham, as usual laughing so much my ribs ached. I'll never forget the big plates of food the three of us had in Cromford!' (AS to BS, 31 January 1999). He told Bill Daleski of how pleased he was that HarperCollins had agreed to launch the novel in Nottingham, 'where else and where better?'

It makes an opportunity to see my brothers. The three of us put on our caps and go into a pub, and have a pint or two, and a smoke if we wish [a ban was already being discussed] – to show Mr Blair and his puritanical politically correct ponces that the old England is not dead and will boot him out if he goes on thinking so. [AS to BD, 5 March 2004]

The closing speech, when they are in the pub, goes to Arthur. Its mood – aggressively nonconformist, just for the sake of it – echoes Sillitoe's letter to Bill, but there is something of Brian Sillitoe there too. It ends with a passage that incorporates Sillitoe's and Brian's opinions on life, the afterlife and – tongue only slightly in cheek – themselves.

> He'll be in hell as long as anybody thinks it exists. It'll be a shame that after we've snuffed it there'll be nobody to remember him, though the more we drink to him the better, so we'd better look sharp and sup up. When Burton's decided his leave from hell is over he'll walk away saying: 'It was nice to see you chaps again, but when Old Nick calls time for the three of you you'll know where to find me. I'll be waiting.' [p. 378]

Brian's only daughter, Debbie, had died from cancer aged thirty-seven in 2001, barely two years after he lost his wife. He was a decent, stoical man treated unfairly by life, and if nothing else the novel he helped create stands as a fitting memorial to him. He died from cancer in 2007, at the age of seventy-three.

It goes without saying that lives of living, working authors must be open-ended, so I shall here return to the point in the Introduction where the subject of this one made his entrance to the book. The third volume of the Moggerhanger trilogy is complete and he is presently working on a novel that is 'probably' set in Nottingham and whose principal figure is yet another bequest to his vast assembly of enigmas. All that Sillitoe will disclose is his occupation, 'a carpenter', but by the time this book is in print so will the novel that will bring him properly to life.

This biography was written with Sillitoe's authorization and cooperation, and he has read the first draft, not to censor it or refashion the image of him it presents – as he puts it, generously and rather ominously, 'it's your book' – but to make sure I have correctly cited and marshalled the facts. In this he has been heroic and meticulous and on only one occasion did he offer his thoughts about my impressions of him. 'I wonder', he writes in the margin, 'if I am as transparent as you think. I can be a different person for different people.' Overcoming a fleeting moment of panic and after pondering this for a while I feel I understand what he means. There is in his Majorca notebooks of the mid-1950s a curious anomaly. Sometimes we encounter a figure who boils with anger and discontentment.

> What are our rights? They include: the right to live in solitude. The right to die when we want to. The right to resist, violently if necessary, those who try to enslave us with solutions, from the pseudo utopianism of the Communists to the nationalism of imbeciles such as Franco. The only

acceptable form of government is the dictatorship of the self. [Private diary, June 1955]

This might sound like a discomforting blend of nihilism and narcissism, but such passages are outnumbered by disclosures of quixotic tenderness. There are, for example, five dense handwritten pages written over a few days during late October 1955, in which he reflects on the death of a kitten, one of four that he and Ruth had adopted as companions for Nell.

They were beggars but they live by what we give them. They think that by sitting on the window ledge they can induce us to give them food, that the mournful pleading looks on their faces will be answered with charity. And so it is.

When prayers are offered up to God to stop or avert disasters, they are not answered. We must help each other. God will not listen.

The death of the kitten appears to sadden him greatly, but with an admixture of unease at the depth of his distress: it was, he had to keep telling himself, only a cat.

On the way to town I made some joke about him now wandering the Elysian fields for cats, scattering the mice ... But the joke fell flat. The cat had been so wild that we had not even given him (or perhaps her) a name.

Why should I be so sad because a kitten had died? Because, I said, I would no longer see it with the other three eating the scraps, or the four of them sitting together on the garden bench. This is true but not the absolute truth. I am upset because even the death of a kitten is an event, a reminder, positive proof that all we have in common is death. There is no heaven for cats and no heaven for men; your only possession at death is the space of ground on which you fall or the bed in which you die. It is a hard fact to face but it reinforces another certainty, or rather an obligation. Be good to others, allow them to live as they wish and, if you can, help them. [Private diary, October 1955]

The last sentence comes closest to a description of the real Alan Sillitoe, despite the fact that his public image is generally that of the unaffiliated rebel. But he is certainly not a chameleon. He does not dissimulate or create roles for himself, and I recall an episode less than a year ago in Belfast International Airport. Alan and Ruth were returning to London after giving talks and lectures in Northern Ireland and in his hand luggage was one token of the province's appreciation, a bottle of rare Russian vodka. After being reminded that fluids of any kind were forbidden from the boarding area he politely replied to the official that his only option now was to consume the valuable liquid before departure, with the assistance of any fellow passengers who cared to join him. Quite a number were sufficiently charmed and amused to take up his offer, and it was joyful indeed to witness the expressions on the faces of the security staff who had clearly not been primed to deal with something quite like this; not a tirade or a rant or indeed a breach of regulations, more like something from an Ealing comedy. This companionable mood proved infectious, and the official joined in to the extent that he summoned an airline employee from the check-in desk and persuaded her to have this large bottle of 'special medicine' placed in Alan's hold baggage.

Had this been engineered by anyone else one might have commended their performance, but, entertaining as it was, Alan was not performing. There is only one Alan Sillitoe, yet he is neither a predictable nor an intractable figure. This was why he was drawn to the profession of writing and has triumphed in his craft. He has the rare quality of being able to create characters, and narrators, who are not extensions or permutations of their creator. They do, however, share with him the quality of capricious, though not irresponsible, self-determination. We feel that we know them as well as we would a real person, but by the same token there is something authentically unknowable about them. They can, like their author, 'be a different person for different people'.

BIBLIOGRAPHY

Without Beer or Bread, Outposts, 1957

Saturday Night and Sunday Morning, W.H. Allen, 1958

The Loneliness of the Long Distance Runner, W.H. Allen, 1959

The General, W.H. Allen, 1960

The Rats and Other Poems, W.H. Allen, 1960

Key to the Door, W.H. Allen, 1961

The Ragman's Daughter, W.H. Allen, 1963

A Falling out of Love and Other Poems, W.H. Allen, 1964

Road to Volgograd, W.H. Allen, 1964

The Death of William Posters, W.H. Allen, 1965

A Tree on Fire, Macmillan, 1967

The City Adventures of Marmalade Jim, Macmillan, 1967

Guzman Go Home and Other Stories, Macmillan, 1968

Love in the Environs of Voronezh, Macmillan, 1968

Shaman and Other Poems, Turret Books, 1968

All Citizens are Soldiers (adaptation of 'Fuente Ovejuna' by Lope de Vega, translated by Ruth Fainlight and Alan Sillitoe), Macmillan, 1969

A Start in Life, W.H. Allen, 1970

Poems (with Ted Hughes and Ruth Fainlight), Rainbow Press, 1971

Travels in Nihilon, W.H. Allen, 1971

Raw Material, W.H. Allen, 1972

Barbarians and Other Poems, Turret Books, 1973

Men, Women and Children, W.H. Allen, 1973

Storm and Other Poems, W.H. Allen, 1974

The Flame of Life, W.H. Allen, 1974

Mountains and Caverns: Selected Essays, W.H. Allen, 1975

Down to the Bone, Wheaton, 1976

The Widower's Son, W.H. Allen, 1976

Big John and the Stars, Robson, 1977

The Incredible Fencing Fleas, Robson, 1978

Three Plays (The Slot-Machine, The Interview, Pit Strike), W.H. Allen, 1978

Poems for Shakespeare, Bear Gardens Museum and Arts Centre, 1979

Snow on the Other Side of Lucifer, W.H. Allen, 1979

The Storyteller, W.H. Allen, 1979

Marmalade Jim at the Farm, Robson, 1980

Israel: Poems on a Hebrew Theme, Steam Press, 1981

Her Victory, Granada Books, 1982

The Lost Flying Boat, Granada, 1983
The Saxon Shore Way, Hutchinson, 1983
Down from the Hill, Grafton, 1984
Sun Before Departure, Grafton Books, 1984
Life Goes On, Grafton Books, 1985
Tides and Stone Walls, Grafton Books, 1986
Alan Sillitoe's Nottinghamshire, Grafton Books, 1987
Every Day of the Week: An Alan Sillitoe Reader, W.H. Allen, 1987
Out of the Whirlpool, Hutchinson, 1987
The Far Side of the Street: Fifteen Short Stories, W.H. Allen, 1988
Three Poems, Words Press, 1988
The Open Door, Grafton Books, 1989
Lost Loves, Grafton Books, 1990
Leonard's War: A Love Story, HarperCollins, 1991
Collected Poems, HarperCollins, 1993
Snowstop, HarperCollins, 1993
Collected Stories, Flamingo, 1995
Leading the Blind: A Century of Guide Book Travel 1815–1914 (reprinted in 2004
    by Bookcase Editions), Macmillan, 1995
Life Without Armour, HarperCollins, 1995
Jewish Influences on My Writing: Memoirs of a Philo-Semite (The Parkes Lecture),
    Univeristy of Southampton, 1996
Alligator Playground, Flamingo, 1998
The Broken Chariot, Flamingo, 1998
The German Numbers Woman, Flamingo, 1999
Birthday, Flamingo, 2001
A Flight of Arrows: Essays and Observations, Robson Books, 2003
New and Collected Stories, Robson Books, 2003
A Man of His Time, Flamingo, 2004
Gadfly in Russia, J.R. Books, 2007

INDEX

Abse, Dannie, 253, 365
Abse, Joan, 253, 365
Adcock, Fleur, 312
Adkin, Ernie (cousin), 97
Adkin, Jack (cousin), 97
Akiba ben Joseph, Rabbi, 32, 147
Allsop, Kenneth, 140
Alvarez, Al, 228
Amichai, Yehuda, 256, 258–9, 265
Amis, Kingsley, 82, 108, 115, 136–7,
    140–41, 143, 153, 180, 199, 267,
    283, 328, 330, 332
Amis, Martin, 328, 343
Anderson, Lyndsey, 140
Andjaparidze, George, 233–42,
    246–7, 371
D'Arcangeli, Francesca, 329–30
Ash, Sholem, 255

Bacall, Lauren, 158
Bailey, C.F., Chief Constable, 358
Baker, Roy Ward, 157
Bakewell, Joan, 270
Banks, Lynn Reid, 267–8
Barnes, Julian, 328
Barstow, Stan, 279
Bartelot, Major, R.G., 275
Baskin, Leonard, 220
Bayliss, Ima, 143, 160
Beckett, Samuel, 129
Behan, Brendan, 154
Begin, Menachem, 296
Begon, Iosif, 271
Belfrage, Sally, 188
Bellow, Saul, 268
Bennett, Arnold, 93
Berman, Ed, 270
Bidwell, Brigadier Shelford, 275
Black Dwarf, 251–2, 255

Blair, Betsy, 180, 252–3
Blair, Tony, 13, 371
Blake, William, 13, 175
Bloomsbury Group, 34–5
Boak, Mr, 104–5
Böll, Heinrich, 268, 342
Bowles, Jane, 186–7, 194–5
Bowles, Paul, 186–7, 194–5
Boyle, Jimmy, 273
Bradbury, Malcolm, 156
Bratby, John, 220
Braine, John, 140–41, 150, 153,
    154–5, 157, 159, 181–2, 268, 279
Brett-Jones, Anthony, 136
Brezhnev, Leonid, 246
Brickman, Miriam, 171
Brown, Bill, 67, 68
Brown, Gordon, 13
Burroughs, William, 186, 195
Burton, Emily (aunt), 288
Burton, Ernest (grandfather), 11,
    21–30, 38, 203, 288, 304, 352–3,
    373–6
Burton, Jack (cousin), 60
Burton, Mary-Ann (grandmother),
    21–2, 24, 26, 33, 373
Burton, Oliver, (uncle), 25–6, 288,
    352–3, 373–4
Bush, George, 371
Bussey, Hilary, 77–80, 135, 324–6,
    328, 363–4
Butler, Samuel, 137
Buttita, Tony, 143
Byron, George Gordon, Lord, 81

Callow, Philip, 154
Camus, Albert, 105, 108
Caton, L.S., 82
Chapman-Mortimer, Charles, 127

Chekhov, Anton, 20
Churchill, Winston, 282
Coleman, Ron, 76
Coleridge, Samuel Taylor, 70
Colin, Rosica, 127, 134, 136, 139–40,
    147–53, 158, 160
Conan-Doyle, Arthur, 28
Conquest, Robert, 168, 169, 175
Corbetta, Mrs, 162
Corso, Gregory, 195
Courtenay, Tom, 177, 181
Couzyn, Jeni, 312
Coward, Noël, 148
Crompton, Richmal, 28
Culff, Robert, 104
Cutts, Mr and Mrs, 37–40, 56–7

Daleski, H.M. 'Bill', 275–6, 279–80,
    280–81, 281–2, 293, 295, 296–8,
    301, 310, 333, 337, 338, 339, 340,
    341, 346, 347, 351, 357, 361, 363,
    368, 372
Dankworth, Johnny, 172
Dante Alighieri, 70
Davidson, Basil, 15
Davie, Donald, 115
Delaney, Shelagh, 154, 181
Denny, Arthur, 305
Dickens, Charles, 17, 79, 93
Dillon, Millicent, 313
Diniyva, Mary, 271
Doherty, Len, 154
Donovan, Jim, 114–15
Dostoevsky, Fyodor, 13, 20, 96
Drabble, Margaret, 267, 268, 288, 361
Dragadza, Tamara, 194–6
Dumas, Alexandra, 27–8
Dundy, Elaine, 188

Edmonds, Mike, 118, 127–8, 129, 185
Eliot, George, 34
Evnine, George, 256

Fainlight, Harry, 143–4, 195, 310–11,
    315
Fainlight, Ruth, 11, 89–93, 101–6,
    111, 117–19, 124, 127, 128–30,
    142–3, 147–9, 151, 164, 180–81,
    185–91, 194–7, 207–8, 217–21,
    253, 257, 259, 272, 283–6, 287–91,
    295, 297, 302–3, 310–13, 315–17,
    321, 326–7, 330, 333–5, 351–2,
    362, 369–71, 377 and passim
Feinstein, Elaine, 225, 313
Field, Shirley Ann, 47, 171
Finney, Albert, 171–3
Firman, Bert (engineering works),
    53–5, 57
Fishman, Jerry, 262–3
Fishman, Rachel, 262
Fitzgerald, Edward, 79
Fitzgerald, Scott, 129
Florence, Peter, 343
Forster, E.M., 89
Fowles, John, 330
Francis, Freddie, 171
Fraser, Antonia, 268
French, Billy, 18
Fussell, Paul, 336

Gable, Clark, 158
Gale, S.J., 164
Garbo, Greta, 158
Gaskell, Elizabeth, 93
Gilbert, Martin, 371
Giles, Frank, 270
Ginsberg, Allen, 195, 311
Gladstone, Ron, 67
Golding, William, 330
Gorky, Maxim, 233
Gormley, Joseph, 268
Goulden, Mark, 150
'Gowa', 104, 105
Graves, Beryl, 129, 207, 217, 363
Graves, Lucia, 128–9

Graves, Robert, 11, 116–17, 129, 134, 136–7, 185, 207, 217, 362–3
Green, Peter, 152
Greene, Graham, 246

Haggard, Rider, 28
Hales, Flight-Lieutenant, 76, 82, 105
Hales, Madge, 82
Hardman, Leslie H., 258
Haslam, Doreen (née Greatorex), 47, 365–8
Hastings, Michael, 188
Hardy, Barbara, 271–2, 336
Hazak, Avi, 269
Heaney, Seamus, 362
Hemingway, Ernest, 108, 129, 156
Henderson, Paul, 89, 91, 96, 105
Henry, G.A., 28
Hoggart, Richard, 34
Holt, Seth, 171
Homer, 99, 285
Hopkin, Willie, 92
Hopkins, Bill, 140
Hope, Francis, 210
Howard, Trevor, 174
Hughes, Carol (see Carol Orchard)
Hughes, Ted, 180, 208, 220, 221, 222–9, 259, 267, 268, 269, 272, 281, 292–3, 303, 310, 311, 314, 315–16, 323, 331, 333, 351, 362
Hugo, Victor, 28
Huxley, Aldous, 35, 79, 108, 137, 249

Ivasheva, Valentina, 237, 272

Jacobsson, Ulla, 138–9
'Janet', 52–3
Jardine, Lisa, 344
Jennings, Elizabeth, 143, 312
Jenry, Joseph, 158
Johnson, B.S., 182

Johnson, Paul, 199
Joyce, James, 83, 161, 249

Kafka, Franz, 100
Kant, Immanuel, 79
Kaufman, Shirley, 298
Knight, Tom, 214, 366
Koestler, Arthur, 252
Kollek, Teddy, 260, 265
Kuznetzov, Anatoly, 246–8, 371

Larkin, Philip, 60, 82, 108, 115, 332, 344
Laski, Marghanita, 268
'Laura', 38–9
Lawrence, D.H., 34–5, 83, 89, 92–3, 101, 105, 108, 135, 154, 346, 361
Lear, Edward, 80
Leavis, Q.D., 296
Lehrain, Max, 206, 302, 338
Lessing, Doris, 220–21, 330
Lesser, Wendy, 313
Levin, Bernard, 168
Lindesay, Andrew, 343
Lodeizen, Frank, 138
Logue, Christopher, 129, 180–81, 188, 220
Loneliness of the Long Distance Runner, The (film adaptation), 160–63, 177–80
Lowry, Malcolm, 211

Macedo, Helder, 193–4, 255, 264–5, 284, 314
Macedo, Suzette, 193
Markowitz, Wolf, 174
Mansfield, Katherine, 35, 111
Margolies, David, 212
Martin, Philip, 148–9, 161
Marshal, Helen, 148–9
Maschler, Tom, 140–2, 147

Maupassant, Guy de, 79
Mayne, Richard, 152
Mayol, Dona-Maria, 128
Mays, Jane, 349
McGuinness, Frank, 210
McEwan, Ian, 328
Megged, Aharon, 256, 265, 276, 268–9
Meir, Golda, 270
Menuhin, Yehudi, 268
Mercer, David, 249, 267, 268, 269, 279
MI5, 248–9
Middleton, Lord, 29
Monroe, Marilyn, 158
Moore, Dudley, 172
Morrell, Lady Ottoline, 35
Mosley, Oswald, 169
Mullan, Brenda, 111
Murdoch, Iris, 211, 267, 268, 330
Murdoch, Rupert, 345
Murry, John Middleton, 35

Nietzsche, Friedrich, 112, 120
Nicholas, Nick, 104
Noyes, Stan, 104
Nudel, Ida, 270–71, 272

Olivier, Laurence, 60, 268
Orchard, Carol, 224, 311, 315, 335
Orwell, George, 17, 111, 187, 249
Osborne, John, 140, 143, 153, 154, 157, 199, 332
Owen, David, 270
Oz, Amos, 297–8

Pagett, Clarence, 157, 159
Parkin, Patricia, 330–31, 374–5
'Pauline', 113–20, 123–4
Perrott, Roy, 163–4
Petty, John, 154
Pink, Flying Officer, 51
Pinter, Harold, 268
Pitman, Robert, 153

Plath, Sylvia, 180, 222, 224–6, 228, 229, 292–3, 312, 316
Power, Flight-Lieutenant, 73
Priestley, Jacquetta, 268
Priestley, J.B., 75
Progressive Intellectuals' Study Group, 278–9
Price-Jones, David, 268

Radio Times, 27
Raleigh factory, 32, 45–6, 47–8
Rank, J. Arthur, 157–8
Raphael, Frederick, 267
Raphael, Gideon, 268
Reade, Charles, 27
Redgrave, Vanessa, 270
Reid, Alec, 324
Reisz, Karel, 158, 170–7, 180, 252–3, 332
Rekunkov, Alexander, 271
Reynolds, Mack, 129–30
Richardson, Amy (aunt), 98, 99
Richardson, Richard (uncle), 98, 99
Richardson, Richard (cousin), 349
Richardson, Tony, 157, 170, 174, 177–80, 181
Richie, Harry, 328
Roberts, Rachel, 171
Roitkov-Fodoryachick, Dina, 271
Rome, Warrant Officer, 53
Rowe, Percy, 44
Ruben, V.P., 271
Rubens, Bernice, 267
Rushie, Salman, 328
Russell, Bertrand, 35, 78

Sachs, Arieh, 260
'Sally', 52, 59–60
Salt, Mr, 28
Saltzman, Harry, 158, 159, 170, 174, 180
Sartre, Jean-Paul, 105, 120, 268

Saturday Night and Sunday Morning
(film adaptation), 170–73
Scargill, Arthur, 345
Schlachter, Ann, 320
Schlachter, Ronald, 67–8, 318–24, 368
Sears, Lawrence, 350
Segal, Clancy, 188
Selvon, Samuel, 154
Sellers, Peter, 270
Sergeant, Howard, 143
Sergeant, Jean, 143
Shakespeare, William, 60, 144
Shapiro, Lamed, 255
Shaw, George Bernard, 201
Shelton, Arthur, 40–41, 44, 47, 51
Sherifa, 186
Shtromas, Alexander, 270–71
Silk, Denis, 260
Sillitoe, Ada (grandmother), 17
Sillitoe, Alan
    Life:
        birth, 17
        relationship with Grandfather
            Burton, 21–30
        childhood experiences and home
            life, 18–44
        factory work; first girlfriends and
            experiences in Air Training
            Corps, 45–58
        transfer to RAF and posting to
            Malaya, 59–74
        diagnosed with TB, meets Hilary
            Bussey and begins to write,
            75–89
        meets and begins relationship with
            Ruth Fainlight, 89–101
        Sillitoe and Fainlight move to the
            Côte d'Azur, 101–106
        Fainlight returns to England and
            Sillitoe moves to Majorca,
            106–13
        begins affair with 'Pauline', 113–14

        meets Robert Graves, 116–17
        begins work on *Saturday Night and
            Sunday Morning*, 117–24
        Sillitoe arrested in Barcelona and
            Fainlight joins him in Majorca,
            124–7;
        'The Match' published, in French,
            in *Carrefour*; Rosica Colin
            becomes his agent, 127–8
        continues with work on *Saturday
            Night and Sunday Morning*,
            several short stories and four
            other novels, 127–39
        visits London and meets Tom
            Maschler, 139–42
        *Saturday Night and Sunday
            Morning* rejected by Maschler,
            147–8
        returns briefly to mainland Spain,
            148–9
        Saturday Night and Sunday Morning
            read by Jeffrey Simmons and
            published by W.H. Allen,
            149–57
        *The Loneliness of the Long Distance
            Runner* and *The General*
            published, 157–63
        his father dies, 164–5
        writes sequel to *The Loneliness of
            the Long Distance Runner*, 165–9
        involvement, with Karel Reisz, in
            the filming of *Saturday Night
            and Sunday Morning* and, with
            Tony Richardson, in filming of
            *The Loneliness of the Long
            Distance Runner*, 169–82
        moves with Fainlight and their son
            David to Tangier, 185–97
        first visit to Soviet Union, 197–20
        begins *William Posters* trilogy, 202
        buys house in London, 207
        adopts Susan after his sister

Peggy's death and buys the
rectory in Wittersham, 216–21
friendship with Ted Hughes,
222–32
further visits to Soviet Union and
other Eastern Bloc states;
becomes friends with George
Andjaparidze, 233–50
involvement in Kuznetzov
defection, 246–8
Travels in Nihilon, 249–50
becomes interested in Judaism and
makes several visits to Israel,
251–67
begins friendship with H.M.
Daleski, 275
campaigns on behalf of political
prisoners and writes The
Widower's Son, 268–76
works on The Storyteller, 277–83
becomes involved in education of
David and Susan; plans and
completes Her Victory, 289–95
David and Susan leave school and
Sillitoe becomes preoccupied
with parts of the East Midlands
in which he had grown up –
reflected in The Second
Chance, The Lost Flying Boat,
Down from the Hill and Out of
the Whirlpool, 296–310
death of his sister Pearl and their
mother, 310
death of Ruth Fainlight's brother
Harry, 310–12
Ruth Fainlight becomes Visiting
Professor at Vanderbilt, and
she and Sillitoe tour the USA,
311–14
sells Rectory in Wittersham and
buys house in St Pargoire,
Languedoc, 315–17

revisits Malaya with Ronald
Schlachter and writes Lost
Loves, 318–23
writes The Open Door, the sequel
to Key to the Door, 324–7
divides time between England and
St Pargoire; spends period
alone in latter while Ruth
Fainlight is at Vanderbilt and
writes Leonard's War, 328–38
reaffirms his unorthodox political
beliefs and writes Snowstop, a
novel on terrorism, 339–46
writes memoirs, Life Without
Armour, and becomes involved
with Daily Mail in dispute over
serialization, 347–50
sells St Pargoire house and buys
ancient property in West
Chinnock, Somerset, 351–2
he, Brian and Michael begin to
research their family history,
352–3
honorary degrees from several
universities; appointed Visiting
Professor at Leicester
DeMontfort University and at
the University of Ulster, 353–5
The Broken Chariot, inspired by his
friendship with Bernard
'Bunny' Sindall, 359–61
death of Ted Hughes, 362
resumes contact with Hilary
Bussey, 363–4
Birthday, semi–autobiographical
sequel to Saturday Night and
Sunday Morning, 365–8
sells house in Somerset and buys
cottage in Diseworth,
Leicestershire, 369
he and Ruth Fainlight visit South
and Central America, 369–70

invited back to Moscow and sees George again, 370–71
continues with researches into family history, particularly Burton, as the basis for *A Man of His Time*, 373–6
death of Brian, 376
Tastes, attitudes and affliliations:
'Angry Generation' of the 1950s, relationship with, 140–41, 143–4, 153, 175, 324
aviation, interests in and involvement with, 51–5, 55–6, 59, 67–8, 73, 305–7, 319–20, 332–3
'Beat movement', encounters with, 185, 195
class, attitudes towards, 54, 66–7, 92–3, 100, 105, 140–42, 145, 147, 150, 154–6, 162–4, 237, 239, 277–9, 326, 342–4, 359–61
clothes, taste in, 13, 322, 374–5
Communism and socialism, attitudes towards, 12, 66–7, 106–7, 167, 168, 187–90, 233–50, 251, 253–5, 261, 277–9, 307, 342, 344–6
daily routine, 11–12, 218, 331, 335
family, relationship with, 17–44, 190–91, 207–8, 212, 214–15, 216–19, 283–9, 301–5, 309–12, 317, 349–50, 352–3, 355, 356–7, 365–8, 373–6
fascism, contempt for, 111–12, 125–6, 128, 166–8, 185, 191, 262–3, 341–2
institutions and authority, defiance of, 35, 40, 41–3, 46, 57, 119, 125–6, 137–8, 205–6, 286, 377–8

Islam, attitude towards, 186, 267, 279–80
Judaism and Israel, 12, 44–5, 138–9, 240–44, 246, 251–73, 275–6, 283, 292–8, 341–2, 371–2
literary tastes and influences, 78–9, 82–3, 91–3, 96, 101, 104–5, 108, 116–17, 144–5
maps and topography, interest in, 29–30, 38, 44, 47, 65, 107
Morse code, interest in, 60–61, 67, 70, 107, 212, 281, 361–2
religious belief in general, attitude towards, 32, 45, 75, 119–20, 363
terrorism, views on, 297, 323, 339–41
Novels and short stories:
'Mr Allen's Island' (unpublished novel), 135, 136
Alligator Playground, 288, 356
Big John and the Stars, 113, 115
'By What Road?' (unpublished novel), 84–6, 91–2, 131
Birthday, 355, 365–8
Broken Chariot, The, 355, 359–61
Death of William Posters, The, 194, 196, 202, 205, 227
'Decline of Frankie Buller, The', 144–6
'Deserters, The' (unpublished novel), 92, 105, 108, 115
Down from the Hill, 307
'Fishing Boat Picture, The', 98, 105, 134
General, The, 95–6, 149, 159, 160
'General's Dilemma, The', 95–6, 105, 127, 134
German Numbers Woman, The, 355, 361–2
'Guzman Go Home', 190

Her Victory, 291–6, 301
'Ivy', 356–7
Key to the Door, 69–70, 71–2, 77,
    81, 194, 210, 233, 315, 319
'Letter from Malaya', 134
Leonard's War, 329, 335–8
Life Goes On, 84, 112, 301–2
Loneliness of The Long Distance
    Runner, The, 35, 97, 98, 127,
    134, 160, 187, 210, 222, 234,
    236, 255, 329, 354
Lost Flying Boat, The, 305–6, 332
Lost Loves, 318–23, 329, 359
'Man's Life, A' (unpublished
    novel), 165–8
Man of His Time, A, 288, 355,
    373–6
'Man Without a Home'
    (unpublished novel), 105, 108,
    161
'Match, The', 97, 98, 105, 109
'Mimic', 98–9
'Mr Raynor The School Teacher',
    115–16
Open Door, The, 77, 80, 86–8, 89,
    134, 323, 324–7, 329, 331,
    333, 363
Out of the Whirlpool, 308–9, 310,
    329
'Palisade, The' (unpublished
    novel), 135
'Pit Strike', 253–5
Saturday Night and Sunday
    Morning, 13, 32, 35, 42, 47, 49,
    54, 57, 87, 88, 100, 108,
    123–7, 131–3, 134, 138,
    139–42, 147, 149–56, 157–9,
    162, 165, 185, 187, 210, 223,
    225, 236, 255, 329, 341, 353,
    354, 360
Second Chance, The, 303–4
Snowstop, 329, 339–40

Start in Life, A, 84, 112, 125–6,
    301–2
Storyteller, The, 277–81, 291, 293
Travels in Nihilon, 249–50
'Uncle Ernest', 19, 93–5, 105, 109,
    134
Widower's Son, The, 273–6
Tree on Fire, A, 196, 205–13, 227
Poetry:
'Dead Man's Grave', 214
'Lancaster', 307
'Learning Hebrew', 295
'Left Handed', 294–5
'On First Seeing Jerusalem', 265
Poems (with Ruth Fainlight and
    Ted Hughes), 229
'Rats', 131, 175–6
Rats and Other Poems, 161, 180,
    189–90
Snow on the North Side of Lucifer,
    291
Sun Before Departure 1974–83,
    264, 294–5
'Surveying', 291
'Wild Cat', 224
Without Beer or Bread, 143
Non-fiction:
Alan Sillitoe's Nottinghamshire,
    309–10
'First day in Israel', 256
Flight of Arrows, A, 362
Gadfly in Russia, 249, 355
Leading the Blind: A Century of
    Guide Book Travel 1815–1914,
    355
Life Without Armour, 18, 27, 55,
    58, 61, 72–4, 95, 119, 137,
    150, 185, 347–50, 357, 360,
    363, 374
'Maps in a Writer's Life', 30
Mountains and Caverns, 66–7, 71
'My Israel', 256

'No Shot in the Dark', 81–2

Raw Material, 18, 23, 24, 32, 261, 262, 289, 296, 352, 374

Road to Volgagrad, 197–202, 204, 234, 241, 243, 258

Saxon Shore Way, The, 301, 304

Drama:

The Interview, 270–1

Sillitoe, Bert (uncle), 19, 20

Sillitoe, Brian (brother), 17, 37, 48, 81, 131–4, 139, 152, 171–3, 174, 185, 186, 189, 190, 191, 192, 193, 194, 195–6, 197, 207–8, 213, 214–15, 216, 277, 284–5, 309, 317, 341–2, 345, 350, 351, 352–3, 355, 365–7, 371–2, 373–6

Sillitoe, Christopher (father), 17–22, 30–33, 37, 39–43, 81, 85–6, 93–4, 110–111, 139, 164–5, 214–15, 277, 317, 349–50

Sillitoe, David (son), 190–91, 217–19, 223–4, 247, 256, 258–9, 283–6, 293, 302–3, 309, 317, 341, 345, 352

Sillitoe, Edgar (uncle), 19, 20, 21, 41, 93–5, 165, 174

Sillitoe, Frederick (grandfather), 19

Sillitoe, Frederick (uncle), 19, 20, 21, 83–4

Sillitoe, Jed (grandson), 369

Sillitoe, John (great-grandfather), 18

Sillitoe, Julia (daughter-in-law), 369

Sillitoe, Mary Jane (great-grandmother), 18

Sillitoe, Michael (brother), 17, 32, 33, 48, 81, 132, 139, 165, 171–3, 190–91, 214–15, 216–17, 247–8, 309, 317, 350, 365–6, 373–6

Sillitoe, Pearl (sister), 17, 31, 37, 139, 165, 310, 317, 365

Sillitoe, Peggy (sister), 17, 30, 31, 37, 81, 139, 165, 216, 304, 317

Sillitoe, Sabina (mother), 17–33, 37, 39–43, 48, 81, 93–4, 119, 165, 174, 214–15, 288, 310, 317, 349–50

Sillitoe, Susan (daughter), 206, 212, 216–19, 223, 224, 229, 247, 286–8, 289, 301–2, 317

Simmons, Jeffrey, 149–51, 153, 157–60

Sindall, Bernard 'Bunny', 219–20, 335, 359–61

Sindall, Jeanetta, 219–20, 335, 359

Singer, Israel Joshua, 255

Sisson and Parker, bookshop, 79

Škvorecký, Josef, 248

Smith, D., 278

Smith, Egerton, 79

Socrates, 78

Sophocles, 78

Spectator, The, 168

Spector, Maurice, 188

Spedding, Mrs, 219, 290

Spender, Stephen, 267

Spruce, Peter, 87

Steinhoff, Ilsa, 105, 108, 127, 207

Stevenson, Ann, 228

Stewart, Donald Ogden, 188

Stoppard, Tom, 268, 270

Storey, David, 279

Strang, Herbert, 28

Strawson, Otto, 149

Surel, Jacques, 314

Suzman, Janet, 270

Swingewood, A., 278

Tacitus, 78

Tarr, Dorothy, 106, 110–11, 116, 118

Tarr, John, 106–7, 110–11, 112, 118

Thackeray, William Makepeace, 79

Thatcher, Margaret, 323, 339, 343, 344, 345, 359

Thorpe, Jeremy, 268

Tolstoy, Lev, Nikolaevich, 79, 238–9
Toone, A.B. and Company, 48–9
Towle, Bill, 48–9
Tressell, Robert, 66–7, 93, 155
Trocchi, Elizabeth, 129, 130
Turgenev, Ivan, 79, 89, 239, 245–6
Tynan, Ken, 188
Tyre, Amy, 18

'Uncle Dima', 237

Van Dreil, Jup, 115
Vaverka, R.D., 278
Vincent, Sally, 344
Virgil, 78
Voltaire, 79

Wain, John, 108, 140, 143, 152
Waterhouse, Keith, 279
Waugh, Evelyn, 202
Wells, H.G., 75, 79, 201
Wesker, Arnold, 188
West, Anthony, 156
Westbury, Schotness and Company,
      187
Wevill, Assia, 224–6
Wilde, Oscar, 78
Willis, Ted, 268
Winter, Ella, 188–9
Wiseman, Thomas, 228
Wodehouse, P.G., 66
Wollaton Hall, 304–5
Woolf, Virginia, 83, 161, 211
Wordsworth, William, 69, 70, 79
Wore, Frank, 33, 44

Xenophon, 78, 285

Yacoubi, Ahmed, 186
Yevtushenko, Yevgeny, 272

Zelichenok, Roald, 271